THE
ZEEBRUGGE
RAID 1918
'THE FINEST FEAT OF ARMS'

To all Ranks and Ratings concerned.

Operation Z.O.

The object of the enterprise we are about to undertake is the blocking of the entrances of Zeebrugge and Ostend. These ports are the bases of a number of Torpedo Craft and Submarines, which are a constant and ever increasing menace to the communication of our Army and to the trade and food supply of our country. The complete achievement of our aims would have the most favourable and far reaching effect on the Naval situation. I am very proud to command the Force which has the great privilege of carrying out this enterprise. Drawn as this Force is from the Grand Fleet, the Harwich Force, the Dover Patrol, the Three Depots, and the Royal Marine Artillery and Light Infantry, it is thoroughly representative of our service. I am very confident that the great traditions of our forefathers will be worthily maintained, and that all ranks will strive to emulate the heroic deeds of our brothers of the Sister Service in France and Flanders.

Vice Admiral Roger Keyes, General Order, 7th April 1918

May I say that if the operation for which you said you might want some of my men is eventually undertaken, I should very much like to take part in it. I would willingly accept the same conditions … that I should not expect to come back.

Captain Henry Halahan, killed at Zeebrugge

Your son Edward lived and worked, shoulder to shoulder with us, for many months. It was given to a few of us to know him as he really was, and to we few, his intimates, he endeared himself by every word and act. We knew him for a man among men; who took every twist of fortune, standing upright; who faced the world, at all times, unafraid. Truthful, sincere and resolute, he hated with a vehement, impassioned abhorrence anything that savoured of dishonour, cowardice, corruption. This last great act of fearless, matchless heroism, proved to the world what we already knew – that through his veins flowed the blood of a thoroughbred.

Letter of condolence to the parents of Leading Seaman Edward Gilkerson, killed at Zeebrugge, from his shipmates of HMS *King George V*

THE
ZEEBRUGGE
RAID 1918

'THE FINEST FEAT OF ARMS'

PAUL KENDALL

SPELLMOUNT

The author is always looking to gather further information relating to the Zeebrugge and Ostend raids of 1918. If you are related to any of the participants of these raids and have photographs, personal testimonies, letters, diaries or any relevant information please contact Paul Kendall at zeebrugge1918@aol.com.

For the families of the men who raided Zeebrugge on 23rd April 1918

Dedicated to the memory of my uncle
Ray Hunt 1936–2005

British Library Cataloguing in Publication Data:
A catalogue record for this book is available
from the British Library

Copyright © Paul Kendall 2008, 2009
ISBN 978 0 7524 5332 3

First published 2008
Reprinted Spring 2008
This paperback edition published 2009

Spellmount
The Mill, Brimscombe Port
Gloucestershire
GL5 2QG
www.thehistorypress.co.uk

Spellmount Limited is an imprint of The History Press

Typesetting and origination by The History Press
Printed in Great Britain by Henry Ling Limited,
at the Dorset Press, Dorchester, DT1 1HD

CONTENTS

ACKNOWLEDGEMENTS

This work on the Zeebrugge raid is the culmination of six years of research. I would not have been able to have written such a book without the internet and its ability to make the world a smaller place, bringing me in contact with archives, museums and people who are related to the men who took part in these operations. I am indebted to many individuals who have supported me. I would like to thank Yves Fohlen for awakening my interest in the Zeebrugge raid and for his friendship, support and counsel. His own quest for knowledge of the First and Second World Wars and the knowledge that he has acquired has been a great inspiration to me.

I would also like to thank Dominic Walsh for his help in writing this book. He is a man with a great passion for learning about the Zeebrugge raid and the men who took part in the operation. I am very grateful for his help in reconciling the correct names on our Zeebrugge casualty lists and for introducing me to several descendants of those men who raided Zeebrugge.

I also appreciate Norbert Kruger for his kindness in photocopying and sending to me German documents relating to the raid and I am thankful for his efforts in translating some of these fascinating documents into English. I would like to extend my thanks to Johan Ryheul and Alain van Geeteruyen for photos and information on the Flanders Flotilla and for sharing their views on the German perspective on the Zeebrugge raid.

I am grateful to the following individuals for information that they have kindly provided: John Soanes for providing me with a copy of the diary of Petty Officer Harry Adams; Peter White for allowing me access to a transcript of an interview that featured Corporal George Moyse and Air Mechanic Francis Donovan; and Richard Davison for supplying me with a copy of a presentation given by Private Beau Tracey. Beau Tracey's presentation about the Zeebrugge raid was enthralling. I would also like to thank Dr. Tony Heathcote, Bill Pollington, Jim Clay and David Slade.

I would like to thank the Trustees of the Imperial War Museum, London for permission to use material from the Department of Documents and Sound collections, in particular Emma Golding from the Imperial War Museum Department of Documents for assisting me in contacting copyright holders; John Stopford-Pickering for his advice regarding copyright issues relating to the IWM sound archives; and Yvonne Oliver for her advice relating to reproduction of IWM images. Thanks also to Matt Little (Documents Archive) and John Ambler (Pictures and Photographic Librarian) at the Royal Marines Museum, Eastney, Portsmouth. I am grateful for their hospitality on my numerous visits. My thanks also extend to Dominiek Dendooven of the 'In Flanders Fields' Museum, Ypres, for his hospitality during my visits to the museum archives, for his assistance in translating some German documents and for his support.

I thank Nicholas Coney at the National Archives for advising me on copyright issues and Judy Nokes of the Office of Public Sector Information for confirming copyright status of *London Gazette* material.

I am very grateful to Mark Frost and his team at the Dover Museum for their warm welcome. It was a very emotive occasion for me when he showed me the White Ensign from HMS *Iphigenia*, still stained with Sub Lieutenant Maurice Lloyd's blood. I thank them for their help and allowing me to quote from the account written by Leading Seaman Beaumont.

I also thank Matthew Sheldon from the Royal Naval Museum, Portsmouth for allowing me to quote from Captain Grant's papers; and Klaus-D. Postupa at Bundesarchiv, Germany for permitting me to use material.

I would like to extend my thanks to Charles Keyes, the grandson of Vice Admiral Sir Roger Keyes and Sandra Powlette from the British Library for allowing me to quote from *The Naval Memoirs of Admiral of the Fleet Sir Roger Keyes 1916–1918*.

I would like to thank the staff of the British Newspaper Library at Colindale. It was a great thrill for me to read accounts of the Zeebrugge raid as they were written nearly ninety years ago. Since many of the newspapers that I viewed are no longer in circulation, it was a great challenge for me to identify the copyright holders of this material. I am pleased that in most cases I was able to establish the identity of the copyright holders and I thank the following individuals for their generosity in allowing me to quote or use images from their publications. Charles A Garside, Assistant Editor of the *Daily Mail*; Joanne Douglas, *Ashton Reporter*; Simon Finlay, *Herald Express*, Kent Regional Newspapers; Martin McNeill, Editorial Director, *Southend Standard* (Echo Newspapers); Helen Burton, *Warrington Guardian*; Rebecca Smith, *Thanet Times*; Margaret Parsons, *Burnley Express & News*; Tony Lennox, Trinity Mirror Midlands Weekly Newspapers; Peter Franzen, Editor of the *Eastern Daily Press* / Archant Norfolk; Graham Smith, Editor of the *East Kent Mercury*; Joy Yates, Editor of the *Hartlepool Mail* for quotes from the *Northern Daily Mail*; John Furbisher, Editor of the *Halifax Courier*; Mark Acheson, Editor of *The News Portsmouth* for allowing me to quote from the *Hampshire Telegraph & Post*. Alex Ballard, *North Wales Chronicle*; Chris Bright, editor of the *Jersey Evening News* for granting permission to quote from the *Jersey Weekly Post*; Mervyn Kay, editor of the *Accrington Observer*; Kate Bryson, Deputy Editor *Kentish Times* Newspapers; Diane Nicholls, Editor of *Medway News*; Brian Aitken & Paul Robertson of the Newcastle Evening Chronicle and Journal Limited. I would also like to thank Matthew Eastley for including an article on my research in the *Post Office Courier*.

For permitting me to include photos and quote from an article that he wrote in the *Cross & Cockade* Magazine relating to Air Mechanic Sidney Hesse, I thank Peter Chapman.

I thank Geraldine Thompson of Manchester Royal Infirmary for allowing me to reproduce the image of Leading Mechanic John Wilkinson

I would like to acknowledge John Hillier, Editor, for allowing me to quote from the *Globe & Laurel*. I also appreciate the assistance given by Trevor Muston, archivist at *Navy News* in assisting me in my attempts to contact Mrs Marlene Gostelow, the daughter of Able Seaman Fred Larby.

I am grateful to Gary Buckland of The Naval & Military Press for allowing me to quote from their publications *The German Submarine War 1914-19*, *The Blocking of Zeebrugge* and *The Royal Naval Division*.

I would like to thank Graeme Hosken, the editor of the *Digger* magazine and Secretary of the Families and Friends of the First AIF for including my article on the sailors from the Royal Australian Navy who took part in the raid. I am also grateful to The Royal British Legion.

I am indebted to all the families who have kindly helped me in providing photos and information relating to their brave ancestors. They have entrusted their valued photos and documents for me to study. I appreciate their trust in me and for allowing me to ask questions about their forebears. I also thank them for reviewing the relevant draft pieces and for their patience when I have sent them further revisions. They include the following individuals:

Len Allbones, son of Private Charles Allbones
Diane and Brian Allbones, nephew of Private Charles Allbones
George Antell, son of Petty Officer George Antell DSM
Brian Bennewith and June Castle for their help in guiding me to the family of Able Seaman Harry Bennewith who live in South Africa. I am also grateful to Harry's nephew Neville Bennewith and great nephew Ian Bennewith for information and photos

Danny Webber, great grandson of Able Seaman Frederick Berry

Commander R.G. Boddie, Agnes Palmer and Janet Carlisle regarding their father Engineer Lieutenant Ronald Boddie

Norman Bonham-Carter, relative of Lieutenant Stuart Bonham-Carter DSO

Tim Bonham-Carter, relative of Lieutenant Stuart Bonham-Carter DSO

Suzi Henshaw, relative of Lieutenant Stuart Bonham-Carter DSO

Ian Botley, relative of Able Seaman William Botley

Jonathan L Bradford Cremer, nephew of Lieutenant Commander George Bradford VC

Carole A Allen, granddaughter of Able Seaman Thomas Bradley

Jean Brown, Daughter-in-law of Able Seaman Norman Brown

Lynne and Freda Burnell, sister-in-law of Private Arthur Burnell

Stewart Burnell, nephew of Private Arthur Burnell

Michael Anson, grandson of Lieutenant Harold Campbell DSO

Nigel Calverley, grandson of Corporal George Calverley

Nicky King, great niece of Able Seaman Arthur Cassell

Hugh Chevallier, distant relative of Lieutenant Felix Chevallier

David Clist, nephew of Private Jim Clist

Doreen Burrow, daughter of Lieutenant Theodore Cooke DSO

Godfrey Cory-Wright, son of Lieutenant Alan Cory-Wright DSC

Dorothy Cardoo, daughter of Private William Cuthbert

Michael McLaren, relative of Private William Cuthbert

R. Demery, relative of Private David Demery

Michael Dunkason, grandson of Master at Arms Charles Dunkason DSM

Clive Hughes & William Francis, son of Deckhand William Francis DSM

Graham Marsden, great nephew of Private Maurice French

M.C. Friday, son of Able Seaman Edward Friday

Linda Butcher, granddaughter of Able Seaman William Frost

Jack Simmonds, son-in-law Able Seaman William Frost

Mark Ferguson, grandson of Engine Room Artificer John Ferguson DSM

Emma & William Garland, nephew of Sergeant Isaac Garland

Brian Brown, great grandson of Private William Gallin

Rodney Gilkerson, nephew of Leading Seaman Edward Gilkerson

Mr. D. Gillard, nephew of Able Seaman Harry Gillard

Kevin Gordon, grandson of Private Alexander Gordon

Philip Gough, son of Air Mechanic William Gough

Tom Greenway, son of Buglar Frederick Greenway

Brian Gumm, nephew of Corporal Percy Gumm

Derek Handford, grandson of Able Seaman Frederick Handford

Diane Ellison, granddaughter of Stoker William Hancock

Jacqueline Oldman, granddaughter of Private Parowmas Harris

Heather Helliar, niece of Able Seaman Hubert Helliar

Neil Helliar, nephew of Able Seaman Hubert Helliar

Captain O. W. J. Henderson, son of Lieutenant Oscar Henderson DSO

Neville Hoath, son of Private Fred Hoath

Betty Thornton & Tony Hopewell, daughter & great nephew of Private William Hopewell CGM

Linda Kelly, granddaughter of Plummer Alexander Horne

Karen Morris, great niece of Private Samuel Hopson

Bill Inge, great nephew of Petty Officer Percy Inge DSM

Dave Eastman, relative of Lieutenant Hope Inskip

John Hammond, nephew of Private George Jones

Des Donovan, nephew of Private Tommy Keegan

Charles Keyes, grandson of Vice Admiral Sir Roger Keyes CB, CMG, MVO, DSO

Ivor Kelland, son of Able Seaman Francis Kelland DSM

Sally Purchase, granddaughter of Leading Seaman Fred Kimber

Marlene Gostelow, daughter of Able Seaman Fred Larby DSM

John Linkin, great nephew of Private Percy Linkin

Colin McKenzie, great nephew of Able Seaman Albert McKenzie VC
Gordon Mabb, nephew of Petty Officer Henry Mabb DSM
Patricia Webber, niece of Petty Officer Henry Mabb DSM
Steve Marling, grandson of Leading Seaman William Marling
Tom Marshall, son of Stoker Andrew Marshall
John & Sally Messer, grandson of Petty Officer Alfred Messer DSM
Ron Moyse, son of Corporal George Moyse
Jean Stout, daughter of Corporal William Mitchell
Ron Nicholls, nephew of Stoker Sidney Nicholls
Paul Ormerod, grandson of Gunner Vincent Ormerod
Irene Conners, nece of Stoker Petty Officer Harold Palliser
Edward Peshall, grandson of Chaplain Charles Peshall DSO
Neil Prangnell, great cousin of Private Harold Prangnell
Sheila Kitchener, niece of Private Harold Prangnell
James Quarrington and Joan Lever Sullivan, son & daughter of Private Robert Quarrington
Nigel Rhind, grandson of Private Ernest Rhind
Beryl Rendell, daughter of Private Percy Savage
Elizabeth Sparrow, daughter of Commander Ralph Sneyd DSO
Ralph Wykes-Sneyd, grandson of Commander Ralph Sneyd DSO
The late Hannah Spencer Latour & Iris Spencer, daughters of Lieutenant George Spencer DSC
Catherine La Tour granddaughter of Lieutenant George Spencer DSC
Jasper Evans, nephew of Commander Ralph Sneyd
Derek Stingemore, relative of Able Seaman William Stingemore
Bryan Stoddart, son of Private Lewis Stoddart
Paul Lamplough, grandson of Stoker George South
Dennis Summerhayes, son of Able Seaman Frederick Summerhayes DSM
Richard E. Taylor, son of Able Seaman Walter Taylor
Eric Taylor, son of Able Seaman William Taylor
Tammy Higginbotham, Great granddaughter of Stoker Ernest Thornton
Gordon Toach, nephew of Private Archibald Toach
Philip Solomon, grandson of Able Seaman Henry Undey
Major General N. Vaux, nephew of Lieutenant Philip Vaux DSC
Mary Twells, daughter of Private William Warren
Andrew Warrington, son of Air Mechanic George Warrington
Adrian Stammers, great nephew of Mate Sidney West DSC
Andrew Bruton, grandson of Private John Weaver
Ms. Wendy Frew, great niece of Able Seaman John Yeadon.

I extend my gratitude to Shaun Barrington and the team at Spellmount Publishers for their enthusiasm. I am grateful to Simon Bellamy for his friendship over the years and for providing guidance and advice regarding publishing. I appreciate the support given by my friend and colleague, Gary Shaw, who has taken a keen interest in this project. I would also like to thank my parents, David and Sylvia Kendall, for their support and for accompanying me on numerous battlefield tours during the past six years. I have enjoyed their companionship while embarking on these pilgrimages. I would also like to thank Tricia Newsome for her friendship, companionship and support.

Please note that when referring to the men who participated in the raid on Zeebrugge I have referred to the ranks that they held at the time; and the British medals that were awarded for the operation.

Paul Kendall, London

INTRODUCTION

During the last year of the Great War on the 23rd April 1918, St. George's Day, officers and men from the Royal Navy, Royal Marines Light Infantry, Royal Marines Artillery, Royal Naval Reserve, Royal Naval Volunteer Reserve, Royal Naval Air Service and an eleven-man contingent from the Royal Australian Navy carried out a daring raid upon the ports of Zeebrugge and Ostend. This book concentrates on the raid on Zeebrugge. The purpose was to block the canal entrances that connected the German Naval Base at Bruges to the sea, entrapping the submarines and torpedo boats of the Flanders Flotilla in an effort to prevent them from scouring the North Sea and English Channel for Allied merchant shipping. By the end of 1917 the submarines of the German Imperial Navy was on the brink of starving Great Britain into defeat by sinking Allied merchant vessels in the North Sea, English Channel and Atlantic Ocean. Korvettenkapitän Hans Bartenbach was commander of the U-Flotilla Flanders and the naval facility at Bruges was an ideal location for short range German UB and UC-boats from the Flanders Flotilla to be based, for it provided easy access to the merchant shipping lanes in the English Channel and along the eastern coast of Britain. Werber Fürbringer who was a commander of various UB and UC Boats based at Bruges from 1915 to 1918 later wrote:

> Probably of all the German arms of service it was the U-boat arm which caused them the worst of their headaches and of these the Flanders boats gave them the most grief. From Bruges, Zeebrugge and Ostend we streamed out to attack Britain's lifeline in the English Channel; a U-boat flotilla based on the Isles of Wight could have been only a morsel more troublesome than the weapon wielded by Bartenbach at Bruges.[1]

The operation to counter this threat to the passage of Allied shipping was an audacious plan and for the officers and men who took part, the odds were distinctly against them. There was a great risk of not returning home. The operation was commanded by Vice Admiral Roger Keyes and the only prospect that he could offer to those who took part was death or capture.

As they crossed the Channel during the afternoon of the 22nd April Admiral Keyes acknowledged the fact that the following day was St. George's Day, sending a signal from his flagship HMS *Warwick*, 'St. George for England', to which Captain Carpenter onboard HMS *Vindictive* replied, 'May we give the dragon's tail a damned good twist.'

Indeed, the men of the Royal Navy and Royal Marines did give the dragon's tail a damned good twist, but paid a high price. The long casualty list of 227 killed and 356 wounded showed that the operation was a bloody sacrifice, especially for an action that lasted less than an hour. For their efforts, eight Victoria Crosses were awarded solely for the raid on Zeebrugge, which was and is the second highest number of Victoria Crosses ever awarded for a single action. (The record for the most number of Victoria Crosses is eleven for the action at Rorkes Drift, 1879.) Zeebrugge marked a revival of the raid as a strategy of warfare once associated with Sir Francis Drake and Horatio Nelson; it planted the seed that would become the achievements of the Commandos twenty years later, during the Second World War. For Vice Admiral Roger Keyes, commander of the Dover Patrol and architect of the operation, the raid on Zeebrugge would be the pinnacle of his naval career. Throughout that career, during the Boxer Rising in China and at the Heligoland Bight, Gallipoli and at Zeebrugge, he displayed great courage and leadership in the spirit of Nelson.

U-boats were at the turn of the century unorthodox weapons, some thought unethical. The German U-boat crews who volunteered for submarine service were regarded with great contempt and were looked upon as pirates. It was a hazardous form of warfare and it required a special type of man to live within the claustrophobic confinements of these small submersibles. The risk of death was a very real prospect with hazards such as being torpedoed, depth charged or being sunk by a mine. There is a great mystique that surrounds the men that left from the port of Zeebrugge in these small craft that were described as iron coffins, to venture in the open sea to prey upon Allied shipping. They had to endure long days within the close confines. The effectiveness of the Flanders Flotilla was terrible: it is estimated that submarines based at Bruges were responsible for the destruction of 2,554 Allied vessels, amounting to 4,400,000 tons. This was one third of the number of Allied ships sunk during the War.[2]

By early 1918 the British Grand Fleet had contained the German High Seas Fleet within the waters of Heligoland Bight and Baltic Sea, however Allied merchant vessels transporting vital supplies to Great Britain were continually suffering harassment from German submarines. There existed a danger that the enemy could starve Great Britain to capitulation. The Alliance was dependent upon British merchant vessels to transport Empire and American troops, together with food and supplies, to the European theatre. Lloyd George quotes the First Sea Lord Admiral Sir John Jellicoe in his support for Haig's Flander's offensive, pessimistically advising the War Cabinet on 19th June 1917 that 'if we did not clear the Germans out of Zeebrugge before this winter we should have great difficulty in ever getting them out of it. The reason he gave for this was that he felt it to be improbable that we could go on with the War next year for lack of shipping.'[3]

Haig's plan to break out from the Ypres Salient and capture the Bruges and the Belgian ports of Zeebrugge and Ostend was thwarted in the muddy quagmire at Passchendaele during November 1917. The Allied forces were exhausted by the Third Ypres campaign and were in no fit state to carry out a further campaign to capture these objectives. The only hope for the Allies to stop German submarines at Bruges from sinking Allied vessels was to block the entrances at Zeebrugge and Ostend. It was therefore left for the Royal Navy and Royal Marines in 1918 to stop the Flanders-based submarines.

Vice Admiral Roger Keyes and his staff displayed great initiative in their daring and innovative plan to block and entrap the Flanders Flotilla submarines in their own port. The planning phase was an enormous logistical task. The objective was to sink three old depleted blockships across the entrance to the Bruges canal. In order to succeed, these blockships must pass the Mole where British intelligence estimated to be a garrison of a thousand men and numerous gun batteries. On passing the Mole they were then within range of the coastal and harbour batteries as they proceeded to the entrance. Surprise was the key to success. In order for this plan to work a diversion would be created by launching a direct assault upon the Mole batteries by storming parties from the Royal Marines Light Infantry and the Royal Navy. A further diversion was necessary to enable the Mole storming parties to carry out *their* diversion, for it was necessary to prevent German reinforcements from getting access to the Mole and this was done by detonating explosives aboard HM Submarine C3, which blew a 30-foot-wide gap in the Mole viaduct. This would give the three blockships a chance to get within the harbour. The plan required great attention to detail when coordinating the attack within the limited time frames. Restricted by the tidal and weather conditions to certain days in each month, the operation was complicated because there were two targets. In order to ensure that the German submarine menace was blocked at Bruges it was necessary simultaneously to block the entrance at Ostend as well as Zeebrugge at the same time. All the participants were heroes. Many of these men had volunteered for this secret operation. Among the volunteers were sailors and Royal Marines who were veterans from the Gallipoli campaign in 1915 and the great sea battle at Jutland in 1916.

The German personnel from the Flandern Marinekorps demonstrated their own dogged heroism, defying the British raiders in defending the Mole. These men had defended Zeebrugge for four years through all seasons, including harsh winters. They braved icy cold weather fronts which were blasted from the North Sea onto this most northerly bastion of the Western Front.

Churchill considered the raid to 'rank as the finest feat of arms in the Great War, and certainly as an episode unsurpassed in the history of the Royal Navy.'[4] The raid on Zeebrugge featured in many local and national newspapers in the months that followed. The funerals of the fallen were reported across the country and in each community journalists sought out those who took part for interviews. As the Kaiser Offensive was driving deep into France towards Paris during Spring 1918, the minds of the British public were focused on these brief raids.

The operation, however, was deemed to have achieved limited success, for the passage at Zeebrugge was cleared to enable submarines and torpedo boats from the Flanders Flotilla to pass through the lock gates from Bruges within a day after the raid. Nevertheless, despite being a partial success and only blocking access to the Bruges canal at low tide, Keyes had given the British public a great morale boost. After the disappointment of the anti-climactic stalemate that was Jutland in 1916, there was no other large-scale naval battle. The German Imperial Navy sought refuge in their ports and rarely ventured out to sea. The German submarines still operated to devastating effect despite the efforts of the Royal Navy and the Dover Patrol who were continually implementing measures to confront this threat to the nation's supply. These Bruges-based vessels were sunk in large numbers, through the efforts of the Royal Navy; however the British public could not understand these initiatives or their gradual effectiveness during four years of war.[5] The operation at Zeebrugge would alter the British public's perception of the Royal Navy and the way it was confronting the German submarine menace.

I first read about the Zeebrugge raid twenty years ago as a schoolboy. Since then I have passed through the port of Zeebrugge via the Bruges canal, en route to Bruges, while serving as a Midshipman with the University of London Royal Naval Unit. During this deployment in 1991, it took an hour for our P2000 Patrol Craft, HMS *Puncher*, to proceed up this canal to berth where the submarines and destroyer torpedo boats of the German Flanders Flotilla were based during the First World War. In 1994, during my final deployment, I was at the helm of HMS *Puncher* as we entered Ostend when I noticed the bow section of HMS *Vindictive*, which stands as a memorial to the raids, near the entrance to the Ostend–Bruges canal. It was not until 2001 that my interest in the raids was strongly awakened. My friend Yves Fohlen asked me for any information relating to the raid on Zeebrugge in British archives. Yves is a French military historian, author and battlefield guide who was brought up in St. Nazaire. His grandfather Roland Prigent bore witness to the explosion of HMS *Campbeltown* in the Normandie Dock on 27th March 1942. Roland Prigent belonged to the French Underground and would observe the movements of German U-boats as they operated from St. Nazaire during World War Two. Information that he was involved in collecting was used by the Allies in London to sink two German U-boats that departed from St. Nazaire. He was working in the dockyard during the morning after the raid and watched HMS *Campbeltown* explode killing the German personnel and their girlfriends whom they had taken aboard as sightseers. The German occupiers ordered Roland and fellow dockyard workers to clear up the horrific mess, which involved recovering the scattered human remains that had been blown across the dockyard. Yves was interested in the Zeebrugge raid, because the operation has certain parallels with the raid on St. Nazaire. The objective of the raid on Zeebrugge was to block the canal entrance at Zeebrugge to prevent German submarines from using the port at Bruges as a base to launch attacks on Allied merchant vessels. The St. Nazaire raid twenty-four years later had a similar objective, which was to destroy the Normandie Dock facility and to deny its use as a base and a repair facility for the German Battleship *Tirpitz*, which was harassing Allied shipping.

The purpose of this book is to explore the role of the German Flanders Flotilla and provide an account of the Royal Navy's plan to counter the German submarine menace. The most important objective is to tell the stories of some of the men from the Royal Navy and Royal Marines who raided Zeebrugge in 1918. All these brave men were ordinary men who led extraordinary lives. They originated from across the social spectrum and from communities throughout Britain; and in some cases they came from different parts of the British Empire, from Australia, Fiji and South Africa. It has been a great revelation for me to discover where they came from and what jobs they did before the war. Many of these men took part in land actions, in Antwerp in 1914, Gallipoli in 1915, the Somme in 1916 and Gavrelle in 1917. They also took part in the sea battles of Heligoland Bight in 1914, Dogger Bank in 1915 and Jutland in 1916. I have researched with great interest the journeys of these men before destiny brought them to Zeebrugge. Of those that were fortunate enough to have survived the ordeal of the raid, their later lives have been equally intriguing. Many adapted back into civilian occupations and settled down to family life after the First World War; but when the Second World War erupted some who had witnessed the horrors of the Great War were willing to fight for freedom and democracy once again. Twenty years later, some of the Zeebrugge raiders returned to serve in the armed services to fight Nazi Germany. For those who were too old, they played their part by serving in the Home Guard. In the year of the 90th anniversary of the raid on Zeebrugge I hope that in this book I have paid tribute to their courage and ensured that future generations will remember the men who twisted the dragon's tail.

NOTES

1. Geoffrey Brooks, *Fips: Legendary U-Boat Commander, 1915-1918*, p53: Leo Cooper, 1999.
2. Statistics quoted from the following sources: R H Gibson & M Prendergast, *The German Submarine War 1914-1918*, Naval & Military Press, 2003, *Evening Telegraph*, 23rd September 1948.
3. David Lloyd George, *War Memoirs of David Lloyd George* Vol. 2, p1292, Odhams Press Limited, 1938.
4. Winston S Churchill, *The World Crisis 1911–1918*, Vol. 2, p1242, Odhams Press Limited, 1938.
5. See Appendix 4 for a list of Flanders-based submarines sunk during the First World War.

CHAPTER 1

THE FLANDERS FLOTILLA

The German Marine Division, commanded by Admiral Jacobsen, entered Bruges on 14th October 1914. From this day until 19th October 1918 Bruges was occupied and under the jurisdiction of Admiral Ludwig von Schröder, who was appointed military governor. Schröder governed the region with an iron fist and was known in Germany as the 'Lion of Flanders'. The objective of the German advance in 1914, known as the Schlieffen Plan, was to reach the French ports of Calais and Dunkirk before turning south to strike at Paris. If the Schlieffen Plan succeeded the Germans would utilize these ports. By the end of October 1914, however, when the First Ypres Campaign lost momentum, the German Navy was forced to use Belgian ports as a base for launching their offensive against Allied shipping. The German Admiralty realised that Bruges would provide an ideal base for German submarines, destroyers and torpedo boats. Connected by canals to Ostend and Zeebrugge, they could feel secure six miles inland at Bruges, but could gain access to the English Channel and North Sea with great ease.

The harbour at Zeebrugge had been cleared of mines by 7th November 1914. U-12, commanded by Kapitänleutnant Walter Forstmann, was the first German submarine to enter Zeebrugge on 9th November. The following day U-12 left Zeebrugge and sailed towards Dover looking for a target. Two days later Forstmann sunk HMS *Niger*, a torpedo gunboat, near to the Deal Light Vessel in the English Channel. The *Niger* was the first victim of a German submarine based at Zeebrugge. Thousands of people from Kent lined the cliffs to watch the spectacle of black smoke billowing from the stricken vessel as she sank in the Channel.

A second German Marine Division was sent to Flanders on 15th November 1914 and together with the first they became known as the Marines Corps Flandern, commanded by Admiral von Schröder. U-5, -6, -11 and -24 used Zeebrugge during the last months of 1914. U-24, commanded by Kapitänleutnant Rudolf Schneider, was the first German U-boat to attack an unarmed merchant vessel without warning during the war, the French SS *Admiral Ganteaume*. On 26th October, Schneider came into contact with this vessel off Cape Gris Nez, which was transporting 2,000 Belgian refugees. There was panic amongst the Belgian civilians as soon as the torpedo struck the hull. A disaster was averted when a nearby vessel came alongside and rescued all passengers with the exception of 40 persons. The vessel was damaged but able to be towed to the nearest port. Schneider defended his actions by claiming that he mistook the vessel for a troopship.

On 23rd December, U-24 departed Zeebrugge to embark on another patrol. Schneider was in the western sector of the English Channel when he encountered the 5th Battle Squadron comprising eight battleships and two light cruisers, under the command of Vice Admiral Sir Lewis Bayly. This squadron was undertaking gunnery practice off Portland, Dorset and it was assumed that the Western Channel could not be reached by German U-boats and therefore there were no escorts allocated to protect these vessels as they sailed in line. They were vulnerable targets and at 2.00 a.m. on New Years Day 1915, Schneider fired a torpedo amidships into HMS *Formidable* while in Lyme Bay. The battleship started to list immediately. Captain Arthur Loxley, the commander of HMS *Formidable*, gave the order

U-24 commanded by Kapitänleutnant Rudolf Schneider sank HMS *Formidable* off the Dorset coast on 1st January 1915. *Formidable* was the first Royal Naval battleship sunk during the war. Note the periscope of U-24 to the left.

to abandon ship. He supervised the evacuation of his crew into small boats. Two light cruisers from the 5th Battle Squadron assisted in this rescue operation. Within a couple of hours the dynamos were flooded by water, causing the lights on board to flicker and then extinguish, plunging the ship into total darkness. The crew aboard maintained their calm as they evacuated the vessel. At 3.15 a.m. Schneider fired another torpedo into the sinking battleship, which caused her to sink faster. Strong winds and rain fell during that morning. The sea conditions were severe causing thirty-foot waves, which battered the stricken vessel. Only 199 sailors had been evacuated when *Formidable* capsized, rolled over and sank at 4.45 a.m. The remaining 550 crew, including Captain Arthur Loxley, perished with her.

HMS *Formidable* was the first British battleship to be sunk during the war and was the first Royal Naval ship to be sunk by a German submarine based at Bruges. It was the first great U-boat achievement during those initial months of the War. For the German Navy, it highlighted the potential of using Bruges as a naval base for launching an attack on Allied shipping in the English Channel. The British Admiralty learnt a great lesson from this tragedy, for this incident demonstrated the vulnerability of the Home Fleet within English waters. As a response to the loss of *Formidable*, seventeen miles of indicator nets, patrolled by drifters, were installed to bolster the defences around Dover.

A German U-boat offensive was declared upon the shores of Great Britain during the New Year of 1915. There would be no restrictions made upon U-boat commanders and their areas of operation. On 24th January 1915 Chief of Naval Staff Admiral Hugo von Pohl stated that

The waters around Great Britain and Ireland, including the whole of the English Channel, are herewith declared to be in the war zone. From February 18 onward, every merchant-ship met with this War Zone will be destroyed, nor will it always be possible to obviate the danger with which the crews and passengers are thereby threatened.[1]

It was not until March 1915 that the German Admiralty in Berlin authorised the establishment of a Flanders Flotilla based at Bruges. The plan was to use the port as a base for smaller submarines. So far they had been reluctant to use the Flanders ports because of the close proximity to the English coast and the increased activity of the Royal Navy off the Belgian coast. Royal Naval gunboats shelled Ostend quite often and any German vessels based in Flanders were susceptible to attack. With the construction of bunkers and artillery installations along the Belgian coast the German Admiralty reviewed their decision and decided to send a limited number of small submarines to the region. Being near to the English Channel, fuel consumption and passage time to enemy shipping lanes would be greatly reduced, allowing German submarine crews more time to patrol Allied shipping lanes. The Germans established their main submarine base at Bruges with the construction of concrete submarine pens, floating docks and workshops for maintenance and repair. The Germans chose Bruges as their principal naval base because being six miles inland from Zeebrugge it would not be threatened by Allied naval bombardments from the sea. Here the German vessels could find refuge when not on patrol. The facility at Bruges was very large. Fourteen thousand employees worked at Kaiserliche werft in Bruges Harbour providing logistical support to submarines of the Flanders Flotilla; 5,000 German technicians and 4,000 civilians were also employed at the German naval base.[2]

It was necessary for seaplanes to escort submarines entering and leaving the naval facility at Zeebrugge for two reasons. Firstly, seaplanes were deployed as a protective measure against Allied aeroplanes operating in the area. The second purpose was to inform submarines of any Allied shipping in the vicinity. So a seaplane base was also constructed on the Mole at Zeebrugge.

HMS *Formidable* was also the first Royal Naval vessel to be sunk by a submarine based at Bruges. She was laid down in Portsmouth dockyard in 1898 and completed in 1901. When War broke out, she acted as an escort vessel protecting the transportation of the British Expeditionary Force to France. On 25th August 1914 *Formidable* transported the Portsmouth Royal Marine Battalion to Ostend.

ADMIRAL LUDWIG VON SCHRÖDER, COMMANDER FLANDERS COAST.

Ludwig von Schröder was born in 1854. He emerged from retirement when war broke out in 1914 to command German Naval forces along the Belgian Flanders coast. During October 1914, soldiers from von Schröder's Marinekorp were responsible for the capture of Antwerp. For the rest of the war von Schröder was responsible for the defence of the German naval bases at Bruges, Ostend and Zeebrugge. He was awarded the Pour le Mérite in October 1915 and Oakleaves in December 1917 in recognition. The German press regarded von Schröder as the 'Lion of Flanders' after he repelled the British attack at Zeebrugge and Ostend. As the Allies were breaking the German line into Belgium during October 1918, von Schröder and his Marinekorp were forced to withdraw. After the Armistice, von Schröder retired. He died in 1933.

Both Ostend and Zeebrugge were vulnerable to bombardments from the sea. Ostend was closer to England and was within range of aerial attacks from Allied planes based in northern France. For this reason Ostend was less useful to the Germans than Zeebrugge. Bruges was connected to the sea by canals to Ostend and Zeebrugge. The Ostend canal was more narrow and shallower than the Bruges canal. The Bruges–Ostend canal was 11 miles long and could be used as an alternative access to the sea.

Construction of the canal started in 1896 and was completed in 1907. The Zeebrugge–Bruges canal cost 42 million Francs to build. It was 6☐ miles long, 230 feet wide and 26 feet deep, big enough for the submarines, destroyers, light cruisers and torpedo boats that used it. Locks were built at Ostend and Zeebrugge that would allow these vessels to enter or leave the canal at any time, irrespective of the state of tide, without lowering the water level of the canal.

From 29th March 1915 the Flanders Flotilla was regarded as a separate entity from the German High Seas Fleet. The Flotilla consisted of UB and UC boats. These types of German submarines were restricted to patrolling the English Channel and as far as the Scilly Isles because they only had short-range capabilities. While on the surface they did not have the speed to chase steamers. When these vessels submerged there was not sufficient power to make headway against strong currents. The batteries would be exhausted after travelling for an hour at 5 knots. In order to achieve good performance the best that they could accomplish was 50 miles at 2.5 knots. This would be ineffective against the strong 8-knot current that flowed through the Straits of Dover. UB boats were coastal submersibles, with a limited radius of action. They were very small craft and were manned by 20 sailors, so small they were often referred to as sewing machines.

Most Flanders submarines had an eye painted on the bow. The eye originated from a U-boat commander serving in the east who ordered that an eye be painted on the bow for luck. He was right: when his submarine was mistakenly attacked by another German submarine; she surfaced and was recognised when her eye was seen as the bow broke the surface. The design was later adopted as an identification insignia by Flanders-based submarines.

The construction of the UB boats was a fast process. UB-10 was the first UB Class to arrive at Bruges. More submarines used Bruges as a base during April 1915 including UB -2, -4, -5, -6, -10, -12, -13, -16 and -17. They were transported from Kiel, Hamburg and Bremen in Germany in parts by railway to Antwerp, where they were reassembled and then taken by barge to Bruges.

UC-1, -2, -3, -5, -6, -7, -9 and -11 were the first UC boats to arrive at Bruges during May 1915. UC boats were used as minelayers and operated off the coast of Britain. The routine of these minelayers consisted of three to four days at sea laying 12 mines close together, then spending up to 10 days in harbour refitting and preparing mines for the next patrol. The objective of laying mines was, of course, firstly to sink enemy vessels; but secondly, to keep British minesweepers occupied, diverting this resource from scouring the seas around the British Isles for German submarines. Each submarine commander was given a specific area where to lay mines. Being the only commander to lay mines in a certain region meant that they knew where they laid mines on previous patrols and would have local knowledge and be aware of them when they returned to their designated patch.

UC-11, commanded by Oberleutnant zur See Walter Gottfried Schmidt, was the first Flanders vessel to lay a minefield. Mines were laid off the Goodwin Light Vessel on 31st May 1915. This operation was very effective, for within 24 hours it caused damage to the British destroyer HMS *Mohawk*. An explosion ripped through the engine room killing five men and injuring four. This caused bewilderment at the Admiralty. It was a sensitive situation, there was no explanation for the mine's presence in this area. Mrs Ethel Hollyer was the widow of Leading Stoker George Hollyer, who was one of the sailors killed by the explosion aboard *Mohawk*. She requested further details as to how her husband had died.

It was standard procedure for the Accountant General of the Navy to respond to bereaved relatives requesting information about the loss of their loved ones. He responded to Ethel Hollyer during July 1915 and wrote:

> I regret to have to state, for your confidential information, that he was killed by the explosion of a mine in the North Sea on the 1st... and that according to a report received from the commanding officer, his death must have been instantaneous. He was buried at Dover on the 4th.
> I have to request that you will be good enough to refrain from communication of the foregoing information to anyone else and from inserting any notice in the Press except in the following form:-
> 'Lost his life on duty while in one of H.M. ships on war service, George William Hollyer, Acting Leading Stoker, Official Number K4857.' Accountant General of the Navy.[3]

The request to keep the details of death from parties other than the next of kin shows the Admiralty's intention to deliberately deny the enemy reports that their mines were effective. If the British press was aware of these mines, then they might ask the Admiralty questions which they could not answer.

The Flanders Flotilla laid more mines off Dover and Harwich, which caused the loss of 23 merchant ships, 16 fishing vessels and two Royal Naval torpedo boats. For three months the British were unaware of the cause of the losses. It was not until 30th June 1915, when UC-2 commanded by Oberleutnant zur See Karl Mey was destroyed by detonation of its own mine, that the answer as to how a mine had drifted and caused damage to HMS *Mohawk* was found. The British raised the wreck of UC-2 that had sunk with all 15 crew onboard and discovered that the Germans were deploying a new form of minelayer.

Until July 1915 German submarine operations from Bruges were restricted to the south-east coast of England. Korvettenkapitän Hans Bartenbach, commander of the U-Flotilla Flanders, was keen to bring disruption to Allied convoys in the English Channel. Werner Fürbringer commanding UB-2 later wrote

> The life artery of Britain, the English Channel, ebbed and flowed directly at our Belgian doorstep. Nevertheless Bartenbach had not been able to make the decision to deploy his flotilla there while the doubt existed as to whether our small submarines were technically up to the task. We were aware of his burning desire to extend operations into the Channel if at all possible.[4]

Intelligence reports indicated that the British had laid anti-submarine nets across the Straits of Dover and Bartenbach was anxious to learn if submarines from the Flanders Flotilla could penetrate these defences and operate within the English Channel. Bartenbach sent Oberleutnant Erich Haecker commanding UB-6 to investigate whether the Straits of Dover could be entered. In July 1915 Haecker confirmed that the British had closed the passage into the English Channel; however, during this dangerous reconnaissance mission, he discovered a breach in the nets near the French coast between Calais and Cap Gris-Nez. On receiving Haecker's report Bartenbach ordered four UB Boats from the Flanders Flotilla to penetrate the English Channel via this gap in the nets. The UB Boats were each given a port to sail to, Boulogne, Le Havre, Dover and Folkestone, the principal ports where Allied shipping transferred troops and supplies between England and France. Their orders were to fire torpedoes into enemy troop and supply ships. UB-2 commanded by Werner Fürbringer was ordered to patrol Le Havre. He left Zeebrugge in July with the expectation that the patrol would last three days. Instead, this patrol was plagued with problems and lasted eight days. After successfully entering the English Channel, Fürbringer was presented with two opportunities to sink Allied vessels and in each instance the only two torpedoes fired by him missed their targets. Feeling very disappointed he later wrote:

German submarine approaching the Mole at Zeebrugge. Note the net cutters on the front of the submarine.

Lt. Kurt Zehmisch, an officer from Infantry Regiment 134, took this photograph of the German submarine UC-66 leaving the canal at Zeebrugge during June 1917 while on leave from the Western Front. UC-66 was leaving Zeebrugge for the last time, for on 12th June the trawler *Sea King* observed UC-66 off the Lizard. Oberleutnant sur See Herbert Pustkuchen, who sank the packet ship *Sussex* in the English Channel in March 1916, was now in command of her. *Sea King* approached UC-66 with great speed, forcing Pustkuchen to submerge. Depth charges detonated the mines being carried on UC-66. She was destroyed with her crew.

> *I felt weak at the knees. Both torpedoes wasted. It was wretched luck. The men had slaved to get the boat here safely, and I had fired wide twice. What would the Flotilla Chief say? And the other three commanders? How would they amuse themselves at my expense! I stood in the tower, slumped against the bulkhead, brooding. Thoughts chased each other through my head. This was bad: I was in the blackest humour.[5]*

Unbeknown to Fürbringer, the other three commanders returned to Bruges to report to Bartenbach that their torpedoes had also missed their targets.

Misfiring two torpedoes would be the least misfortune for Fürbringer and the crew of UB-2 during this operation. They were 120 miles away from Zeebrugge and the main engine had broken down. With no means of power they were at the mercy of the tide of the English Channel and vulnerable to the threat of Allied patrol vessels. Fürbringer made the decision to drift back to Zeebrugge when the tide ebbed eastwards. This would mean that twice during the day for a period of six hours UB-2 would need to sit on the bottom of the English Channel while the tide ebbed westwards. Fürbringer estimated that they could drift between 16 and 20 miles each day, which meant that they would arrive at their home port within eight to ten days; which posed another problem. They had embarked with food and water provisions for three days. Now they had to make those provisions last for a lot longer. Water was rationed to one cup per man per day. They succeeded in making their provisions stretch and they reached Zeebrugge eight days later. Near the Belgian Coast they were met by Hans Valentiner in UB-16 who had been sent out to look for the missing vessel. Valentiner nearly mistook her for an English submarine when UB-2 rose to the surface and was about to fire a torpedo into her bow. On seeing the Flanders Eye painted on her bow he recognised her as a friend and withheld fire.

Entrance to the Zeebrugge sluices. This was where German submarines from the Flanders Flotilla left the Bruges Canal to enter the North Sea. It was the objective of the Zeebrugge operation to block this entrance.

Above: The entrance to the Bruges Canal at Zeebrugge photographed in 2006.

Left: German submarines at Bruges.

German submarine pens at Bruges, known as 'the eight salvations'.

German Torpedo Boats from the Flanders Flotilla berthed at Bruges.

Aerial view of the German Naval Base, Bruges, home of the Flanders Flotilla. Note the bomb craters that are dotted around the surrounding countryside.

Above: The Bruges Canal from Zeebrugge lock gates, today. The German submarines from the Flanders Flotilla passed through this canal from their base in Bruges and were responsible for sinking a third of all Allied merchant ships lost during the First World War.

Right: German submarine in the Bruges Canal.

Left: Bruges Canal in 2003.

Below: German submarine waiting to pass through the lock gates at Zeebrugge prior to patrol.

Left: The lock gates at Zeebrugge today. This photograph was taken in the same position as the one featured opposite, below.

Below: German submarines moored alongside the Zeebrugge Mole.

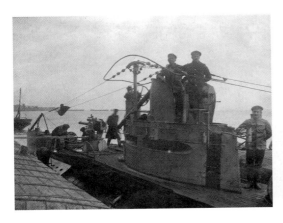

Above: German destroyers and submarine berthed alongside the inner Mole at Zeebrugge.

Left: German submarine departs from the Mole after patrol in the English Channel and is heading for the entrance to the Bruges canal.

German Torpedo Boats at Zeebrugge, 1917.

German submarines berthing alongside the Mole at Zeebrugge. Submarines based at Bruges would stop at the Mole before a patrol and on their return, before going back to their Bruges base.

By October 1915, 16 German submarines were operating from Zeebrugge and Ostend. The strategy of sowing minefields was reaping rewards. During 1915, UC boats from the Flanders Flotilla had laid a total of 648 mines along the eastern coast of England stretching as far north as Grimsby, on the Yorkshire coast. These mines were responsible for the sinking of 94 vessels. The casualties comprised 32 British steamships, ten fishing vessels, and 15 mine sweepers. Mines do not discriminate: they sank 24 vessels from neutral countries. On 17th November 1915 the British hospital ship *Anglia*, transporting cot cases from the Western Front in France to Britain, succumbed to mines laid by UC-5 with the loss of 85 lives.

The Allies were powerless to stop the significant and costly loss of shipping caused by the Flanders Flotilla. However the Flotilla did suffer one setback when on 6th November UC-8 ran aground off Terschelling. This boat was sent from the periscope school at Kiel to bolster the flotilla and was en route to Bruges when she ran aground. This was the first Bruges-based submarine whose crew was interned in neutral Holland. On 9th November UB-17 sank the French destroyer *Branlebas* by torpedo.

The German submarine operations unleashed from Flanders began to step up the pace in 1916. On 24th March 1916 UB-29 commanded by Oberleutnant zur See Herbert Pustkuchen damaged the 1,353-ton Channel packet ship *Sussex* by firing a torpedo into her bows. He later said that he mistook the *Sussex* for a troopship because her decks were crowded. Those onboard thought that the vessel struck a mine and it was not until they limped to Boulogne that they realised they had been torpedoed, when torpedo fragments were found in a lifeboat. Fifty lives were lost as a result of the explosion when the torpedo from UB-29 struck her hull. Twenty-five American casualties were among the dead. This attack on a civilian vessel provoked international condemnation. President Wilson, who was stung by the loss of American lives, including women and children, voiced his discontent. On 19th April 1916 Wilson threatened to sever diplomatic relations with Germany if it did not abandon the strategy of attacking passenger and freight carrying vessels. As a result of this threat to German–American relations German submarine commanders were given the following instruction on 20th April 1916:

In accordance with the general principle of visit, search, and destruction of merchant-vessels recognized by international law, such vessels, both within and without the war zone, shall not be sunk without warning and without saving human lives unless the ships attempt to escape or offer resistance.[6]

Oblivious to the international furore, Pustkuchen continued his patrol and sank the British steamer *Salybia* before returning to Bruges.

During April 1916 the Flanders Flotilla suffered a double setback. The first occurred on 5th April when the propellers of UB-26 commanded by Oberleutnant zur See Wilhelm Smiths were entangled in the nets of the British drifter *Endurance* at Le Havre. The French torpedo boat *Trombe* dropped three bombs near to UB-26, which forced Smith and his 21 crew to surface and surrender to the Allies. Before abandoning the stricken submarine Smith made an effort to destroy all documentation that could prove useful to the enemy, but failed. French divers were sent down to search the wreck and found charts detailing the location of German minefields. UB-26 was renamed the *Roland Morillot*, after the French submariner who served with the French Navy throughout the war until killed in the Adriatic.

UC-5 ran aground on the Shipwash Shoal, near Harwich on 27th April 1916. The time was 9.00 a.m. and the tide was falling. Oberleutnant zur See Ulrich Mohrbutter, commander of UC-5, made every attempt to dislodge his vessel from the shoal. After using his engines and discharging weight overboard he failed to get free. Throughout the morning Mohrbutter sent out wireless signals requesting assistance from German vessels. Instead these signals revealed C-5's position to the Royal Navy. At 1.00 p.m. HMS *Firedrake* approached the stranded vessel. Resigned to surrender, Mohrbutter ordered his crew on deck. The crew was told to wave at the approaching British vessel to ensure that they were not fired upon. Before surrendering to HMS *Firedrake*, Mohrbutter ordered that explosive charges be placed against particular apparatus. He was anxious to destroy this equipment and intending to scuttle the vessel. As a boat from *Firedrake* was lowered into the water to accept the surrender of the crew Monrbutter ordered the fuses to be lit and the crew to dive overboard. The last man onboard detonated the charges and everyone followed the order. However, this effort to scuttle only succeeded in blowing a hole in the hull. *Firedrake* towed UC-5 into Harwich harbour where she was repaired. This captured Flanders vessel became an important tool in the Allied propaganda war. After her repairs she was put on display at Temple on the River Thames in London. Later she was taken to New York where she was exhibited and used to sell Liberty Bonds. Useful intelligence was gathered from the captured crew of UC-5 relating to the laying of mines and the attitude of the crew. The British learned that mines were laid at high water at a speed of two knots, one mine being dropped every two minutes in groups of 4. Intelligence reports based on the interrogation of prisoners captured from UC-5 reported that, 'the men state that minelaying work from submarines is very trying and frequently they are unable to get practically any sleep for three days. Most of them seem glad to have finished even at the expense of capture.'[7] It was also ascertained that except for one crewman, all of the men captured aboard UC-5 did not volunteer to serve on submarines.

Submarines from the Flanders Flotilla did have some success during April 1916. On 25th April, UB-18 commanded by Kapitänleutnant Otto Steinbrinck and UB-29 commanded by Oberleutnant zur See Pustkuchen (the commander who damaged the *Sussex*) were stationed off the Suffolk coast near to Lowestoft. Pustkuchen in UB-29 fired a torpedo into the light cruiser HMS *Penelope* causing her damage on 25th April 1916.

Steinbrinck in UB-18 saw four submarines from the Royal Navy on the surface off the coast of Yarmouth. Steinbrinck was a Flanders Flotilla submarine ace ranked within the first dozen aces of the War. He was responsible for sinking 210,000 tonnes of Allied shipping from Flanders. UB-18 fired a torpedo at the leading submarine, E22; however the British commander had seen her periscope and manoeuvred his boat to avoid the torpedo. E22, commanded by Lieutenant Reginald Thomas Dimsdale, turned to ram UB-18.

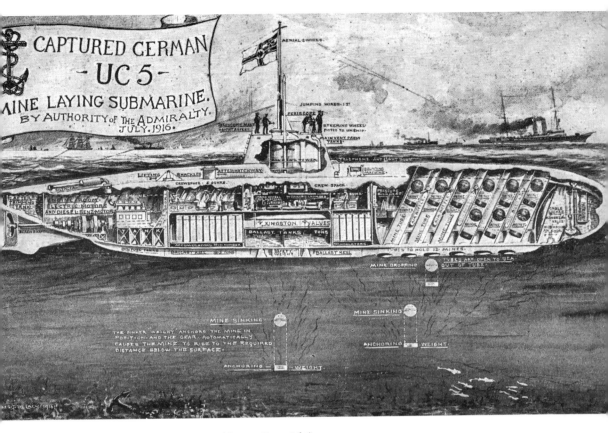

Captured German Submarine UC-5. (Crown Copyright)

As hunter became hunted, Steinbrinck in turn took evasive action and dived under E 22. Steinbrinck then brought UB-18 to periscope level and saw E 22 heading towards his position, at which point he fired two torpedoes. One torpedo struck E 22 while the other missed its target. E 22 blew up at 11.45 a.m. on 25th April 1916. As E 22 sank, Steinbrinck observed two British sailors fall into the sea. Steinbrinck was aware of the presence of the three other submarines and was in position with his stern pointing towards them and ready to fire another torpedo. Instead of attacking the three other vulnerable submarines, perhaps killing their crews, he decided to save life and surface to pick up the two survivors to prevent them from drowning. He then quickly dived to escape. Signaller William Harrod and E.R.A. Frederick Buckingham were the two sailors who were rescued by Steinbrinck. They were initially presumed lost, so it was a welcome relief for their families to later learn that they were captured and imprisoned at Dulmen Prisoner of War Camp in Westphalia, Germany.[8] Dimsdale, aged 30, sank with the remainder of the crew. Steinbrinck's selfless action to save the two British seamen was respected by his British adversaries who bore witness to this extraordinary rescue.

The Flanders Flotilla continued to lay mines throughout the summer in 1916 and was responsible for the sinking of 70,000 tons of shipping.[9] UB boats continued to stalk troop ships in the Channel and destroy navigational aids. The first successful use of hydrophone and depth charges occurred on 6th July 1916 when the Flanders boat UC-7 was sunk by depth charge from HMS *Salmon*.

British sailors onboard captured Flanders Submarine UC-5.

During July 1916, Captain Charles Fryatt, the British commander of SS *Brussels* was executed in Bruges. The SS *Brussels*, a steamship that belonged to the Great Eastern Railway Company that ferried passengers between Harwich and Rotterdam was harassed by the German Navy. A routine passage on 2nd March 1915 was interrupted when a German submarine signalled the SS *Brussels* to stop. Fryatt was aware that his vessel was faster than the enemy submarine. He ordered 'full steam ahead' and evaded the German U-boat. Later that month on 28th March 1915 Fryatt was once again harassed by the enemy, when U-33, commanded by Kapitänleutnant Konrad Gansser, ordered SS *Brussels* to stop. U-33 was a larger vessel and was much faster. Fryatt knew that he could not outrun this submarine, so he steered his vessel directly towards U-33. Rockets were fired as it approached the submarine. The commander of U-33 hesitated then began to dive as SS *Brussels* approached fast, but his initial delay resulted in Fryatt ramming the submarine. Fryatt continued his journey to Rotterdam as U-33 headed towards Belgium with a list. Fryatt continued to sail between Harwich and Rotterdam until 22nd June 1916 when SS *Brussels* was surrounded by a fleet of German destroyers from Bruges. Fryatt was unable to repeat his previous brave deeds, for he was not in a position to offer resistance. There was no chance of escape and SS *Brussels* was forced to surrender. The vessel was escorted to Zeebrugge. On arrival at Zeebrugge, Fryatt and his crew were initially taken to the Naval Headquarters in Bruges. Although they were prisoners in German custody, they were regarded as non combatants as merchant seamen. Nonetheless, Fryatt was arrested and taken to Ruhleben Prison along with his crew.

On 26th July 1916, Captain Fryatt was brought before a Court Martial in Bruges where he was tried for being a non combatant responsible for ramming the submarine U-33 on 28th March 1915. In the view of the German authorities Fryatt was a civilian who had exceeded his remit in attacking the U-boat. The German Captain Neumann defended Fryatt, but it was a vain attempt. Fryatt was unaware of the sentence until at 7.00 a.m. on 27th July when German officers brought him from his cell and escorted him to the Mur des Fusilles in Bruges. It was here that he was informed that he had been found guilty and had been sentenced to death for his brave attack upon U-33. Commander Freiherr von Butlar was in command of the firing squad. Captain Fryatt, aged 43, was executed. Fryatt's body was brought back to England for burial near his family home at Dovercourt (All Saints) Churchyard, Essex. After the execution, Fryatt's widow received her husband's personal possessions, including a nickel watch and chain. She also received a breathtakingly callous letter from the German authorities in Berlin offering to return Fryatt's pipe on receipt of payment for twenty pounds. After being captured, the SS *Brussels* was berthed near the seaplane base on the inner Mole at Zeebrugge where she served as living quarters for German military personnel.

September 1916 saw the delivery of the new batch two UC Boats to Bruges. Half of the first batch had been lost during operations from Flanders. The UC (II) boats was larger than the previous boats. They displaced 450 tons instead of 160 tons and had the capacity to carry more mines, 18 instead of 12. Unlike the first batch they were fitted with two torpedoes and were able to defend themselves while on patrol. They had greater range, which meant that operations could now be extended as far north as Flamborough Head in Yorkshire and off the coast of Southern Ireland. These UC boats could lay minefields outside the ports of Portsmouth, Portland, Dartmouth and Falmouth. The living conditions onboard were greatly improved. Towards the end of 1916, further batches of UC Submarines (UC-16 to -33) were deployed in Flanders ports. With additional submarines the Flanders Flotilla was of course able to increase its operational capabilities and sink more Allied ships.

During the closing months of 1916 the Flanders Fleet suffered further losses. On 30th November UB-19 commanded by Oberleutnant zur See Erich Noodt was sunk by the Q ship *Penshurst*. Seven men were lost, but 16 crew, including Noodt were captured. A Q Ship was a Royal Naval decoy vessel that would pose as a trader and sail under the flag of a neutral country. Once the U-boat's surfaced and fired warning shots across the bow of the 'trader' some of the crew would abandon ship. Assuming that the vessel was unmanned the U-boat would draw closer to the vessel before destroying it. However, the remaining crew members on the Q Ship were waiting for the U-boat to draw closer before opening fire with armament that included twelve-pounders, Lewis guns and depth charges. As soon as the U-boat was close, the White Ensign was raised and the crew fired. This deception was successful on numerous occasions during the war and accounted for the loss of a small number of Flanders-based submarines. The Admiralty conceived this naval strategy in December 1914 and 220 vessels including steamers, trawlers and fishing smacks were requisitioned by the Royal Navy to be deployed as Q Ships.

Starving England to defeat, by cutting off all supplies into the country was a very real prospect. It was anticipated that at the current rate of sinking merchant vessels, England would capitulate by the end of 1917. On 1st January 1917 Germany had declared unlimited submarine war against the Allies. Twenty-two submarines were based in Flanders by January 1917. That number had increased to 38 by March 1917.

The first months of 1917 saw losses amongst the coastal minelayers based in Flanders. The Q Ship *Penshurst*, which had sunk UB-19 a month earlier, scored another kill and sank UB-37 commanded by Oberleutnant zur See Paul Günther on 14th January 1917, with all 21 crew onboard.

UC-39 had arrived at Bruges on 3rd February after being newly built at Kiel. Commanded by Oberleutnant zur See Otto Ehrentraut, she left Zeebrugge on 6th February for the first time to patrol the British East Coast. This was regarded as a 'shake down' patrol for Ehrentraut and his crew. During the following days she sank a number of vessels. The first success came on 7th February when UC-39 encountered the Norwegian SS *Hans Kinck*. Ehrentraut fired three initial shots and time was allowed for the crew to abandon ship. Once they had disembarked from the vessel a torpedo was fired into the bows of the vessel and she sank. During the evening of 7th February Ehrentraut apprehended the British registered vessel the SS *Hanna Larsen*. The Master and Chief Engineer of this merchant vessel were taken onboard the UC-39 before the British vessel was sunk by gunfire and torpedo. During the afternoon of 8th February Ehrentraut sighted the SS *Ida* and opened fire. As the crew of this Norwegian vessel was preparing to abandon ship the UC-39 continued to fire upon them. As a result the Chief Mate and Steward were killed, and two men were wounded as they lowered their small boat into the sea. Ehrentraut's Second in Command then boarded *Ida* and sank her with bombs.

KAPITÄNLEUTNANT OTTO STEINBRINCK, FLANDERS FLOTILLA U-BOAT ACE.

Otto Steinbrinck was born on 19 December 1888 in Lippstadt. During World War One he commanded the I Flotilla submarine U-6 and later the Flanders Flotilla boats UB-10, UB-18 and UC-65 and was responsible for sinking 204 Allied vessels, which equated to 210,000 tons during 24 patrols. To commemorate the first anniversary of the creation of the Flanders Flotilla Steinbrinck received the Pour le Mérite from Kaiser Wilhelm on 29th March 1916 in recognition of the Allied tonnage that he had sunk. During his successful attack upon the British submarine E 22 he risked UB-18 to save two of the surviving British seaman who fell into the sea. After the war he became a prominent businessman within the German steel industry. Because of his friendship with Heinrich Himmler and because he was awarded honorary membership of the SS he was interned at the end of the Second World War. He felt uncomfortable about wearing SS uniform and during the war preferred his naval uniform. Accused of using slave workers, he was sentenced to five years imprisonment. Confined to a small prison cell he existed on a diet of bread and water. He did not serve the full five years and died on 16th August 1949 as a result of ill health caused by the poor conditions he endured. (Kapitänleutnant Otto Steinbrinck: Photo from U-boote Am Feind, 1937).

Ehrentraut's luck ran out later the same day. Locating a target while patrolling off Flamborough Head he was about to sink a merchant vessel when the destroyer HMS *Thrasher* surprised him. As Ehrentraut tried to take evasive action and dive, *Thrasher* launched a depth charge that exploded and caused damage to the conning tower and control room of UC-39. The explosion had caused casualties amongst the crew. With the hull ruptured by the impact of the explosion, water poured into the boat. There was a state of panic inside the crippled submarine and Ehrentraut made the decision to surrender. As UC-39 surfaced and Ehrentrant climbed out of the conning tower, he was killed by British fire. The three men who followed him were also killed and there were several wounded casualties. Onboard were the Master and Chief Engineer of the *Hanna Larsen*, sunk previously. With a white handkerchief in his hand the Master waved frantically at the British, who ceased fire. These two prisoners were rescued unharmed. Three German sailors dived into the sea, but drowned. Seven men were killed out of the 24 crewmen. The 17 remaining crew were taken onboard *Thrasher*. UC-39 sank while being towed.

Another Flanders submarine, UC-46, was sunk on 8th February 1917 when she was rammed by the destroyer HMS *Liberty* near to the Goodwin Sands. Her commander Oberleutnant zur See Friedrich Moecke and his 22 crew were all killed. On 23rd February UC-32 commanded by Oberleutnant zur See Herbert Breyer was destroyed when one of her own mines blew up off the coast of Sunderland. Another Flanders submarine was interned by the Dutch on 13th March when UB-6 commanded by Oberleutnant zur See Oskar Steckelberg ran aground off Hellevoetsluis.

Captured UC-5 pictured on the River Thames. UC-5 was displayed to the public at Temple. Blackfriars Bridge is in the background.

On 5th April President Woodrow Wilson brought the US into the conflict by declaring war on Germany. By April 1917 the German U-boats had sunk 155 British vessels altogether, amounting to 516,394 tons. Mines were responsible for sinking 14 ships of 28,888 tons. The human cost amounted to 1,125 lives.[10] During the first six months of 1917 in excess of two million tons of British shipping was lost to German U-boats.

The Royal Navy fought back. During the month of April, two German submarines from Flanders were sunk. On 5th April 1917 the Royal Naval submarine C7 was waiting off the Schouwen Buoy for any German submarine entering or leaving Zeebrugge. At 3.30 a.m. UC-68 commanded by Oberleutnant zur See Hans Degetau was returning from a patrol and was sunk by a C7 torpedo.

Above: During early February 1917 the American Steamer SS *Illinois* started her passage from Port Arthur, Texas, bound for England with a cargo of much needed supplies. On 18th March 1917 *Illinois* was sailing through the English Channel 20 miles north of Alderney when she encountered Flanders-based submarine UC-21. Oberleutnant sur See Reinhold Saltzwedel was the highly decorated commander of UC-21. During his career he would be awarded the Iron Cross (1st and 2nd Class) and the Pour le Mérite. The sinking of SS *Illinois* was photographed by a German officer from UC-21. When the submarine returned to port the German officer asked a Belgian photographer to develop the images and was threatened with his life not to duplicate them for his own use. The Belgian photographer was aware of the importance of these images and was determined to preserve copies to show after the War the destructive capability of the German submarine campaign. To hide them from the German occupiers he persuaded a gravedigger from Bruges to hide them in a family vault in a cemetery until the Armistice. These images formed part of the photographic collection of the Zeebrugge Museum.

On 19th April UC-30 struck a mine and sunk with all 27 crew including its commander Kapitänleutnant Heinrich Stenzler. She had been attacked twice by two Allied seaplanes, but managed to evade her pursuers without any damage caused. During the patrol the UC-boat had also experienced problems with her motors, but this had not prevented her from laying mines off Le Havre, Ouistreham and Cherbourg.

On 9th May UC-26 was sunk by HMS *Milne*. UC-26 had suffered numerous setbacks since joining the Flanders Flotilla in November 1916. While being repaired at Ostend, on 4th February 1917 she was crushed against the pier by a German steamer, damaging her oil fuel tanks and two torpedo tubes. The repair operation would continue into the beginning of April. Commanded by Kapitänleutnant Matthias Graf von Schmettow she departed Bruges on 30th April 1917 at 4.30 p.m. and sailed along the canal to Zeebrugge, leaving at 8.00 p.m. Her mission was to lay mines in the English Channel.

Schmettow torpedoed the Norwegian vessel SS *Certo* off Le Havre during the night of 2nd May. Three other torpedoes were fired at the two escort trawlers, but missed their targets. It is thought that the reason that these torpedoes missed was because the torpedo tubes were not repaired properly in Ostend. In fact the entire repair operation was botched: as well as the defective torpedo tubes the broken fuel tanks were not fixed.

Before heading towards Flanders UC-26 laid some mines off Cherbourg. This operation proved fruitful for within a couple of hours the British merchant vessel SS *Ussa* struck one. En route to Zeebrugge at 1 a.m. on 9th May UC-26 was intercepted by HMS *Milne* as she sailed on the surface near Calais. Schmettow misjudged the situation and was convinced that the British destroyer had not seen them. When Schmettow finally made the decision to dive it was too late. As she slowly submerged *Milne* approached UC-26 and clipped the inner pressure hull. UC-26 was submerged to the base of the conning tower when she was struck, causing the UC-boat to sink. Depth charges finished her off as she sank to the bottom of the English Channel. Nineteen crew, including Schmettow, perished. However, two men survived, Leutnant zur See Heinrich Peterson and Maschinistenmaat Acksel. It is reported that Acksel was afraid after his capture that he would be poisoned and refused to eat or drink anything that was given to him by his British captors. It was not until a British officer drank from the same cup that he drank and he had to be assured by Peterson that the food was safe to eat.[11]

As the submarine offensive from Flanders intensified, German losses increased. After May 1917 the Flanders Flotilla were losing an average of three boats each month. The volume of Allied shipping being sunk began to decline. Many of the submariners from 1914 had perished during three years of war. The rushed training of new submarine crews was inadequate and the poor standards at sea were one reason for their declining performance.

At 8.30 a.m. on 7th June 1917 UC-29, commanded by Kapitänleutnant Ernst Rosenow, fired a torpedo at close range into the bows of a small steamship off the southern Irish coast. The vessel was badly damaged, causing a 40-foot wide hole on her starboard side on the water line. Her boiler room, engine room and No. 5 hold flooded immediately upon impact. The explosion killed Stoker Petty Officer Isaac Radford who was stationed in the engine room. The weather conditions were misty with a wind and rough sea. A lifeboat containing the panic party under the command of Lieutenant F. Hereford was used as bait to lure the UC-boat to reveal its position. With great caution Rosenow waited for half an hour before surfacing to pick up these survivors in the lifeboat. Unbeknown to Rosenow this small vessel was not a merchant vessel but was in fact the Q Ship *Pargust*, commanded by Commander Gordon Campbell. His remaining crew lay still on the deck waiting for the order to man their gun and fire upon the unsuspecting submarine.

At 8.15 a.m. the periscope of UC-29 could be seen by Campbell at a range of 50 feet from the *Pargust*. At 8.33 a.m. Rosenow surfaced. He approached the lifeboat as the occupants started to row towards their damaged vessel. Rosenow made an attempt to shout instructions to the occupants of the boat through a megaphone, but they ignored his instructions. Rosenow gave the order to fire upon the lifeboat. Lieutenant Hereford continued to act as a decoy despite the fire. As soon as UC-29 was in line with the Q ship Campbell gave the order to open fire with all guns. The crew rose from the deck and fired their gun at the submarine. The first shell scored a direct hit on the conning tower of UC-29. Oil discharged from her side as she listed badly to port after receiving three direct hits at point blank range. Passing the *Pargust*, her crew rushed out from the conning tower with their hands in the air, indicating their intention to surrender. Campbell ordered his gun crew to cease-fire. As soon as fire had been withheld Rosenow tried to make a dash to escape through the mist. The German sailors standing on her aft deck were washed into the sea. The guns of *Pargust* shelled the fleeing UC-29, sinking her and the crew, with the exception of two survivors. One German sailor was seen to be clinging to her bow as she sank. The *Pargust* was assisted by the American destroyer USS *Cushing*, HMS *Zinnia* and the British sloop *Crocus*, who towed her to a safe port. The crew of *Pargust* was awarded medals for the action. Lieutenant Ronald Stuart and Seaman William Williams received the Victoria Cross following a ballot. Officers and men from the *Pargust* selected these two individuals to receive this prestigious honour on behalf of the ship. Campbell was awarded the DSO.

By 1917, Herbert Pustkuchen who sank the *Sussex* was in command of UC-66. On 12th June the trawler HMT *Sea King* observed UC-66 off the Lizard. *Sea King* approached UC-66 with great speed, forcing Pustkuchen to submerge. Depth charges detonated the mines being carried on UC-66 and she was destroyed with all her crew.

July was a bad month for the Flanders Flotilla. Losses were high. Five British seaplanes intercepted UC-1 in the Thames estuary on 24th July 1917; though she may have hit a mine. On 29th July 1917, two seaplanes bombed UB-20 and sank her; though again, mines may have done the damage.

The U-boats were not only in the Channel to harass the Allied shipping. The Channel was also the direct route for submarines to travel to hunting grounds in the Atlantic Ocean and it was estimated that at least one German submarine would pass through each night to this end.

On 4th August 1917 UC-44 was sunk by a German mine after laying eight mines off Waterford, Ireland. The irate commander Kapitänleutnant Kurt Tebbenjohanns was angry that his vessel should have succumbed to a minefield laid by UC-42. He was the only survivor to be rescued from the water. The Allies had deliberately not swept this stretch of sea in percipient anticipation that a German U-boat would return and sow another minefield. Documents retrieved from UC-44 indicated that German submarines were passing the Straits of Dover despite the mines and patrols. This was dispiriting evidence that the measures implemented by Vice Admiral Sir Reginald Bacon to restrict the use of the Dover Straits by barrage obstructions was a failure.

A duel was fought in the Bay of Biscay on 8th May between Captain Gordon Campbell VC DSO and the Flanders submarine ace Oberleutnant zur See Reinhold Saltzwedel, commanding UC-71. Campbell had already received the Victoria Cross and Distinguished Service Order, while Saltzwedel had been awarded the Iron Cross 1st and 2nd Class for his work with the Flanders Flotilla. Campbell was in command of the Q ship HMS *Dunraven* masquerading as a merchant steamer. Campbell observed an enemy submarine on the horizon, but continued to act as a merchant vessel by approaching the UC-boat's position in a zig zag pattern. Saltzwedel submerged but remained in her position. When *Dunraven* was within 5,000 yards UC-71 surfaced at 11.17 a.m. and opened fire upon her. The *Dunraven* returned fire from her gun. Campbell decreased speed to allow the submarine to pass, while simultaneously sending out distress signals which read 'Help! Come quickly – submarine chasing and shelling me.'[12] As shells from UC-71 fell near, *Dunraven* stopped her engines and dispatched a panic party in a small boat to give the impression she was sinking and that her crew were abandoning ship. A fire broke out aft onboard *Dunraven* as a result of the shelling. The submarine approached to a distance of 400 yards under the cover of smoke that was billowing from *Dunraven*'s stern.

Campbell did not give the order to fire at this stage for he wanted the UC-boat to get clear from the smoke. Before he could give that order an explosion on the aft deck destroyed the gun crew positioned there and was mistakenly interpreted by the remaining gun crews as the signal to fire. Saltzwedel cautiously submerged immediately. Twenty minutes later a torpedo struck the *Dunraven*'s engine room. Another panic party was sent out to try to entice the submarine. Saltzwedel remained submerged as he observed the situation through his periscope. Captain Campbell and a small complement of crew remained concealed onboard while the aft deck blazed. Fifty minutes later he brought UC-71 to the surface astern of *Dunraven* so that the submarine could not be fired upon. For twenty minutes the crew of UC-71 fired shells upon the Q ship, before submerging once more. Throughout this time Campbell refrained from returning fire. When UC-71 submerged Campbell decided to fire a torpedo, which narrowly missed the target. Another torpedo was fired as the submarine crossed her bows, but missed. Saltzwedel submerged yet again and Campbell sent a third panic party in the hope of luring UC-71 to destruction, but the extraordinary engagement ended when American and British destroyers arrived to evacuate the wounded and extinguish the fire onboard *Dunraven*. An effort was made to tow her to a port, but this failed when the weather deteriorated the following morning and she sank flying the White Ensign. Lieutenant Charles Bonner and Petty Officer Ernest Pitcher were selected by the crew of HMS *Dunraven* to receive the Victoria Cross for this action. Campbell received a bar to his Distinguished Service Order.

During September 1917 the Flanders Flotilla suffered further losses. UC-42 sank when she hit a mine that she had laid off the coast near Cork on 10th September. All hands including the commanding officer Oberleutnant zur See Hans Albrecht Müller perished in the accident. A bomb sank UC-72 commanded by Oberleutnant zur See Ernst Voigt from the seaplane 8695 off the Sunk Light Vessel on 22nd September.

On 26th September 1917 the British patrol vessel PC 61 fired upon UC-33, hitting the conning tower. PC 61 then rammed the mine layer at a speed of 20 knots, causing the vessel to role over. As she rolled her mines detonated causing her to explode and sink. PC 61 succeeded in rescuing one sailor and the commanding officer Oberleutnant zur See Alfred Arnold.

Lt. Kurt Zehmisch, an officer from Infantry Regiment 134 took this photo at Zeebrugge during June 1917 while on leave from the Western Front. It shows German submarine UC-62 in the sluice at Zeebrugge after a collision with a French vessel.

Towards the end of September UC-63 commanded by Oberleutnant zur See Karsten von Heydebreck embarked on her ninth patrol from Zeebrugge. This was an extremely prolific voyage for Heydebreck and his crew. After laying her mines near the Isle of Wight, UC-63 proceeded towards the Bay of Biscay. During the 14-day passage the submarine sank four ships, the *Europa*, *Dinorah*, *Italia* and *Perseverance*, which amounted to 14,000 to 16,000 tons. However, her tenth patrol from Zeebrugge was to be her last. Departing during the night of the 16th/17th October, UC-63 headed for the English Channel. During the following night while submerged she sailed through the Dover Barrage. The next morning she surfaced and steered a course to return to the Isle of Wight. During the day she was forced to dive by air attacks and was pursued by three armed trawlers. On reaching the coast near to the Isle of Wight UC-63 laid mines in two positions within the area. These mines would prove hazardous to Allied ships travelling from south coast ports such as Southampton and Portsmouth to Le Havre. As in previous voyages, Heydebreck sailed towards the Bay of Biscay searching for an opportunity to unleash his torpedoes against any unsuspecting enemy merchant vessel. A three-masted sailing vessel from the US was sunk off Bayonne as a result. On returning to Zeebrugge UC-63 sunk two steamers off the Normandy coast between Cherbourg and Le Havre. For two days she sailed along the south English coast looking for prey but did not encounter any. Heydebreck and his crew succeeded in passing the Dover Barrage while submerged, but she was sunk by HM Submarine E52 on the clear, moonlit night of 1st November. On passing the barrage UC-63 surfaced. Petty Officer Fritz Marsal was on the bridge with the officer of the Watch and a *matrose*. Marsal was keeping watch on the starboard side. The officer of the watch sent the *matrose* down for some coffee. During this time the boat's engineer came to the bridge to talk to the Officer of the Watch. This would prove a fatal distraction. Marsal, by chance, glanced to port and to his shock observed the British submarine E52 on the surface and turning her bow towards them in preparation for firing off a torpedo. Marsal immediately gave the alarm, but it was too late. A torpedo had been discharged by E52 and hit UC-63 amidships. The impact of the explosion threw him against the submarine, knocking out several teeth and gashing his chin. He found himself in the sea where he had to wait fifteen minutes to be recovered by the crew of E52. The Navigating Officer went down with the remainder of the crew.

Petty Officer Fritz Marsal was the sole survivor and during interrogation he revealed some useful information regarding UC boats based at Bruges. It was confirmed by Marsal that submarines would load their mines and torpedoes at Bruges. It was also discovered that submarine crews were billeted in a convent located near the German naval base.

UC-65 was another Flanders boat sunk during November 1917. Like her sister boat UC-63, she was also torpedoed by a Royal Naval submarine, C 15. UC-65 left Zeebrugge on 21st October and passed over the Dover Barrage while sailing on the surface at high water. Once through the Dover Straits the commander Kapitänleutnant Claus Lafrenz proceeded towards Le Havre, where mines were laid off the coast. Lafrenz was a successful U-boat commander and had received the Iron Cross (1st and 2nd Class). He was also reputed to have taken the first photograph of a British Q Ship. During the patrol Lafenz had fired all five torpedos onboard. On 31st October he sank a vessel off Start Point and on the 2nd sank two other vessels near to Prawle and Start Points. On 3rd November UC-65 was returning to Zeebrugge and the crew was looking forward to some well-earned leave when a torpedo fired from C15 sank her. The torpedo struck aft and Lafenz was blown into the air by the explosion and landed in the sea. As he fell he bruised his chest. Twenty-four men sank with UC-65. Five survivors were captured, including Kapitänleutnant Claus Lafrenz, Leutnant Diedrich Braue, Obermatrose Willy Ostergaard and Erich Fugner. A telegraphist named Theodor Bremer was also captured. During interrogation Lafrenz revealed how German submarines broke through the Dover defences when entering and leaving the English Channel. The intelligence gathered from Lafrenz prompted Vice Admiral Bacon to order the illumination of the Dover Barrage at night and to increase the number of mines positioned alongside the nets.

At sea, submarines were either being mined or intercepted by convoy operations and patrols. On 18th November HMS P 57, a patrol boat that was built with hard steel bows for ramming submarines encountered the Flanders-based UC-47 off Flamborough Head. UC-47 was commanded by Oberleutnant zur See Günther Wigankow. Some have questioned why an experienced submarine commander such as Wigankow should be caught on the surface, but since the radio mast was fully raised it is suspected that he was trying to send a message to German Naval HQ in Bruges. P 57 struck UC-47 perpendicular to the hull near to the conning tower, at a speed of 15 knots. Wigankow and his crew sank with the stricken submarine. A depth charge was fired to ensure her destruction, confirmed when oil rose to the surface.

Left: Sluice at the Zeebrugge end of the Bruges Canal where Lt Kurt Zehmisch took his photo in 1917 (page 39), taken in 2003.

Below: Photograph by Lt. Kurt Zehmisch of a German Torpedo Boat in the sluices at Zeebrugge, June 1917.

Sluice at the Zeebrugge end of the Bruges Canal taken in 2003, where Lt. Kurt Zehmisch took the photograph on page 41.

As Bacon's orders to increase the strength of the Dover Barrage defences were being executed with the installation of minefields and deep barrage nets across the Straits of Dover, German submarines were still accessing the English Channel. A deep minefield was laid during November 1917, but this counter-measure did not deter or obstruct the U-boat menace, for within the first two weeks of it being laid in position, 21 U-boats had successfully passed through. UB-56 commanded by Oberleutnant zur See Hans Valentiner was the first victim to strike a mine in the Channel on 19th December. As the mine barrage was strengthened across the English Channel, the passage of Flanders submarines into the Straits of Dover became more perilous.

During November and December, the British continued to improve their anti-submarine measures with a barrier that consisted of three lines of defence. The barrier ran between Folkestone and Cape Gris Nez. Rear Admiral Roger Keyes, Director of Plans at the Admiralty, was responsible for the Barrage and reported to the Dover Patrol Commander Vice Admiral Bacon. The first line comprised nets hung with mines. They were laid very low so that submarine commanders would not see them so easily. British patrol vessels patrolled along this first line looking for any submarines that were ensnared, or any submersible bold enough to overcome this obstacle by sailing over the net. Some submarines took a great risk in attempting to sail *under* the net, but the most common method was under the cover of darkness to sail over the nets and try to avoid the Allied surface fleets patrolling the vicinity. Many submarines would pass the Dover Straits by night and sail on the surface over the Barrage. For this reason the Dover Barrage was considered a failure during the early stages and as a consequence Bacon was replaced by Keyes as Commander of the Dover Patrol.

As soon as he took up his new role Keyes ordered a review of the Dover Barrage. Magnesium flares would burn across the Channel, illuminating the night sky, making it more difficult for U-boat commanders to pass. Wing Commander Frank Brock from the Royal Naval Air Service created these flares. This measure was not entirely effective for the magnesium would give an inconsistent blaze and at times the barrier was in darkness and German submarine commanders could exploit the moment.

The second line of defence consisted of a minefield with the mines positioned at various random depths. The third barrier consisted of two large searchlights that beamed concentrations of light onto the narrowest part of the English Channel. As these beams scoured the Dover Straits, Allied patrol vessels looked for prey. The Flanders Flotilla was losing one submarine every week during the early part of 1918. The average life expectancy of a submarine crew was six patrols.

UB-35 was destroyed six miles north of Calais by depth charges from HMS *Leven* on 26th January 1918. Commanded by Oberleutnant Karl Stöter, she left Zeebrugge on her final patrol on 16th January 1918 bound for the English Channel and the Bay of Biscay. Once UB-35 had navigated through the Dover Barrage Stöter looked for Allied targets. On 19th January Stöter fired two torpedoes into the hull of SS *Mechanician* off Start Point. Displacing 9,044 tons, the vessel was forced to return to port. Stöter continued his successful patrol sinking two vessels off the Isle of Wight. On 22nd January SS *Teelin Head* displacing 1,718 tons was sunk and the 3,677-ton SS *Serrana* was damaged, but was able to reach a friendly port. On the following day UB-35 fired a torpedo into the 3,405-ton SS *Corton*, damaging her but not fatally.

Stöter's luck ran out on 26th January 1918 when UB-35 stopped a Greek merchant vessel 20 miles south of Portland. At 2.00 a.m. Stöter brought his boat alongside and ordered the crew to abandon the vessel. Stöter intended to detonate charges onboard in an effort to sink her. As the fourth crewman from the Greek vessel boarded UB-35, HMS P 34 suddenly appeared at a distance of 1,500 yards. Stöter was forced to submerge immediately, discharging the four Greek crewmen and two crewmen from UB-35 into the sea. All six men were rescued by P 34. One member of the crew was left onboard the Greek vessel, as Stöter with great haste was forced to submerge. This crewman was taken prisoner and it was his capture that would save his life. At 10.30 a.m. during the following day Lieutenant Commander A Melsom commanding HMS *Leven* sighted the periscope of UB-35. Melsom was obsessed with sinking a German submarine and this was his chance. Initially he made an unsuccessful attempt to ram the submarine, then he swung the stern over her and launched depth charges. An explosion tore UB-35 apart. Stöter and six men were brought to the surface in an air bubble. Only one man was recovered from the sea but died soon later. Melsom was awarded the DSO for sinking UB-35.

Unidentified Allied vessel sunk by German submarine, photograph from the Zeebrugge Museum.

Oberleutnant zur See Günther Bachmann commanding UB-38 tried to pass the Straits of Dover on the French side of the Channel on the evening of 8th February 1918. Her position was revealed by magnesium flares and she was spotted by nearby patrol vessels. In a desperate attempt to evade capture Bachmann dived; three explosions were heard and UB-38 sank after being hit by a mine. All crew were killed. Admiral Scheer later wrote that it was at this point in the war that most realised 'the Straits were almost impassable'.[13] Only German submarines from Flanders would attempt to pass the Straits of Dover during 1918. With the increase in U-boat losses through the Dover Straits German U-boats based in the Heligoland Bight were forced to sail around the north coast of Scotland in order to reach the Atlantic instead of passing through the perilous obstacles in the English Channel.

The medieval town of Bruges with its lattice-work of beautiful canals was a refuge for German submarine commanders and their crews from the dangers of the war. While in Bruges they would live ashore; the officers would billet in hotels and the crew lived in a designated house for submarine ratings. The mortality rate of the crews from the Flanders Flotilla was high and Bruges must have seemed a kind of paradise for a time. However, during 1918 Bruges became the target of incessant air raids that focused their attention upon the concrete submarine pens that had six-foot-thick walls and roof, considered bomb proof. These shelters proved effective in protecting the submarines of the Flanders Flotilla.

Another strategy was therefore sought to counter the submarine menace. To impede their freedom of access to the open sea and destroy their bases was the counter measure decided upon. The British were determined to beard the 'Flemish' lion in his den.

NOTES

1. R H Gibson & M Prendergast, *The German Submarine War 1914-1918*, p27: Naval & Military Press, 2003.
2. Gregory Green: *On the War Path in Bruges*: Dienst Museum, Bruges.
3. National Archives: ADM 1/8423/152. HMS *Mohawk* casualty report 1915. Letter to Ethel Hollyer from the General Accountant of the Navy.
4. Geoffrey Brooks, *Fips: Legendary U-Boat Commander, 1915-1918*, p15: Leo Cooper 1999.
5. Ibid p18.
6. R H Gibson & M Prendergast, *The German Submarine War 1914-1918*, p89: Naval & Military Press, 2003.
7. National Archives: ADM 137 / 3876. Interrogation of survivors of German submarines.
8. National Archives: ADM 1/8455/92. Loss of submarine E 22.
9. R H Gibson & M Prendergast, *The German Submarine War 1914-1918*, p104: Naval & Military Press, 2003.
10. Ibid p161.
11. National Archives: ADM 137/3876. Interrogation of survivors of German submarines.
12. 'The London Gazette, No.31021', dated 20th November 1918.
13. R H Gibson & M Prendergast, *The German Submarine War 1914-1918*, p289: Naval & Military Press, 2003.

CHAPTER 2

A PLAN TO BLOCK BRUGES

An attempt to deal with the German submarine problem that emanated from the Bruges canal was proposed towards the end of 1916. In a report dated 24th November 1916, Commodore Reginald Tyrwhitt called for the destruction of Zeebrugge lock. Artillery bombardments and aerial bombing had proved ineffective. The attack would take place 1 ½ hours prior to sunrise and his intention was to 'sink a ship of slightly less beam than the width of the lock itself. This proposal at first sight may appear to be an impossibility, but, on going into details it is not so difficult as it appears.'[1] A ship of the Apollo Class was identified as a potential vessel to ram the lock gates, with a crew of 11 men. The attack would be preceded by an aerial bombardment and a barrage involving all Monitors from the 3rd Battle Squadron. Tyrwhitt considered this action would provide an adequate distraction while the blockship passed the Mole and approached the mouth of the canal. Tyrwhitt also proposed the use of gas to debilitate German gun crews stationed in shore batteries before the arrival of the blockship.

The designated blockship would be escorted by two fast minesweepers and guided by the breakwater as it approached the canal entrance, the vessel would be rammed into the lock gate, then exploded. Tyrwhitt was optimistic that, 'the lock gates will be utterly irreparable and the ship, being jammed in the entrance, will be very difficult to remove.'[2] Two fast motor boats would be carried as a means of escape after the completion of the operation.

At a meeting of Admiral Jellicoe the First Sea Lord, Vice Admiral Bacon, the Commander of the Dover Patrol and Commodore Tyrwhitt, the Commander of the Harwich force, the plan was vetoed. Bacon did put forward the proposition that if there were to be a future raid on Zeebrugge, Coastal Motor Boats should attack the lock gates with torpedoes.

Tyrwhitt made a further proposal during May 1917 suggesting that an amphibious operation be carried out to seize the Mole and Zeebrugge with the purpose of using the port as a base to carry out further operations to seize Antwerp and break the stalemate on the Western Front. The approach of the amphibious force would be covered by a smoke screen and a gas screen, devised by Wing Commander Frank Brock from the Royal Naval Air Service. Bacon responded negatively; however, he was interested in developing the idea to seize the Mole for the purpose of destroying the lock gates of the Bruges canal.

By the end of 1917 it was reported by intelligence sources that 38 submarines and 28 destroyers were based at Bruges and were using the exits at Zeebrugge and Ostend to gain access to the sea. The Allies had two options for preventing enemy vessels from Bruges from going to sea. The first option was to capture the Belgium coast and the port of Bruges. The Third Ypres offensive in the later months of 1917 had not succeeded in capturing these objectives. In the early part of 1918, another military operation was not viable because the Allied armies were not strong enough to initiate a further campaign. The only feasible option that remained was therefore either to destroy or obstruct the enemy's exits to the sea. If the Royal Navy could succeed in such an operation, then the German Navy would be ensnared within the confines of Bruges.

Vice Admiral Bacon submitted his plan to block Zeebrugge on 3rd December 1917, a month after the Third Ypres campaign had run its course. The plan involved bombarding German shore batteries east of Zeebrugge, deliberately leaving batteries west of the Mole to deceive the enemy and conceal the intended objectives. The operation would be executed at night and aided by a smokescreen. The northern half of the Mole would be temporarily captured and held. The raiding party would assault the Mole in two Monitors. While on the Mole, all enemy vessels berthed on the inner Mole and all guns would be destroyed. The seaplane base and any German buildings, equipment and defences would be sabotaged. A light beacon was to be erected on the Mole to guide blockships and escorts into Zeebrugge harbour. The objective of the raiding party was to hold the Mole for as long as possible and destroy as much as possible as the blockships passed to their sinking positions across the canal entrance.

A ship of the Blanche class would act as blockship and proceed towards the canal entrance. Once the vessel had blocked the entrance, her crew would try to reach the Mole and escape on the Monitors berthed alongside the outer sea wall. Once the retirement signal had been given and the raiders safely embarked, destroyers would tow the Monitors off the Mole.

The last days of 1917 brought a change in command at the Admiralty. With the approval of PM Lloyd George, Geddes replaced the First Sea Lord Jellicoe with Sir Rosslyn Wemyss. On 28th December 1917 Rear Admiral Roger Keyes was appointed to Dover Command replacing Vice Admiral Bacon. Promoted to Vice Admiral, Keyes was now responsible for the passage of all Allied shipping through the English Channel. This appointment would give Keyes the chance to focus his energies on tackling the German submarine menace. The First Sea Lord Admiral Sir Rosslyn Wemyss ordered Keyes to devise a plan to attack Zeebrugge and Ostend. Wemyss's predecessor First Sea Lord Jellicoe had approved of an attack on these ports during December 1917.

Keyes was the ideal man for coordinating this operation. Firstly, during this time Keyes was already playing an important role in the preparations for this dangerous enterprise. He provided a list of suitable and available cruisers in the Royal Navy that were obsolete and could be utilized as blockships during the operation. Secondly, he had inspected the Bruges canal entrance at Zeebrugge when HMS *Lurcher* called at the port in October 1914.

It was decided that simultaneous raids would be carried out on Zeebrugge and Ostend to sink ships containing concrete to obstruct the canal entrances. It was necessary to block Ostend to prevent smaller German vessels from entering and leaving Bruges using the smaller canal. If one raid were carried out then the enemy would be alerted to further raids, so it was important that these raids were carried out at the same time, in order to take the enemy by surprise and block the canals simultaneously. For the raid on Zeebrugge Keyes proposed a diversionary attack upon the Mole in order to divert attention from the blocking operation and to destroy the guns that would prevent the blockships from reaching the entrance to the Bruges canal. This plan would greatly assist the blockships to pass the Mole itself, before they ran the gauntlet of the barrage from shore batteries. If the guns on the Mole were either not captured, destroyed or their attention diverted, then the blockships stood little chance of entering the harbour and reaching the entrance to the Bruges canal. The secondary objective for the Zeebrugge raid was to inflict enough damage on the Mole facility to render it useless to the enemy in the future.

It was learnt through intelligence that approximately 30 submarines and 35 surface vessels including destroyers and torpedo boats would be present at the naval facility at Bruges at the beginning of 1918. Keyes submitted his proposal to block the Zeebrugge and Ostend canals to the Admiralty on 24th February 1918. The meeting lasted for two long hours. Keyes later recalled:

I explained my proposals in detail, was severely catechised and after the meeting, left the attached paper with the First Sea Lord who circulated it, returned it to me with the remarks of the Sea Lords, and informed me that my plan of attack was approved.[3]

German 6-inch gun defending the port.

Any initiative to block the Bruges canal would involve passing the heavily defended Zeebrugge Mole. The Mole at Zeebrugge was an enormous breakwater built to protect the harbour from severe sea conditions from the north and west. Construction began in 1893. Concrete blocks weighing 3,000 tons were used. It was completed in 1903 and opened with great pomp by King Leopold of Belgium. Semicircular in shape and 1½ miles in length, the Mole extended half a mile in a northeasterly direction towards the sea; it was regarded as the longest in the world. Barrie Pitt, in his book *Zeebrugge* points out that the length was greater than the distance between Marble Arch and Tottenham Court Road. An anonymous German serviceman wrote:

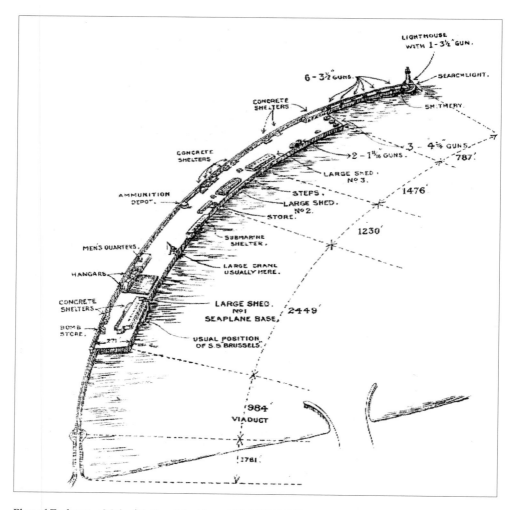

Plan of Zeebrugge Mole. (National Archives ADM 137/3894)

The two thousand four hundred metre long white wall extends into the sea and you need almost half an hour to reach the lighthouse, with the open water in front of you and with small and colourless houses along the coastline behind you. The road is so wide we could easily have organised a car race next to the railway lines. Outside, at quite some distance from land the wall becomes as broad as the market square of a large city. Many rails cut through the pavement.[4]

At the start of the War, it was transformed by the conquering Germans into a fortress to defend the canal entrance and harbour from attack. According to intelligence, it was estimated that a thousand men occupied the garrison on the Mole. Aerial reconnaissance photographs showed that the Mole was strongly fortified. The Mole was divided into four sectors. A 300-yard causeway consisting of a road and a double track railway led to the steel viaduct. The road and railway continue along the viaduct, which measures a further 300 yards, traversing a breach in the Mole. The purpose of this breach was to allow the tidal flow to flow through and to prevent silting within the Mole perimeter. The viaduct leads to the broad Mole itself. A 16-foot high, 10-foot-thick concrete wall was constructed on the outer seaward side to protect the harbour

German soldier wearing a gas mask; the sheepskin looks like it provided good protection from the harsh North Sea winds that battered the Zeebrugge Mole.

complex from severe northerly gales. The top of the wall contained a nine-foot-wide roadway and a further parapet wall measuring four foot high. At high tide, the top of the parapet would be 30 feet above sea level and would be 15 feet higher than the deck of any warship. This section of the Mole also served as a seaplane base and the former passenger terminal was converted for this purpose. A long shed constructed of reinforced concrete was built by the Germans to accommodate up to a thousand soldiers. Submarines from Bruges and torpedo craft would berth at the Mole before proceeding to the open sea. The enemy garrison was based at the seaward end of the Mole, where stone trenches, machine gun and anti-aircraft installations protected by barbed wire entanglements were installed. The fourth sector leading to the lighthouse contained two 3.5-inch guns and four 4.1-inch guns, which could be rotated 360 degrees, enabling them to fire seawards and towards the inner harbour and shoreline. The Germans also mounted a 6-inch Verey cannon near to the lighthouse, to illuminate any approaching assault force.

The lighthouse at the end of the Mole was used as a signal and observation station. Before the lighthouse on the promontory that connected the lighthouse to the broad section of the Mole the Germans had established a battery of six guns of calibre 3.5 & 4.1 inches, which were thought to be able to fire seawards and to the shoreline as required. This would prove a dangerous hazard for any raiders, because they would be forced to sail up the deep channel that passed this battery to within a few yards, exposed to fire at point blank range. If a vessel planned to berth alongside the outer Mole wall then she too would need to approach close to this battery. If a vessel succeeded in passing these guns, she would then encounter three heavy guns, which were positioned on the eastern extremity of the broad section of the Mole. They would fire on any vessel that passed the lighthouse and entered the port.

If a vessel got this far, then she would need to avoid net and barge booms that were positioned between the eastern end of the Mole and a buoy located 270 yards south. If a vessel sailed into one of these barge booms her propellers would be entangled in the nets, which would significantly reduce speed or disable her sufficiently for the guns on the Mole and the shoreline to fire upon and sink her. Together with all these defences, any raider would also have to overcome navigational problems, such as the strong tidal stream and uncharted shoals; and during a night-time attack, would be required to recognize reference points in darkness, which would require great seamanship skills. Once the Germans were alerted to a raid, their searchlights and flares would illuminate the sky and expose the attackers' position, making them vulnerable to enemy batteries.

The canal entrance was closely defended by artillery. By early 1918, 225 German guns defended the Belgian coast from Nieuport to the Dutch border; 136 of these guns were of calibres ranging from 6 to 15 inches, with ranges up to 24 miles. The coastline defences in and around the port included trenches protected by dense barbed wire entanglements, machine gun batteries and emplacements. Keyes and his staff would have been acutely conscious of these myriad challenges as they planned the raid on Zeebrugge.

NOTES

1. National Archives: CAB 45/268: Admiral Sir Roger Keyes' original letters and comments on the Eastern Mediterranean (Dardanelles and Gallipoli), the Ostend and Zeebrugge raid, and the Dover Straits, 1915-1930.
2. Ibid.
3. Ibid.
4. Anonymous German testimony. In Flanders Fields Museum, Ypres.

CHAPTER 3

VICE ADMIRAL ROGER KEYES

The raid on Zeebrugge was the defining moment in Roger Keyes' life, but he displayed daring, innovative leadership and a capability to devise strategy throughout his naval career. Keyes was born in the Punjab, India on 4th October 1872. His career with the Royal Navy began in July 1885 as a cadet on HMS *Britannia*. Two years later he was assigned to HMS *Raleigh*. During his service on this frigate he was promoted to midshipman in 1887. From 1889 he served on the cruiser HMS *Turquoise*, which patrolled the east coast of Africa with the mission to thwart the transportation of slaves. Keyes quickly climbed through the ranks, promoted to acting sub-lieutenant in November 1891 and two years later Lieutenant in 1893. During the Boxer Rebellion in 1900 Keyes was a Lieutenant in command of the gunboat HMS *Fame*. Together with sister ship HMS *Whiting* he was deployed to China as part of the international effort against the Boxers. Nationals from Britain, America, France, Italy and Germany were isolated when the Boxer Rebels besieged Peking during June 1900. 3,500 foreigners threatened by the Boxers sought refuge in a compound defended by a military force of just 407 men, 56 of them Americans. Chinese Christians also sought refuge in the compound. The Boxers killed 250 foreigners and their campaign against westerners reached its climax when they murdered German Minister Ketteler on 20th June 1900.

An international task force led by Royal Naval Officers rushed to Peking to relieve the city, but was thwarted by strong resistance at Tientsin between 10th and 26th June. It was necessary to sail along the River Peiho to Tientsin, a passage strongly guarded by a series of forts. An effort was made to pass this river and a Royal Naval task force led the international initiative. The campaign began with the bombardment and capture of Taku Fort, the first fort that defended the river. Keyes volunteered to take the next fort at Hsi-Cheng with two gunboats, but was forbidden to do anything. Unperturbed, he continued to press his proposal by trying to interest Russian Staff Officers. They laughed at Keyes' idea and pointed out that at least five thousand soldiers with strong artillery support were required to overcome these defences.

Despite his youth, Keyes was a determined, zealous individual who believed in his abilities and in his plans. Acting against orders he took it upon himself to take HMS *Fame* up the River Peiho and attack Hsi-Cheng Fort with an assault force of 34 men. He succeeded in blowing the guns with explosives. Such was the force of the explosion that it blew out the portholes of the flagship HMS *Barfleur* that was moored twenty miles away. On his return Keyes was presented with a case of champagne and invited to dine onboard *Barfleur* with the Admiral. This was the moment Keyes began to make a name for himself within the Royal Navy. The Admiralty was so impressed by his conduct that they promoted him from the rank of Lieutenant to Commander. When Peking was relieved on 14th August 1900, Keyes was the first person through the sluice gates to reach the compound where the westerners were besieged.

During the first decade of the twentieth century Keyes held numerous posts within the Royal Navy. In November 1910 he was appointed Inspecting Captain of Submarines. Keyes began the First World War with the rank of Commodore with command of the Eighth Submarine Flotilla, based at Harwich. Keyes was never afraid to confront the enemy and during the first months of the war he plotted to bring the German Navy to battle. To counter the threat from German naval patrols in the North Sea he sanctioned an attack on these vessels in the Heligoland Bight, with the purpose of enticing German Naval Command to deploy its larger vessels in response. Keyes ordered his submarines to wait for the German heavy ships. It was Keyes' strategy that generated the first naval battle of the First World War. The Battle of Heligoland Bight took place on 28th August 1914 and involved Rear-Admiral Beatty's First Battle Cruiser Squadron and Commodore Reginald Tyrwhitt's Harwich Force. It resulted in the sinking of the German light cruisers *Ariadne*, *Mainz* and *Koln* and the destroyer *V-187*. 1,000 German sailors were also lost in this action. With such significant losses in men and ships the Kaiser was forced to revise his naval strategy, which would result in his surface vessels playing a defensive role, moored for most of the time in German ports.

Admiral Sir Roger Keyes.

Keyes would look for any opportunity to go to sea. During the Battle of Heligoland Bight, he was aboard the destroyer HMS *Lurcher*, contravening Admiralty policy that forbade high ranking officers from taking part. He was present when *Lurcher* went alongside the sinking *Mainz* to rescue 220 German survivors from the stricken vessel. On his return to his dismay he was ordered not to go to sea in a destroyer because of his high rank. Werner (Fips) Fürbringer, First Watch Keeping Officer onboard U-20, wrote of the effect of the action at Heligoland Bight: 'The adverse effect of the action on our morale, the so-called Battle of the Heligoland Bight, was immense. We had lost four ships without reply in a daring coup and one had to give the enemy full credit for the careful reconnaissance and planning which must have gone into it.'[1]

During October 1914 Keyes was responsible for escorting the 7th Division and the 3rd Cavalry Division from England to Zeebrugge. When the time came to abandon Zeebrugge before the advancing German Army it was Keyes who suggested that the lock gates of the Bruges canal be destroyed, but he was told that the British Army would require use of the canal when it was reoccupied and his idea was not approved.

In 1915 Keyes was appointed Commodore Chief of Staff to Rear Admiral Sackville Carden, the Allied naval squadron commanders stationed off the Dardanelles. The Gallipoli Campaign was underway as he arrived. Carden had to resign his position through ill health in March and Vice Admiral Sir John De Robeck was his successor. Keyes devised a plan to break through the Dardanelles Straits that led into the Black Sea. The aim was to open access to the Black Sea, attack the Turkish fortifications and guns from the rear and cut the Turkish Army supply route. It was his intention to send three Naval Squadrons into the Dardanelles Straits under the cover of a smoke screen and attack the Turkish fortifications and guns that were harassing Allied passage. Minesweepers would sweep a passage though the straits. Surviving battleships would then concentrate their firepower upon the Turkish fortifications. Churchill the First Lord of the Admiralty and architect of the terrible Gallipoli campaign supported Keyes' proposal. 'The Keyes plan was remarkable for its audacity.'[2] However, the Admiralty and Cabinet were more cautious about embarking on further schemes and rejected the plan. Keyes was awarded the DSO and CMG for his role in the Gallipoli campaign.

In June 1916 Keyes returned to Britain to command HMS *Colossus*, a battleship of the Grand Fleet. In 1917 he was promoted to Rear Admiral and given command of the Fourth Battle Squadron. Keyes was then assigned the role of Director of Plans at the Admiralty based in London. As Director of Plans he was already involved with work he would continue in his next command. He believed his remit was to

…make the passage of the Dover Straits dangerous to submarines, but to strike at the root of the evil, by attempting to block the sea exits from Bruges, which the Germans had developed into a most formidable and well equipped base for destroyers and submarines.[3]

He took up his role as Commander Dover Patrol on 1st January 1918. Keyes was anxious to prevent enemy vessels entering the Channel. He wrote in his memoirs that:

Modern war is too costly in life and treasure to prolong the agony by inaction. Thousands of our men were fighting desperately in other areas, and I felt that a decision must now be fought for in the area confided to my charge. I had learnt my lesson off Gallipoli, where I had watched a campaign that had infinite possibilities peter out through irresolution; and, cost what it might, I was determined to put an end to the peaceful inaction in the Dover Straits, for which our shipping farther afield was paying so heavily.[4]

There was a distinct difference between the command of Keyes and Bacon. Bacon adopted the defensive approach to war, while Keyes preferred to fight and win. Although Bacon played a role in conceiving the plan to seize the Mole and block Zeebrugge, Bacon could not put his plans into action. Keyes had the ability to get things done. Conscious of the bitter campaigns fought by the British Army on the Western Front he wanted the Royal Navy to take an offensive approach. He would show the British public that the Royal Navy was fighting as hard as their British Army counterparts mired in the trenches.

One of his first tasks was to close the Straits of Dover to German U-boats that were passing over the nets and mines on the surface at night time. As mentioned earlier, he revised the structure of the Dover Barrage. Mines were laid at varying depths and the Dover Straits was illuminated at night by magnesium flares and searchlights. These measures assisted the Dover Patrol to observe any German U-boats passing on the surface and force them down into the minefields and their destruction. From 1st January to 23rd April 1918 several submarines from Flanders were sunk in the Dover Straits as a result of the changes that he implemented.

UC-50 was one of the German submarines from the Flanders Flotilla that was sunk. On 4th February 1918, while patrolling the Channel off Dungeness, HMS *Zubian* sighted UC-50, commanded by Kapitänleutnant Rudolf Seuffer. Seuffer and her crew had patrolled the Bay of Biscay when she was depth charged by *Zubian* at 5.30 a.m. Oil appeared on the sea's surface, indicating the destruction of UC-50. A Royal Naval diver confirmed the sinking.

As UC-50 was being hunted Keyes was taken in a seaplane to watch from the air. During this flight the aircraft experienced engine failure and was forced to ditch in the sea. The conditions were extremely unfavourable and the sea was rough. Although there were Royal Naval vessels in the vicinity chasing the UC boat Keyes and the crew of the downed seaplane could not see one. 'It was a couple of hours before we were picked up, and I was haunted by a horrible fear that a German submarine might come up and take us prisoners to Germany.'[5] When their Chief failed to return, Keyes' Staff in Dover launched a frantic search operation and within a few hours Keyes and the downed crew were found by a Coastal Motor Boat and brought to safety.

During the early months of 1918 Keyes and his staff were busy preparing for the raids. Keyes insisted on leading the armada in his flagship HMS *Warwick* during the operation. Leading by example, Keyes was in conspicuous danger throughout the raid on Zeebrugge as *Warwick* sailed off the Mole. On his return from Zeebrugge he was awarded the KCB (Knight Companion of Bath) by King George V. As mentioned earlier, the propaganda value of the raids, despite their failure in their key objectives, was immense. The Kaiser's offensive launched on 28th March had seen the German Army break through the Allied lines pushing them back deep into France and towards Paris; the audacious raid on Zeebrugge initiated by Keyes showed the British public that the Allies were on the offensive in these difficult times and for this reason Keyes was regarded as a national hero.

Keyes continued with his career in the Royal Navy after the First World War. In May 1935 he retired with the rank of Admiral of the Fleet. In 1934 he was elected as the Conservative Member of Parliament for Portsmouth North. During October 1938 Keyes was among the Conservative MPs who abstained in the vote to sanction the Munich agreement. During October 1939, soon after the outbreak of the Second World War, Keyes approached Winston Churchill, First Lord of the Admiralty with a proposal to lead an attack on Trondheim in Norway, using obsolete Royal Naval vessels, but his offer was declined. On 7th May 1940 Keyes initiated a debate on the competency of the cabinet after the Allied defeat in Norway during the previous month. Keyes was dressed in the uniform of Admiral of the Fleet. It was this debate that resulted in the collapse of Neville Chamberlain's administration and the creation of a coalition government led by Winston Churchill. Churchill appointed Keyes to overseas Combined Operations Command during July 1940. Keyes, the man who masterminded the raid on Zeebrugge in 1918, was now responsible for the organisation and training of the Commandos. His remit covered the planning of raids on the coastline of Nazi-occupied Europe. In this role Keyes contributed to the devising of landing craft for this revolutionary type of warfare. However, other Chief of Staff Officers considered Keyes' plans to be unfeasible and in October 1941 Churchill was influenced by these officers to replace him. Captain Lord Louis Mountbatten took over the role. Keyes felt betrayed and criticized Churchill and his government's running of the war from the back benches of the House of Commons. It was Keyes who proposed a vote of no confidence in Churchill's administration in July 1942, which was defeated. In an effort to appease and prevent him from causing further trouble, Keyes was offered a peerage in January 1943. Keyes accepted the peerage with good grace and was known as Baron Keyes of Zeebrugge and Dover.

Keyes did get to go to sea again. With the support of the Ministry of Information, he embarked on a lecture tour of North America, Australia and New Zealand during the summer of 1944. He was invited to spend some time with the United States Pacific Fleet and was aboard USS *Appalachian* during the Battle of the Philippine Sea, 19th–20th October 1944. On 25th October USS *Appalachian* took part in the landings at Leyte and was attacked by Japanese aircraft. Anti-aircraft smoke covered Keyes who was standing on the ship's bridge and this smoke inhalation damaged his lungs. Keyes returned home to England, but died on 26th December 1945 from a heart attack. His wish was to be buried with his fellow Zeebrugge raiders and this was granted when he was buried in St James's Cemetery, Dover.

During the fiftieth commemoration of the Zeebrugge Raid in 1968, Lord Mountbatten commented: 'Twenty-four years after 1918, when it fell to me to lay on the great raid on St. Nazaire, I did my best to emulate Zeebrugge. It was one of the Navy's proudest battle honours.'[6] Keyes was a man who would try to tackle the impossible in order to win the war. He was an innovator, who would devise strategies and would have the courage and conviction to implement those plans. His style of command and his character may be construed as reckless, the Zeebrugge operation itself of course sustained many casualties. But the path to victory is paved by the tragic loss of men. L. Carlyon wrote of Keyes with reference to his time at Gallipoli, but the judgement is as relevant to Zeebrugge:

HMS *Warwick*, Flagship of Vice Admiral Roger Keyes during the Zeebrugge raid. This cruiser was sunk by U-413 on 24th February 1944 off Trevose Head, North Cornwall.

Every navy needs a Roger Keyes, just as every army needs a George Patton. They provide the Homeric stuff; they make war seem grander than a trip to the abattoir. All that really matters is that such people never become supreme commanders. Keyes had a buccaneering spirit that was at odds with the caution of de Robeck. Throughout the Gallipoli campaign that was to come, Keyes wanted to try things when others wanted to do nothing.[7]

In numerous newspaper articles written soon after the raid in April 1918, Keyes was compared with Nelson. Some articles declared that Keyes had displayed the Nelson touch. If Keyes had been killed at Zeebrugge, he might well have achieved something like Nelson's immortality.

NOTES

1. Geoffrey Brooks, *Fips: Legendary U-Boat Commander, 1915-1918*, p5: Leo Cooper 1999.
2. Winston S Churchill, *The World Crisis 1911-1918*, Vol 2, p911: Odhams Press Limited 1938.
3. Sir Roger Keyes, Admiral of the Fleet RN, *The Naval Memoirs 1916-1918*, p199: Thornton Butterworth Ltd, London, 1935.
4. Ibid p162.
5. Ibid p173.
6. Lord Mountbatten, the *Daily Telegraph*, Monday 22nd April 1968.
7. L.A. Carlyon, *Gallipoli*, p94: Bantam books 2003.

CHAPTER 4

PREPARATION FOR THE ZEEBRUGGE RAID

The organisation for the raids on Zeebrugge and Ostend fell to Vice Admiral Roger Keyes and the Dover Patrol. It was an enormous undertaking, something that could not be done by Keyes alone. Therefore, Keyes assembled a large staff of officers to assist in planning the finer details of the operation, the training of personnel and the preparation of all vessels involved. Keyes chose his Staff from officers he served with during his extensive naval career. They were people whom he had known and could trust. He needed support from a Staff Officer and initially requested Major Godfrey from the Royal Marines. Keyes served with Godfrey at Gallipoli in 1916; however Godfrey was unavailable. Keyes then asked for Captain Alfred Carpenter to be appointed to this role. Carpenter had served as Keyes' navigator aboard HMS *Venus* prior to the First World War. Keyes respected him for his attention to detail and ability to absorb complex information. Captain Wilfred Tomkinson was appointed as Keyes' Chief Personal Aide. Tomkinson was commander of HMS *Lurcher* during the Battle of Heligoland Bight in August 1914, when Keyes was Commodore onboard.

Captain Henry Halahan was selected to lead the naval assault team. Halahan first saw action as a Midshipman while serving aboard HMS *Aurora* in 1900. He participated in the siege of Tientsin. During 1914 he commanded HMS *Bustard* during the bombardment of German positions on the Belgian coast. He received his DSO for his command of Naval heavy batteries based in Belgium from January 1915. When Halahan received a request from Keyes for volunteers he immediately volunteered himself. 'May I say that if the operation for which you said you might want some of my men is eventually undertaken, I should very much like to take part in it. I would willingly accept the same conditions … that I should not expect to come back.'[1]

The transport of reinforcements, supplies and ammunition to France and the responsibility of ensuring that these transports were free to sail across the English Channel unmolested from enemy vessels and submarines was the remit of the Dover Patrol. The preparation for the raids placed incredible strain upon the Dover Patrol to such an extent that assistance was required from the Grand Fleet, Harwich Force and the naval dockyards at Portsmouth and Chatham.

There would be no purpose in blocking the entrances to the canal if the blocking ships could easily be removed. So it was important to decide on the type and dimension of vessels used and what damage would be required in order to sink them and to make it difficult for the enemy to attempt to remove them. In order to achieve the objective the blockships should be too large to be lifted by hawser or lifting equipment. Measures should be taken to ensure that the enemy was denied the option of cutting away and dismantling the vessel. The use of cement would make the vessel too heavy to lift and placing cement in awkward places to counter the use of cutting equipment would satisfy these requirements. To facilitate the swift sinking of each vessel on an even keel, a hundred tons of cement and rubble were evenly distributed in the bottom of each of the blockships. They would be scuttled so that the vessel rested on a damaged portion of the hull.

Five obsolete light cruisers, originally constructed under the Naval Defence Act of 1889, were selected for the task of blocking the canal entrances. Initially they were on standby to block the French ports of Boulogne, Calais and Dunkirk if the German Army broke through at Ypres and captured these ports. The success of the Kaiserslacht launched in March 1918 made the loss of these ports a real threat. HMS *Thetis*, *Intrepid* and *Iphigenia* were designated to block the Zeebrugge entrance, while HMS *Brilliant* and *Sirius* would block the Ostend entrance. These old light cruisers were of the required length to block the Bruges canal at Zeebrugge and the harbour entrance at Ostend. They were modified with extra ballast in the bilges and 50 tons of concrete on the upper deck to prevent enemy shipping sailing over them at high tide once they were sunk. All the blockships contained explosive charges in the bottom of each ship. The charges were all connected electronically to various positions on each ship so that if one position was disabled, the charge could be activated at an alternate position onboard. Once at their intended destinations these charges would be blown to blow the bottom out of each vessel, so that their hulls would sink and rest on the seabed. The Germans did not carry out regular dredging operations at the canal entrance at Zeebrugge. This resulted in silt accumulating in this location, so if the blockships could be sunk across the central channel of the canal entrance, then silt would build up around the sunken blockships, causing further impediment to their removal.

The personnel required for the blockships, storming and support vessels amounted to 86 officers and 1,698 men, including 718 Royal Marines. Keyes was responsible for recruiting officer volunteers and later recalled in his memoirs the enthusiastic attitude of the officers interviewed.

> It was very interesting to watch their reactions of the various officers – whom I interviewed singly – when I told them that the enterprise would be hazardous, and finally said that the best chance of escape I could offer them after it, was a German prison until the end of the war. With one exception only, they appeared to be simply delighted and most grateful for the honour I had done them in offering them such a wonderful prospect! Then I got them an outline of the plan, and said that although I would make every endeavour to save them after they had sunk the ships, I felt that it was a very forlorn hope. They took everything for granted, asked few, if any questions and went away apparently full of joy and gratitude.[2]

Lieutenant Ivan Franks from HMS *Dolphin* was the first officer appointed to command a blockship after a recommendation from Sir David Beatty. Franks, who had previously commanded a submarine, was designated Commander of HMS *Iphigenia*. On passing the interview for the appointment, Franks requested that his colleague Lieutenant Edward Billyard-Leake be appointed as his second in command. Franks played an important role in the supervision of the preparation of all the blockships at the early planning stages.

Lieutenant Stuart Bonham-Carter was recommended by Captain Carpenter to command *Intrepid*. It was Captain Fuller, Keyes' liaison officer at the Admiralty who recommended Commander Ralph Sneyd for command of *Thetis*. Sneyd was very inquisitive during his interview with Keyes. He was a man of great experience and asked numerous pertinent questions pertaining to the raid. Keyes misunderstood Sneyd's concerns as negativity and was not prepared to appoint him, but Sneyd's concern was only for the operation's success. Sneyd was adamant that no one else was going to command *Thetis* and convinced Keyes to appoint him commander of the blockship.

The preparation of the blockships at Chatham before the raid was an enormous task. All metal, fittings and machinery surplus to requirements had to be removed from all five blockships to provide space for rubble and cement to be placed in the hulls. The removal of the masts and the installation of alternative steering positions was also carried out. If one steering position was knocked out then an alternative position could be used to steer the ship to the mouth of the canal.

To ensure the success of the blocking of the canal it was crucial that the guns on the Mole be captured or destroyed, or at the very least diverted. Without this there was a danger that the blockships would be sunk before they reached the canal entrance. Lieutenant Colonel Bertram Elliot was appointed commander of the 4th Battalion Royal Marine Light Infantry and Royal Marine Artillery force whose objective was to assault the Mole. Major Alexander Cordner was appointed his second in command. Many of Elliot's ancestors had served in the Royal Marines since 1707. Major C Shelton RMLI was a friend of Elliot's and described him as 'A man of steel nerve, with an absolute contempt of fear and danger.'[3] Elliot had seen action during the early part of the war, as a major he was part of the British Naval Mission that was sent to Serbia in 1915. With Admiral Trowbridge and 25 marines he was involved in the defence of Belgrade and supervised mining operations that took place on the River Danube. During the evacuation of Belgrade, Elliot and his Royal Marine Light Infantry contingent were the last to leave. It was a long and arduous journey as they marched from Kragushevatz through Albania, before reaching Monastir. For his service in Serbia, Elliot was awarded the Distinguished Service Order.

It was planned to land assault troops on the Mole on the seaward side. Ships usually berthed on the inner Mole, and the seaward side was not built to accommodate the berthing and securing of vessels. After Keyes was appointed Vice Admiral Dover, he abandoned the idea of using a Monitor to attack the Mole. He later wrote:

> Plans Division made efforts to find me a fast hardy merchantman passenger vessel with high free board, designed to go alongside jetties, for a boarding vessel. I also sent an officer on my staff to Liverpool to inspect ferry steamers which he suggested would be admirably suited for carrying large bodies of men owing to the shallow draft, double hulls, hardiness, etc. Finally no suitable merchantman being available, I decided to use Vindictive, which had been destined to block Ostend, as the main boarding vessel, and Liverpool ferry steamers as tenders as their shallow draft would take them over minefields at high water. [4]

HMS *Vindictive* was an old 6-inch gun Arrogant-Class cruiser which, prior to the raid, had an uncertain future. The Royal Navy regarded the Arrogant-Class cruisers as the 'Fleet rams'. *Vindictive* was built at Chatham Dockyard in the same dock where HMS *Victory* had been built 159 years earlier. Keyes had a dilemma regarding the chain of command. Captain Henry Halahan had been appointed commanding officer of the Royal Naval assault team that was to storm the Mole from *Vindictive* and was senior to Commander Carpenter. Under Naval regulations the senior officer was meant to be in command of a vessel. Keyes had promised command to Carpenter and was sensitive to his disappointment, so he made the irregular move to allow Carpenter to command *Vindictive*, with the provision that the senior Captain Halahan was in command of the naval assault team. These areas of responsibility were clearly defined before the operation. Carpenter was responsible for navigating the vessel to Zeebrugge, while Halahan had overall control of the assault operation when *Vindictive* was berthed alongside the Mole. Lieutenant Commander Robert Rosoman was appointed First Lieutenant with Engineer Commander William Bury as engineer officer.

Various modifications were made to *Vindictive* at Chatham. The foretop had been raised to enable machine gunners to fire over the sea wall onto the Mole. The foretop, bridge and flame-thrower compartments were heavily strengthened with mattresses and reinforced with steel for additional protection. Flame-throwers would be used to project jets of fire onto the Mole to clear German personnel as *Vindictive* came alongside. A special deck was installed above the upper deck on the port side from the forecastle to the quarter-deck to enable fourteen gangways (27 inches wide), positioned at a 45-degree angle, to be lowered onto the outer sea wall of the Mole. The attack would be carried out at high tide, which meant that there would be a distance of between four and seven feet separating the false deck and the Mole parapet. This false deck would also be used to shelter the assault force from enemy fire during the approach to the Mole. Access to this deck was via three wide ramps, which elevated from the starboard side of the lower deck. Commander Edward Osborne, Gunnery Officer on the Staff of Vice Admiral Dover, was responsible for the fitting out of *Vindictive* with howitzers, mortars, pom-pom and machine guns. Two 7.5-inch howitzers were positioned on the forecastle and quarterdeck, one 11-inch howitzer was installed on the quarterdeck. Two 6-inch B.L. and two 6-inch Q.F. were fitted on each side of *Vindictive* to fire heavy shells. Five 1½-pounder pom-pom guns designed to fire pointed shells was also incorporated in the armaments as well as six Lewis guns deployed in the fortified foretop. Ten Lewis guns were positioned on the port side of the vessel to cover the Mole assault force with machine gun fire. Stokes Mortars were added to the ships' armament in order to bombard the Mole and shore batteries while they were alongside. Twelve Stokes Mortars were set up to fire at short-range targets on the Mole, while the remaining four Stokes Mortars were set to fire long-range shells at shore batteries. Special fenders were made to allow the *Vindictive* to berth along the seaward side of the Mole. They were very large and measured 12 feet in circumference, enough to act as a cushion between *Vindictive* and the Mole. Supplies of ammunition and equipment for smoke screens were all stored on the upper deck. Engineer Lieutenant Boddie recalled that that '*Vindictive* looked more like a Christmas tree than a cruiser.'[5] Carpenter recalled:

> The Vindictive *rapidly changed her appearance. Every unessential fitting that could be removed in the time at our disposal was wafted away. The foremast was cut off just above the fighting-top. The mainmast was removed altogether and a large portion of it was fitted horizontally across the deck, extending several feet over the port side of the ship, as a bumpkin designed to prevent the port propeller from bumping against the Mole at Zeebrugge ... I can well remember the astonished look on their faces as these men boarded my ship. Even the heavy downpour of rain seemed to be unnoticed. One man remarked as he came aboard. 'Well, it's darned good to be aboard a blessed something, but I'm blowed if I know what she is'.[6]*

Navigational hazards on the way to the Mole included shifting sands, enemy mines, and the lack of navigational night-lights, which the Germans had removed. Keyes had confidence in the navigational skills of his Royal Naval Officers and their ability to get the fleet to Zeebrugge. However, as a result of these dangers and as a precaution against the loss of HMS *Vindictive*, two Liverpool ferries, the *Iris* and *Daffodil*, were requisitioned to carry some of the storming party. It was also intended to use these robust vessels as tugs to assist in the securing operation, ensuring that *Vindictive* was pushed alongside the outer wall of the Mole. Each of these Mersey ferries could transport 1,000 troops and because they had a shallow draft with double hulls were considered unsinkable. The *Iris* and *Daffodil* were twin-screwed pleasure steamers. It was unusual for large vessels such as these to have hinged funnels. *Daffodil* was built in Newcastle in 1906. Captain Herbert Grant, Keyes' intelligence officer, identified these two vessels as suitable for the raid. There was a public outcry in Merseyside when it was announced that these two ferryboats were to be requisitioned by the Royal Navy. A story was circulated indicating that these ferryboats were to be used in the US to assist in bringing troops to Europe. According to Sir George Anston in *Secret Service*, Sir Douglas Brownrigg, the Chief Naval Censor, was told that these Mersey ferryboats were required for a raid. Anxious that the press may bring attention to the fact that these two vessels were being removed from service on the Mersey, he decided to inform the Directors of the Press Bureau that they were to take part in the raid and appealed to their patriotism, asking that no more articles were to appear in the press regarding the disappearance of the steamers from the River Mersey. The raid on Zeebrugge was hardly the best kept secret, for Brownrigg also found it necessary to make efforts to prevent Members of Parliament from asking awkward questions regarding the removal of the vessels. Brownrigg told the Speaker of the House of Commons of the secret operation, who agreed to meet any MP with a question on the subject, to tell them of the raid in private and appeal to them to not to raise any questions regarding the matter in the House of Commons. It is remarkable that while sailors and marines were being trained to embark on a deadly operation, where the chances of returning home safely were remote, the Chief Naval Censor was openly discussing the plan with journalists and politicians.

Once Captain Grant had secured the *Iris* and *Daffodil* for service they were renamed HMS *Iris II* and HMS *Daffodil IV*. Commander Valentine Gibbs and Lieutenant Commander Harold Campbell were chosen to command respectively. Keyes knew both these officers before the raid on Zeebrugge. Gibbs (who had won the Cresta Run in 1913), served as a Midshipman in the China Seas under Keyes. Campbell served as First Lieutenant aboard HMS *Lurcher* during the Battle of Heligoland Bight on 28th August 1914, when Keyes served as Commodore on the same vessel.

It was planned that *Vindictive* would tow *Iris* and *Daffodil* to Zeebrugge. Once they were released and proceeded under their own power, *Iris* would berth alongside the Mole to land her raiding party and *Daffodil* would ensure that *Vindictive* was firmly secured against the Mole by pushing on her starboard side. Both were sent to Portsmouth for refit to prepare for the raid. They required only minimal alteration for the purpose of the operation, which included the installation of steel plating and mattresses on the structures to protect against shrapnel, splinters and bullets.

In order to prevent the enemy reinforcements entering the Mole during the raid, a plan was devised to destroy the viaduct that linked the Mole to the mainland. Two C Class submarines with their bows containing high explosives were designated to approach the viaduct, light time fuses, and escape in motorised dinghies before the viaduct was destroyed. Each submarine carried a complement of two officers and four men. Two were used as a precaution in the event of one of them breaking down.

Additional vessels were required to support the operation by protecting the principal vessels from attack by enemy surface vessels at sea, rescuing blockship crews and executing diversionary measures such as smoke screening to conceal the raiders' approach, and long range bombardment from the sea. Monitors, Coastal Motor Boats (CMBs) and Motor Launches (MLs) would form part of the support fleet. CMBs were lighter and faster than MLs. Monitors would provide a barrage upon German shore batteries. They would work in conjunction with the Royal Air Force who were assigned bombing targets from the air. A grand total of 168 vessels were used in the operations to block Zeebrugge and Ostend.

The most important and critical factor of the entire operation was the ability to maintain the element of surprise right up to the moment the assault vessels approached the Mole. To ensure that the armada was concealed from the German batteries on the Mole and on the shore, a smoke screen was essential. Wing Commander Frank Brock from the Royal Naval Air Service was the pyrotechnics expert who was responsible for the production of smoke screens. He was a suitable candidate for such a role – many will recognise his name from childhood – his family had established the company Brock's fireworks. Brock was a boffin, a well-read man who could comment upon most subjects, according to Captain Carpenter. Brock was a unique character: he held the rank of Lieutenant Commander in the Royal Navy, Lieutenant Colonel in the Army and Wing Commander in the RAF. He was the founder of the Royal Naval Experimental Station at Stratford and was responsible for developing Very pistols, signal flares and floating flares that illuminated vast areas on contact with water. In 1914, while posing as an American tourist, he attended a Zeppelin demonstration in Germany. As a result of this spying operation Brock developed the anti-Zeppelin bullet that could penetrate a Zeppelin and bring it crashing to the ground. This bullet succeeded in shooting down several Zeppelins.

HMS *Vindictive* in Dover Harbour after the raid on Zeebrugge. Built in 1899 at Chatham, HMS *Vindictive* was an Arrogant-class cruiser. When World War One broke out she served as part of the 9th Atlantic Cruiser Squadron and was responsible for capturing the German merchant ships *Schlesin* and *Slawentziz* during August 1914. Her superstructure was converted for the raid on Zeebrugge. Length: 342 feet, Beam 57 ½ feet. Displacement: 5,750 tons. Power/speed: 10,000 hp/19 knots. Crew: 480 men.

Brock's greatest achievement was the invention of the flameless smoke screen, which was a fundamental element in the planning for the raid on Zeebrugge. The screen was created by a stream of chloro-sulphuric acid injected under pressure onto the hot interior surface of the funnels of larger vessels or in the exhausts of Motor Launches and Coastal Motor Boats. The smoke would gather on the sea surface and conceal the fleet. The development of a smoke screen that would conceal Keyes' fleet was carried out by three officers and 87 men from Brock's Royal Naval Air Station Experimental Base. The preparation of the chemicals for the smoke screens was done in a specially constructed workshop in Dover Dockyard. The installation of smoke apparatus in the MLs and CMBs took place at short notice in Dover dockyard under the supervision of Flag Captain Ralph Collins. Keyes later wrote that 'the value of Brock's contribution to the undertaking was simply incalculable.'[7] As well as producing smoke to conceal the raiding armada as it approached Zeebrugge, Brock also devised light buoys to denote the course and flame-throwers that would fire flames of burning oil upon the Mole as *Vindictive* secured alongside. Brock played an important part in the operation and his contribution was concomitant upon the condition that he would go to Zeebrugge with the raiders. Keyes agreed with great reluctance to permit Brock to take part in the actual operation, but he was the only person who understood the scientific practicalities of the application of the smoke apparatus. Regarded as something of a genius, it would be disastrous to lose such a great mind, but Keyes had no choice but to allow him to take part. There was another valid argument for Brock's presence during the operation. Intelligence reports had identified unexplained metal tubes positioned on the Mole. It was thought to be a German device used for sound ranging for shore batteries. These metal tubes had to be investigated during the raid and Brock was the only person of a suitable scientific background to carry out this inspection. Keyes recalled 'Brock's one plea, which I would have preferred to have refused – as his genius for inventions was so valuable – was that he should be allowed to get on to the Mole, in order to try and find out the German method of sound ranging, so I reluctantly consented to his going on *Vindictive*.'[8]

Volunteers were sought from all sections of the Royal Navy. Men were drawn from the South Coast Commands and the Grand Fleet at Scapa Flow, with the strict stipulation that they were to be unmarried single men of very good character. Able Seaman Bernard Devlin later recalled that 'preference was given to men who practised boxing and were fond of sport.'[9] Ninety-one personnel from the Admiralty Experimental Stations at Dover and Stratford and eleven men from the Royal Australian Navy were also selected to take part. Due to the sensitive nature of the operation and necessity for strict security the men could only be told that they were volunteering for 'a dangerous venture'.[10]

Commander Patrick Harrington Edwards was an RNVR officer who had served in Gallipoli and was seriously wounded on the Western Front in France. Keyes described him as 'a one-eyed bearded warrior'.[11] When Keyes was searching for volunteers Edwards was recuperating from wounds that he sustained in trench fighting in France and was keen to get back into the war. Keyes was aware of Edwards' experience and wanted him to train the Royal Naval landing party that was to assault the Mole. Edwards wrote of his feelings towards the operation after being assigned by Keyes:

> When I arrived back in Chatham I was full of it. I thought it was quite hopeless, but, oh my goodness, it was quite gloriously hopeless. It was desperate; but I realized our position and the frightful losses the U-boats were inflicting on our shipping were also desperate. The boats engaged were of no great fighting value; the officers and men? Ah! That was another matter. I went off to my cabin that night, but I could not sleep. How lucky I was to be in it.[12]

For some sailors serving with the Grand Fleet, the opportunity to volunteer for a dangerous operation was appealing. The routines of gunnery drills, ship maintenance and convoys with no contact with the enemy were tedious and this venture would break the monotony of their quiet war. Some sailors had not seen any action while serving with the Royal Navy and this mission would give them their chance to confront the enemy face to face. Petty Officer Harry Adams was one of forty volunteers from the Grand Fleet battleship, HMS *Royal Sovereign*, who later wrote that he 'had nearly four years of War and was ready for all that was going – to hasten its end.'[13] Adams explained the selection process:

> Personally, I was one of the 'Grand Fleet' contingent and this is how we of the Royal Sovereign volunteered. Quite a number of us (about forty), were detailed to muster at the sick bay to pass the Doctor – late one night. Ten of us passed a very stiff medical examination, and we were bundled off to the Commander's Cabin.
>
> He gave us to understand that some volunteers were required – he couldn't tell us any more, (he didn't know), but he said more or less these words. 'Any of you who are fed up with being stationed with the 'Grand Fleet' (and some of us had had almost four years of it), and want Action, Medals, etc, now is your chance. However if any of you ten don't care about it, say so.'
>
> Well, two preferred to remain in the ship leaving eight of us. The Commander needed only six; (it seemed six, from each ship was the required number). He proceeded to arrange us according to our height; Yours truly came sixth and just caught the boat, leaving the remaining two to fill our places if we fell out, or fell sick. He told us, that whatever it was, we should have at least a fighting chance – an even chance, but personally, I don't think anyone of the whole outfit had even a dog's chance.[14]

Leading Stoker Henry Baker had experienced three landings in the face of hostile fire in Gallipoli and did not think that this operation could be any worse, so he volunteered. For Engineer Lieutenant Arthur Lougher, from Cardiff, it was a matter of national pride that drove him to volunteer. Seeing that no officer from Wales was taking part, he felt obligated to represent the Welsh in this enterprise. He later recalled, 'I looked at the group of officers who were going to take part in this stunt and seeing no one representing Wales there I said to myself "I am going to have a hand in this if only for the sake and the credit of my own little country".'[15]

Fifty sailors from HMS *Neptune* answered the call for volunteers for this dangerous operation. Among them was Leading Seaman William Childs who was recruited for the Zeebrugge stunt on 12th February. Lieutenant Arthur Chamberlain was the recruiting officer and once he had established that Childs was not married or engaged he asked him if he would be interested in participating in a secret operation. Childs asked for more information, but Chamberlain was restricted to what he could tell him, but all he could say was 'if we came back alive we should be pretty lucky'.[16] Six other sailors from *Neptune* were selected for the raid. They were Able Seamen J. Day, A. Everest, A. Hilling, C. Reed, E. Young and Albert McKenzie. McKenzie had recently served seven days punishment in the cells onboard *Neptune* for misbehaving before volunteering for this operation. He would more than redeem himself at Zeebrugge.

Not all men who volunteered for this dangerous mission were single. Some married men did not mention their marital status when volunteering. Stoker Petty Officer Harold Palliser who was assigned to the blockship *Intrepid* was married and his wife was living in London. Petty Officer Frank Lucas had recently married before joining the *Iphigenia*. Both men would make their wives widows.

There were some sailors who did not volunteer of their own accord. The prospect of volunteering for a dangerous operation, with no knowledge of the task and with the potential to risk loss of life was not appealing to everyone. Engineer Lieutenant Ronald Boddie, who would be the Chief Engineer aboard HMS *Thetis*, had to persuade six reluctant eligible men to volunteer. He recalled, 'To my astonishment, the secret nature of the venture discouraged the men from volunteering, and I had great difficulty in persuading and cajoling six eligible but rather indifferent men to accompany me.'[17]

Able Seaman Henry Groothius, a sight setter from HMS *Benbow* and a veteran of the Battle of Jutland was selected for the raid. During an interview in June 1971 he recalled, 'They said that we were volunteers but weren't volunteers, we were picked. If you are a picked man you can't be a volunteer can you? And there were six of us.'[18]

Ordinary Seaman William O'Hara, from Lurgan, Armagh, was one of seven men from HMS *Conqueror* who took part. O'Hara, who was also a Jutland veteran, indicated in his testimony written in December 1931 that he did not volunteer for the Zeebrugge raid. 'Service in the Grand Fleet during the war was dull, I was young and wanted to see something of the war; therefore when I was sent for in Feb 1918 and told I was selected for special service I was very pleased indeed.'[19]

Chief ERA Thomas Farrell had served eighteen years in the Royal Navy and was a willing volunteer. He confided in a friend before embarking for Zeebrugge 'I'm off on a suicide job.'[20] Lieutenant Edward Hilton-Young, a Royal Naval Siege Gun officer based at Nieuport, wrote of sailors' unwillingness to volunteer. It was his opinion that

Usually the sailorman is reluctant to volunteer, and dislikes to be asked whether he will do so. It is due in part to his reluctance to make himself conspicuous before his mates; in part it is due also to a superstition. He thinks that if he volunteers he is 'asking for it', and tempting Providence to 'take it out of him'; but if he is 'tolled off' he is quite content, because it is then a question of common luck.[21]

Hilton-Young received a request from Captain Halahan for thirty volunteers 'for an undertaking of real danger'. He did not find any difficulty in finding thirty volunteers, despite the fact that his men had been serving on the Western Front for two years under continuous shellfire and after suffering heavy casualties. At the time of Halahan's request these men had been given leave to return to England for rest and to spend time with their families, but many decided to volunteer nevertheless.

Sailors from various corners of the British Empire took part. Ordinary Seaman Harry Bennewith was a volunteer who was born in Uitenhage, Cape of Good Hope in South Africa, volunteered. So did Chief Motor Mechanic Eric McCracken and Air Mechanic Oliver Griffiths who came from Fiji. Chief Motor Mechanic Sydney Fox who served in the RNVR came from New Zealand. Stoker Albert Wilson who served on HMS *North Star* was born in New York, USA. A token force of eleven sailors from the Royal Australian Navy was among those selected. On 23rd February 1918 HMAS *Australia* had returned to the Grand Fleet base at Rosyth after escorting a convoy between Bergen and Aberdeen. After the 48-hour passage a communication was received by HMAS *Australia* requesting eleven volunteers for special service. The request was sent to *Australia* because she was the flagship of the Second Battle Cruiser Squadron. The requirements were for seamen and stokers. There were many volunteers for this special duty, but all those enthusiastic men who stepped forward were not accepted, to their dismay. Instead, the eleven men were selected. They were Warrant Officer Artificer Engineer William Edgar, Leading Seamen Bush and Rudd, Able Seamen Harry Gillard, Newland and Staples, and Stokers Bourke, Hopkins, Lockard, McCrory and Strong. They had no knowledge of the impending operation and later that day they received orders to leave on the 9.25 p.m. train for London. In London they were granted two days leave and instructed to report to Chatham depot at the conclusion of their leave.

The 4th Battalion Royal Marine Light Infantry was formed initially for service in Ireland, but from 8th February 1918 it was to prepare for the raid on Zeebrugge. 'Volunteers' were apparently sought throughout the Royal Marines Light Infantry and Royal Marines Artillery. However, according to Captain Arthur Chater, the men were not volunteers, unlike their Royal Naval counterparts: they were selected, or ordered to volunteer. Many of these Royal Marines were married men, such as Private John Bostock.

Private Jordan Daniel from Merseyside was one of the Royal Marines selected. In an interview years after the raid he indicated that he did volunteer. He originally joined the Royal Marines Light Infantry aged 17 in 1914 through economic necessity. Prior to the Zeebrugge operation Daniel served on a ship that received mail from mainland Britain and distributed it to the Grand Fleet. This was a backwater post for young men who wanted to play a fighting role in the war. 'An order came round asking for volunteers for special service. I myself volunteered for this special service. I did not know what it was for or anything like that.'[22]

There were other motivations for volunteering. Vengeance for the loss of family members during the War was a factor for some men. Private William Hopewell said to a journalist after the raid, 'I volunteered for this particular job, because I lost two brothers at the front in six months, and I wanted to get my own back.'[23]

Some RMLI volunteers for the operation had already seen action during the war, which made them suitable candidates. Private Jim Clist is a good example of an experienced combat Royal Marine. Clist from Taunton was a Mons Star recipient who had served in France and Belgium in 1914. He was a keen boxer who had enlisted in the RMLI during July 1914, because he was advised it would help him pursue his interest in the sport. During 1915 he took part in the Gallipoli campaign while attached to 4 Company, Plymouth Battalion. On 4th March 1915 he landed at Sedd-el-Bahr providing protective support for the demolition party whose objective was to destroy the fort and the Turkish guns that guarded the entrance to the Dardanelles Straits. Lieutenant Lamplough, who was also selected for the Zeebrugge Raid, landed with Clist and No.4 Company. This was one of a series of preliminary minor raids to destroy Turkish gun batteries that threatened the safety of Allied minesweepers tasked to clear mines in the Dardanelles Straits prior to the main landings. During this particular raid a party of Turkish snipers fired upon them from ruined houses as they ascended the cliffs. Lamplough's company lost three men during the minor raid.

Both Clist and Lamplough, along with Plymouth Battalion, took part in the landings at Y beach on 25th April 1918. Their objective was to establish a bridgehead four miles north of the four landing beaches, named S, X, V and W, located near Cape Helles. Their purpose was to prevent Turkish reinforcements from the north reaching these beaches. The landing was opposed and as the day progressed the Turks counter-attacked as they tried to consolidate the position on the cliffs overlooking Y Beach. Determined to push the RMLI back into the sea, they attacked persistently throughout that night. Suffering many casualties and with stocks of ammunition fast becoming exhausted they were forced to evacuate Y Beach the following day. Clist later recalled the landing at Y Beach:

When the Turks attacked it was Hell let loose. At the same time some of our battleships opened fire on us. I think it was the Goliath, Triumph *and* Swiftsure. *They must have killed and wounded hundreds of our men. The authorities issued us with a scarf, which could be used when folded as a cap. The consequence was the navy could not tell us from the Turks, who had similar headgear. And at dawn on the 26th April we had the Turks in front of us and the navy firing at us from the sea. They were using high explosive shells …Private Wright who knew a bit of semaphore went on the beach and managed to get a message through to the Navy. The Turks drove us onto the beach and the Navy who had knocked all the fighting out of us made amends by rescuing us from the beaches. I think we had been ashore for about thirty-six hours and must have lost over four hundred men of our battalion. As soon as I got on the rescue boat I started drinking from my bottle. During the time I had been ashore I had not used or opened this bottle, then I could not stop drinking and I continued drinking when I got aboard* HMS Goliath *or* Triumph, *I can't remember which. I felt awful with all the water that I had drank, but after vomiting it up, at least a gallon of liquid, I felt much better.*[24]

On the following day (the following day!) Clist and Lamplough took part in a second landing at Sedd-el-Bahr which was named V Beach for the Gallipoli operation. Clist regarded his commanding officer highly and referred to the 'courageous' Lamplough decades later. Lamplough was wounded on 21st May 1915.

Clist would continue to serve throughout 1915 in the Gallipoli campaign. During this period he lost many comrades. Plymouth Company landed at Y Beach on 25th April with a force comprising 1,100 men. When the Company was withdrawn from the region, Jim Clist was one of ten veterans from the Y Beach landing who had fought and survived through the ordeal of Gallipoli. It was difficult to make friendships, because within a short space of time, they would either become casualties or succumb to illness. Jim later remembered: 'I never seemed to be able keep a mate for more than a few weeks. If they were not killed or wounded they developed dysentery, jaundice or some other kind of illness. I was often envious of men who got what we used to call a Blighty wound, which meant a wound serious enough to take you back to England.'[25]

The ordeal of the Zeebrugge raid lasted for less than an hour. This was a short time in comparison to the eight months that he endured in Gallipoli, where his only hope was to get through and survive each day. Clist later described the weekly routine in Gallipoli, and how terrible it was to endure the deprivations and dangers of life in trenches. The hazards of stray Turkish bullets, living in squalid conditions, dealing with lice and scarce food supplies were daily realities for Jim Clist at Gallipoli:

Life in the trenches was horrible. We would usually do seven to ten days in the firing line and about four days in the reserve trenches, which was only about a mile from the firing line. We could not go any further back without going into the sea. Turkish bullets that missed the firing line would often land in or near the reserve trenches. On one occasion I was sitting on the bank of the reserve trench talking to a chap who had only just came out from England. He was asking what it was like on the firing line. We were both cleaning our rifle at the time. I turned to speak to him, he was crumpled up on the ground. A stray bullet had hit him in the head. I never heard a sound from him when he was hit. He was taken away unconscious. In the firing line you would do two hours on the lookout, we used small periscopes for this, and two hours trying to eat or rest, but before doing either of these we would have to take our clothes off, turn them inside out and run a lighted match or cigarette along the seams. As you did this you could hear the lice cracking as their bodies full of blood burst. It was also impossible to eat food without including several flies … For the first six weeks after landing we only had dog biscuits and corn beef, plus some plum and apple jam. We had to soak the biscuits most times as they were very hard … We were sometimes able to swap our jam with the French troops over on our right flank for some tins of meat and veg. I think that they were called Maconochies.[26]

The Gallipoli campaign would prepare Clist mentally for Zeebrugge. Despite the dangers of the trenches Jim Clist considered himself lucky to be alive. 'I continue to have a charmed life, but on several occasions I was lucky. Once I was in the firing position, a bullet went through the sleeve of my forearm and continued through the sleeve of my upper arm without grazing the skin.'[27]

It was towards the end of 1917 that Clist responded to a request for volunteers to serve aboard Defensive Armed Merchant Ships. During January 1918 Clist was ordered to report to Plymouth. When he reached Plymouth it was apparent that he would not be serving aboard merchant ships, and he was assigned to 4th Battalion Royal Marines Light Infantry, which was training for a night landing at an undisclosed location.

The 4th Battalion comprised three companies, A, B and C, with the men drawn from Chatham, Portsmouth and Plymouth respectively. During the raid each company would wear insignia on their arm to denote which company they belonged to. A white square was worn by A Company, a white circle by B Company and a white triangle by C. A machine gun section from the Royal Marines Light Infantry and a Trench Mortar and Pom-pom section from the Royal Marines Artillery were also components of the 4th Battalion. Based at Deal, Kent, they commenced their six-week training at the end of February 1918 at Freedown, near Deal. Men from the Royal Marines Artillery were trained how to operate howitzers and pom-pom guns on ranges at Shoeburyness in Essex. In order to maintain secrecy, they were not told of their task during the training.

The shape of the Mole was taped out at Freedown near Deal, and the men of the 4th Battalion were told that it resembled the part of a drained canal bed that was employed by the enemy as an advanced ammunitions dump in France as a cover story. This caused great intrigue amongst the sceptical Royal Marines. Private Alfred Hutchinson recalled, 'A lot of us couldn't understand why they were sending about 1,000 Marines when we had all those troops already in France.'[28] Corporal George Moyse remembered that 'they told us it was a dried-out canal! We'd volunteered for what was described simply as a very risky job, but I was so inquisitive that I searched the map of Europe for dried out canals.'[29] The efforts by senior officers to conceal the true nature of the operation caused great problems for Lieutenant F. J. Hore, the battalion Quartermaster. 'Personally I experienced the greatest difficulty in obtaining satisfactory intelligence as regards my future transport details, pioneers, etc. Col. Elliot contrived to bluff me most successfully on these points. I quite forgave him when he explained later that he had not misled me from choice!'[30]

The battalion practised assaulting the simulated target at Freedown both night and day. They also practised drills in ascending ramps and jumping over ramps that would be a vital skill when assaulting the Mole from *Vindictive*. Private Hutchinson recalled: 'Most of our training was done at night. We had a mock up of the Mole and we trained each day with bayonet practice, and strangleholds. We even did it in gas masks with smoke screens and starshells going off everywhere. When we weren't training at night we were doing twelve-mile route marches.'[31]

The seamen storming party, including the eleven Australian sailors, were ordered to report to HMS *Hindustan* at Chatham Depot for training. Also known as the Bluejacket storming party, they were 200 seamen commanded by eight officers. The sailors were forbidden to leave the confines of the dockyard at Chatham. They were permitted to use the canteen in the dockyard. There was high-spirited banter between the men selected for the Zeebrugge raid and the other sailors serving in the dockyard. Although they were not aware of the details of where they were going, they were called the Suicide Club or Jellicoe's Light Horse. The seamen force was divided into four Companies designated A, B, C, and D, containing 50 men. Groups A and B were transported to the Mole by *Vindictive*, *Iris* and *Daffodil* transported C and D respectively. Each Company was subdivided into four sections consisting of twelve men. Ordinary Seaman William O'Hara later recalled the moment when he reported at Chatham Barracks:

> There was great speculation as to what we were there for but no one could satisfy our curiosity. We were eventually detailed off into four sections, men belonging to ships of the same squadron being detailed to the same section. As I belonged to the 2ⁿᵈ battle squadron I formed 4 section under the command of Lieutenant Commander Bradford and Lieutenant Hawkings.[32]

As a security measure the First Sea Lord ordered the destruction of any written material about the operation during the early phases. As a consequence there is not much material that gives any details concerning the training program, although some are revealed in personal testimonies. The first week of training involved route marches and swimming. Lieutenant Commanders Arthur Harrison, George Bradford and Bryan Adams were responsible for their training. Training staff from the Army assisted them. The seamen were inducted through a rigorous physical training schedule that incorporated trench warfare, bomb throwing, rifle and bayonet combat. There was a night exercise in Raynham, Kent, in which the sailors were pitched against the 5ᵗʰ Middlesex Regiment. During the sixth week of training the shape of the Mole was simulated in the chalk pits at Wouldham in Kent. Here they used live ammunition in an exercise observed by the Lord Commissioners of the Admiralty.

The working day for all seamen under training was long and arduous, beginning at 5.30 a.m. and concluding at 7.30 p.m. in the evening. There was a distinct difference between Army and Naval discipline, and some of these seamen found it difficult to adapt to Army methods. Able Seaman Henry Groothius recalled an incident during battle formation training: 'We had a row with the army instructor … He started bullying the sailor. We knew that a hell of a lot weren't going to come back and he found out to his cost that he was surrounded by 100 men with fixed bayonets. Our Lieutenant came up and asked what was the matter and we told him that he was bullying the sailor.'[33]

Leading Seaman William Childs later wrote of the gulf between Army and Royal Navy discipline, but regarded his Army instructors with high respect and affection.

> Within a very short space of time, soldiers and sailors were working as one. Our instructors were army sergeants and sergeant majors, who very soon won favour with the sailors; in fact, I know Sergeant Major Green used to turn blue in the face trying to drill Army discipline into us. (It was of no use, as Naval Discipline and Army Discipline are like chalk to cheese), and I must say that a finer set of instructors one could not wish to drill under.[34]

The differences between Army and Navy methods were overcome during six weeks of training. There were some sailors from the Royal Naval Division who had served on the Western Front in the trenches. During this period sailor and soldier was trained to fight together. The training for the storming party consisted of trench warfare and close quarter combat. Ordinary Seaman William O'Hara:

Every morning we proceeded to the army drill ground and there were taken charge of by army instructors from the 5th Middlesex Regt. We were given a thorough soldier's training for five weeks, special men were picked for bombing, Stokes gun, and Lewis gun, training. After three weeks we were given khaki uniform, great trouble was experienced at first with our new uniform, but we soon got used to it.[35]

The tasks of the seamen during the raid were various. Their duties included securing *Vindictive*, *Iris* and *Daffodil* alongside the Mole. Once berthed on the Mole it was their task to position the gangways for disembarkation. Once the gangways were secure they were expected to storm the Mole and cover the assault of the Royal Marine force. While on the Mole they were to destroy the battery at the end of the Mole, demolish cranes, stores, sheds and attack any enemy craft berthed on the inner Mole. On capturing the end of the Mole they were to light beacons to guide the blockships into Zeebrugge Harbour. During the retirement it was their task to cover the withdrawal of the Royal Marines and slip the lines of assault vessels.

Each element of the operation was trained separately. The storming party, the CMB crews, crews from *Vindictive*, the Mersey ferries and the blockships did not know what the others were doing. The stokers from HMAS *Australia* were to be part of the engine crew aboard the blockship, HMS *Thetis*. Their training involved learning about the ship from forecastle to stern and was separate from their colleagues who were selected for the storming party on the Mole.

Lieutenant Cecil Dickinson, commander of the team designated to demolish the naval facilities on the Mole trained the demolition party. Some of the Australian seaman would form part of this demolition team. Their orders were to destroy the three batteries on the Mole, the lighthouse at the end, cranes, stores and sheds. Petty Officer Harry Adams was part of the Demolition team under training and remembered Dickinson to be 'a jolly fine fellow … He gave you all the confidence in the world – "Secure" in short, a grand character, splendid leader, the kind one would serve under, go anywhere with, under any and all circumstances.'[36] The demolition team experimented with gelignite and tried to ascertain the appropriate place and angle to place the high explosives upon cranes, cables and iron bars for maximum destruction.

The Royal Marines were put through intensive training. Without revealing any operational details of their objective, the Adjutant General Royal Marines gave anyone who did not want to take part in this perilous endeavour the opportunity to withdraw. No man took advantage of this offer, so they were all volunteers.

During early March 1918 Winston Churchill, Minister of Munitions at the time, visited the 4th Battalion RMLI. Private Ernest 'Beau' Tracey later recalled that they were formed up at the North Barracks Parade at Deal, where Churchill inspected them. He spoke to every man, taking one and a half hours to inspect the battalion. After the inspection they closed in around Churchill en masse. Churchill stood on a platform and addressed them. Tracey recalled his exact words in 1979:

You are going on a daring and arduous stunt from which none of you may return, but every endeavour will be made to bring back as many of you as possible. Should any of you, for any reason whatsoever desire not to go you may on dismissal of this parade go to your company office, hand in your name and not a word will be said.[37]

According to Ernest Tracey not a man dropped out.

Strict security measures were enforced to such an extent that when King George V in his role of Colonel in Chief of the Royal Marines inspected 4th Battalion RMLI at Deal on 7th March, he was not informed of the impending operation. Lance Corporal George Calverley from A Company remembered the Royal visit. 'I was standing in the supernumerary rank two paces behind my section. He had a very gruff voice. He looked at me for a couple of seconds and as he passed on I heard him remark to the accompanying General about someone being very young and I assumed that it was me he was referring to.'[38] Private Jim Clist from No.12 Platoon remembered: 'The King inspected our battalion at Deal. I was wearing the Mons Star ribbon at that time and he mentioned something to me about the Mons Star and would have shook hands with me had I put my hand out, but I was too flustered to do anything.'[39]

During the rigorous training prior to the raid there were breaches of discipline. All personnel involved with this operation were denied shore leave. The men would either march to destinations or be transported in lorries. Harry Adams heard a rumour that 'some lads in a certain lorry, held up the driver with a revolver that they might stop to purchase mouth-organs.'[40] Some sailors went absent without leave. Ordinary Seaman (later Petty Officer) William O'Hara recalled ways of obtaining unofficial leave. 'While at Chatham no leave was given, but trust a sailor to find a way out, the most simple was putting up a leading badge and change of cap ribbon which was very easy as there were many ships in the yard. As no one knew what we were going to do there was no reason in stopping our leave.'[41]

A more serious incident occurred during the afternoon of Friday 15th March. The 4th Battalion War diary records that during the first battalion exercise on the Lynch, on this day, 'No.7 Platoon failed to fall in as ordered.'[42] The entire No.7 Platoon disobeyed orders with the exception of two privates. There is no further explanation as to why the men from this platoon that belonged to Portsmouth Company refused to take part in the first battalion exercise, but there was a severe breach of discipline. Maybe the men from this platoon were unhappy about the conditions, the harsh training. Maybe they were reluctant to continue training without knowing what they were training for. The incident brought disgrace not only upon the participants, but also showed their Commanding Officers in a poor light, who took no action. Lieutenant Robus reported the incident to Major Hobson at 5.40 p.m. on 15th March; however, Hobson did not in turn report the matter to Lieutenant Colonel Elliot. Elliot, CO of the 4th Battalion, was not aware of the incident until two days later. How Elliot discovered this mutinous conduct is a cause for further embarrassment. It was Sergeant Major Thatcher who overheard the rumour in the Sergeants' Mess that a platoon from B Company had disobeyed an order to fall in. Thatcher reported the story circulating around the Sergeants' Mess to Captain Chater, the battalion's Adjutant. Chater reported it to Elliot at midday on 17th March. Elliot later wrote 'I sent for Major G. R. Hobson, R.M.L.I. and inquired as to the truth of the rumour. He appeared to know little about it although the affair occurred on Friday 15th and was reported to him by Lieut. Robus at about 5.40 p.m. 15th.'[43]

Elliot ordered Hobson to carry out an investigation immediately and submit a report. Major Cordner, the battalion 2nd in Command and the Adjutant Captain Chater were present when Elliot gave Hobson this order. The fact that an entire platoon had disobeyed an order was a serious matter; the fact that Hobson did nothing is even more serious. Elliot was aware of the serious implications to the overall operation and as soon as he received Hobson's report on Monday 18th March he ordered a Court of Enquiry to convene that day. No.7 Platoon was placed under open arrest and their platoon sergeant sent back to Divisional Headquarters with no further part to be played in the operation. Lieutenant Colonel Elliot ordered two further Courts of Enquiry, the second being held on 20th March and the third on the evening of 21st March. Realising his negligence in failing to report the incident or deal with the mutinous conduct of No.7 Platoon, Hobson tried to cover for his slackness by claiming that he would have written a report after an investigation had taken place. This claim did not stand up in the Court of Enquiry, because when Hobson was summoned by Elliot to confirm or deny the rumour, he knew very little and it was Elliot who ordered him to write a report in the presence of Cordner and Chater. Elliot sent the proceedings of the second and third Courts of Enquiries to Brigadier General H.S. Neville White, the Adjutant General Royal Marines. The Royal Marines Museum holds the covering letter, but not the detail of the Courts of Enquiry. In the covering letter Elliot made the following observations regarding Major Hobson's conduct:

No adequate action appears to have been taken by either the Platoon Officer or the Non-commissioned Officers to enforce this order … No investigation of the matter was held by the O.C. Company until ordered by the Commanding Officer. It appears doubtful if the matter would have been reported had the rumour not begun to spread that the incident had happened.[44]

Elliot wrote of the men of No.7 Platoon. 'No matter what grievance the platoon may have had, no possible justification can be found for their action.'[45] The motivation behind the disobedience remains unclear from all extant documents; a report written by Brigadier General Neville White to the Commandant Royal Marines of 23rd March simply confirmed that there was 'an outbreak of collective insubordination in a Platoon belonging to the Portsmouth Company of the 4th R.M. Battalion.'[46] It was White's personal opinion that 'the whole case … shows a lamentable want of decision and control on the part of some of the Officers and N.C. Officers in that Company.'[47]

Despite holding three Courts of Enquiry the individuals responsible for leading this mutiny were not identified: 'It is regretted that it has been impossible to discover who are the ringleaders.'[48] One thing is certain, the officers and men from No.7 Platoon were withdrawn from the battalion and the search for replacements began. On 18th March the battalion's war diary recorded that Lieutenant Colonel Elliot arranged leave, pay and changes of officers. On 19th March Major G Hobson, Lieutenant Dewhurst, 2nd Lieutenant H Robus and G Hollamby from No.7 Platoon left the battalion. Hobson was reprimanded for his conduct and this reprimand was recorded on his service record, which also notes that while serving aboard the battleship HMS *Canopus* he was present at the Battle of the Falkland Islands on 14th December 1914 and during the bombarding of Turkish Forts defending the Dardanelles Straits; and covering the Allied landings at Anzac and Cape Helles on 25th April 1915. The Adjutant General of the Royal Marines recorded in his service record on 30th March 1918 the following:

This regrettable occurrence took place on the 15th March 1918, and apparently Major G. S. Hobson, R.M.L.I. took no steps in the matter until the morning of the 17th, and no report made to the Commanding Officer until the 18th. It is inexplicable that such a very gross act of insubordination which might have had the most serious consequences was not dealt with by Major Hobson immediately it was brought to his notice, even assuming that, as he supposed, four men were involved, this does not exonerate him for not having taken steps to enquire into it, and the fact that his Platoon Commander was a very young inexperienced Temporary Officer, should have put him on his guard. I therefore consider that Major Hobson displayed a very serious lack of judgement in dealing with this case and is thereby shown that he is wanting in those powers of leadership and command of men, which reflects adversely upon his abilities as an Officer and a note to this effect will be recorded in his service.[49]

Hobson was sent on leave and on his return ordered to rejoin his Divisional Headquarters at Chatham. Hollamby and Robus were returned to Portsmouth Divisional Headquarters. Lieutenant George Hollamby, who had served in Gallipoli in 1915, was transferred to France after leaving 4th Battalion RMLI. He was wounded on 16th April, but after recovery returned to active duty. He was killed on 27th September 1918 when a bullet went through his left thigh and pierced his heart. Dewhurst was sent on leave until arrangements were made for his re-embarkation on HMS *St. Vincent*. The replacement officers included Captain Edward Bamford who was designated Commanding Officer of No.7 Platoon, Captain F. Law, and Lieutenants B Claudet, H. de Berry and A. Norris.

The NCOs and men of No. 7 Platoon who failed to parade on 15th March do not appear to have been disciplined. Instead of facing a court martial they were transferred back to Portsmouth Division in disgrace. There is a reference in the battalion war diary on 3rd March to Chater, the

Adjutant who 'conducted 3 N.C.O.s and 30 men of No. VII Platoon to Portsmouth'.[50] Brigadier General Neville White remarked in his report dated 23rd March: 'As regards the Portsmouth Platoon withdrawn should it be found impossible to deal drastically with any of these N.C. Officers or men for mutiny, I would strongly urge that they be subjected to a vigorous course of close order drill for a month or two in order to discipline them.'[51]

During the period that they were training with No.4 Battalion for the Zeebrugge Raid these men were recorded as being of very good character. Private John Flynn, an apprentice joiner from Blackburn and Private William Halliday, a packing case maker from Rochdale, both belonged to No.7 Platoon. They both joined under-age on 21st May 1917 in the same Manchester recruiting office. They were sent away to Portsmouth for not parading yet they have unblemished service records. The only 'forfeit' they would ever pay was for lying about their age when they enlisted, losing pension entitlement for the number of days they served as under-age soldiers. These men continued to serve with the 3rd Royal Marine Battalion for the remainder of the war.

Private Arthur Higgins from Kings Norton Birmingham also refused to parade, but there is no record of him being disciplined on his service record. He was transferred to the 1st Royal Marine Battalion and served with the corps until 1922. Private William Swadge, from Burton on Trent, another individual who lied about his age when he enlisted, was also transferred to the 1st Battalion. He was killed in action on 2nd September 1918.

There were some veteran Royal Marines who were sent back to Portsmouth. Private William Harvey from Birmingham had served on HMS *Monarch* from 26th December 1913 to 31st December 1917. He was onboard when U-15 made an unsuccessful attack on HMS *Monarch* off the Fair Isle in August 1914 and when the Dreadnought took part in the Battle of Jutland in May 1916. Similarly, the NCOs Sergeant Thomas Cooper and Corporal William Sole had served for more than six years and had very good character references on their records. Such men did not parade for a reason. I believe that these men were not cowards or trying to avoid their duty. Some had lied about their age to enlist and were keen to play their part in the war, some possessed considerable experience with the Corps. After this incident they were moved on to serve elsewhere and in some instances died in battle. It is my theory that the mutineers from No.7 Platoon were protesting for a valid reason. There may have been an individual, possibly an instructor during the training, who was either bullying the men, or was negligent and causing accidents.

As Chater escorted No.7 Platoon to Portsmouth, four NCOs and 27 Privates joined the 4th Battalion to replace them. These men were all volunteers and Lieutenant Colonel Elliot took part in the selection process personally. The four NCOs were taken from the NCO School of Instruction Class. Sergeant Frank Bessant and Corporals Samuel Smith and Frank Regan were all from Portsmouth Division. Elliot selected Corporal Bert Wells from Plymouth Division on the basis that he knew him and that he could be trusted. Bert Wells had served on HMS *Exmouth*, which bombarded Zeebrugge on 23rd November 1914 and later supported the Gallipoli operation in May 1915.

The men chosen to replace No.7 Platoon were made up of 17 recruits from Deal Machine Gun Company, 10 ex-buglers, six spare men from the 4th Battalion and two privates from the original No.7 Platoon who had paraded as ordered on 15th March. Private James Feeney was one of the replacements and according to his diary he volunteered for the 4th Battalion RMLI at Deal on 19th March. He was among thirty volunteers, of which only eleven was selected for the Zeebrugge raid (Feeney, McDowell, Burgess, Whitely, Goodwin, Lightbown, Morris, Mitchell, Wilson, Poole and Smullen). The Royal Marine buglers were not trained for a combat role when they joined the Corps. Brigadier General White was confident of their value to the operation despite their lack of training. He wrote, 'any deficiency in specialist training such as bombing is more than counter-balanced by the keenness and absolute fitness of the men.'[52] These men were keen to play a fighting role in the War and were enthusiastic to bear arms.

It was thought these inexperienced volunteers might be more dangerous to their colleagues than to the Germans. They were therefore issued with cutlasses only.

A week after No.7 Platoon's indiscretion the men training for the Zeebrugge raid were given four days leave. Special trains were arranged to take them to London Bridge and Charing Cross railway stations in London. It is an unusual state of affairs to train a group of men for a secret special operation; then half way through the training, allow them to leave barracks. With approximately two thousand men returning home on leave, drinking in local pubs, there was clearly a great risk that some of these men might reveal that they were about to embark on a special operation, although they were not aware of the precise nature of their business. The leave may have been granted because of No.7 Platoon's refusal to parade. Morale may have been low and Keyes and Elliot may have decided give the men a fillip.

Petty Officer Harry Adams returned to his home in the market town of Hailsham in Sussex: 'It was during those four delightful days, I became engaged to be married – to a 'Sweet Soul' … And so those few days drew to an end far too quickly. Still, an over-hanging cloud – one felt so full of important secrets; but knew nothing.'[53]

While the men were given leave, the officers continued to prepare for the operation. Major Cordner acted as RMLI liaison officer with Captain Herbert Grant, who was Keyes' intelligence officer. During the afternoon of 22nd March, Cordner visited Grant to discuss the preparations. Grant wrote of Cordner: 'Our frequent meetings gave me a great regard both for him and his ability, though he was the most quiet and unassuming man, whose manner cloaked real ability and leadership. I knew that he felt he would never return, if *Vindictive* got alongside the Mole, but this never interfered with his unremitting work for the welfare of his men, and the object in view.'[54]

Cordner was dedicated to his men. Two weeks later cigarette supplies were dwindling. There were no cigarettes to be found on *Vindictive* so he personally visited the canteens at Deal and Chatham to search in vain for supplies. He then asked tobacco companies in London for supplies, but they too were unable to help. On 4th April, Cordner told Grant that 'there was not a single cigarette in the *Vindictive* and other ships at the Swin, and [the] men would be fagless for a week or more.'[55] Grant asked how many cigarettes were needed. Cordner placed an order for 25,000 and Grant was able to supply them to him two days later.

Throughout the training there were numerous instances of absence without leave reported in the daily Battalion Orders amongst RMLI personnel. On 30th March 17 men from Portsmouth, Plymouth and Chatham Divisions were punished with seven days confinement to barracks and a forfeit of one day's pay for the offence. On the same day three men from Chatham Divison were punished more severely for the same offence. Private Frank Rolfe, a No.7 Platoon replacement, was disciplined on 2nd April for being absent without leave with seven days confinement to barracks and loss of two days pay. It must be remembered that the men training for the operation on Zeebrugge were isolated from the world and had no contact with loved ones. At the end of each strenuous training day, the men were beginning to prepare themselves mentally for the onslaught they would have to endure. The impending operations made these volunteers think of their mortality and face the realistic prospect that they may not return home. So for many men breaching military discipline in order to say good-bye to a loved one was worth the punishment. One of these men was Private John Bostock, who was awarded 10 days confinement to barracks and forfeit two days pay for being AWOL on 30th March. Bostock was punished once again on 9th April when he was deprived of a good conduct badge for breaking out of barracks while a defaulter and remaining absent. Bostock had been married for two years, during most of that period he was serving on HMS *Intrepid* patrolling the Russian coast. He had not spent much time with his wife Dorothy, who lived in Deal, and his reasons for absconding were understandable.

During Easter Monday on 1st April a terrible setback befell the RMA detachment to the 4th Battalion RMLI when four men from a Stokes mortar team were killed and five wounded during a training exercise on Freedown, when a Stokes Mortar bomb prematurely exploded. Bombardier Fred Belfield and Gunners Albert Aldridge, Samuel Houchen and Arthur Large were killed. Gunner Ernest Cassey died two days later of injuries sustained. The epitaph on Gunner Samuel Houchen's tombstone at Deal Cemetery reads:

WHEN THE STOKE GUN PRIMED FOR ACTION
BURST AND SHATTERED ALL HIS LIMBS
ALL HIS COMRADES AROUND HIM DYING
NE'ER A MURMUR CAME FROM HIM
NO ONE SAW HIS SHATTERED FEATURES
SHOWING WHERE THE SHELL BORED
BUT HIS NOBLE LIFE IS ENDED
NOW HE'S RESTING WITH THE LORD

Lieutenant Daniel Broadwood who was standing behind No 2 Gun at the time of this tragic incident reported that 'The battery of 4 guns had received the order 'Four rounds gun fire' and were carrying out this order when No 1 gun burst killing 4 men and injuring 6. The shell must have been placed in the gun in the correct way as the cartridge container was found in the bottom half of the gun.'[56] Lieutenant Colonel Elliot wrote in his report to the Adjutant General, Brigadier General H.S. Neville White on 2nd April: 'I was present at the time of the accident, and can offer no other explanation than that the burst was due to a premature explosion due to faulty ammunition.'[57] An inquest into the deaths of these four men was carried out at the Royal Marines Infirmary, Deal, during the afternoon of 2nd April and a verdict of accidental death was given.

A full rehearsal of the operation took place on 2nd April. The raiding party on the Mole would comprise three elements. A party of seaman led by Captain Henry Halahan would be the first to land on the Mole to secure the vessel for berthing, in conjunction with the tugs *Iris* and *Daffodil*. They were also responsible for lowering scaling ladders from the Mole to *Iris* so that A Company (Chatham) led by Major Charles Eagles could land. Once this was done, they were to lead the storming parties along the Mole to the lighthouse, where they would launch flares as a navigational aid to assist the blockships in their approach to the harbour.

The Royal Marine Light Infantry storming party led by Lieutenant-Colonel Bertram Elliot would then follow them. B and C Company sailed on *Vindictive* while A Company sailed on *Iris*. They were ordered to achieve their objectives at all costs. Each Company had drawn lots to lead the initial assault on the Mole. Major Weller's C Company, from Plymouth won and would be the first to disembark. The first platoons to go ashore would be Nos 9 and 10 who were assigned the task of capturing and consolidating strong enemy positions two hundred yards along the Mole to the west shore end, inclusive of Shed No. 3. Captain John Palmer with Platoon Nos 11 and 12 was assigned to knock out the three 4.1-inch guns on the eastern extremity of the Mole. B Company led by Captain Edward Bamford would disembark and secure all bomb ammunition dumps, sheds and shelters two-thirds along the Mole towards the viaduct. A Company led by Major Charles Eagles, once disembarked from the *Iris* would follow and support B Company, but was tasked with occupying the seaplane base and aircraft personnel quarters. Each man wore an india-rubber swimming belt. All platoons were armed with a Lewis gun and a flame-thrower. They also carried two ladders and four ropes; as soon as they landed on the parapet, there would be a four-foot drop onto the concrete wall, then a further twenty-foot descent to the ground level on the Mole. The advanced units at each end of the Mole would fire red Very lights to signal the extent of their progress and indicate that the Portsmouth and Chatham Companies should come ashore, and also to act as a guide to the gunners on *Vindictive* who were providing covering fire.

The third party consisted of a demolition unit commanded by Lieutenant Cecil Dickinson. The principal aim of this raiding force was to disable or destroy enemy batteries on the Mole, preventing them from firing upon the approaching blockships as they passed the Mole and headed toward the canal entrance. Their secondary objective was to cause maximum damage and destruction of the naval facility. Knowledge of the number of enemy guns was approximate. It was difficult to ascertain the exact number of enemy vessels that would be berthed alongside the Mole on the night of the assault, but it was expected that most of the vessels would be prepared to slip immediately during an attack. It was estimated that there would be three Torpedo-boat destroyers, three dredgers, three small craft and the *Brussels*. There were also two floating cranes weighing 55 tons and 10 tons moored to the Mole. There were three large sheds, 11 cranes, hangars for seaplanes, bomb stores, ammunition dumps and storage facilities to be destroyed. For this task the demolition team carried ammonal, guncotton detonators, and fuses. It was planned that the *Vindictive* would arrive at the Mole 20 minutes prior to the arrival of the blockships, to allow time for securing alongside and landing storming parties to silence the batteries.

On 6th April the 4th Battalion RMLI were paraded before Lieutenant Colonel Elliot at 6 a.m., then marched behind a band through the streets of Deal to the train station. They marched to the tunes of 'Rule Britannia', 'Auld Lang Syne' and 'The Girl I Left Behind Me'. The people of Deal, including whole families, lined the streets early that morning to give the Royal Marines a good send off on their journey to Dover. The Marines from the 4th Battalion has still not been told of their destination as they embarked on the Clyde ferry steamer *King Edward* at Dover later that day. They suspected that they were destined for France. The Captain of the *King Edward* shouted from the bridge to the Colonel 'Am I to proceed direct to France?' The Colonel replied 'proceed to sea and I will give you your orders'. The presumption that France was the intended destination amongst the Royal Marines was confounded when the ship set a course towards Sheerness. At the Mouse Lightship they were transferred to the *Daffodil*, which then transported them to the Swin, eight miles south of the Essex Coast, where A and B Companies were transferred to the battleship HMS *Hindustan*, and C Company were put on HMS *Vindictive*. *Vindictive* became very crowded when C Company joined the crew on board. The *Hindustan* was moored in the Thames estuary with other vessels seconded to the operation. They were out of sight of land and there was great confusion amongst the ranks. The men were put at ease as soon as they transferred aboard HMS *Hindustan* when Lieutenant Colonel Elliot assembled the men and finally told them the purpose of their mission. He received a round of applause from his men.

On 7th April Vice Admiral Keyes visited these ships to brief them in great detail on the task that lay ahead. A clay model of the Mole was used to show them their objectives for the operation. Captain Carpenter stressed how perilous the operation would be and that everyone had a decisive role to play. Sergeant Wright recalled Carpenter's briefing: 'We are going on a very dangerous errand, and any hitch in the operation may mean a naval disaster, so it is everyone's duty to do his best.'[58]

Private 'Beau' Tracey recalled that Vice Admiral Keyes gave every man one last opportunity to pull out of the operation if they so desired. Nobody opted out. Private Feeney caught the mood: 'The general opinion here at the moment is that it will be either completely successful or we shall be all wiped out.'[59]

During the briefing Captain Carpenter advised the men on misinformation to disseminate if they were captured.

It may so happen that some of you men may have the misfortune to be captured during this operation. If so, bear in mind you must not give any information to the enemy, especially concerning our Fleet. On the other hand, there is certain information we should like you to pass on. In the first place, tell them we are capturing their submarines, taking them to England, putting English crews on board, and sending them to sea again as decoys. Secondly, tell them that on every merchant ship putting to sea there is fitted an instrument, which can detect a submarine at a two-mile radius. This information must be tactfully passed on letting the enemy bring up the subject first.'[60]

Although no one requested to drop out during the initial briefing, the men who waited aboard the vessels moored in the Thames Estuary now had time to think about the operation and their chances of survival. The close, claustrophobic confines of the ship where all they could do was sit, smoke idly and wait for the operation to begin was the time when their doubts and anxieties manifested. Private Feeney wrote of his dissatisfaction with life at sea and there is a hint of second thoughts: 'Mess 50. Number of men, twenty-eight. No room. Don't like ship life. No room to even change your mind.'[61] Petty Officer Harry Adams learned that he was assigned to *Daffodil* and later recalled:

Finally, I suppose, we knew for the first time which ship we would man. There was a funny feeling running through our veins by this time, I don't think we spoke much, just ready–set for the go, and the sooner we got stuck into it, the better. Truth to tell, we wanted more than ever now, to get on with the job; whichever way it was going to end for us … We saw guns, ate guns, and dreamt guns – they were constantly in our thoughts … I'm sure it began to dawn on every man separately – in his own way – that it was no 'jam puff' ride; but not one would have turned back now, (even if he had the chance).

One sort of became quietly – more sober and serious – even more keen to get on and get it done. A most peculiar feeling deep down. You realised this 'Arsenal' would greet you – hard and heavy. One even began to think of those at home quite a bit more sincerely – I know lots of men (myself included) who addressed wee parcels – keep-sakes maybe, forwarded if there was no return for them. This was kindly undertaken by the Chaplain of the 'Hindustan'.[62]

Lieutenant Philip Vaux was navigating officer aboard the blockship HMS *Iphigenia*. He had considerable experience with the Royal Navy throughout the War. He began his service as a Midshipman on HMS *Lion* and his first experience of action was at the Battle of Helioland Bight on 28th August 1914. Four months later he was at the Battle of Dogger Bank on 25th January 1915. Transferring to HMS *Warspite* as a Sub Lieutenant, he saw further action at Jutland on 31st May 1916 prior to volunteering for the Zeebrugge raid. He wrote a letter to his father on 8th April before leaving:

By the time you get this epistle it will be all over and I shall either be home or a prisoner of war or no longer … If the Hun is not expecting us I think we ought to do it O.K., but if he is all ready it's going to be a pretty tough proposition as we have to steam past their guns at practically point blank range. Getting away is also a bit of a problem – if the cutter is seaworthy I pull away in her like blazes after the ship is blown up and sunk, out to sea and hope to get picked up by a destroyer or something – if I can't manage that I shall row to Holland – only 7 miles – walk ashore, demand 24 hours to repair damages (this is quite O.K. by International Law a warship may put into a neutral port for 24 hours to repair damages – my cutter will certainly be a man of war as I will have pistols on board! – and probably a broken oar as damages!) … I shall pay a visit to the British Attaché or what not and get him a cable for a destroyer or motor boat to take me back – quite simple – Of course that is assuming we are lucky enough to get in and lucky enough to get away again.[63]

While the storming parties trained for the assault on the Mole and the blockships and supporting vessels were being prepared for the operation, the 61st Wing of the Royal Air Force flew regular reconnaissance sorties over Zeebrugge. In the weeks prior to the raids, they took photographs of the port at different tide times. These images greatly assisted the planning of the operation and were used to make models for training purposes. Keyes had prior experience of the utility of aerial recon. General Hamilton in his *Gallipoli Diary* recalled how he, Commander Samson and Chief of Staff Keyes spent hours poring over photographs, 'trying to digest the honey brought back by our busy aeroplane bees from their various flights over Gallipoli'.

There were five nights every two weeks when the appropriate combination of weather, tide, and wind might come together. The direction of the wind should be towards Zeebrugge to ensure that the destroyers could effectively use their smoke screens. There could be no moon and had to be high water to enable the gangways on the assault ships to reach the wall of the Mole to disembark the storming parties. At high tide there would be only one hour and twenty minutes for them to attack the Mole and depart; if they stayed longer they would run aground on the sandbank beneath the Mole.

Prior to the raid Keyes insisted on viewing the entire operational area around Zeebrugge. Captain Alick Bowater RNAS was the pilot who took Keyes on a reconnaissance flight despite the potentially heavy anti-aircraft fire that made the flight hazardous.

Keyes wife, Eva, paid a visit to *Vindictive* and presented a horseshoe on a shield as a gift to the crew. By the consensus of all onboard this lucky charm was fixed to the middle funnel on the side that would approach the Mole during the impending raid. This charm worked – for the funnel at least – which received little damage in comparison to the fore funnel that was completely destroyed as it approached the Mole and the aft funnel that suffered substantial damage. The middle funnel was not touched by shells or bullets around the horseshoe.

The men were kept on standby at a moment's notice. The assault was postponed three times because of adverse weather conditions. Twice, on the 11th and 13th April, postponement took place once the raiding force had sailed. Favourable weather conditions on 11th April allowed the operation to proceed. At 4.00 p.m. HMS *Warwick* led the armada towards Zeebrugge. *Warwick* was followed by *Vindictive*, who at 10 knots was towing the Mersey ferry boats *Iris* and *Daffodil*. *Thetis* followed close behind leading the five blockships. The flotilla sailed in single file as they headed towards the Belgium coast. The blockships were closely escorted by a CMB each. Destroyers and MLs from the Dover and Harwich flotillas joined the armada in the English Channel. On board *Thetis* Captain Sneyd in a morale-boosting gesture provided his officers a special dinner of grouse together with delicacies from Fortnum & Mason.

At 10 p.m. the fleet was approaching the minefields off the Belgian coast. Surplus crew members aboard the blockships were transferred into MLs. Only a skeleton crew was required to take the blockships to the canal entrance. At this point the flotilla split into two, with the *Brilliant* and *Sirius* heading for Ostend and *Vindictive* destined for Zeebrugge. A passage had been cleared through the minefield. The *Thetis*, *Iphigenia* and *Intrepid* reduced speed to ensure that they arrived in the inner harbour 30 minutes after *Vindictive* had reached the Mole.

The conditions remained favourable until Keyes' task force was 16 miles off Zeebrugge, when the wind changed direction, blowing from the south, which would have blown the smoke screen towards the sea and exposed the fleet to the German gun batteries along the Belgian coast. Monitors and the RAF had begun bombing targets in Zeebrugge. Keyes was in a terrible dilemma, for if he abandoned the operation at this stage, there was a risk that the Germans may have discovered the effort and destroy the element of surprise for any future attempts. The order to abort would mean that a fleet of 74 vessels would have to turn away from the coast and head back home. This in itself would be a difficult and dangerous operation, when undertaken at night and when the majority of the larger ships were towing smaller vessels without navigational lights.

He called it off. As the armada altered course for home there were near collisions between vessels. Lieutenant Calvin, second in command of ML 558, described it as a 'hair raising affair … The experience of seeing the destroyers miss ramming us by inches as they scraped by both stem and stern at the same time will remain in my memory to my dying day.'[64] Keyes:

I went through a pretty difficult time during the next few moments. I knew that every man in the expedition felt, as I did, keyed up for the ordeal. How they would hate to be called off and then asked to undergo it all over again – or perhaps, worse still, have to go back to their ships having achieved nothing; we still might have been seen by an enemy submarine; we knew that the Swin force had been seen by neutrals, and if the Admiralty thought for a moment that the expedition would be no longer be a surprise, they would be absolutely certain to declare it off. What would our feelings be, if the weather proved favourable after turning back. These thoughts crowded through my mind and I was horribly tempted. It would be so much easier to go on and trust to the God of Battles and the good fortune of the British Navy for a happy issue. An Admiral afloat has one great advantage over his brother the General, who of necessity in modern war, must remain in safety at his headquarters many miles behind the line. At least I could share some of the risks I was asking others to undertake.[65]

These are the words of a leader who would not ask his men to do things that he was not prepared to do himself. Although he was an innovator willing to take a risk, he was not reckless and considered the consequences of this changing situation with great prudence. To have carried on could have resulted in a disastrous failure that would have risked the lives of many brave young men. In Keyes's memoirs he refers to Nelson's failed amphibious landing at Santa Cruz in July 1797, when he pressed on to capture the port on Tenerife despite unfavourable weather conditions. Nelson's failure to abandon the operation led to disaster and the lesson from history helped Keyes to make his decision. There was a moment of anxiety when Keyes lost communication with *Brilliant* and *Sirius*, but they did receive a message to abort the operation. If Keyes had proceeded with the operation and the changing wind direction had blown the smoke screen out to sea, the entire fleet would have been blown out of the water.

Not all vessels, however, had received the signal to abort. CMBs 2, 4, 10, 12, 20 and 33A from the Ostend units did not receive the communication to abandon. At 1.00 a.m. in accordance with their orders each of these Coastal Motor Boats proceeded with their designated task off the Belgian coast. CMBs 4 and 12 dropped the first smoke floats. At 1.05 a.m. CMB 20 dropped a calcium buoy alongside the Stroom Buoy causing a smoke screen near to the shore. It took some eight minutes for the buoy to function accordingly and establish a smoke screen. CMB 20 then laid a further calcium buoy near to Bell Buoy and again it took some time for a smoke screen to become effective. CMB 33A commanded by Lieutenant Robert Angus accompanied CMB 20. Angus had been ordered to position two calcium buoys near to the eastern pier at Ostend. At 1.20 a.m. CMB 33A was seen for the last time as she approached the pier. No pigeons or messages were received from the vessel. Lieutenant F. Harrison commanding the Ostend units reported that 'The enemy fired star shells almost on the arrival of CMBs at Stroom Buoy. They opened fire from the forts on what appeared to be a barrage system and kept it up intermittently during the whole operation. Shrapnel was bursting over the inshore boats most of the time.'[66]

The Germans were awakened by the heavy bombardment from the British Monitors on the Ostend coast. During the night it was reported that a British motor boat entered the entrance to Ostend harbour and fired its machine guns at the searchlight on the pier. German guns responded and achieved a direct hit. This was CMB 33A. After being hit the vessel ran aground in Ostend Harbour, with all six crew killed.

Midshipman Andrew Cunningham was among the crew who died that night. He had served three years with the Royal Naval Reserve as a Midshipman on HMS *Changunola* patrolling between Iceland and Glasgow and was waiting for promotion to Sub Lieutenant. Aged 19, Midshipman Cunningham had been ordered by Lieutenant Harrison not to be aboard prior to the Ostend operation. His youthful spirit and enthusiasm to experience battle led him to disobey Harrison's order and as a consequence he would lose his life.

Cunningham's body was lost to the sea and his name is commemorated on the Portsmouth Naval Memorial. The German machine gunners who poured deadly fire onto CMB 33A were awarded Iron Crosses.

The loss was even greater than it first seemed. It is suspected that the Germans captured this vessel with detailed documents relating to both raids, on Zeebrugge and Ostend. Lieutenant Angus had disobeyed the order not to have aboard operational details. If so, he had compromised the success and safety of the entire fleet and raiding personnel. Admiral Keyes stipulated that no patrol vessels should carry secret documents. There was no doubt that the Germans were well aware of British intentions to attack Ostend and Zeebrugge according to *Trutzig und Treu!* by Admiral A.D. Jacobsen, (Berlin 1935). It would appear the British plans were in the hands of Admiral Ludwig von Schröder's chief of intelligence on 12th April. The documents were marked ZO and any German intelligence officer could guess the exact locations of the intended landing ground. Within 24 hours all battery crews were warned to expect an imminent attack.

The capture of these documents possibly resulted in the German Navy re-locating the Stroom Bank Buoy. This would have disastrous consequences during the attempt to block Ostend Harbour on St. George's Day two weeks later, when *Sirius* and *Brillant* would run aground in the area. CMB 20 had placed a calcium buoy near the Stroom Bank Buoy as planned and then took a dead reckoning from this navigational buoy in the approach to the piers. There is no mention in Lieutenant Harrison's report that the Stroom Bank Buoy had been moved, but it can be assumed that the Germans had indeed moved the Buoy.

On the journey back home aboard *Vindictive*, Leading Seaman Reuben Pearce who was in charge of A Company's Lewis Gun received an accidental bullet wound through the thigh. A main artery had been severed and he died two days later. Pearce was 43, a veteran of the Siege of Ladysmith and the Boer War.

The order to abort was a blow for everyone concerned. To have spent six weeks of strenuous training and to embark on the passage to the target only to be halted at the last moment affected the men greatly. Petty Officer Harry Adams recalled: 'We were all, I'm sure, Officers and Men very irritable, and bitterly disappointed – "Nerves" just about at breaking strain.'[67] Lieutenant F. J. Hore:

CMB 33A washed ashore at Ostend after the aborted attempt to block Ostend on 11th/12th April 1918.

CMB 4 is a First World War Coastal Motor Boat at the Imperial War Museum, Duxford, Cambridgeshire. This CMB took part in the Kronstadt raid on 18th August 1919.

Naturally everyone was much down in the dumps until the following morning when the Vice Admiral came on board. Our spirits rose when he told us that he never had a more poisonous decision to make than the one overnight, but as the wind was against us the whole squadron would have been sunk, so much did success depend on the smoke screen.[68]

Another attempt was made two days later on 13th April. This was cancelled because of strong winds and deteriorating seas, which would have greatly hindered the smaller vessels in the fleet. Once again, Keyes was right.

Sir Rosslyn Wemyss advised Keyes on his return from the second aborted attempt that the operation was cancelled and ordered him to disband the raiding force on the grounds that the element of surprise had been lost and that the Germans may have knowledge of the operation. Another factor in the decision to abandon was that the next date for another attempt with favourable tide and moon conditions was three weeks away. This was too long a period to keep the men aboard ships. Keyes was determined that his plan to seal the German Flanders Flotilla in Bruges would be followed through. Desperate to keep his operation alive he made the declaration that he would make another attempt within ten days under a full moon and persuaded Wemyss to revoke the order to cancel the operation and disband the force. With the operation still active there was the problem of keeping several hundred sailors and marines accommodated in cramped conditions aboard vessels for those ten days. In order to maintain security, no one was permitted to go ashore, which caused great frustration. HMS *Dominion* was deployed to the Swin to ease the overcrowding and provide more comfortable living space. The ten days spent in the Swin waiting for the next attempt was psychologically demanding nevertheless, for all involved. These men had been trained, stood up and stood down on two occasions. The lack of space aboard the vessels meant there could be no more training. Their nerves were strained and uncertainty caused further anxiety as they idly waited. They could not see land and the men were not allowed contact with their loved ones at home. Petty Officer Harry Adams:

All we knew and saw, were 'Guns', waiting to blow you to bits and the ensuing days were really days of waiting for your death. About the nearest approach I should say, to a man in the 'condemned cell'. Those men knew, and those that are left know that feeling, and I bet could sympathize only they hadn't committed any crime – that's all.[69]

During those long hours waiting the men passed their time boat racing, organising concert parties and gambling. Gambling was considered a serious offence in the Royal Navy, but in the circumstances a blind eye was turned. Crown and Anchor was a game played by the Zeebrugge raiders while they waited for the next attempt. Others took the opportunity to attend hymn-singing sessions organised by Chaplain Charles Peshall. Private James Feeney was a Roman Catholic, but there was no service to accommodate his faith. Feeney attended one of the sermons given by the Church of England Chaplain Peshall on 14th April. During that service Peshall asked the congregation to pray for Leading Seaman Reuben Pearce who had died after an accident on the last attempt. Feeney recalled his feelings at having to wait a second time for the operation to begin and of his concerns for his own fate:

We shan't make another attempt before ten days. I expect to be barmy by then, for want of something to interest me. All my speculations are in the future. Am I to be, or not to be after the landing? Went to evening prayers at the Seamen's Mess Deck, conducted by the Chaplain (Church of England). He is a real fine type of a man's man. His mind is as broad as the sea.[70]

Air Mechanic William Gough later recalled that the enthusiasm to fight began to wane after the abortive attempts to raid the Belgian ports. With time to contemplate their situation and realise that death could be a consequence, many of the men like Gough began to rethink:

We felt, to use a now common expression, somewhat 'windy'. This was not the case on the first occasion [the 10th]. Then, everyone was worked up to the highest pitch of excitement and was eager to have the opportunity of fighting. On the second attempt the general feeling was a great desire to get the job over and done with. But between these abortive attempts, there had been time to think over things and when we finally set out, we felt anything but ready for heroics. Nevertheless, we were determined to do our best.[71]

Although postponement caused disappointment for all those who took part, some valuable lessons were learnt, such as lack of communication between Royal Naval and Royal Marine Officers. Captain Arthur Chater:

Zeebrugge Mole; it takes little imagination to understand how daunting a landing target it made.

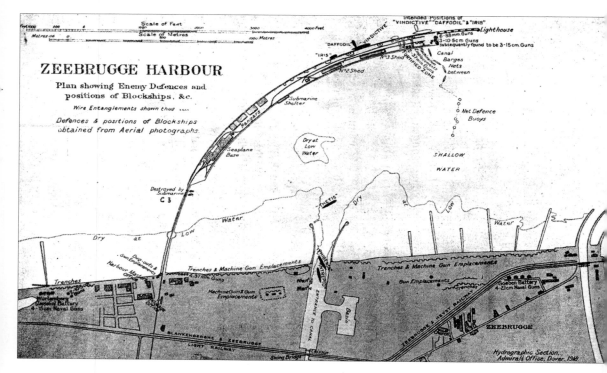

Zeebrugge Harbour – the plan of attack. (From *The Story of Zeebrugge* by Colonel G.M. Stinglhamber DSO).

One of the lessons learned from this abortive attempt was this: prior to our arrival, and without consulting us, the Captain of the Vindictive *had announced that before the ship reached the Mole, a double tot of rum would be issued to all hands. As the operation was one in which all would need clear heads and steady hands and feet, we felt this to be a mistake, but there was no going back on it. We learnt however that the rum issue would need far closer supervision than had been given to it on 11th April.[72]*

A tot of rum was a good tonic to steady the nerves, to calm the senses of a soldier before he engaged in battle during the Great War. To over-indulge was clearly madness. This problem had been highlighted during the first attempt on 11th April, when the over-consumption of alcohol became a serious problem aboard the blockship *Thetis* and the cause of friction between the seamen and the stokers. The stokers had been working in the engine room during the passage across and faced a seven-hour passage during the return journey home. Engineer Lieutenant Boddie, Chief Engineer onboard, detailed some seamen to trim coal in the bunkers to assist the stokers in their work during the passage. To the annoyance of the stokers the chosen seamen were of no use, for they were drunk.

It turned out that about the hour we had seemed definitely committed to the operation, the Coxwain, a Chief Petty Officer with an excellent war record, had with some of his seaman cronies raided the spirit room, breached the rum cask, and issued to his friends a supply of rum sufficient for the entire ship for two days. We got back to the Swin at noon on the 12th, with all hands exhausted. The Coxwain was immediately discharged, and incidentally his successor was one of the killed at Zeebrugge, 10 days later. The stokers felt indignant about the rum incident, mainly because they had not been invited to participate in the orgy, and partly because the seamen were unfit to assist them in the stokeholds.[73]

Ordinary Seaman William O'Hara also reported that many of the men were not in a fit condition to assault the Mole due to the effects of the rum issued aboard *Iris*.

> *In our second venture we got within about 15 miles of our objective but the wind turned again and so we could do nothing but return again, I really think it was just as well that we had to return for on the crossing the rum was served out neat and as no check was kept on it most of the men were very far from sober and therefore in no condition to land on the Mole.*[74]

On 18th April, two days prior to the third attempt, Lieutenant Ivan Franks had developed appendicitis and was sent to hospital for an operation. Deeply disappointed, he missed the actual raid and command of *Iphigenia* passed to the twenty-one-year old Lieutenant Edward Billyard-Leake. Billyard-Leake had held the rank of Lieutenant for only one year and this command was a tremendous responsibility for a man of that age.

That surprise was probably lost caused great concern amongst senior naval officers at the Admiralty, who were reluctant to proceed with further attempts. The First Lord of the Admiralty Sir Eric Geddes visited the fleet to ascertain the morale of the men. On the basis of this visit he sanctioned one more attempt.

NOTES

1. Sir Roger Keyes, Admiral of the Fleet RN, *The Naval Memoirs 1916-1918*, p219: Thornton Butterworth Ltd, London, 1935.
2. Ibid p220.
3. *Globe & Laurel* 1918, p106.
4. National Archives: CAB 45/268. (Admiral Sir Roger Keyes' original letters and comments on the Eastern Mediterranean [Dardanelles and Gallipoli], the Ostend and Zeebrugge raid, and the Dover Straits, 1915–1930).
5. Engineer Lieutenant Boddie papers IWM Ref. 96/47/1.
6. Captain A F B Carpenter VC RN, *The Blocking of Zeebrugge*, p117: Herbert Jenkins Limited, London, 1925.
7. Sir Roger Keyes, op cit, p240.
8. Ibid p240.
9. The *Newcastle Daily Chronicle*, 29th April 1918.
10. Lieutenant Boddie papers IWM Ref. 96/47/1.
11. Sir Roger Keyes, op cit, p221.
12. Ibid p222.
13. Petty Officer Harry Adams Papers.
14. Ibid.
15. *South Wales Daily News*, Tuesday 30th April 1918.
16. Philip Warner, *The Zeebrugge Raid*, p87: William Kimber, 1978.
17. Engineer Lieutenant Boddie papers IWM Ref. 96/47/1.
18. University of Leeds Archives Able Seaman Henry Groothius Tape 93.
19. Ordinary Seaman William O'Hara Papers.
20. *Chatham, Rochester & Gillingham News*, Saturday 27th April 1918.
21. Edward Hilton-Young MP, *By Sea and Land, Some Naval Doings*, p273: T.C. & E.C. Jack Ltd, London & Edinburgh, 1920.
22. IWM Sound Archives Private Jordan Daniel 8552.
23. *Hampshire Telegraph & Post*, Friday 26th April 1918.
24. Private Jim Clist interview, courtesy David Clist.
25. Ibid.

26. Private Jim Clist interview.

27. Ibid.

28. Max Arthur, *Lost Voices of the Royal Navy*: Hodder & Stoughton, 2005.

29. Corporal George Moyse interview. Courtesy Peter White.

30. *Globe & Laurel* 1918, p104.

31. Max Arthur, *Lost Voices of the Royal Navy*: Hodder & Stoughton, 2005.

32. Ordinary Seaman William O'Hara Papers.

33. University of Leeds Archives Henry Groothius Tape 93.

34. Philip Warner, *The Zeebrugge Raid*, p88: William Kimber, 1978.

35. Ordinary Seaman William O'Hara Papers.

36. Petty Officer Harry Adams Papers.

37. Private Ernest (Beau) Tracey interview. Courtesy of Richard Davison.

38. Lance Corporal George Calverley, IWM Ref: 02/30/1.

39. Private Jim Clist interview, courtesy David Clist.

40. Petty Officer Harry Adams Papers.

41. Ordinary Seaman William O'Hara Papers. .

42. National Archives: CAB 45/268 & Royal Marines Museum.

43. Letter from Lieutenant Colonel Elliot to Adjutant General, Brigadier-General H.S. Neville White, 23rd March 1918, Royal Marines Museum.

44. Ibid.

45. Ibid.

46. Brigadier General Neville White letter to the Commandant Royal Marines written on 23rd March 1918. Royal Marines Museum.

47. Ibid.

48. Brigadier General Neville White report dated 23rd March 1918, Royal Marines Museum.

49. National Archives: ADM 196/63: Major G S Hobson Service Record.

50. National Archives: CAB 45/268.

51. Brigadier General Neville White report dated 23rd March 1918, Royal Marines Museum.

52. Ibid

53. Petty Officer Harry Adams papers.

54. Royal Naval Museum RNM, Ad. Lib. MSS 217. Papers of Captain Herbert Grant.

55. Ibid.

56. Lieutenant Daniel Broadwood report, Royal Marines Museum.

57. Lieutenant Colonel Elliot's report, Royal Marines Museum.

58. Sergeant Wright, Royal Marine Museum Arch 10/2/W.

59. Private Feeney's diary, quoted in *The Zeebrugge Raid* by Philip Warner, p119: William Kimber, 1978.

60. Sergeant Wright, Royal Marine Museum Arch 10/2/W.

61. Private Feeney's diary, quoted in *The Zeebrugge Raid* by Philip Warner: William Kimber, 1978.

62. Petty Officer Harry Adams Papers.

63. Lieutenant Vaux IWM Ref: P447.

64. William Guy Carr, *Out of the Mists*, p104: Hutchinson & Co., 1940.

65. Sir Roger Keyes, Admiral of the Fleet RN, *The Naval Memoirs 1916-1918*, p252: Thornton Butterworth Ltd, London, 1935.

66. National Archives: CAB 45/272. (Zeebrugge correspondence reports, 1918-19).

67. Petty Officer Harry Adams Papers.

68. *Globe & Laurel* 1918, p105.

69. Petty Officer Harry Adams Papers.

70. Private Feeney's diary, quoted in *The Zeebrugge Raid* by Philip Warner, p121: William Kimber, 1978.

71. IWM Museum Department of Documents: Acting 1st Class Mechanic W H Gough, IWM 91/11/1.

72. Captain A.R. Chater, RMLI, IWM Museum: 74/101/1.

73. Engineer Lieutenant Ronald C. Boddie, IWM Museum: 96/47/1.

74. Ordinary Seaman William O'Hara Papers.

CHAPTER 5

'MAY WE GIVE THE DRAGON'S TAIL A DAMNED GOOD TWIST'

After the postponed attempt on 13th April, the next date with suitable tidal conditions was Monday 22nd. On that day at 10.45 a.m. the order to proceed was received by the main force assembled in the Swin. The task force destined to assault Zeebrugge and Ostend was disposed in three columns. The central column was comprised of the main attacking force. *Vindictive*, towing the ferryboats *Iris* and *Daffodil* led the central column. The five blockships, the minesweeper *Lingfield* and five motor launches followed behind *Vindictive*. The role of Lingfield and the Motor Launches was to evacuate surplus crew from the blockships before the final passage to the canal entrances at Zeebrugge and Ostend.

The flagship HMS *Warwick* led the starboard column. Private Beau Tracey who was aboard *Iris* remembered the proud moment as he looked in the direction of HMS *Warwick*, flying the Vice Admiral's flag. This flag was presented by the commander of the battleship HMS *Centurion* to Keyes, a large battleship flag now being flown from the mast of a smaller destroyer. It was an impressive sight according to Beau Tracey. 'It gave one a certain degree of pride to be able to look in that direction and see that massive Admiral's flag.'[1]

Warwick was followed by *Phoebe* and *North Star*. These three vessels were to protect the *Vindictive* from torpedo attacks while she was berthed alongside the Zeebrugge Mole. *Trident* and *Mansfield*, towing the submarines C1 and C3, also formed part of the starboard column, together with *Tempest*, the escort for the Ostend blockships *Brilliant* and *Sirius*. The fleet sailed towards the Belgian coast at a rate of 10 knots.

The port column contained vessels that were detailed to protect the northern flank of the attacking force. *Whirlwind* led *Myngs* and *Moorson* as well as the other escort for the Ostend blockships, *Tetrarch*. In an effort to conserve fuel, each vessel in all three columns towed one or two coastal motor boats. While CMB 35A was about to get into tow by *Thetis*, she fouled her propellers with 4½-inch thick rope. At 5.20 p.m. *Thetis* proceeded while Lieutenant E. Hill commanding CMB 35A tried to clear the propeller. Unsuccessful in clearing it, they were towed back to Dover by the drifter *Gideon* at 6.30 p.m. CMB 35A arrived at Dover at 8.00 p.m. Hill and his crew were bitterly disappointed by this setback, but made a determined effort to join the raiding force. On arrival at Dover the vessel was hastily hoisted from the water and the propeller was cleared of the entangled rope. They were designated to put up the western smokescreen and Hill headed for Zeebrugge at full speed in order to carry out their orders. Despite the delay, Hill succeeded in getting his vessel to Zeebrugge in time for the attack later that night. At 4.30 p.m. CMB 5 commanded by Sub Lieutenant C. Outhwaite developed a problem with a red hot piston in No 5 cylinder. Outhwaite departed from the raiding flotilla and made his way to Ramsgate where the problem was rectified. CMB 5 went full steam ahead as she tried to catch up with the rest of the fleet.

The Harwich Force was deployed as a safeguard to prevent German vessels attacking the raiding force from the North Sea. The 61st Wing RAF provided air cover. As Keyes' fleet sailed on, British airmen patrolled and bombed the Belgian coastline. These air patrols ensured that enemy planes did not observe the fleet as it crossed the English Channel. Sopwith Camels from No. 204 Squadron patrolled the coast. Handley Page Aircraft from

No. 214 squadron bombed Zeebrugge, while No. 213 and No. 217 Squadrons contributed to the bombing sorties during that evening.

Navigational buoys had been laid ahead of the operation. Each vessel was given defined orders to a strict timetable of movement. This was done to reduce the need for communications en route. The transmitting of wireless signals was prohibited and the use of visual signals was reduced to a minimum.

For many, the journey to Zeebrugge would be their last, and thoughts of family and sweethearts were uppermost in their minds. Keyes had forewarned them that this was an unusually hazardous operation and the best chance of survival would be to be taken prisoner and spend the rest of the war as a POW. Private Alfred Hutchinson who was aboard *Iris* remembered, 'It was a beautiful morning, but it really hit us when the No. 1 ordered us to cover the top deck with sand to soak up the blood. Later that afternoon we watched the sun set. Everyone was very quiet. I think we were wondering if we would see it rise in the morning.'[2] Lieutenant F.J. Hore, Quartermaster for 4th Battalion RMLI recalled, 'We were under no delusion as to our mission. Everyone knew he was in for a tough job, but all were in the highest spirits. We hoped to surprise the Bosche. We knew that having left our cards at the Mole, he would, with his usual courtesy, be anxious to return our call.'[3] The crews were under no illusion. Lieutenant Hilton-Young: 'People did not talk about their chance of coming through – people never do. I think that everybody was fairly sure that the ship would go down with a great many casualties, and that a certain number would get picked up by the small craft or struggle ashore and be made a prisoner.'[4]

While training for the raid, Private Jim Clist had developed a friendship with Private Fred Freeman, who also belonged to No.12 Platoon. Jim remembered playing cards with Fred as they sailed aboard *Vindictive* towards Zeebrugge on the night of 22nd April.

> My mate in the section was a chap called Curly Freeman. He was a strong well built chap with dark curly hair. He was serving on HMS Tiger when he volunteered. About two hours before the actual landing we were playing cards. I remember finishing up with a lot of coppers. I put them in my breast pocket, they might help to protect one part of my body. My mate Freeman got very serious as the time drew near for the landing. And insisted that he should cut off one of his curls. I tried to laugh it off and told him that we would be having a pint together when we got back to Deal, but he was sure he was going to be killed and cut off some of his hair himself and gave it to me. He was killed that night.[5]

HMS *Vindictive* leaving for Zeebrugge, 22nd April 1918, photographed by R. Perkins.

The men were also wondering if this third attempt would be cancelled. With two aborted attempts, many of the sailors and Marines were acutely conscious that the Germans could be waiting for them. Petty Officer Harry Adams on board *Daffodil*: 'Was it too much to even hope that the Germans couldn't possibly have got 'wind' of our coming? Seemed almost ridiculous this being the third try, to even waste time 'hoping' – in any case by this time, we were past caring whether they knew or not. We wanted to get on with the job.'[6]

Vice Admiral Keyes had intended to sail on *Vindictive* as his flagship, however this was deemed impractical, because it would deny him the ability to oversee the entire operation. With *Warwick* positioned near the Mole, Keyes would be in a position to observe, appraise and respond. Earlier, his wife Eva reminded him that the following day was St George's Day as she walked with him. She recommended that Keyes use St. George as his battle cry. As soon as the armada was under way Keyes duly sent a signal from *Warwick* by semaphore, 'St. George for England', to which Captain Carpenter aboard *Vindictive* replied, 'May we give the dragon's tail a damned good twist.'

Private Philip Hodgson No 12 Platoon was aboard *Vindictive* and recalled the impressive sight of the armada as it sailed across the Channel:

> *It was a fine spring afternoon, when we set off, 'Vindictive' with 'Iris' and 'Daffodil' in tow to save their limited supply of fuel followed in line ahead by the old gun boats, to become blockships, 'Thetis', 'Iphigenia' and 'Intrepid' sailing down outside the Goodwins to our rendezvous off Dover with the remainder of the attacking force consisting of lines of destroyers and MLs with their special smoke generators. It was indeed a thrilling sight to see this armada of small ships sailing in perfect order in an almost calm sea as the sun set and darkness fell.*[7]

Aboard *Vindictive* preparations were still being made. Leading Seaman William Childs organised the construction of sandbag defences for the two Lewis Gun teams in his charge. He separated the two emplacements with a 3/8th-inch Zinc plate as a precaution if a shell exploded nearby. Instead of two teams being wiped out by the same shell, the plate would provide an adequate shield to absorb any blast and enable the other team to continue to man their gun.

Before dusk, Wing Commander Arthur Brock the pyrotechnics specialist was transferred to *Vindictive* from the whaler of an accompanying destroyer. There was no reason for Brock to take part in the operation, but he insisted on the grounds that he could ensure that the smoke screen worked. And as previously mentioned, he also wanted to inspect a new range-finding apparatus that the Germans were suspected to be using. He hoped to find this apparatus on the Mole. He had in his possession a box that was marked with the warning 'Explosives – Handle with great care'. This box was hoisted onto the upper deck of *Vindictive* with extreme caution. Brock brought this allegedly hazardous box to Captain Carpenter's fore cabin where he opened it to reveal several bottles of vintage port, which he generously shared amongst his fellow officers during dinner. Captain Halahan, Lieutenant Colonel Elliot, Major Cordner and Commander Osborne dined in Captain Carpenter's fore cabin. Six hours later, only Osborne, the gunnery officer, would be alive.

A tot of rum was served out to those men who requested it at 8 p.m and two hours later at 10 p.m. In order to maintain a tighter control of the rum issue, Platoon Sergeants were responsible for ensuring that each man received his daily allocation. Private Beau Tracey aboard the *Iris* remembered that the men did not have a choice, they had to drink the allocated ration.

> *When we were on the way over there we had to have two tots of rum. I think that those tots of rum were two hours apart and you had to drink it. There was no question of you being a teetotaller and saying well I give my tot to somebody else because you just went up there, the Company Sergeant Major had the roll and as you went up your tot was poured out, you drunk it right in front of him.*[8]

Ordinary Seaman O'Hara also aboard HMS *Iris* remembered that the issuing of rum was more organised in contrast to the two previous attempts to raid Zeebrugge. 'Neat rum was issued, but we had learned our lesson over our second attempt and only two tots were issued to each man and his name ticked off so it was a more sober and better disciplined force ready for the attack.'[9] Only one Royal Marine exceeded his ration. Chater:

> *As the result of experience on 11th April, very careful precautions were taken to ensure that no man got more than his own ration of rum. In spite of this, one old soldier must have borrowed someone else's tot, for when I went round the mess decks with the Sergeant Major as the men were closing up, he shouted at us, 'We are just going over the top. We are all equal now'. I remember catching sight of the same man some three hours later, and thinking what a changed and sober man he looked.*[10]

Lieutenant Campbell commanding *Daffodil* trusted the men to know their own limitations. While checking that no one over-indulged, he said before returning to the bridge 'Well men, there's the rum, it's your lives, and you know what is expected of you.' Nineteen years later Campbell confided to Petty Officer Adams that only a small amount of rum had been consumed by the men aboard *Daffodil* that evening. However, the ship's cat found an opportunity to splice the main brace. Petty Officer Harry Adams remembered, 'Several more dirty rolls and dips, nearly turning the ship completely over and on one occasion the roll was so violent that the store room door burst open and a jar or two of rum broke bounds and smashed; which brings me to our black cat Mascot. His four legs, were about forty not enough – but he enjoyed the "Bubblie".'[11]

At 8.45 p.m. the assault fleet reached its rendezvous position where the blockships began to tow two coastal motor boats to economise on fuel. The fleet stopped at 9.55 p.m. for surplus crews from the blockships to be evacuated to other ships; however, a developing swell prevented *Intrepid* from disembarking crew members not essential for the actual blocking operation. (Blockship surplus crews were transferred to the minesweeper *Lingfield*.) ML 555 commanded by Lieutenant G. Goodwin was assigned to take off surplus crew from *Intrepid*, but her propellers had been fouled by lines used to tow coastal motor boats.

By 10.30 p.m. the fleet was 15 miles from Zeebrugge and the Ostend force altered course for their destination. Hot soup was distributed to the men aboard *Vindictive*. Thirty minutes later 4th Battalion RMLI and the Bluejacket assault party fell in on the deck of *Vindictive* and went to action stations. At 11.00 p.m. the destroyer escort had disappeared into the darkness and Acting 1st Class Mechanic William Gough remembered that those onboard *Vindictive* 'felt very lonely indeed.'[12]

At Buoy D, located 15 miles north west of the Zeebrugge Mole, the flotilla stopped for ten minutes where the *Iris* and *Daffodil* tow ropes were released. From this point all ships sailed towards their destined targets under their own power in total darkness and without radio communication.The hawser that was used by *Vindictive* to tow the *Iris* and *Daffodil* was released at 11.10 p.m. First Lieutenant R. Rosoman coordinated the release. Captain Halahan had already received a wound before the battle had begun. While he was on the quarter deck he had tripped and fallen over the hawser, cutting his eyebrow which required stitches.

During the evening slight rain fell, reducing visibility, which interfered with the long-range bombardment of Zeebrugge. At 11.35 p.m. the Monitors *Erebus* and *Terror* were bombarding the coast near Zeebrugge. The destroyers *Termagant*, *Truculent* and *Manly* supported the two Monitors in the barrage. Owing to the tide and the poor visibility the bombardment commenced later than scheduled. The Germans were not alerted to the raid by this bombardment because naval bombardments had been carried out at exactly the same time at Zeebrugge on nights before the raid. As soon as the British naval barrage began, men from the Matrosenartillerie-Regiment I were called to action. Their guns at the coastal batteries, Kaiser Wilhelm II, Schleswig-Holstein and Freya, fired upon the British Monitors HMS *Erebus* and *Terror*.

The rain also hampered the RAF in their ability to deploy aircraft and identify bomb targets. Major W E D Wardrop DFM served as an RNAS observer with No.7 Squadron:

> Zeebrugge was the one that we actually took part in, but our role there wasn't very – how can I put it – a means to do any damage, but just to attract the searchlights and force them to put their searchlights up while our Navy tried to get in as close as they possibly could without being found. But as soon as the first shot was fired by the Navy, so all the searchlights went down on the sea and they started bombarding them, of course. So far as we were concerned we were just left alone. We had no more to do so we came home. All we were doing was going round dropping one bomb at a time, coming in and going out again. There were several of us, we were doing that in turn, to keep on making a nuisance of ourselves to force them to put the searchlight up and the guns.[13]

Aboard *Vindictive* shipmates wished each other good luck and said goodbye to each other in case they did not survive. At 11.15 p.m. the order for 'action stations' was given. Rifles were loaded with magazines and the order was given to fix bayonets on arrival on the Mole. One officer from the Royal Engineers, Lieutenant Arthur Eastlake, and 34 RNAS personnel charged with operating the flame-throwers secured on the port side of the vessel got into position.

Everybody waited silently on deck for the assault upon the Mole. The raiding parties were under cover standing shoulder to shoulder in five ranks. Only the drone of the propellers broke the silence. On deck sailors were stationed with flares ready to illuminate the Mole at the last minute and a cable party was standing by on the forecastle ready to drop anchor at the foot of the high seaward wall. Those manning the howitzers, bomb mortars and flame-throwers on the decks and the guns in the foremast were instructed to fire as soon as the enemy had detected their presence. Lieutenant Hilton-Young was concerned about the dangers of overcrowding around the gun battery that he commanded on the forecastle of *Vindictive*. The overcrowding could slow down the landing parties who stood around the gun or impede the gun crew in carrying out their duties.

> Looking down the battery deck I could see or rather feel that they were crowded with men, mostly of the marines' landing parties, and presently a lot more of them came tumbling into our bay through a door out on to the forecastle. They filled our cramped space so full that we could not move in the dark without treading on somebody, but the decks were so full also that there was nowhere else for them to go, and they had to stay. They crowded so closely round the gun that there was hardly room to load, and if we had to fire in a hurry they were in danger of injury from recoil. All the time we had to be telling them to stand clear, and often to be feeling about in the dark in order to make sure that there was nobody in the way; and that was our chief external occupation and anxiety during the approach.[14]

Sergeant Harry Wright aboard *Vindictive* later recalled the tension as they approached the Mole.

> Our little Sergeants' Mess was crowded. We hastily shook hands and then went out to get our men on to the upper deck, into the darkness. Rifles were loaded and bayonets fixed. No lights were showing on any of the ships, and everyone spoke in whispers. Our nerves were strained almost to breaking point. Would we get alongside the Mole without the Germans seeing us? We stood shoulder to shoulder, rifles in hand ready for the dash forward – not a movement, and only the noise of the propellers breaking the silence.[15]

Coastal motor boats and motor launches sailed on ahead to to lay the smoke screen in advance of the main assault force. At 11.40 p.m. the smoke screen operation began. The Germans fired a star shell towards the sea, illuminating the sky. They could not see anything through the smoke and the Royal Navy was not detected, although the illumination greatly assisted navigation. The Germans did fire shells into the fog. The speed, size and manoeuvrability of the motor launches and coastal motor boats meant a direct hit was unlikely. However, some of the smoke floats laid near the Mole were sunk by German fire. At the same time the wind changed direction and this and the destruction of the smoke floats began to break up the smoke screen.

As they approached the Mole, visibility was extremely poor because of the rain and the smoke screen. The forecastle could not be seen from the bridge. The sea was becoming rough. The wind had changed to off shore. The enemy were continually firing star shells and beaming searchlights into the murk. Accompanying Motor Launches acted quickly to add to the smoke screen each time the enemy launched a star shell. Ordinary Seaman O'Hara aboard the *Iris* described the approach:

> The Germans must have known something was about to take place as we were under continuous star shell fire all the way in; it seemed like day with the sun trying to break through a thick fog; one could not see very far ahead on account of the smoke floats dropped from the motor launches and CMBs, therefore we were invisible to the enemy.[16]

Although the sky was illuminated, the Mole could not be seen from *Vindictive* and the enemy could not see them. At 11.56 p.m. *Vindictive* sailed out of the smoke screen and the Mole could be seen in the darkness approximately 300 yards off the port bow. Captain Carpenter, who was conning the ship from the forward port flame-thrower hut, increased to full speed and altered course so that the vessel would approach the Mole on a 45-degree bearing.

Fire was still withheld onboard. Air Mechanic William Gough belonged to a detachment of 34 men from the Admiralty Experimental Station at Stratford. He was waiting to land on the Mole with flame-throwers and phosphorus grenades:

> On the port side we could see a dark mass looming large through the fog, and knew that we were nearing the Mole. Minutes seemed like eternities. Then came the order to get ready and load our weapons. It was a welcome relief to have something to do to divert one's thoughts from outside happenings. Excitement was at fever-heat and our nerves strained to the utmost. The silence was appalling.[17]

Someone loading his revolver accidentally discharged a shot. This caused another marine to fire his weapon by accident. Yet still the Germans were not alerted to their presence, thanks to the density of the smoke screen.

As *Vindictive* passed the lighthouse and the six-gun battery, at last, the inevitable, she was observed: a searchlight beam illuminated the vessel like daylight. Beau Tracey recalled that there was a minute of silence from the Mole after the armada was discovered. This delayed German response could have been either because the German gunners were changing star shells for high explosive shells – or they were just too staggered to do anything.

The German soldiers on watch on the Mole described *Vindictive* appearing from the fog like a 'phantom-ship'.[18] Kapitänleutnant Felix Glatzer telles a different story, in that during that night the motors of boats and aircraft were heard. Kapitänleutnant der Reserve Robert Schutte from German Marine Artillerie was commanding officer of the battery on the Mole. The noise of ships' engines could be heard around 11.30 p.m. Schutte was alarmed by the sight of the artificial fog and ordered the guns on the Mole battery to fire blind. All that could be seen was Brock's wall of fog. The coastal batteries were alerted. The Württemberg Battery fired shells to illuminate the sky. The guns on the Mole battery fired six shells in the direction of the engine noise.

When *Vindictive* was 500 metres from the outer Mole, German soldiers and sailors on the Mole battery and on the shore batteries unleashed a horrific barrage. Shells and machine gun fire were aimed at the foc'sle. Battery fire from the Mole struck the deck and upper structure many times. Private Hodgson was assembled with No.12 Platoon underneath a wooden lifeboat stowed on the upper deck. It was this wooden boat that protected them from the inferno:

> It seemed as if hell had been let loose, as the ship closed in against the wall and was struck by heavy shells around the forecastle, the control top and the foremost funnel, flame-throwers on the port-side and flaming pieces of metal flying everywhere, luckily for our group that old ship's boat bore the brunt of this, no wonder that it was so full of holes when I saw it next morning.[19]

Sergeant Wright later wrote of the moment the enemy discovered their presence:

> No sooner had that light died down than another went up. The silence was broken by a terrific bang followed by a crash as the fragments of shell fell in among us, killing and maiming the brave fellows as they stood to their arms, crowded together as thick as bees. The Mole was just in sight, we could see it off our port quarter, but too late. Our gunners replied to this fire, but could not silence that terrible battery of 5-inch guns now firing into our ship at a range of less than 100 yards and from behind concrete walls. A very powerful searchlight was turned on us from the sand dunes at Zeebrugge and the powerful batteries there began to fire. The slaughter was terrible.[20]

Private James Feeney from No.7 Platoon, Portsmouth Company:

> Then there was a noise when our guns opened fire, and a German destroyer about 200 yards from us replied. I had cotton wool in my ears, and it sounded as if someone pulled the props from under the sky and I fell down. I dropped on the deck, and kept as low as I could. I often heard of people feeling small. I never felt so uncomfortably big in my life before. These thundering and banging and ear splitting sounds continued for nearly ten minutes, and even then we could hear the wails of anguish of the wounded and the dying.[21]

The sound of the guns firing at Zeebrugge could be heard with horrible clarity and distinctly felt in Dover and along the Kent coast. In Calais, Emily Rumbold was a clerk serving in the Women's Army Auxiliary Corps at Queen Alexandra's Camp, Calais. She recalled, 'We could tell that they were naval guns, because they were so terrific, the noise – it shook the huts, because really it wasn't very far up the coast.'[22]

Engineer Lieutenant Arthur Lougher was down below in the engine room of *Vindictive*. He had separated the engine room crew into two teams, one detailed to attend to the engines, while the other team stood by to tackle any fires that might occur onboard. 'The whole of the time we were alongside the Mole we were continually shelled … the noise of the firing was something terrific and although I was sorely tempted to go up and see how things were going on, I had to stick to my duties below. The noise was deafening, and the ship rocked like a cradle.'[23]

It must have been almost unbearably testing for Lougher and the men in the engine room to work down below, not knowing anything about the action going on above deck, (often the lot of the stoker). If *Vindictive* received a hit that resulted in her sinking, it would have been incredibly difficult for these men to escape. Some shells penetrated the engine room and caused damage and casualties. Lougher later praised his men: 'They worked like Trojans and stuck to their posts like glue. Men with gaping wounds treated them as of no account, and insisted on carrying on.'[24]

Gunners commanded by Lieutenant Rigby in the fore top immediately responded, which signalled other gunners onboard also to return fire. Among those gunners was Sergeant Finch in the fighting top, who would later be awarded the Victoria Cross for his actions that night.

Lieutenant Edward Hilton-Young R.N.V.R. was a gunnery officer aboard *Vindictive*, commanding the forward 6-inch B.L gun crew. He could remember 'the eruption of sparks where the shells struck, the crash of splintering steel, the cries and that smell which must haunt the memory of anyone who has been in a sea-fight – the smell of blood and burning.'[25] Hilton-Young was to receive a wound to his arm that later required amputation. Captain Carpenter recalled the moment when he brought *Vindictive* alongside the Mole:

> The noise was terrific and the flashes of the Mole guns seemed to be within arm's length. Of course it was, to all intents and purposes impossible for the Mole guns to miss their target. They literally poured projectiles into us. In about five minutes we had reached the Mole, but not before the ship had suffered a great amount of damage to both material and personnel.[26]

While they were standing on the exposed fore bridge port side aboard *Vindictive*, Captain Chater tried to warn his Commanding Officer Lieutenant Colonel Bertram Elliot and Major Alexander Cordner second in command, to take cover. Chater remembered his own earlier experiences of the hazards of shellfire. During 1914 in Antwerp he foolishly looked over the parapet and was wounded. He sustained a further wound in Gallipoli when shrapnel struck him in the back. He knew that as they approached the Mole through the shell fire they had to keep their heads down as much as practicable and he tried to advise them, but to no avail. 'A moment later a shell appeared to hit the front of the lower bridge beneath us. My two seniors dropped to the deck on either side of me. I grasped hold of them and spoke to them in turn, but neither answered me.'[27] It was sheer folly that the Commanding Officer and his second in command should be together, so that both were killed by the explosion from the same shell. The two most senior officers of the battalion had been wiped out before the battle commenced and before they gave the order to advance. Command of the 4th Battalion RMLI now fell upon Major Weller, commander of C Company.

Private Jim Clist belonged to No.12 Platoon and was Major Weller's runner:

> We were packed like sardines. When the Germans got on target they gave us Hell. The roar was deafening. Someone shouted out it is all right lads, that is our guns. That was not much consolation to us, about thirty to forty of our chaps were laid out on the deck killed or wounded. I thought that someone had hit me in the chest with a brick. My left shoulder became numb, but I was able to carry on all right. I was supposed to keep close to Major Weller as I was his runner and as it turned out he was in sole charge of the landing party as his two senior officers were killed before the landing.[28]

Many more shells struck the *Vindictive* causing further damage and casualties. Sergeant Camfield from No.5 Platoon was standing on the starboard side of the funnel casing amidships. A shell hit the aft funnel, and then ricocheted down towards the deck where he and No.5 Platoon were positioned. The shell exploded destroying the two platoon flame-throwers. A piece of shrapnel or debris from the explosion tore away Camfield's jaw. He lost his lower teeth and his jaw bone, and was wounded in the right shoulder.

Leading Seaman Dowell was one of an eight-man crew manning a 6-inch gun on *Vindictive*'s port side. He remembered the attitude he tried to adopt as they approached the Mole. 'Before we went into the affair, I thought to myself, "If I start by thinking I'll be sure to get killed or wounded – well, most likely it'll come true." So I went in with a good heart.'[29] Dowell and his gun crew were only able to fire three rounds, for once *Vindictive* had reached her berth, their 6-inch gun was below the level of the Mole. One of Dowell's comrades had received a leg wound. Unable to fire their gun they turned their efforts to helping secure *Vindictive* to the Mole.

> There came the signal arranged for, which took us to the job of trying to make fast alongside. A derrick had been rigged out to let down a specially made anchor by means of a 3-½ in. cable. The idea was to

make the anchor fast against something or other on the Mole. But the derrick, though it held the anchor some 18 or 20 feet off the ship, didn't quite go far enough. You see, there is a part of the Mole which projects under water, so it was impossible for the Vindictive *to come closer than she did. The special brows projected a good deal further than the derrick, so the landing parties were able to get out all right. But the anchor hung just short. Some men on the Mole tried to draw it in, but when we lowered away the anchor proved too heavy for them, and there it hung alongside the Mole instead of on it.*[30]

For some gunners, the battle was over before it had begun. The crew manning the 7.5-inch howitzer on the forward deck was not firing. Captain Reginald Dallas Brooks discovered that the entire crew was either dead or wounded. The same shell that killed Elliot and Cordner also wiped out the forward 7.5-inch howitzer crew and Stokes Mortar Battery. Dallas Brooks ordered Dowell's crew of seamen to put this gun into action, while exposed to enemy fire. Dowell:

Seeing we couldn't do anything more with the anchor, a marine officer told us to go and man the howitzer on the forecastle, as its crew had been wiped out. In all that firing, with dazzling light one minute and darkness the next, and with the decks covered with dead and wounded, it wasn't easy to get our chaps together. The gun layer was by my side, and, strangely enough, in all that noise and confusion I could hear the sight-setter's voice, though I couldn't see him. So I shouted to him, and it wasn't long before we seven had got together again and taken up our positions at the howitzer. Five of the seven went down at once. I don't know if it was shrapnel bursting overhead or whether we got splinters from a shell that had struck the superstructure. Anyway, only two of us were left standing, and when the marine officer saw that he ordered us to come away.[31]

Captain Dallas Brooks also aligned the 11-inch howitzer on the quarter-deck in the direction of the Goeben Battery. The Goeben Battery was located on the shore immediately opposite the end of the Mole. The howitzer fired 25 rounds at this target and Commander Osborne wrote in his report that he believed that these shells fell close to the Goeben Battery.

As a result of the initial engagement most of the gangways were destroyed and many others were so badly damaged that they could not be used. Only two could be used to disembark the assault force onto the Mole. The structure of the upper decks bore the brunt of German gunfire, because they were on the same level and the nearest target the enemy gunners could fire upon. Captain Carpenter described the hits:

The material damage was very great … Two heavy shells penetrated the ship's side below the upper deck. One passed in just beneath the foremost flame-thrower hut and burst on impact. The other came through within a few feet of the first and wrecked everything in its vicinity. Two other heavy shells came through the screen door to the forecastle and placed one of the howitzer guns out of action. The funnels, ventilators, bridges, charthouse and all such were riddled through and through.[32]

Air Mechanic John Lomax aged 20 was in charge of a flame-thrower, but his apparatus had been destroyed by shellfire. 'It was an hour of inferno, not only for us, but for the Germans. I don't know how we did get through. The boat was an absolute shambles.'[33]

The dead and wounded lay around the deck. Those who were unhurt were unable to aid the wounded as they were pinned down by enemy fire. This did not deter Leading Seaman Dowell and his surviving comrade from helping the other five men from their gun crew who became casualties:

The five who went down almost at once were not dead, and some had started to drag themselves off the forecastle. We half lifted, half carried the others, one by one, into shelter, and then beckoned to some stretcher bearers to come and take charge of them. There were a lot of bearers passing here and there all the time, and very busy.[34]

Staff Surgeon James McCutcheon had designated areas aboard *Vindictive* as sick bays. He set up the foremost dressing station in the stokers' mess and an aft dressing station in the warrant officers' mess. He chose them because they were well protected, easily accessible from the upper deck, well lit by electric light and in the case of power failure could be lit by candles and magazine hand lamps. The port side of the mess deck was sectioned as a place to accommodate the wounded and medical supplies were stored there. All personnel that participated in the raid received lectures on the application of first aid and each person was supplied with a field dressing. Medical supplies were not only stored in the dressing stations but all over the vessel. Neil-Robertson stretchers and first aid bags containing tourniquets and dressings for wounds and burns were positioned at every gun, in the fore top and conning tower for ready use. The medical team had rehearsed procedures in advance of the operation. Preparations had been made for treating casualties suffering from severe burns from flame-throwers. It involved using a paraffin wax which was sprayed on a thin layer of cotton wool and formed an airtight coating. This treatment invented by Dr. Berthe de Sandfort, a French Army medical officer, was applied to the burnt skin. The first wounded were taken to the dressing quarters at 11.50 p.m. Within a short time all dressing stations were full to capacity and other areas of the vessel were used to attend to the wounded. Darkness and overcrowding in these small sick bays impeded the work. Staff Surgeon McCutcheon wrote in his report that 'most of the cases had multiple wounds of an extensive nature, accompanied by severe haemorrhage, which had been caused by bullet, shrapnel, high explosive, or what appeared to be an explosive bullet.'[35] He later confirmed to King George V, when he visited the wounded at Chatham after the raid, that during that night he treated the wounds of 170 men. In one section of *Vindictive* where surgeons and medical staff were working, part of the ship's structure had been shot away, which resulted in highly inflammable liquid deluging the compartment. Fortunately, that part of the ship was not hit, but despite the danger the surgeons continued to operate on the wounded. One shell passed through the ship's galley and a sailor was wounded when a tin of sardines blown out of the galley stores struck his leg.

Percy Kenworthy from Durkenfield had enlisted in the Royal Navy on 1st January 1918 and was Steward's Assistant aboard *Vindictive*. During the operation he performed the role of stretcher bearer. This was a horrific experience for a young eighteen-year-old who had so recently enlisted.

> *Although I belonged to the victualling or steward's department, I was for the purpose of the raid actually a stretcher bearer. The enemy opened fire at about 300 yards. We had no other choice then but to go ahead. We steamed through the smoke screen along the Mole in order to disembark the landing parties. The Germans shelled the* Vindictive *for about 20 minutes, and there were casualties on all sides. The work of the stretcher bearers began amid an inferno of shells and quick firing guns from the land batteries and the Mole. I was with Staff Surgeon McCutcheon, and killed and wounded were lying all over the ship, I saw an injured man being attended to by one of our stretcher parties when a shell killed the whole lot of them. I helped to fetch the dead and wounded from the upper decks to temporary hospitals below after rendering first aid.*[36]

The deck of *Vindictive* was a scene of bloody carnage as the tightly packed men waiting for disembarkation were slaughtered by shellfire. Air Mechanic William Gough was assigned to a platoon containing 40 men ready to land upon the Mole with portable flame throwers and phosphorus bombs. During the ferocious bombardment this platoon was reduced to 10 men.

Among those killed was Stoker Jonathan Hughes from East Ham in London. He had joined the *Vindictive* just before the vessel sailed for Zeebrugge. He counted the number of stokers in the mess and discovered that he was the thirteenth man out of the whole party of stokers onboard. He said to his new mess mates, 'Well, I've got some chance of coming out of this lot, I have. I'm blowed if I'm not the thirteenth man of No.13 mess.' During the raid Hughes was given a job to do on deck and was the only stoker to be killed from that mess. Leading Stoker Henry Baker was also given duties on the deck of *Vindictive*:

> For an hour it was undiluted hell. If the wind had not shifted, our fog screen would have kept us from observation. Of course when it lifted our ships became targets, and the batteries found the range in quick time. Shells penetrated our steel armour. One of these, a gas shell, burst in the canteen, and another in the naval steward's stores.[37]

No.10 Platoon comprised one officer and 44 men. When the first shell fired from the Mole Battery exploded over the deck, it killed 30 men of the Platoon, including the commanding officer Lieutenant Robert Stanton. Sergeant Wright who went to his aid: 'As I knelt beside him he had just time to whisper "Carry on, Wright", before he died. And so died a gallant young officer who thought more of his duty than himself. He was well liked in the Platoon.'[38] Sergeant Wright assumed command of the remnants of No 10 Platoon.

Captain Henry Halahan commanding the storming party was killed by machine gun fire, together with many other senior officers who were positioned on the false deck. Commander Patrick Harrington Edwards suffered bullet wounds in both legs, but ordered that he should be carried ashore onto the Mole. This order was disobeyed to save his life as he was taken below decks to seek medical attention from the surgeon instead. With so many senior officers becoming casualties at the onset of the assault, replacements were established rapidly to ensure that the operation continued. It is a testament to the training and the calibre of the sailors and marines that the operation carried on despite the loss of senior commanders at such an early stage.

Despite orders for the raiding parties to remain under cover until the ship had arrived alongside the Mole, senior officers had positioned themselves where they could observe proceedings and would be able to lead and direct the assault. As a consequence Captain Carpenter could see that they 'were exposed to the full blast of the hurricane fire from the Mole battery.'[39]

The Captain knew this because through the maelstrom of bullets, shells and splinters he coordinated the approach to the Mole from the port forward *flammenwerfer* hut, where he in turn was exposed to the enemy fire. Sergeant Wright witnessed the courageous conduct of *Vindictive*'s Commanding Officer: 'During all this time Captain Carpenter stood on the bridge giving orders to the engine room staff and doing his utmost to get the ship alongside and was calm and collected as if he was taking her alongside the Mole in peacetime. No man ever did their work more bravely.'[40]

Leading Stoker Henry Baker was working on deck and could see Carpenter commanding the ship amidst the blast of bullets and shells. In this tribute to Carpenter he said: 'We did our duty, but the world ought to know how brave he was. He stood on the bridge of *Vindictive* all through that hell. The men that stood beside him were shot down one by one, whilst those in the foretop were killed and toppled beside him on the bridge.'[41]

As *Vindictive* approached the Mole, Carpenter could see six feet above the parapet. His First Lieutenant Rosoman and Coxwain Petty Officer Edwin Youlton, who was steering the *Vindictive* from the conning tower, closely supported him. Carpenter went full speed ahead to get alongside the Mole as quickly as possible. A swell caused her to go beyond her allotted position to disembark the storming parties. At one minute past midnight, one minute behind schedule, *Vindictive* arrived alongside the Mole at a speed of 16 knots. The engines were immediately reversed and the ship's hull gently bumped the Mole on the two specially installed fenders fitted on the port bow. It was a gentle mooring and the bump was not felt as she came alongside. The vessel pitched erratically up and down because of the speed of the approach. This movement caused further damage to some of the gangways. She berthed 300 yards west of the intended position, west of the Leitstand (the fire-directing post of the Friedrichsort battery on the Mole). This may very well have been a blessing in disguise for if they had moored nearer to the gun battery, they would have been an even easier target. There would have been German sailors and soldiers firing upon them from the sea wall.

Captain Carpenter had manoeuvred *Vindictive*'s stern against the Mole. A three-knot tide was flowing. She was rolling heavily with the swell and was now attracting heavy enemy fire from several directions. Captain Carpenter was conducting this difficult berthing operation from an unprotected and exposed bridge: 'The din had now reached a crescendo. Every gun that would bear appeared to be focused on our upper works, which were being hit every few seconds. Our guns in the fighting top were pouring out a continuous hail of fire in reply.'[42]

Captain Carpenter was fantastically lucky to survive such ferocious fire; as he conned the vessel from the bridge a bullet passed through the rear of his cap and exited through the front. The bullet missed his scalp by a fraction of an inch. (The cap is displayed in the Imperial War Museum, together with his binocular case, which was also hit by a bullet.) As soon as *Vindictive* berthed, Carpenter immediately gave the order to release the starboard anchor.

An exploding shell caused a fire that contained fused Stokes bombs near the bridge where Petty Officer Edwin Youlton was steering *Vindictive*. It was his actions that prevented a disaster. Youlton's CGM Citation reported, 'He averted a catastrophe by stamping without the slightest hesitation on the burning parts. This brave action was repeated shortly afterwards, when the fire restarted, just before he was struck down and severely wounded by a shell.'[43]

So much of the deck was shot away that Stoker William John Maxey could see the stars in the night sky from the engine room. (Maxey, who served with the Middlesex Regiment during the Second World War landed on the Normandy beaches on 6th June 1944.) The stokers in the engine room were wearing goggles and respirators to protect them from the ammonia fumes in the engine room.

Five minutes after the berthing, *Daffodil* appeared from out of the smoke screen and sailed for the *Vindictive*'s foremast straight at the Mole. At the beginning of the voyage there were concerns that *Daffodil* would not attain a sufficient head of steam to push *Vindictive* onto the Mole. Artificer Engineer William Sutton made efforts to overcome this problem and *Daffodil* managed to operate at a 160 lbs of steam in order to do the job. Sutton kept up the pressure despite the engine room being holed and two compartments flooded.

Although *Daffodil* was shielded by *Vindictive* from enemy fire, the reverberations of German fire striking her hull were strongly felt aboard the Mersey ferry. Harry Adams recalled, 'Being on the outboard side of the old ship, we were somewhat sheltered but every time they hit her, we caught the lot, you could feel the bits hitting your body with a sharp thud – an uncanny feeling.'[44] It was extremely difficult keeping upright for Harry Adams and the demolition teams onboard as *Daffodil* pushed her foc'sle onto *Vindictive*. Fast flowing swells destabilized the vessel. Adams wrote:

We bounced off her time and time again like a tennis ball from a racket – would steam 'full ahead' again, only to meet her with more shuddering bumps that would shoot all hands off in different directions. Great is the wonder she didn't smash herself to bits; her boilers must have been near explosion point – and the Huns still blazing away unceasingly at us.[45]

The vision of dying comrades, torn torsos, and broken bodies amongst the debris would haunt the survivors of that night for the rest of their lives. Harry Adams remembered the scenes 21 years later, in 1939:

I was stationed on the F.X. of the 'Daffodil' and on more than one occasion as we rammed her, I came up in line with one of her port-holes and the sight that met my eyes was ghastly – Good God! Have I got to come to this, I thought! For it was terrible – made you very sick at heart, you forgot the guns and the din for the second. I can't ask you to imagine this – you couldn't. There was about a foot and a half to two feet of water on her mess-deck, and every time she rolled, it 'swished' from side to side with a mixture I never wish to see again as long as I live – yet I have it so clearly in my mind's eye as I write.

The water, was no longer water, it was the blood of British seamen – who until a moment or so ago, were alive and well. Their heads – arms – legs and trunks torn to bits and separate, mixed up with loaves of bread – bread – barges, potatoes, stools, mess utensils, and so it went on – the guns still craving for more victims (nor did they 'crave' in vain) many – many more brothers or sweethearts.[46]

Lieutenant Campbell looked on the large quantities of Stokes mortar ammunition was stored in *Daffodil*'s fore peak with trepidation. Fearful of an explosion that would have catastrophic consequences for those aboard he ordered the crew to dump the Stokes mortars and ammunition over the side. Harry Adams was a member of the demolition team and was one of four men who went below decks to assist: 'Four of us went down below and racked out these boxes of shells and passed them up for others to pass over the side and whilst down there, we had a German shell pay us a visit – luckily it didn't explode, but left us a filthy load of gas.'[47] This gas would afflict Harry Adams health for the rest of his life. Over the following two decades Harry was hospitalized eight times as a result of the gas attack.

All but two of the gangways had been destroyed by the shellfire. Lieutenant Commander Arthur Harrison was positioned on the exposed bridge to coordinate the lowering of the gangways onto the Mole. The two foremost gangways were lowered until they reached the parapet of the high seaward wall. Once these gangways were secured the order was given: 'Storm the Mole.'[48] A short blast on a boatswain's whistle was the signal for the storming parties to assault. Lieutenant Commander Bryan Adams led a party of seaman tasked to secure *Vindictive* to the Mole using grappling anchors. The men not only had to deal with enemy fire, they had to cross the unsteady gangway that was rising and falling several feet as the vessel rolled. The ends of the gangways were sliding backwards and forwards on top of the wall. While on the narrow gangway they had to maintain their balance or drop thirty feet to certain death. Once on the Mole parapet they attempted to secure *Vindictive* with the grappling anchors, but the heavy swell made it impossible. The foremost grappling anchor barely reached the Mole and because of the movement of the vessel the party lost control and it fell between the ship and the wall.

It was left to *Daffodil* to push *Vindictive* onto the Mole to enable the storming parties to get ashore. Lieutenant Campbell, who had received a wound that blinded him in one eye still remained at his post to supervise the operation. With her first task done, she berthed alongside *Vindictive* and transferred her demolition parties onto *Vindictive* so that they too could get access to the Mole. Sub Lieutenant Felix Chevallier and four Able Seamen, Bone, Butter, Patton and Salter, were the only members from the Bluejackets' assault team from *Daffodil* who transferred to *Vindictive* as soon as she came alongside. It was important that *Vindictive* was held in position by *Daffodil* so that when the signal for withdrawal was sounded, these men could get back aboard. If *Vindictive* drifted away then the storming party would be left stranded on the Mole without any means of escape.

Once *Vindictive* was hard alongside the Mole, the high seaward wall shielded her hull from enemy gunfire and no further damage could be sustained to hull or deck. Carpenter had manoeuvred *Vindictive* into a blind spot where guns at the end of the Mole were unable to fire. However, two 3.7 cm Anti-Aircraft machine guns operated by Oberartilleristenmaat Scheidt could fire upon the upper structure above the wall. The bridge and forecastle were targets for Scheidt.

The other potential danger to *Vindictive* was from German motor boats with torpedoes, based at Blankenberghe, which was within five minutes sailing time. The smaller craft were present to counter this threat. Since *Vindictive* had berthed in the wrong place on the Mole, the high parapet prevented the use of the larger guns on the deck. It would mean that the storming force would assault the Mole without heavy fire support. Lance Corporal George Calverley was aboard *Iris* with a fine view of the drama:

> The 'Vindictive' took the brunt of the fire from the guns on the Mole at point blank range as she went alongside and the 'Daffodil' took up her position. As we passed them to take up our position ahead of her, flames were coming out of her funnel. All hell seemed to be let loose, her troops were climbing the wooden scaling ladders onto the Mole and flame-throwers were shooting flames across the Mole. It was like 'Dante's Inferno' must have been.[49]

At 12.15 a.m. the *Iris* dropped anchor 100 yards westward ahead of *Vindictive*, near to the Mole. Royal Marines from the Chatham Division were anxious to land and get to work. Private Herbert Peryer later told his son that he and his comrades from No.1 Platoon were armed with Paterson Colt Revolvers and coshes. He also recalled that they wore plimsolls to keep their footing on the deck of *Iris* and as they climbed onto the Mole. They could not land until *Iris* was securely moored. The *Iris* could not berth alongside the Mole in front of *Vindictive* because the grappling irons on her lines were unable to secure her. As she bumped heavily alongside, the considerable swell made it difficult to attach the parapet anchors. Ordinary Seaman O'Hara explained: 'Alongside, strenuous efforts were made to make fast but with the heavy swell we found this impossible; our means of making fast was by a grapnel attached to a long heavy pole, but owing to the swell and the height of the Mole this pole with the heavy grapnel became unmanageable.'[50] He also observed British sailors and Royal Marines who had landed from *Vindictive* passing along the parapet. 'Several men passed up on the Mole which we took to be British as they were wearing white arm bands, our identification for the attack, but they made no attempt to help us to make fast.'[51]

Unsuccessful efforts were made to secure her berth under heavy fire from soldiers from the Hafenkompanie. Lieutenant Commander Bradford, leader of the storming party aboard *Iris*, climbed up onto a gangway that was swinging over the parapet and jumped down upon the Mole in a desperate attempt to secure the vessel. Bradford was killed as soon as he stepped onto the Mole, according to Petty Officer George Warrington. However other accounts state that he sat on her grapnels while under fire to secure the vessel. Bullets were pouring into the funnel of the *Iris*. Sailors aboard advised Bradford to slide back aboard to avoid the intense fire. He took no notice of their warning and he was shot dead as soon as he reported *Iris* secure to Commander Gibbs. Bradford fell between the Mole and *Iris*. Ordinary Seaman O'Hara witnessed Bradford's courageous act, which would win him the Victoria Cross.

> I heard a cheer and looking up saw our section commander, Lt Comdr Bradford climbing up our derrick which was trained over the Mole; he was successful in reaching the Mole and immediately made fast our grapnel; unfortunately as he finished he stood up, and therefore became a target for enemy snipers, he was shot and fell between the ship and the Mole; we managed to get a line to him which he grasped but as he was badly wounded he did not have the strength to hold on and be pulled up; a ladder was procured and placed over the side but unfortunately just as a volunteer was descending to his aid a rather heavy swell dashed 'Iris' against the Mole and he was crushed between.[52]

Petty Officer Michael Hallihan was the man who made the brave attempt to save Bradford, but was also crushed to death. Both these men's remains were recovered; Hallihan was buried in St. James's Cemetery, Dover. Bradford's body was recovered and later buried in Blankenberge Town Cemetery. Lieutenant Commander Edward Hilton-Young later paid tribute to the 'dark, smiling' Bradford, 'whose manner had ever the graciousness and gentleness with which the true warrior spirit is wont to surround itself in order to save it from hurting other spirits less finely tempered than itself.'[53]

Iris was bouncing alongside the Mole so vigorously the grapnel broke away. Lieutenant Claude Hawkings, who was 22 and second in command of the assault party, bravely repeated Bradford's deed, by running along the swinging gangway onto the Mole and trying to secure *Iris* to the parapet. He too was killed in the attempt and fell on the parapet of the Mole. Lieutenant Oscar Henderson reported that 'when last seen, he was defending himself with his revolver.'[54] According to Bradford's Victoria Cross citation, Lieutenant Hawkings made the first attempt to secure *Iris* and once he was killed, Bradford made his attempt.

It was evident that the use of scaling ladders to ascend the Mole was impossible. Many of these ladders had broken. An eight-knot current was running along the outer wall of the Mole and greatly hindered the berthing operation. Assaulting parties assembled on the deck of *Iris* were hit as bullets ricocheted. Air Mechanic Harry Bascombe was one of six men from the Royal Naval Experimental Station who was aboard *Iris*. It was his role to 'work the flame-throwers which are slung over the shoulder and to throw Phosphorous hand grenades on to the Mole and set light to any building that they came in contact. Unfortunately we were not able to get on the Mole owing to the tide, but managed to get the grenades on the Mole with a few good throws.'[55]

To prevent further casualties the berthing operation was abandoned at 12.35 a.m. The situation deteriorated and it was decided that *Iris* should berth at the stern of *Vindictive* where she could shelter from enemy fire. Gibbs brought *Iris* alongside *Vindictive* to allow Royal Marines from A Company to cross her deck and assault the Mole. Only a few men from A Company transferred onto the *Vindictive* before the retirement signal was given.

Rigby's gun crew in *Vindictive*'s fighting top directed unrelenting fire against the heavy gun battery at the end of the Mole and on the lighthouse extension. Parallel to *Vindictive*'s berth at a distance of 80 yards on the inner Mole the German Torpedobootszerstorer V 69 was berthed. Leutnant d. Res. Zimmermann was positioned in the Leitstand control battery located east from where the *Vindictive* was moored. It was from here that Zimmermann informed Gunner Westphal in the Mole battery on the ranges and bearings of the enemy assault. He also relayed this information to the crews aboard the German vessels berthed alongside the inner Mole. On hearing this alert, Kapitänleutnant Benecke, commander of V 69, prepared the only gun onboard that was able to fire at *Vindictive* between the sheds on the Mole. Junior officer Fahnrich Klintzsch assisted him. V 69 could be clearly seen from the fighting top, where Lieutenant Charles Rigby RMA was in command of seven men with the two pom-pom guns and six Lewis guns, directing fire at her structure. Captain Carpenter:

We could see the projectiles hitting the Mole floor whenever the gun was temporarily depressed, and the shower upon shower of sparks as they tore through the destroyer's upper works. The vessel appeared to have sunk, as very little of her upper deck could be seen, although we had such an elevated view-point, but now I think it possible that the wall protected her vitals and that she escaped complete destruction from our gun fire.[56]

Once *Vindictive* was secured, the howitzer guns commanded by Captain Reginald Dallas Brooks RMA bombarded specially assigned targets. Their work was disrupted by shellfire directed at *Vindictive* and the Mole from the German shore batteries. Sergeant Knill was part of the gunnery team aboard *Vindictive* and despite suffering the effects of gas remained at his post to fire his gun.

The Royal Marine crew manning the 7.5-inch howitzer forward on *Vindictive* was all wiped out at the outset of the attack by German shellfire and splinters. A naval crew resumed firing from this gun but soon suffered heavy casualties. The flame-throwers aboard were disabled before they could be used. A shell severed the nozzle of the forward flame-thrower operated by Lieutenant Arthur Eastlake from the Royal Engineers. The aft flame-thrower supervised by Wing Commander Brock could not be used when oil failed to ignite because the ignition mechanism was shot away.

Above: Guns on the Mole battery at Zeebrugge.

Left: Two German personnel pose next to one of the Mole guns at Zeebrugge. These guns caused considerable carnage aboard HMS *Vindictive* as she berthed alongside the Mole.

Rockets were fired from *Vindictive* to guide the blockships into the harbour by one of Brock's party. The rockets illuminated the lighthouse at the end of the Mole, which assisted the blockships in their passage into the harbour. At 12.15 a.m. Captain Carpenter gained a 'momentary glimpse' of the blockships as they safely passed the Mole and cleared the lighthouse. The diversionary assault still had to continue until all the blockships had been sunk and their crews had been rescued. Once this had been successfully achieved, the storming parties would carry out further demolition work. At 12.30 a.m.,

> *Although the ship was still being hit continuously and the inferno showed no signs of abatement one can say that the conditions had become stabilised. Shells were still hitting us every few seconds and many casualties were being caused by flying splinters. Large pieces of the funnels and ventilators were being torn out and hurled in all directions – one wondered how much more of this battering the ship could stand.'[57]*

First Lieutenant Rosoman received bullet wounds to both of his ankles but refused medical attention to remain in the *Vindictive*'s conning tower. Lieutenant Edward Hilton-Young was wounded in the right arm while supervising the firing of the foremost 6-inch guns. Collapsing on the battery deck he had to be taken to receive medical attention by force after having refused to have his wound attended. He later ventured back on deck to continue supervising the gun crew, with his right arm dressed with bandages and smoking a large cigar, which contravened naval regulations; due to the exceptional circumstances, Captain Carpenter turned a Nelsonic blind eye. Captain Carpenter ventured down to the mess deck to visit the many casualties.

> *Every available space on the mess deck was occupied by casualties … Many were stretched at full length on the deck, the majority being severely wounded. Some had already collapsed and were in a state of coma. I fear that many had already passed away. It was a sad spectacle indeed. Somehow, amidst all the crashing and smashing on deck, one had not realised the sacrifice that was taking place … The wounded were literally pouring down every available ladder in a constant stream.*[58]

The Belgian civilians living in Zeebrugge were awakened by the awesome firepower that night. A nun who lived in Zeebrugge wrote:

> *On 22 and 23 April the German maid in our house announced from the reading room that there would be a major trial alarm that evening, indeed there was a trial alarm, but after that we experienced something quite different. Shortly after 12 o'clock heavy dull thumps were heard, one after the other projectiles above the port, sea and Mole, constant cracking, terrible bangs, there was fire everywhere, this wasn't a bombardment, it was far worse, fire and flames in the air, it was terrible, hideously cruel. Suddenly, a far more dangerous bang; there was smoke and fire everywhere, people were escaping in all directions but most of them along the bridge of Ramskappele, they were running between the shells and many fell along the route. Now they started bombing, we did not know from where the bombs that were fired came, some said they came from Knocke. The third bomb from the sea fell on a small farm, inhabited by poor people, the mother was alone at home with the children, the father was on duty at the Sas, he was afraid to go home expecting to find nothing but bodies. Thank God, while the mother was taking care of things the children had sought refuge in the cellar and the mother escaped unhurt. The youngest child was pulled unharmed from its crib which had been covered in glass and plaster. Guns were roaring on all sides, shells shuffle above our heads, there is nothing but death and destruction. What had been going on?*[59]

The German defenders and the Belgian civilians living in Zeebrugge had no idea of the true purpose of this British raid. Despite the German barrage *Vindictive* had succeeded in securing alongside the Mole and the landing parties were in position to launch the diversionary assault upon the Mole.

KAPITANLEUTNANT DER RESERVE ROBERT SCHUTTE

Kapitänleutnant der Reserve Schutte from 1st Naval Division was the commander of the Mole Battery at Zeebrugge. For four years he commanded this most northerly German bastion on the Western Front. Here he and his men endured the bad winter months and the good weather during the summer. During the war he would be a familiar figure to submarine commanders and their crews as they left Zeebrugge. He was very welcoming if they returned from their dangerous operation, offering them alcohol. Werner Fürbringer, a Flanders-based submarine commander wrote of Schutte: 'His post was in fact the outermost artillery emplacement of the entire Western Front and by reason of his isolated existence at the end of the two-thousand-metre-long breakwater he was known universally as The Pope of the Mole. He was also the most decent fellow in the world. Crewmen aboard U-boats putting to sea or returning were able to obtain from him all their requirements, including drink. Virtually every U-boat passing the Mole would pull alongside the Molehead to greet the Pope.'[60]

According to German sources as soon as engines could be heard in the fog by German sentries on the Mole, Schutte ordered star shells to be fired in the direction of the noise. It must have been a frightening prospect for this small band of men to be confronted by the RMLI and Royal Naval Storming Parties. To continue to resist their enemy and defend their position, despite being isolated from the mainland, showed great courage. As *Vindictive* appeared from the fog it was Schutte's guns that fired into her, causing massive structural damage and inflicting heavy casualties. As the battle raged on the Mole, Schutte's guns continued to fire. ML 424 was sunk near to the Mole, possibly from shells fired from the guns of the Mole Battery. Once *Vindictive* was moored the guns of the Mole Battery were unable to fire at her, therefore when *Thetis* passed the Mole lighthouse Schutte ordered the guns to be turned 180 degrees to aim at the blockship. Schutte kept his nerve and survived the battle. When Kaiser Wilhelm visited Zeebrugge the following day he awarded Schutte the Knight's Cross with Swords of the Royal Order of the House of Hohenzollern. Schutte survived the war and returned to his civilian occupation as a branch manager for Reichsbank, but died in 1923 aged 43.

Kapitänleutnant der Reserve Schutte, (third from right) the commander of the Mole Battery and the officers under his command, who effectively supported him in countering the British raiders. Oberleutnant Adolf Rodewald was the second officer in command of the Mole Battery and is wearing the bow tie (second from right). Leutnant Zimmerman is standing on the extreme left.

Above left: Large calibre guns of the Mole Battery.

Above right: The men aboard *Vindictive* and the Mersey ferry boats *Iris* and *Daffodil* had to approach the Mole not so much within range of guns such as this one, but – relative to normal naval engagements – more like straight up the barrel.

The Kaiser also bestowed the Iron Cross First Class upon Oberleutnant Rodewald. Kapitänleutnant Robert Schutte had ordered Rodewald to organise a group of Marine Artillerymen to repel the invaders. Rodewald formed a group comprising three officers and ten soldiers. Armed with rifles and hand grenades they held the western approach to the battery at the end of the Mole. They could see the *Vindictive* berthed 200 metres from the battery. Rodewald sent some of his party back to the Battery at the end of the Mole. He and Zimmermann led a counter attack on the upper Mole parapet and along the roofs of a personnel accommodation bunker on the Mole towards *Vindictive*. During this counter attack they captured one machine gun and two flame-throwers. Rodewald recorded German Marine Artillery casualties of eight dead and 16 wounded.

NOTES

1. Private Ernest (Beau) Tracey interview. Courtesy of Richard Davison.
2. Max Arthur, *Lost Voices of the Royal Navy*: Hodder & Stoughton, 2005.
3. *Globe & Laurel* 1918, p105.
4. Edward Hilton-Young MP, *By Sea and Land, Some Naval Doings*: T.C. & E.C. Jack Ltd, London & Edinburgh, 1920.
5. Private Jim Clist interview, courtesy David Clist.
6. Petty Officer Harry Adams Papers.
7. Private Philip Hodgson Royal Marines Museum ARCH 7/17/2.
8. Private Ernest (Beau) Tracey interview. Courtesy of Richard Davison.
9. Ordinary Seaman William O'Hara Papers.
10. IWM Department of Documents Captain A.R. Chater, RMLI: IWM 74/101/1.
11. Petty Officer Harry Adams Papers.
12. IMW Museum Department of Documents: Acting 1st Class Mechanic W H Gough, IWM 91/11/1.
13. IWM Sound Archives Major W E D Wardrop DFM 29.
14. Edward Hilton-Young MP, *By Sea and Land, Some Naval Doings*: T.C. & E.C. Jack Ltd, London & Edinburgh, 1920.
15. Sergeant Wright, Royal Marine Museum Arch 10/2/W.
16. Ordinary Seaman William O'Hara Papers.
17. IMW Museum Department of Documents: Acting 1st Class Mechanic W H Gough, IWM 91/11/1.

18. National Archives ADM1/8525/142. Naval Raids on Zeebrugge & Ostende April & May 1918.

19. Private Philip Hodgson Royal Marines Museum ARCH 7/17/2.

20. Sergeant Wright, Royal Marine Museum Arch 10/2/W.

21. *Globe & Laurel* April 1919.

22. IWM Sound Archives Emily Rumbold 576.

23. *South Wales Daily News*, Tuesday 30th April 1918.

24. *South Wales Daily News*, Tuesday 30th April 1918.

25. Sir J. Hammerton, *The Great War, I Was There*, p1648: The Amalgamated Press Ltd, London, 1938.

26. Captain A F B Carpenter VC RN, *The Blocking of Zeebrugge*, p190: Herbert Jenkins Limited, 1925.

27. IWM Department of Documents Captain A.R. Chater, RMLI: 74/101/1.

28. Private Jim Clist interview, courtesy David Clist.

29. *The Daily Chronicle*, 27th April 1918.

30. Ibid.

31. Ibid.

32. Captain Captain A F B Carpenter VC RN, *The Blocking of Zeebrugge*, p193: Herbert Jenkins Limited, 1925.

33. *Blackburn Times* 27th April 1918.

34. *The Daily Chronicle*, 27th April 1918.

35. National Archives: ADM 137/3894, P145. Staff Surgeon McCutcheon's report.

36. *The Ashton Reporter*, Saturday 4th May 1918.

37. *Folkestone, Hythe, Sandgate & Cheriton Herald*, 4th May 1918.

38. Sergeant Wright Royal Marines Museum Archive 11/12/5(5)).

39. Captain Captain A F B Carpenter VC RN, *The Blocking of Zeebrugge*, p194: Herbert Jenkins Limited, 1925.

40. Sergeant Wright Royal Marines Museum ARC 10/2/W.

41. *Folkestone,Hythe, Sandgate & Cheriton Herald*, 4th May 1918.

42. Captain A F B Carpenter VC RN, *The Blocking of Zeebrugge*, p196: Herbert Jenkins Limited, 1925.

43. *The London Gazette*, No.30807, 23rd July 1918.

44. Petty Officer Harry Adams Papers.

45. Ibid.

46. Ibid.

47. Ibid.

48. Captain Captain A F B Carpenter VC RN, *The Blocking of Zeebrugge*, p202: Herbert Jenkins Limited, 1925.

49. Imperial War Museum Department of Documents: Lance Corporal George Calverley, IWM 02/30/1.

50. Ordinary Seaman William O'Hara Papers.

51. Ibid.

52. Ibid.

53. Edward Hilton-Young MP, *By Sea and Land, Some Naval Doings*, p277: T.C. & E.C. Jack Ltd, London & Edinburgh, 1920.

54. National Archives: ADM 137/3894: Lieutenant Oscar Henderson's Report.

55. University of Leeds Archives: RNMN (REC) 008 Name: BASCOMBE, H F.

56. Captain A F B Carpenter VC RN, *The Blocking of Zeebrugge*, p204: Herbert Jenkins Limited, 1925.

57. Ibid, p208.

58. Ibid, p209.

59. Account from anonymous nun living in Zeebrugge. In Flanders Fields Museum, Ypres.

60. Geoffrey Brooks, *Fips: Legendary U-Boat Commander, 1915-1918*, p50: Leo Cooper, 1999.

CHAPTER 6

STORMING THE MOLE

The primary objective of the diversionary attack on the Mole was to distract the German artillery batteries, which would ensure that the three blockships safely passed the Mole batteries en route to the canal entrance. The *Vindictive* suffered heavy fire directed from the 9.4-inch guns from the Goeben battery. The Germans would be prepared to bombard the Mole indiscriminately with shells, despite the danger of damaging their own property and personnel. The parapet onto which the storming parties would disembark was on a high wall devoid of cover. For the assault parties it was comparable to soldiers leaving their trenches on the Western Front going over the top.

Some German sentries on the Mole were heard by some British attackers to have shouted as they approached 'It's the Americans. It's the Yankees'. Despite CMB 33A being captured two weeks prior to St George's Day at Ostend, it appeared that the Germans on the Mole – or at least the rank and file – were in a state of shock and were surprised by this assault. There were three destroyers lying on the inner Mole and the sailors aboard were seen fleeing their vessels, dressed in their night attire in a state of panic. They had good reason, for the sailors from the seaman demolition party were raring to go. Able Seaman Bernard Devlin was part of the demolition team aboard *Daffodil*: 'While the *Vindictive* was endeavouring to make her grapplings fast, and the *Daffodil* was pushing her into the side of the Mole, the men picked out for the attack could scarcely be held back, so eager were they to get to work.'[1]

The seamen were the first wave to assault the Mole. With Captain Halahan dead, Lieutenant Commander Arthur Harrison was to lead the storming party. However, he too was wounded on the deck of *Vindictive* when a shell fragment struck him on the head leaving him concussed and with a broken jaw. He was not in a position to lead the initial assault. Lieutenant Commander Adams was the first man on the Mole leading the raiders from A and B Companies eastwards along the parapet towards the lighthouse. Immediately the raiding party set to work by bombing some observation huts, which were discovered to be unoccupied. Since *Vindictive* was moored further from the intended targets than planned, Adams had to lead his party 250 yards to attack their objectives. Those that were dying or wounded on the gangways gallantly wished their colleagues good luck in their enterprise. Many of the seamen had been wounded as *Vindictive* approached the Mole. Able Seaman Charles Ellis had been hit, 'but I went over the top despite the wound.'[2]

Lieutenant Walker was lying wounded by a gangway. His left arm had been blown away. Captain Carpenter remembered:

> On the order being given to storm the Mole the storming parties had rushed up every available ladder to the gangway deck. At the tip of the foremost ladder the men, in their eagerness to get at the enemy, were stumbling over a body. I had bent down to drag it clear when one of his men shouted 'That's Mr. Walker, Sir, he's had his arm shot off.' Immediately Walker, who was still conscious, heard this he waved his remaining hand to me and wished me the best of luck. This officer, Lieut. H. T. C. Walker, survived.[3]

Able Seaman William Lodwick was No.1 of the Lewis Crew from No.4 Section, A Company, in a sandbag emplacement aboard *Vindictive*. The Lewis gun that he was manning was blown out of his hands by enemy fire as *Vindictive* approached the Mole. When she berthed, Lodwick rescued the gun and landed. He used it on the Mole but was restricted by lack of ammunition trays. He 'brought the gun riddled by bullets in several places.'[4]

Marines and bluejackets ascend the gangways from *Vindictive* to storm the Mole; an illustration from *The Great War*.

Leading Seaman Childs from B Company was extremely lucky to survive when a 303 bullet hit his tin hat, then ricocheted through the rim, and on exit struck one of his puttees around his ankle. Childs belonged to the assault team commanded by Lieutenant Arthur Chamberlain, which had sustained many casualties. Chamberlain, Childs, McKenzie and Eves were among the remnants of B Company. It was up to these men to carry on with the plan. Childs was carrying a weight of 142 lbs that included a rifle, two bandoliers (50 rounds each), two Mills Bombs, wire cutters, torch, helmet, gas mask and 16 trays of Lewis gun ammunition. McKenzie carried equipment weighing 100 lbs, which included a Lewis Gun with eight cartridges of ammunition (47 rounds in each), a revolver with 100 rounds, gas mask and helmet. These two men had to dodge enemy bullets and shells and climb up the pitching gangway to the Mole parapet. As they reached the top of the gangway they waited for the *Vindictive* to roll before they jumped onto the Mole. In a letter to his brother McKenzie wrote:

Well, we got within about fifteen minutes' run of the Mole, when some marines got excited and fired their rifles. Up went four big star shells, and they spotted us … They hit us with the first two star shells and killed seven marines. They were still hitting us when we got alongside … I tucked the old Lewis gun under my arm and nipped over the gangway aft … I turned to my left and advanced about 50 yd and then lay down.[5]

Wing Commander Brock assaulted the Mole with Lieutenant Commander Adam's first wave (dressed in khaki) and armed with two revolvers and a cutlass. He ran along the parapet towards the lighthouse. Able Seaman McKenzie was with him:

There was a spiral staircase which led down into the Mole, and Commander Brock … fired his revolver down and dropped a Mills. You ought to have seen them nip out and try to get across to the destroyer tied up against the Mole, but this little chicken met them half way with the box of tricks, and I ticked about a dozen off before I clicked.[6]

There was an observation shelter with a range finder above it. Once bombs had been thrown inside the shelter to clear any enemy inside, Brock inspected the range finder. An unidentified member of the landing party saw Brock lead an assault upon a gun emplacement surrounded by barbed wire:

We were one of the earliest crowds to go over and Commander Brock went ahead. It was a fearful job getting over the brow, but the Commander dropped down on to the Mole, a distance of at least ten feet. 'Come on you boys' he shouted, and one by one we followed him. There were Huns near us in a nest surrounded by barbed wire, but we stormed that and reached one of the guns on the Mole. Commander Brock, single handed, attacked the gun's crew and we captured the gun and put it out of action.[7]

Air Mechanic Roland Entwistle witnessed Brock fall near to an enemy machine gun emplacement. German reports record that Matrose Kunne from S-53 was engaged in a confrontation with a British Lieutenant Commander. They fought a savage fight with knife and bayonet resulting in both men being killed. An unidentified German submarine commander recounted his experience to Lowell Thomas for his book *Raiders of the Deep*: 'I have never seen such horrible hand to hand fighting as took place on the Zeebrugge Mole. The sailors from the *Vindictive* swarmed down, and many of the defenders, taken by surprise, were unarmed. I saw an Englishman bayonet a German through the body, and then the dying man sank his teeth in the throat of his adversary.'[8] This officer may have been referring to Brock and Kunnes. Both these men were found dead lying next to each other at the Leitstand Friedrichsort Battery. It is quite possible that the unidentified Lieutenant Commander could have been Brock. Once on the Mole Brock was heading for the blockhouse or the Leitstand Friedrichsort Battery. His intention was to search for the observation range finder. This is where he was last seen and where he died. Kunnes was buried in Zeebrugge Churchyard and it is possible that Brock is one of the two unknown British officers buried in this same churchyard. Brock was a brilliant, charismatic, man whose loss was not only a tragedy for his family and those who knew him, but a national loss. Brock could have achieved great things after the War, had he lived.

Parapet anchor used by HMS *Vindictive* during the attack on Zeebrugge, which stands in the Garden of Remembrance in the grounds of the Royal Marines Museum, Eastney.

The battle continued and Adams led his party 40 yards further along the Mole where he found an iron ladder that descended from the parapet to the ground level of the Mole. Three men climbed down the ladder to prevent German soldiers from reaching the parapet. Lieutenant Arthur Chamberlain was killed when his lung was blown out through his back at the foot of this ladder. Adams left the men to consolidate the position while he returned to *Vindictive* to collect reinforcements. On passing the observation shelter he encountered a small party including two Lewis gunners led by Petty Officer George Antell. Antell had been wounded in the hand and arm before assaulting the Mole and was in great pain, but carried on regardless. Adams detailed the party to advance eastwards along the parapet. At this point Adams and his men were shielded by the observation shelter from enemy fire from the end of the Mole. But they were exposed to machine gun fire from the German destroyers berthed alongside the inner Mole.

Lieutenant Commander Harrison regained consciousness and despite the physical pain he was suffering from the fractured jaw he sustained earlier, he crossed one of the narrow gangways. He resumed command of his landing party, directing the attack on batteries eastward along the Mole in the fortified zone. Harrison met Adams near to the observation shelter. After being briefed by Adams, it was he who instructed Adams to return to the *Vindictive* to seek reinforcements.

Harrison led a charge along the parapet onto a machine gun position. His courageous charge failed to overwhelm the German position. German machine gunners poured cross fire from concealed positions on the Mole. During the battle Harrison was shot in the neck and killed. With the exception of two wounded men, all of his party was killed. For this action Harrison was awarded the Victoria Cross. The official notification reads:

Though already severely wounded and undoubtedly in great pain, [he] displayed indomitable resolution and courage of the highest order in pressing his attack, knowing as he did that any delay in silencing the guns might jeopardize the main object of the expedition, i.e. the blocking of the Zeebrugge–Bruges canal.[9]

Able Seaman McKenzie and Harold Eves were among the survivors from the Royal Naval Landing Party. They were wounded and alone on the Mole. Eves made an effort to carry Harrison's body over his shoulders and run back to *Vindictive*, but he was repeatedly shot at from three different German machine gun positions on the Mole. He could not make it back. Able Seaman William Lodwick witnessed Eves being wounded on the Mole:

I saw Harold Eves rush to the left of the Mole to get Lieut. Comm Harrison who had fallen, he got the body on his shoulder and he staggered and fell heavily to the ground. He was only a few yards from the enemy's gun position. I cannot honestly say he was killed. We could not get to his body on account of heavy fire from machine guns. He was left on the Mole.[10]

Eves was later captured and remained a Prisoner of War for the duration.

Despite his wounds McKenzie continued the fight with his Lewis gun, sweeping an enemy trench with machine gun fire. McKenzie was suffering from a smashed right foot and several shrapnel wounds to his back. With great resilience he continued the fight and accounted for a number of German soldiers and sailors who tried to run from a shelter on the Mole to a nearby destroyer. McKenzie was wounded again in the hands when a German bullet struck the Lewis gun, knocking it from his hands. Leading Seaman Childs and McKenzie fired at the enemy with rifle and revolver. McKenzie:

My Lewis gun was shot spinning out of my hands, and all I had left was the stock and pistol grip which I kindly took a bloke's photo with who looked too business-like for me with a rifle and a bayonet. It half stunned him, and gave me time to get my pistol and finish him off. I then found a rifle and bayonet, and joined up our crowd who had just come off the destroyer. All I remember was pushing, kicking and kneeing every German who got in the way.[11]

The wounded McKenzie was unable to ascend the ladder from ground level onto the Mole parapet. Leading Seaman Childs carried his wounded comrade up the ladder. Once on the parapet, McKenzie had to crawl on his hands and knees back to the *Vindictive*. For his actions, the 19-year-old Able Seaman McKenzie was nominated by ballot by his colleagues to be awarded the Victoria Cross.

All Australian volunteers who formed part of the Naval storming party survived the attack unscathed. Leading Seaman G Bush led No.4 Section in A Company. Leading Seaman Dalmorton Rudd, Able Seaman Harry Gillard and L. Newlands also belonged to No.4 Section. They descended the ladder from the parapet to the Mole, where they killed several of the enemy. Able Seaman G. Staples was the other Australian sailor, who was a hand bomber with A Company. He was commended for his efforts to evacuate the wounded from the Mole.

Oberleutnant Adolf Rodewald was the second officer in command of the Mole battery. Kapitänleutnant Robert Schutte, the Battery Commander, had ordered Rodewald to organise a group of Marine Artillerymen to repel the invaders. Rodewald formed a group comprising two officers and ten or twelve rankers, mostly cooks and ammunition carriers. Armed with rifles and hand grenades they held the western approach to the battery at the end of the Mole. They could see the *Vindictive* berthed 200 metres from the battery. Rodewald observed a British bayonet attack along the upper Mole and saw the officer, a captain, who was carrying a machine gun on his back, killed as he led the charge.[12] Captain Halahan was killed aboard before *Vindictive* berthed alongside the Mole. Therefore this British officer was probably Lieutenant Commander Harrison.

A second group was organised from the occupants of the Leitstand. They formed a defensive position east of the machine guns perched on the Upper Mole. Here they could fire upon raiders disembarking from *Vindictive*. Many of the sailors killed trying to secure *Vindictive* were slain by machine gun fire from the end of the Mole. Continuous fire poured along the top of the Mole – Sergeant Wright called it 'a death walk' – but by some stroke of luck the firing paused, maybe because the gun jammed or the gunner may have changed the belt. At this point Sergeant Wright led the remnants of No.10 Platoon onto the Mole. Before the machine gunner at the end of the Mole recommenced firing Wright and the platoon managed to secure their ladder and descend from the parapet, where they killed two German sailors. No.10 Platoon now turned towards Zeebrugge and the viaduct.

Leutnant Zimmermann watched the raiders from *Vindictive* slowly and with great caution cross the two remaining wooden gangways onto the Mole. Zimmermann was forced to retreat from his observation position in the Leitstand, because it was too close to *Vindictive*. He withdrew to the Friedrichsort Battery where he met Rodewald's party. Rodewald also mentions that the Captain of a German torpedo boat with one member of the crew was firing a gun at the raiders. As previously mentioned, this German Officer was Kapitänleutnant Benecke, who with Fahnrich Klintzsch was firing from the Torpedo Boat V 69. It was normal procedure for the crews of German torpedo boats to shelter in dugouts on the Mole during air raids. The crews of other German torpedo boats moored along the inner Mole were organised and fired upon the raiders with rifles as they appeared on the Mole parapet.

The 4th Battalion RMLI war diary reported that Lieutenant Theodore Cooke led the first party onto the Mole. However, one unidentified Royal Marine told a journalist that he saw Captain Bamford lead the way with No.7 Platoon, followed by Cooke. Cooke led his party of Marines from No.5 Platoon of B Company onto the Mole. It was initially planned that Nos. 10 and 11 Platoons would lead the assault, but because most of the officers and men from these platoons were casualties, it was up to Cooke and No.5 Platoon to lead the RM assault. Corporal George Moyse was one of the few survivors from No.11 Platoon:

Assault parties from the Royal Marines ascend narrow gangways onto the Mole. Drawing by Charles de Lacey from *The Blocking of Zeebrugge* by Captain Carpenter VC.

I was with the storming parties, formed up below deck. A shell burst among us and wiped out almost all the men standing on my right. But when we got alongside every able man dashed through the inferno on the deck and climbed the gangways up to the parapet of the Mole. By that time most of the gangways had been shot away.[13]

The rain that was falling caused further problems as it made the gangways slippery for those men crossing them with steel helmets, box respirators, guns, equipment and bombs. Private James Feeney was part of No. 7 Platoon and formed part of the second wave: 'In the anxiety to keep my balance on the see-saw of the gangway, I forgot about the rain of lead, and felt really comfortable when I put my foot on the concrete.'[14] Private Alfred Hutchinson aboard the *Iris* remembered that 'the gunfire was so heavy, the men were falling off the ladders as they tried to get on to the Mole. As the boats were hit, the ladders fell and the men with them.'[15]

Private Philip Hodgson with No.12 platoon described in some detail the diffculty of getting off the ship:

We moved over to the port side to disembark on to the Mole first climbing the sloped ramp between the funnels up on to the false deck which had been constructed to give access to the boarding prows but some of these had fallen into the sea, others damaged by shell fire, so it was necessary to look for a usable one. These prows were formed of baulks of timber bolted together in pairs to form a gangway some 18 inches wide and 15 feet long, the inner half fastened down with a slight rising slope on the false deck, it had a hinge at the outer end by which a similar pair of baulks were attached to the inboard part, but the outer end of the second prow had to rest on the parapet wall of the Mole, but it was not all just so simple as that, the inner part rose and fell vertically as waves lifted the ship, whereas the outer half pivoted like a see-saw about the end resting on the Mole, so after finding a prow in good order it was necessary to pause and watch this double motion and then make a dash. Loaded as I was with full equipment, small arms, ammunition, rifle and two panniers, with four trays of Lewis gun bullets, it was not easy but somehow I scrambled over and dropped off the parapet wall, almost alongside R.S.M. Thatcher.[16]

The men would face further difficulties once on the Mole descending the scaling ladders, twenty feet from the parapet to the ground level of the Mole. Private Feeney had to wait ten minutes before he could get on a ladder, all the while under enemy rifle and shell fire. They had their backs to the enemy. Heavy casualties had been foreseen, with the added difficulty of recognising friend from foe in the dark, and in this the planners were horribly correct.

Lieutenant Lamplough led No.9 Platoon across the gangways, and it was only at that moment that he realised *Vindictive* was not berthed in the position originally planned. Fortunately for Lamplough, 'On arrival at the brows I realised … we were abreast the centre of No.3 Shed and close to my objective.'[17]

Lance Sergeant Radford from No.9 Platoon, another wounded on *Vindictive*, managed to lead his men behind Lamplough onto the Mole, until he received a further wound.

Lieutenant Charles Rigby's crew in the fighting top greatly supported the storming parties as they raided the Mole. Rigby had experienced action in the Dardanelles during 1915 and at Sailly-Au-Bois during the Battle of the Somme in 1916, but this was a more vulnerable situation. Captain Dallas Brooks ordered Rigby only to fire upon the Mole when certain that he would not cause casualties among the seamen and marines storming party. They fired at numerous targets to ensure that they kept the heads of the enemy down. Lieutenant Lamplough appreciated the covering fire that they provided. 'During my landing there had been a tremendous amount of firing of every sort and the noise had been terrific, but the most encouraging, until unfortunately knocked out, was the firing of the pom-poms from the foretop of *Vindictive*.'[18] The fighting top was on the fore mast. To access the fighting top, the men from Lieutenant Rigby's RMA team had to climb a ladder riveted to the mast then climb through a narrow hole into the firing position. With several men positioned amongst ammunition supplies the fighting top was a claustrophobic environment. Rigby would stand in the centre giving orders while the men prepared to pull the triggers on their pom-pom and Lewis guns.

> Smoke, acrid and asphyxiating, blew back into the faces of the gunners. But they fought grimly on. Occasionally one passed a sleeve quickly across his eyes to wipe away the blinding fog. Continually men tried to spit the choking fumes from their throats. Then suddenly there came a detonation louder than all, followed by a half stifled cry as a man fell across the breech of his gun and rolled lifelessly to the floor. An enemy shell had entered the top and put one of the guns temporarily out of action.
>
> Carefully the wounded gunner was moved aside and another took his place at the firing key. Men might fall but the fight must go on. And it did. Other shells came in. More men dropped. The pathetic heap of mangled humanity grew momentarily larger, yet the outpouring stream of fire and lead continued to roll from every part of the top's periphery. Guns jammed. Men tugged them clear and grasped newly filled belts, rattling these through as quickly as the guns would carry them. By now the floor had become a ghastly litter of spent shell, spent men, and bloodstained clothing. The revolting debris of war piled higher each second.[19]

Although they inflicted considerable damage upon the German destroyer, the fore top was horribly exposed to the enemy guns. It was a shell fired from the destroyer hitting the fore top that killed or wounded all occupants, with the exception of Sergeant Finch, who continued the fight to the bitter end. Finch was in a terrible situation. But he continued to support his colleagues with his Lewis gun. As the *Globe and Laurel* recounted, Captain Carpenter witnessed the extraordinary resolve of this remarkable NCO:

> The only survivor who was not completely disabled – Sergeant Finch R.M.A. – struggled out from the shambles somehow, and without a thought for his own wounds, examined the remaining gun, found it was still intact, and continued the fight single-handed. Another survivor, Gunner Sutton who had again been wounded, fired the remaining ammunition when Finch could no longer carry on; finally, a German shell completely destroyed the remains of the gun position.
>
> After the second shell to blast the fore top, Sergeant Finch found the strength to help Gunner Sutton, who was the only surviving occupant down the battered ladders to the sick bay, where he collapsed from his wounds. Finch and his colleagues in the fore top had displayed great resistance and determination in providing supporting cover fire as the storming party ascended the steep walls of the Mole. Captain Carpenter praised their invaluable contribution to the success of the operation. 'The splendid work of Lieutenant Rigby and his gun's crew had been invaluable, and one cannot but attribute the complete success of our diversion very largely to these gallant men.[20]

Once on the Mole, Cooke and No.5 Platoon advanced west along the Mole parapet where they encountered enemy snipers, who were firing at the parapet from shed number 2. Captain Chater directed an attack upon this shed. They silenced the snipers. As the battle progressed it was apparent to the men of No.5 Platoon that German shells were causing more damage than their own efforts.

Captain Edward Bamford led another party westwards along the parapet to join Cooke's party. Exposed to enemy fire they advanced 200 yards. Cooke received two wounds. The second wound was sustained while trying to assist a wounded man back onto *Vindictive*. He continued to advance until he collapsed unconscious. His batman Private John Press, who was also wounded, carried him back to *Vindictive*.

Lieutenant Charles Lamplough's No.9 Platoon with remnants from No.10 platoon then disembarked. Sergeant Wright remembered:

… passing our dead and wounded lying everywhere, and avoiding big gaps made in the ship's decks by shell fire. Finally we crossed the two remaining gangways which were only just hanging together, and jumped on to the concrete wall, only to find it swept by machine-gun fire. Our casualties were so great before landing that out of a platoon of 45 only 12 landed. Number 9 platoon led by Lt Lamplough had about the same number.[21]

This dramatic depiction of the fight on the Mole was drawn from descriptions provided by Captain Carpenter to the artist de Lacey. The left of the picture shows the commander of V 69, Kapitänleutnant Benecke, with Fahnrich Klintzsch, firing upon *Vindictive* as Royal Marines charge a German position on the Mole. From *The Blocking of Zeebrugge* by Captain Carpenter VC.

Zeebrugge Mole, before the bloody fighting.

Nos. 9 and 10 Platoons amounted to just fourteen men. They dropped onto the ground level of the Mole using ropes from the parapet. They found that many Germans on the Mole withdrew to the safety of their concrete shelters. German reinforcements on bicycles were peddling furiously onto the Mole to repel the raiders and the assault party was trapped between the garrison at the end of the Mole and reinforcements from the west, together with gunfire from enemy ships berthed alongside the inner Mole.

Lieutenant Lamplough captured and consolidated positions near shed number 3 and ensured that the enemy was prevented from approaching westward along the Mole. Some of the Marines from No.11 Platoon assembled near Shed Number 3, where they prepared to launch an attack on a German destroyer that was berthed on the inner Mole, while demolition teams prepared the shed for destruction. Corporal George Moyse was one of two survivors from No.11 Platoon:

> I had a bag of 40 bombs and a pair of insulated wire cutters. As a corporal of the marines, I was supposed to lead a party of twelve men, but only two of us got there – and then it seemed like a nightmare … The worst of it was that the Vindictive moored on the outside – the seaward side – of the breakwater, we had to climb down from the parapet where we landed, to the floor of the Mole. That was 16 feet, and they had machine guns under us. Eventually I ran into a concrete shelter and chucked bombs at a German destroyer moored against the Mole, which was shelling Vindictive.[22]

Lieutenant Cecil Dickinson led No.2 Platoon, C Company, from the Naval Demolition unit with the objective of dealing with the German craft berthed alongside the inner Mole. No.1 Platoon was assigned the task of destroying the gun batteries at the end of the Mole, while No.3 platoon was to target the facilities. Only Sub Lieutenant Chevallier and four men were able to get aboard Vindictive from Daffodil and reach the Mole. The remaining men with Nos. 1 and 3 Platoons were stranded on Daffodil. Dickinson was left with 21 men from the ranks that sailed on Vindictive, together with 22 Royal Marines who were responsible for the transport of explosive equipment. Their objective was to demolish German armaments, stores and buildings. Four trolleys and eight baskets containing explosives were stored on the upper deck aboard Vindictive, but it was impossible to transfer them across the two remaining gangways. This more or less ruined the demolition operation. Although some explosives and flame-throwers were brought ashore the presence of British sailors and Royal Marines on the Mole prevented the demolition of anything for fear of causing casualties among comrades. Shed No.3 was prepared for demolition with the placing of charges, should the opportunity arise. Enemy shells had hit the western side of the shed, causing flames to burn inside. An effort by two men from Dickinson's No.2 Party was made to place explosive charges alongside a German destroyer that was berthed near to Shed No.3, but heavy machine gun fire from this vessel prevented them from causing any substantial damage. Dickinson's team resorted to throwing some bombs onto the deck of the German vessel.

Acting 1st Class Mechanic William Gough was in the leading wave on the Mole, armed with a flammenwerfer (or flame-thrower). He was part of Wing Commander Brock's party of Air Mechanics from the RNAS who had volunteered for this operation. Assigned to Lieutenant Lamplough's Company he was originally given the objective of engulfing some sheds on the inner harbour side of the Mole with deadly fire. It took time for him to reach his objective carrying such a heavy, dangerous piece of equipment. On his arrival he found his work was done, the sheds had already been demolished by shellfire. Instead he used his weapon upon a nearby destroyer, V 69, moored alongside the inner Mole. Most of the German crew, including Kapitänleutnant Benecke, was on the deck and firing upon the raiders with all guns. Others were firing through port holes. Gough deployed his flame-thrower, engulfing the deck with jets of burning petrol and oil, killing sailors onboard.

I must have killed a lot of them. I tried to reach the bridge, from which someone [presumably the Commander] was pointing at me with a revolver, but the range was too great, and my flame-thrower played out. Then, as the bullets from a machine-gun from further up the Mole got too close to be safe, I left my now useless weapon and took cover behind a low wall. From this position, I saw my weapon smashed to pieces by machine-gun fire.[23]

According to Gough some British seaman later boarded this blazing destroyer to explode charges in her engine room, causing the vessel to sink. Two unidentified Royal Marine officers later spoke to journalists regarding the attack on the destroyer. Newspapers reported that these men came from the Plymouth Company, therefore these two officers could be Lieutenant Lamplough and Underhill.

Two German destroyers lay alongside the outer side of the Mole, and both of them kept firing at Vindictive *at quite close range. From these vessels a number of German sailors swarmed up to attack us, but when they found themselves looking at the points of British bayonets they stopped. Our men charged and cleared the space and we then rushed to the first destroyer into which we threw half a hundred hand bombs. A loud explosion followed and the last we saw of her she was heavily on fire and sinking. We were unable to reach the other two destroyers and what became of them we are unable to say.*[24]

One unidentified Royal Marine described the attack on the German destroyer to a journalist:

Our strong party was forming up when a big, burly German loomed out of the semi darkness, and made a dive to the nearest man. Before he could do anything, our captain, who was calmly walking up and down knocked him on the head with a truncheon – a weapon with which some of us had been provided. He killed the man outright. On the other side of the Mole lay another German destroyer. This vessel we destroyed, and we knocked on the head all the men who opposed us.[25]

Another unidentified Royal Marine took a souvenir from a dead sentry on the destroyer:

I belonged to what you might call 'the pirate crew' that boarded one of the German destroyers. The first Hun we saw was the marine on sentry on deck. We quickly downed him, and then made a dash for the hatchway, knocking the German sailors back much quicker than they could scramble up. Before we left I approached our old friend the sentry, and do not know whether he was dead or not, but I said 'sorry old chap, but I am a marine myself, so there is no harm in taking your helmet.'[26]

Able Seaman Bernerd Devlin was part of the Demolition party that climbed on board *Vindictive* from *Daffodil*:

The splendid achievement at Zeebrugge was won because every man knew how to use his fists ... our pom-poms were belching forth as fast as they could. I went over the specially constructed landing stage on my hands and knees and when I got on the Mole was surprised to think how I had escaped injury. ... I saw a lot shot down ... Machine-gun bullets whizzed above us and past us, shells burst over our heads, gas choked those men who in the excitement had allowed their respirators to slip from their faces.[27]

Once on the Mole, Devlin and his party charged along the parapet towards the concrete gun emplacements in an attempt to silence the guns.

With cutlass drawn in one hand and a bomb in the other, each one of us rushed along the Mole towards the concrete gun stations. Those Germans who tried to get away by taking to their heels were blown to atoms by our bombs which we pelted at them. No quarter was shown. German gunners concealed in their concrete batteries were bombed out. Those who showed fight were slain by cutlass. It was a case

Belgian guns captured by the Germans were used to defend the Mole and were incorporated within the Mole battery. The picture (below) gives an impression of the deadly field of fire of these guns, as a German torpedo boat passes the end of the Mole looking like an unmissable target. It shows how imperative it was for the Royal Marines and Royal Naval Landing Party to knock out the Mole Battery to enable the blockships *Thetis*, *Iphigenia* and *Intrepid* to pass.

of teeth, feet, hands or anything, I got into close quarters with these surprised Germans, and like my colleagues, what the bomb failed to do the cutlass accomplished. Any German who showed his head was a dead man. Slashing right and left with the cutlass, and banging their concrete gun emplacements with bombs, we put seven guns out of action before we reached our first objective – the lighthouse.[28]

One man from the demolition team rushed up towards the steps of the lighthouse and used a bomb to demolish the lighthouse lantern. 'The lighthouse was stormed and battered with bombs. The lantern was soon demolished, and afterwards the whole structure was completely wrecked. If there were any Germans in charge of this lighthouse then they surely died at their posts.'[29]

Two lights were positioned at the end of the Mole to guide the blockships into Zeebrugge harbour. Once this was done the raiders turned their attention to the three destroyers that were lying alongside the inner Mole. Throwing bombs onto one of the destroyers they became engaged in a bitter hand to hand confrontation on the deck. The fighting was desperate; one German sailor did not relish the fight and jumped overboard to seek refuge in the cold dark water. Devlin remembered 'Fists and feet were freely used in the scuffle. When the submarine blew up the Mole the men went wild with delight, and if anything, fought harder than ever … our men were always on top.'[30]

Captain Chater was busy coordinating the landing and identified a potential problem that could jeopardize the withdrawal of the raiders once the operation was completed. He went ashore

… to investigate the height of the sea wall [the raised pathway], of which conflicting reports had been received, and the best means of getting down to the Mole and back again. I found there were no steps near to where the ship had been berthed, and that the height was too great to jump down. Returning on board, I gave instructions for hook ropes to be taken ashore and I made Sergeant Major Thatcher personally responsible that, after the men had landed, scaling ladders were placed and maintained in position. Without these ladders, no man who got down onto the Mole would have been able to get back on to the ship. Having given these orders, I returned to the sea wall, slid down a hook rope and crossed over to number 3 shed on the far side of the Mole. My impression is that the sea wall abreast of the Mole was not under rifle or MG fire at this time, but the defenders were shelling the Mole and their shells were striking the sea wall and sheds. Only the funnels and foretop of the Vindictive *were visible over the sea wall.*[31]

Private Hodgson from No.12 Platoon assisted RSM Thatcher with placing the heavy wooden ladder from the top of the sea wall to the ground level onto the Mole.

Loaded as I was with full equipment, small arms, ammunition, rifle and two panniers, each with four trays of Lewis gun bullets, it was not easy but somehow I scrambled over and dropped off the parapet wall, almost alongside R.S.M. Thatcher. He was attempting single-handed to lift a heavy wooden ladder which had been brought in 'Vindictive' over the iron railing, along the inner side of the footway to enable us to get down on to the main part of the Mole. 'Give me a hand lad', he shouted, so I dropped my rifle and the panniers and together we soon had the ladder over, 'Now off you go, it is safer down there', so picking up my things I was soon down on the main part of the Mole, moments later, the R.S.M. was badly wounded, was got back on 'Vindictive' but had to have a leg amputated.[32]

Elements from No.7 platoon commanded by Lieutenant de Berry also assisted Thatcher in positioning ladders so that they could gain access to the Mole ground level and provide support to Nos. 9 and 11 Platoons. An unidentified marine remembered that the Germans 'had the cheek to try to take our scaling ladders. We let them come within 10 yards and then blew them away. Those we found in the open ran like rabbits, but others stuck in corners and sniped at us with rifles and machine guns.'[33]

Left: A different view of the Mole Battery, Zeebrugge.

Below: Personnel relaxing at the Mole Battery.

Above left: Marinekorps Flandern on Zeebrugge Mole. The Matrosen (sailors) of the Imperial German Navy wore a blue naval cap with an Imperial cockade and black cap tally.

Above right: Men from the Marinekorps Flandern who defended the Mole at Zeebrugge. Admiral Ludwig von Schröder was acutely aware of the importance of the Belgian ports and the threat they posed to Allied shipping, but he had a constant battle for ships and support; MarineKorps Flandern had to compete with the Baltic fleet and the largely inactive High Seas Fleet for attention.

The initial objective of the Royal Marine assault team was to capture a fortified position 150 yards from the seaward end of the Mole. It was intended to berth *Vindictive* so that the raiders could surmount the parapet and drop within the fortified sector. Here they would be attacking the stone trenches and machine-gun emplacements from the rear and would be in an ideal position to sabotage the 5.9-inch guns covering the lighthouse. Since *Vindictive* berthed 70 yards away from the intended location, the storming party found themselves exposed to German machine gun fire from trenches at ground level on the Mole. If the *Vindictive* had succeeded in berthing at the scheduled point, then the storming party would have been behind this awkward trench system and could have attacked from the rear. Now they were forced to attack the trenches and cut through intricate barbed wire defences from the front. The Royal Naval landing party was also exposed to machine gun fire from enemy vessels moored alongside the inner Mole wall. Captain Carpenter recalled the confusion: 'The terrific noise, the darkness, the bursting of shell and hail of machine-gun bullets rendered it exceedingly difficult for any one individual to make such observations as would lead to a connected account of the fighting on the Mole itself.'[34]

The close quarter combat was extraordinary.

> *A hefty German fired at me point blank from five yards range. The bullet entered the fleshy part of my left arm, near the muscle. It came through my sleeve, then through my left breast pocket and out by the button, without seriously injuring me: but my mate fixed him properly. Quickly reversing his rifle he gripped the muzzle, bought the butt end square on the German's napper, flopping him out fair. In a joke I cried: 'Right O matey: that's the stuff to give 'em.'*[35]

Another Royal Marine described his close call with death. 'A German bullet struck the rim of my steel helmet. It actually passed under the rim, the across the top of my head and out from the other side of the helmet, making a clean round hole. All it did to me was to singe my hair.'[36]

One RM recalled the use of the *arme blanche*:

> *The whole place was alive with shells. The shore batteries began firing on the* Vindictive *and hit the Mole and their own destroyers inside the harbour. We did not think they would fire on their own crowd. For an hour we chased Germans through sliding doors and underground passages. Every one of us had grenades, and we made the place lively with them. Towards the end my officer was wounded by a sniper at close quarters. I got him right in the chest with my bayonet and left it sticking there while I helped my officer back.*[37]

The Royal Marines were in a vulnerable position as they attacked the fortified zone and were attacked from the rear by German soldiers from the end of the Mole. The *Iris'* failure to berth meant that Marines from A Company could not get ashore, so there were insufficient men to carry out an attack on the fortified zone and establish a wall of defence against German reinforcements coming from the western part of the Mole. However, the success of C3 in destroying the viaduct alleviated this problem. When Major Weller was informed that the naval storming force was experiencing difficulty in securing the fortified positions at the end of the Mole he sent No.12 Platoon and remnants from No.11 Platoon to assist. Lieutenant Underhill commanding No.11 Platoon reached the observation shelter containing the range finder. Adams and his naval force were in a position 40 yards further along the Mole. Underhill and his men could not reach their position because of heavy German machine gun fire that crossed the parapet. With Lieutenant Lamplough's consolidation of the advance position with No.9 Platoon, No.5 Platoon transferred their wounded back to the ship, while those that were not casualties joined Captain Bamford and his force.

Private Jim Clist had lost contact with Major Weller while aboard *Vindictive*, but he found him ashore on the Mole. In his account Clist gives an indication of the decimation of the platoons that assaulted the Mole and refers to two Royal Marines who were suffering from the effects of shell shock.

> *I lost Major Weller in the confusion, but I caught up with him as soon as I got ashore. The first message he gave me was to tell Lieutenant Underhill to take his men to the end of the Mole and destroy the battery that was still firing at the* Vindictive. *I gave him the message, but before he started on the mission he told me to find so and so section, I can't remember the section, but it was the one I was attached to for rations, Corporal Kingshott the clairvoyant was in charge. I had to tell the Corporal to take his section to the end of the Mole and support Lieutenant Underhill, but he only had three or four men left. A few minutes after the corporal had gone I was on my way back to Major Weller I met two more men of that section. I told them where to go, but they were in such a state of shock that they would not move. When I left them they were stood up in what I considered the most dangerous part of the Mole. I shouted and told them to lie down, but they took no notice.*[38]

While Underhill and No.11 Platoon was held up by the observation shelter, Captain Bamford assembled Nos. 5, 7 and 8 platoons for an assault on the fortified area and the 4.1-inch battery at the end of the Mole. Captain Bamford led the assault. An unidentified Royal Marine described it: 'We then received the order to charge, and we rushed along the Mole to the shore. We bayoneted and shot all the men we came across. The noise of the firing intermingled with the shouts and cries of the men was terrible. It was a fair slaughter, and all around us was hubbubs; but we kept our heads, and put the wind up the Boche completely.'[39] However, before the assault could gain any momentum the retirement signal was heard. The withdrawal was hindered by German machine gun fire. Most of the scaling ladders from the Mole to the parapet were destroyed. The raiders sheltered by No.3 shed where they waited for an appropriate moment when the German fire briefly subsided to make a dash for *Vindictive*. The wounded were evacuated in good order.

It is recorded that 200 men were based at the air station on the Mole. It is probable that only a minimum number of personnel guarded the air station, for most personnel slept in accommodation in Zeebrugge. Seventy men from the Hafenkompanie and crews from Torpedo Boats and destroyers moored along the Mole took part in defending the Mole. Rodewald sent some of his party back to the Battery at the end of the Mole. With his remaining men, Rodewald and Leutenant Zimmermann led a counter-attack towards *Vindictive* along the parapet and above the roof of the bunkers that were used as accommodation. During this counter-attack they captured a machine gun from one of the British dead and two flame-throwers. They turned this machine gun and used it against the British.

Belgian civilians were on the Mole at Zeebrugge during the night of the raid. The nun residing in Zeebrugge could testify how fierce the battle raged during that hour:

> *The destruction of the claire-voie lighting prevented people on the Mole from asking for help or using electrical lights, it was only thanks to the Bengal lights and projectiles that they noticed they were in danger, everyone who handed in his weapons was tied up and thrown in MTBs (motor torpedo boats), many were drowned at sea. It was an icy cold night but even if they had been aware of the danger their fear would have been much greater. It was only in the afternoon that this became apparent. No one was allowed to cross the bridge but a Belgian civilian was on watch on a German ship at the end of the Mole; he had realised the great danger he was in and initially fled into a small boat but seeing the English set on the Germans like lions, and stabbing, shooting and throwing hand grenades, the man jumped into the sea and swam up to the shore of Heyst, which he reached safely.*[40]

Officers of 4th Battalion Royal Marine Light Infantry

Back Row – 2nd Lt H. B. Lovatt (wounded), Surgeon F. P. Pocock, MC RN, Lt and Qr-Mr F. J. Hore (wounded), Lt B. S. Claudet, Lt D. Broadwood, Lt.G. O. Stanton (died of wounds), Lt G. Underhill, Lt H.A. P. de Berry, Lt S. H. E. Inskip (killed).

Second Row – Captain J. M. Palmer DSC (Prisoner of War). Lt C. R. W. Lamplough, Lt J. Jackson (killed), 2nd Lt A. G. Norris, Lt I. H. Dollery (killed), Lt T. F. V. Cooke (wounded), Lt W. E. Sillitoe (killed), 2nd Lt W. C. Bloxsom (wounded), 2nd Lt W. H. Boxall, Captain C. P. Tuckey (missing).

Front Row – Captain C. B. Conybeare (wounded), Captain R. L. Del Strother (wounded), Major C. E. C. Eagles DSO (killed), Major A. A. Cordner (killed), Lt Colonel B. M. Elliot DSO (killed), Captain and Adjutant A. R. Chater, Major B. G. Weller DSC, Captain E. Bamford DSO, Surgeon H. St C. Colson RN.

Captain Dallas Brooks and Lt Rigby were away at the time the photo was taken.

NOTES

1. The *Newcastle Daily Chronicle*, 29th April 1918.
2. *Daily Sketch* 1st May 1918, page 2.
3. Captain A F B Carpenter VC RN, *The Blocking of Zeebrugge*, p202: Herbert Jenkins Limited, 1925.
4. National Archives ADM 137/3894: Lieutenant Commander Adams Report.
5. Able Seaman Albert McKenzie VC Papers, Courtesy Colin McKenzie.
6. Ibid.
7. *Northern Daily Mail*, 27th April 1918.
8. Lowell Thomas, *Raiders of the Deep*: Doubleday, 1928.
9. *The London Gazette*, 17th March 1919.
10. National Archives ADM 116/1656: Able Seaman William Lodwick Report.
11. Able Seaman Albert McKenzie VC Papers, Courtesy Colin McKenzie.
12 Oberleutnant Rodewald's report, 'Friedrichgorter Kriegsbuch' by Kapitänleutnant Felix Glatzers.
13. Corporal George Moyse interview. Courtesy Peter White.
14. *Globe & Laurel* April 1919.
15. Max Arthur, *Lost Voices of the Royal Navy*: Hodder & Stoughton, 2005.
16. Private Philip Hodgson Royal Marines Museum ARCH 7/17/2.
17. Lieutenant Lamplough Royal Marines Museum ARCH 11/13/79.
18. Ibid.
19. *Globe & Laurel* April 1919.
20. Captain A F B Carpenter VC RN, *The Blocking of Zeebrugge*, p204: Herbert Jenkins Limited, 1925.
21. Sergeant Wright, Royal Marines Museum Archives ARCH 10/2/W.
22. Corporal George Moyse interview. Courtesy Peter White.
23. IWM Museum Department of Documents: Acting 1st Class Mechanic W H Gough, 91/11/1.
24. *Hampshire Telegraph & Post*, Friday 26th April 1918.
25. Ibid.
26. Ibid..
27. *Thomson's Weekly News* 4th May 1918.
28. Ibid.
29. Ibid.
30. *The Newcastle Daily Chronicle*, 29th April 1918.
31. IWM Department of Documents Captain A.R. Chater, RMLI: 74/101/1.
32. Private Philip Hodgson Royal Marines Museum ARCH 7/17/2.
33. *Daily Mail*, 24th April 1918.
34. Captain A F B Carpenter VC RN, *The Blocking of Zeebrugge*, p204: Herbert Jenkins Limited, 1925.
35. *Hampshire Telegraph & Post*, Friday 26th April 1918.
36. Ibid.
37. *Daily Mail*, 24th April 1918.
38. Private Jim Clist interview, courtesy David Clist.
39. *Hampshire Telegraph & Post*, Friday 26th April 1918.
40. In Flanders Fields Museum, Ypres.

CHAPTER 7

ATTACK ON THE MOLE VIADUCT

The viaduct connecting the Mole to the shore was 328 yards long and 40 feet wide and supported two railway lines. It consisted of six piers across its width and 59 piers along its length. A strong tidal current of six knots flowed beneath. The purpose of this aperture in the Mole was to prevent the accumulation of silt.

It was necessary to destroy the viaduct that connected the mainland and the Mole in order to prevent enemy reinforcements reaching the Mole garrison; and to create a further diversion. Its destruction was part of the demolition work that was taking place on the Mole, which would also reduce the operational capability of the enemy using the facility as a naval and aerial base in the future.

Two old submarines, C1 and C3, were selected to take part in the destruction of the Mole viaduct. C1 and C3 were built in 1906 and 1907 respectively and both displaced 316 tons. C1, commanded by Lieutenant Aubrey Newbold, and C3, commanded by Lieutenant Richard Sandford, each had a complement of two officers and four men, carrying high explosives fitted with timed fuses that would be ignited allowing a delay that would enable the crew sufficient time to escape. Five tons of amatol was positioned as far forward in the bows of each submarine as to ensure that when the submersibles crashed into the piers of the viaduct, the explosives would be positioned directly under it. Each submarine carried a motor boat and scaling ladders, so the crews were given two options for escape, according to circumstance, either to ascend to the Mole and rejoin Allied forces, or escape seaward. Gyro control was installed in both C1 and C3 to enable the submarines to continue their course automatically after the crews had abandoned them and before penetrating the viaduct.

The Torpedo Boat Destroyers *Trident* and *Mansfield* towed C1 and C3 until they were within a mile-and-a-half of the viaduct. It was imperative that the assault force reached the viaduct without alerting the enemy. Along the coast between the Mole and Blankenberge a mere two miles away were positioned 19 5-inch guns and four howitzers of 11-inch calibre. The fortified barracks on the Mole was near to the viaduct so there was a great reliance upon the smoke screens.

C1 was delayed in detaching from her hawser and could not continue her passage to destroy the viaduct. Lieutenant S. Bayford, the First Lieutenant, was washed overboard and had to be rescued from the sea. C3 was left to carry out the attack alone. The destruction of the viaduct depended upon Lieutenant Sandford and the crew. They were Lieutenant John Howell-Price, Stoker Henry Bendall, Petty Officer Walter Harner, Leading Seaman William Cleaver and Engine Room Artificer Allan Roxburgh.

As C3 approached the viaduct at midnight at a rate of six knots, the enemy caught sight of her in the light of a star shell. German 4-inch guns fired shells directly at C3. For a short moment C3 was being tracked by an enemy searchlight and receiving enemy fire. Artificial smoke used to conceal the submarine's approach was blown northwards. However, the firing was of short duration. The steel viaduct was clearly visible amidst the glare of background light caused by star shells and searchlights. When they were 100 yards from the viaduct Lieutenant Sandford altered course on a bearing 085 degrees to ensure that C3 approached the viaduct at right angles at a speed of 10 knots. He decided not to use the automatic gyro steering that would have allowed them to escape into the skiff at a safe distance while the submarine continued its course into the viaduct. Instead, he chose to crash C3 into the viaduct to ensure that the objective was achieved. The crew of C3 risked their lives for if they were anywhere close to the viaduct at the moment of the explosion, the force would have killed them instantly or stunned them, causing death by drowning. Sandford manoeuvred the submarine between two vertical steel girders, wedging the hull underneath the railway line at a distance of 50 yards from the northern end of the viaduct. C3 was secured between the piers and was raised two feet above the surface of the water.

Stoker Henry Bendall recalled the moment when C3 collided with the Mole viaduct. 'She was going at full tilt when we hit the viaduct. It was a very good jolt, but you can stand a lot when you hang on tight. We ran right into the middle of the viaduct and stuck there as intended. I do not think anybody said a word except, "Well, we're here all right".'[1]

C3 did not attract much enemy opposition initially, either because the Germans were distracted from the diversionary assault on the Mole, or they may have thought that C3 was one of their own submarines. Then a small enemy contingent commenced to fire upon them from the viaduct with machine guns. This obviated the possibility of using the scaling ladders to climb onto the viaduct as a means of escape. The only escape option was the sea, so Lieutenant Sandford gave the order to abandon ship. The crew of the C3 was mustered on the deck prior to ramming the viaduct piers. On Sandford's command they lowered the motor skiff into the water and boarded. As his men waited anxiously in the skiff, Sandford experienced problems in lighting the fuse. Once Sandford fired the time fuse, which was scheduled to detonate in twelve minutes, he joined the crew. Leading Seaman William Cleaver:

> We all stood and waited with bated breath. The shouting on the Mole above increased. There was the clatter of rifles. At last we saw the figure of our commander. He was hurrying along the deck towards us bending low. 'Come on, Sir!' we yelled in chorus. There was a fusillade of rifle bullets from the Mole that whizzed menacingly past our heads. 'Everything OK,' said Lt. Sandford as breathlessly he jumped aboard the skiff. He told us afterwards that his delay was due to difficulty in lighting the fuses. He had also seen that the lights were out.[2]

As they made their escape westward Roxburgh discovered a potential disaster. As soon as they abandoned C3, the propeller on the skiff had been damaged and could not be used. This setback prevented a hasty withdrawal. Cleaver recalled, 'It was an awful situation. In less than three minutes the first of the fuses to be lit if it functioned would reach the charge in the bows of C3 and destroy the viaduct and every living thing in the vicinity.'[3]

With only minutes to go before C3 exploded they took to the oars paddling for their lives. The skiff was fixed within the beams of enemy searchlights and the escaping crew became the target of intense enemy machine gun fire from the viaduct and the shore. Although they were clear of hostile fire from the viaduct, the skiff sustained many hits and water was entering the small vessel. Fortunately, the motor pump was operating, which meant that they were able to expel the water rapidly. Lieutenant Sandford, Petty Officer Harner and Stoker Bendall sustained wounds as they paddled frantically against the tide.

> 'The oars!' shouted someone. Bendall and Harner grabbed them from the bottom of the skiff and began to pull madly away from the Mole. Less than two minutes to go now probably. And still the rifles cracked and bullets whistled all around. 'They couldn't hit a pussy cat,' said Lt Sandford derisively. And at that moment he sank back, wounded in the leg. What frantic strokes Bendall and Harner were making …Bendall rolled over with a groan. He was wounded in the thigh. I took his place with the oars. By this time the boat had been hit several times and was leaking badly. Roxburgh and Lieut. Price were having a busy time with the hand pumps. Had it not been for them the boat would undoubtedly have sunk.[4]

Kaiser Wilhem inspecting the damage caused by C3 to the Mole. The picture was taken by De Ghelden of Bruges when the Kaiser visited Zeebrugge hours after the raid on the morning of 23rd April.

At approximately 12.15 a.m., when they were 200 yards from the viaduct, C3 exploded causing a breach of between 60 to 80 feet in the viaduct and destroying the link from the mainland to the Mole and the twenty Germans who were firing from it. Stoker Bendall:

> The lights were now on us and the machine guns going from the shore. Before we had made 200 yards the submarine went up. We had no doubt about that. There was a tremendous flash, bang, crash, and lots of concrete from the Mole fell all round us into the water. It was luck that we were not struck.[5]

Leading Seaman William Cleaver recalled the moment when C3 exploded:

> And then it was as though Heaven came to meet Earth in one momentary upheaval … C3 and the viaduct were no more. Above the din of the raging battle the fearful fulmination rose. Great chunks of masonry fell in the water all around us. The boat rocked and swayed as though possessed. Flames shot up to a tremendous height. In their glare was visible a great break in the Mole. Out of the sea rose great twisted masses of ironwork bent into grotesque shapes.[6]

The moment of the explosion was felt by everyone in the vicinity. Sergeant Wright who was standing on the Mole recalled that the 'explosion was so great that the whole concrete Mole shook from end to end.'[7]

Petty Officer Harry Adams on the deck of Daffodil remembered the 'thud that shook Heaven and Earth – The ships shivered and trembled – the nearest approach to an earthquake one could imagine. We had been warned to expect it, but amongst all this it had passed from one's mind – the concussion threw you to the deck.'[8] Air Mechanic William Gough witnessed the devastating spectacle of the explosion of C3 from the Mole:

C3 and her crew.

HM Submarine C3 with A4 and A5 in Portsmouth Harbour, taken by R Perkins.

It was the grandest and at the same time the most awful sight I have ever witnessed. A huge column of fire – blood-red, through the fog, suddenly shot up, followed almost immediately by the crash of the explosion, and a concussion that seemed to lift the bottom out of everything and that must have rocked Zeebrugge and its surroundings to the foundations.[9]

German Staff Officers were residing in the hotel near to the where the Mole begins. The alarm of an attack had been raised and all were running to the command post which was five minutes away. The force of the explosion destroyed roofs and windows in Zeebrugge.

It has been recorded that many of the German reinforcements on bicycles fell to their deaths into the gap made by the explosion of C3. At this point searchlights were extinguished and any enemy firing within the vicinity subsided. Concrete debris, steel splinters and fragments of human remains fell upon the crew of C3 as they made their escape. The small skiff escaped into the darkness, which was intermittently lit by shell and star shells. Bendall was hit four times.

Within ten minutes the crew from C3 was rescued by a picket boat, commanded by Lieutenant Commander Francis Sandford, the brother of Lieutenant Richard Sandford. Bendall recalled 'We gave a shout of joy when we saw her.'[10] They were promptly taken to the safety of HMS *Phoebe*. The successful destruction of the viaduct denied the enemy the opportunity to send reinforcements onto the Mole and marginally relieved the immense pressure on the Marine and Bluejacket assault force.

LIEUTENANT RICHARD SANDFORD VC RN, COMMANDING OFFICER, HM SUBMARINE C3

Lieutenant Richard Sandford was born in Exmouth on 11th May 1891, the son of the former Archdeacon of Exeter. He had served in home waters in the submarine service for four years during the war. While recovering from wounds sustained in the destruction of the Mole viaduct Sandford later recalled: 'There was no doubt about getting there. I set the fuse myself and I think the thing was done all right. We were lucky in being picked up by the picket boats afterwards. The firing from the shore was a bit severe at 200 yards, and only the fact that the sea was a bit rough and we were up and down a good deal saved us. The crew did their duty, every man. They were all volunteers and picked men. We got in without difficulty and were not found by the searchlights until we were getting away.' Lieutenant Richard Sandford's Victoria Cross Citation reads:

This officer was in command of Submarine C.3. and most skilfully placed that vessel in between the piles of the viaduct before lighting his fuse and abandoning her. He eagerly undertook this hazardous enterprise, although well aware (as were all his crew) that if the means of rescue failed and he or any of his crew were in the water at the moment of explosion, they would be killed outright by the force of such explosion. Yet Lieutenant Sandford disdained to use the gyro steering, which would have enabled him and his crew to abandon the submarine at a safe distance, and preferred to make sure, as far as humanly possible, of the accomplishment of his duty.[11]

Despite his coming through this terrible ordeal, tragically, Lieutenant Sanford would die on 23rd November 1918 of typhoid fever.

Lieutenant Richard Sandford VC, leaving the obsolete submarine C3 loaded with explosives beneath the viaduct of the Zeebrugge Mole. He and his crew, though the target of German machine-gun and rifle fire, escaped in their dinghy and the submarine exploded, destroying a great part of the viaduct. Illustration from *The Great War*.

Stoker H. C. Bendall DCM.

Leading seaman
W. G. Cleaver C G.M. DSM.

P. O. Harner C. G. M.

E. R. A. - AG Roxburgh C. G. M.

STOKER 1ST CLASS HENRY BENDALL CGM,
LEADING SEAMAN WILLIAM CLEAVER CGM,
PETTY OFFICER WALTER HARNER CGM
& ENGINE ROOM ARTIFICER ALLAN ROXBURGH CGM

The CGM citation states:

> *The ratings above mentioned were members of the crew of Submarine C.3. which was skilfully placed between the piles of the Zeebrugge Mole viaduct and there blown up, the fuse being lighted before the submarine was abandoned. They volunteered for and, under the command of an officer, eagerly undertook this hazardous enterprise, although they were well aware that if the means of rescue failed, and that if any of them were in the water at the time of the explosion, they would be killed outright.[12]*

LIEUTENANT JOHN HOWELL-PRICE DSC

John Howell-Price was born on 16th September 1886 at St. Alban's Parsonage, Five Dock, Sydney, Australia. He was the second of five sons born to the Reverend John Howell-Price and his wife Isabel. When he was aged 14 John ran away to sea. Serving an apprenticeship as a merchant navy officer on clippers, he would go on to earn a master mariner's certificate. On 24th March 1915 John enlisted in the Royal Naval Reserve as a temporary Sub Lieutenant. He was later promoted to Acting Lieutenant and served aboard the armed merchant cruiser HMS *Alcantara*. He survived the sinking of *Alcantara* when she was torpedoed in the North Sea on 29th February 1916 during a fierce battle with the German SMS *Greif*. He and the other survivors nearly froze to death as they drifted in an open boat. After being rescued from this ordeal Howell-Price was promoted to temporary Lieutenant on 24th July 1917 and transferred to the Royal Naval Submarine Service. Early in 1918 he volunteered to take part in the Zeebrugge raid and was assigned second in command of the submarine C3. He was awarded the DSC for the part he played. His citation reads:

> *His assistance in placing Submarine C3 between the piles of the viaduct before the fuse was lighted and she was abandoned was invaluable. His behaviour in a position of extreme danger was exemplary.*[13]

After the war from 1918 to 1921 Howell-Price served with the Royal Australian Navy. He then served with the Merchant Navy until his death on 13th November 1937. He died in Liverpool.

NOTES

1. *Daily Mail*, 24th May 1918.
2. *The Sunday Graphic and Sunday News* 1935.
3. Ibid.
4. Ibid.
5. *Daily Mail*, 24th May 1918.
6. *The Sunday Graphic and Sunday News* 1935.
7. Sergeant Wright, Royal Marines Museum Archives ARCH 10/2/W.
8. Petty Officer Harry Adams Papers.
9. IMW Museum Department of Documents: Acting 1st Class Mechanic W H Gough, 91/11/1.
10. *Daily Mail*, 24th May 1918.
11. *London Gazette* 23rd July 1918.
12. Ibid.
13. Ibid.

Above right: Howell-Price pictured when he was a Sub Lieutenant. (AWM ref: AO5732).

Top right: German guns belonging to the Württemberg Battery. Zeebrugge Mole and the railway viaduct can be seen in the background. Lt. Sandford and the crew of HM Submarine C3 had to sail to the railway viaduct within full view and easy range of these guns.

Above right: Aerial view of the substantial breach caused by HM Submarine C3.

CHAPTER 8

SMOKE SCREENING AND SUBSIDIARY ATTACKS

As the diversionary assault was taking place HMS *Warwick*, *Phoebe* and *North Star* sailed near to the end of the Mole to provide smoke screens when and where necessary. HMS *Myng* providing smoke screen cover as the eastern guardship suffered an accident during the operation. Leading Seaman H.C. Beaumont later wrote of this incident: 'Had a very bad accident with the foremost smoke screen, the chap working it jumped overboard and was lost. The ship was enveloped in smoke and gas and nearly gassed all hands, there was no panic. The opinion of everybody is that the smoke from this damaged tank saved us, if it was not for that we would have been blown out of the water.'[1] On the official casualty list, there was one fatality listed from *Myng*, Mechanic Second Class John Rouse and it is most likely that he was the sailor who jumped overboard mentioned by Beaumont. His body was never recovered and his name is one of four listed on the memorial to the missing in Zeebrugge Churchyard.

At 12.05 a.m. *Mansfield* was ordered by *Trident* to produce a smoke screen. As *Mansfield* complied with the instruction, a drum containing acid for the smoke screen exploded and the acid spilled over the upper deck. Fire hoses were immediately deployed to cover the acid with water. A change in wind direction resulted in the smoke produced enveloping the vessel, forcing the crew to use their gas masks. Smoke and acid was drawn into the engine room and after boiler room by air fans. The occupants in these parts of the ship were taken by surprise and were unable to put on respirators in time. Most of those on duty in these compartments were gassed, which took the after boiler room out of operation for twenty minutes, preventing the use of the aft funnels for smoke screening.

Lieutenant Cuthbert Bowlby commanding CMB 26B led an attack upon the seaplane sheds. He brought his coastal motor boat 70 yards abreast of these sheds, stopped the craft and fired shells at them contiuously.

Lieutenant Oswald Robinson commanding M.L 424 was a protective escort for the blockships as they approached the canal entrance. As they appeared from the smoke screen the vessel received a direct hit killing Robinson, Deck Hand Joseph Baxter and Leading Deck Hand Fred Fearn. Lieutenant John Robinson assumed command and ordered the remaining crew to abandon the disabled vessel. Once everyone had disembarked into a dinghy he ensured that the enemy did not capture the stricken vessel by setting fire to the engine room. Lt. Robinson was awarded the Distinguished Service Cross for his actions that night. They left the boat in flames. Later that day the incapacitated vessel was washed ashore and was inspected by German officers. Robinson and the crew were evacuated by ML 128.

ML 110 commanded by Lieutenant Commander James Young was assigned the task of positioning calcium buoys near to the Mole, then to evacuate blockship crews after the ships were sunk at the canal mouth. During the operation this vessel was hit three times by German fire, which disabled the ML. Lieutenant Commander Young and Leading Deck Hand James Daniels DSM were killed by the explosions. Lieutenant Leonard Lee and two deck hands were wounded. Lieutenant George Bowen assumed command of ML 110 when the captain was killed. When the ship was disabled he evacuated his crew in a dinghy

A conventional smoke screen protecting British vessels.

A motor launch demonstrating smoke screen capability. Behind the ML can be seen one of the Monitors that bombarded the Belgian coast during the raid.

before firing two trays of a Lewis gun at the deck of each compartment to ensure that the vessel was holed and would sink. Bowen was awarded the Distinguished Service Cross. ML 110 sank and the surviving crew was recovered by ML 308.

It was expected that the German Navy would deploy destroyers based in Bruges to confront the raiders. The assault upon Zeebrugge had caught the Germans apparently completely by surprise, so there was not sufficient time to steam up the engines of the destroyers berthed alongside the inner Mole. The sailors aboard these vessels assisted the soldiers manning the garrisons. Unit H, comprising CMB 5 and 7, was ordered to enter the inner harbour and sink enemy vessels moored on the inner Mole. Both vessels were to attack in tandem but they lost contact with each other and were forced to act independently. Sub Lieutenant Blake was in command of CMB 7. He reported his torpedo struck the destroyer beneath the fore bridge from a distance of 600 yards. Blake reported that they received heavy enemy fire from the batteries east of the canal. A German dredger positioned north east of the canal entrance also poured machine gun fire upon her. Blake increased speed to 20 knots as they escaped from the inner harbour. During their escape the vessel collided with a large buoy, causing extensive damage to the starboard bow. Blake increased the speed to 32 knots to ensure that the damaged section of the hull was out of the water, preventing the vessel from sinking. In accordance with orders he headed eastwards, but because the vessel was taking in water, Blake turned CMB 7 around and headed for Dunkirk at full speed. When the vessel was off the coast at Ostend an oil gland burst and as a result the engines had to be switched off. Water was entering the disabled vessel rapidly and all attempts at repair failed. Blake ordered that the vessel be prepared for burning and fired two white Very lights to alert nearby British destroyers patrolling in the vicinity. At 2.15 a.m. the distress signal was observed by HMS *Faulknor* whose captain instructed HMS *Tetrarch* to assist the crew. CMB 7 was reached by *Tetrarch* three miles north west of Stroom Buoy. A very short tow was attached to CMB 7 to ensure that the damaged bow was out of the water until its arrival at Dover later that morning.

Sub Lieutenant Outhwaite commanding CMB 5 encountered an enemy destroyer while off the end of the Mole. The CMB was proceeding from out of the smoke at 12 knots when the German destroyer spotted her in the glare of star shells. The destroyer beamed her forward searchlights on the CMB and fired. At 12.05 a.m. at a range of 650 yards Outhwaite fired his torpedo at the German destroyer. The torpedo struck under the forward searchlight; at the moment of impact the searchlight beams were extinguished. Enemy fire from the Mole and coastal batteries concentrated on CMB 5, which turned to port and made eastwards on a course for the Dutch Buoys. After proceeding for five miles CMB 5 altered course westwards on to Dunkirk.

The British destroyers *North Star* and *Phoebe*, in conjunction with several CMBs, sailed near to the seaward end of the Mole to counter the threat of enemy surface vessels inside the Mole. The result was the sinking of two German Motor Launches and a German destroyer sunk by torpedo. Torpedoes struck the steamer *Brussels* and two other German destroyers. Captain Kenneth Helyar, Commander of HMS *North Star*, claimed that his torpedoes struck enemy vessels. Oberleutnant Rodewald recorded in his report of the raid that a destroyer (possibly the *North Star*) fired a torpedo that hit the Mole directly at the battery. He reported that at the same time a shell detonated in the battery where two German soldiers were killed. After firing five torpedoes at enemy vessels moored along the inner Mole, *North Star* was hit in the engine room by a shell from German coastal batteries, which reduced her speed and increased her vulnerability to enemy fire. At 1.25 a.m. *North Star* stopped 400 yards from the end of the Mole. At the mercy of enemy guns she received numerous hits on her port side and was starting to sink.

Lieutenant Commander Hubert Gore-Langton commanding HMS *Phoebe* circled the disabled ship and put up a smoke screen to conceal the vulnerable vessel from the German batteries. *Phoebe* succeeded in towing *North Star* from danger under cover of the smoke screen, but the cable was shot away, and because she was sinking so fast her crew had to be rescued. Helyar's DSO citation records that 'he refused to leave his ship until she was sinking under his feet.'[2] ML 110 and ML 424 were two other Royal Naval vessels sunk near to the Mole during the operation.

CMB's 27A and 32A were tasked with attacking enemy ships moored on the inner Mole. They were detailed to fire torpedoes inside the Mole once the blockships had passed. A defective clutch on the port engine aboard CMB 27A meant that CMB 32A had to execute the attack alone. At 1.40 a.m. CMB 32A commanded by Sub-Lieutenant J. Garriock fired her torpedo into the hull of the steamship *Brussels*. Garriock could not assess the damage sustained by the *Brussels* because of the opacity of the smoke screen and enemy fire. As soon as the torpedo was discharged CMB 32A returned home.

NOTES

1. Dover Museum.
2. *The London Gazette*, 23rd July 1918.

CHAPTER 9

THE BLOCKSHIPS GO IN

The blockships were led by HMS *Thetis* commanded by Commander Ralph Sneyd, which was followed by HMS *Intrepid*, commanded by Lieutenant Stuart Bonham-Carter. HMS *Iphigenia* commanded by Lieutenant Edward Billyard-Leake was the rear blockship. Providing the subsidiary diversionary assault on the Mole was successful and the three blockships could enter the inner harbour unmolested they were to proceed to the canal entrance. Sneyd was instructed to enter the canal and ram the canal gates, if *Intrepid* and *Iphigenia* followed close behind. *Intrepid* and *Iphigenia* were to sink close to the piers across the mouth of the canal. According to local intelligence this was the best place to sink these ships, because it was the narrowest part of the entrance and silt would accumulate around the sunken blockships causing further hindrance to the German Navy in their anticipated efforts to remove the scuttled ships. If *Thetis* could not reach the gates of the canal then Sneyd was ordered to sink the blockship near to them.

Triplicate conning and steering positions were installed in all the blockships, so that in the event of one position being destroyed, then another team would be able to take over and continue the operation.

As they sailed across the channel, gun crews were standing by prepared to defend the vessels against enemy craft and to respond to enemy batteries once their presence was discovered. At midnight, the crew on the blockships could hear heavy gunfire as they approached the Mole, but were not able to observe anything because of the thick smoke screen, which was slowly drifting seaward in their direction. For the next fifteen minutes the blockships passed through an area which was the focus of enemy bombardment. Engineer Lieutenant Boddie aboard *Thetis*, wrote:

> It was a stirring sight, the dark night had been converted into daylight, and the three blockships and the surrounding sea seemed brilliantly illuminated. My first reaction was a sensation of nakedness, and a feeling of certainty we should be immediately fired at from the shore batteries. All that happened however was that my teeth started chattering.[1]

A star shell illuminated the approaching blockships, but fortunately the smoke screen put up by nearby coastal motor boats concealed their passage. The sense of vulnerability was heightened by the fact that the blockships were sailing at only seven knots, so that they would pass the Mole thirty minutes after *Vindictive* had arrived. The stokers had an easy time while travelling at this slow rate. Boddie:

> It was interesting to observe the men; they showed similar symptoms of nervousness to those I had felt, and which I hoped I had not shown; they smoked cigarettes hard, almost violently; they stoked the fires far more vigorously than was necessary for 7 knots. It was very important to maintain this speed accurately, as the hour's run from the gap to the end of the Mole was done on dead reckoning.[2]

Commander Sneyd in *Thetis* sighted the Mole in the glare of explosions and shellfire by the blockships at 12:20 a.m. Captain Ralph Collins, commander of all Motor Launches, guided them into the harbour. Collins, who was aboard ML 558, gave the bearing of the lighthouse to Sneyd. Once they had passed the lighthouse on the eastern extremity of the Mole *Thetis* increased to maximum speed, aiming to steer clear of the barge boom. Enemy light guns on the end of the Mole were still operational and were bearing heavy fire upon the *Thetis*. Gun crews on *Thetis* replied to the German barrage. However, Sneyd did not observe any activity from the 4.1-inch guns at the end of the Mole.

On passing *Vindictive* berthed alongside the Mole, *Thetis* increased to full speed. Engineer Lieutenant Boddie and Chief ERA Frank Gale, assisted by a junior ERA, worked an engine each. As the speed of *Thetis* increased from seven to 16 knots the noise in the engine room was tremendous. With the boilers primed water was spilling over with the steam. The engines pounded loudly, with the piston rod glands gushing boiling water.

German batteries initially thought that they were German vessels as they entered the harbour. A German submarine officer later told Lowell Thomas that a junior officer stationed on one of the gun batteries by the canal entrance thought that the English blockships were German torpedo boats. As *Thetis* attained its full speed on entering the inner harbour, the starboard engine followed by the port engine suddenly stopped. Boddie thought that gunfire had cut through the steam pipes, but a quick inspection of the pressure gauges ruled out that theory. He then thought that maybe they had run aground. A strong easterly tide had caused *Thetis* to sail into the boom of entanglement nets. Although the nets were torn and a barge was sunk, severe damage was inflicted upon the ship's propeller, which was hopelessly entangled in the boom net. Lying motionless within the confines of Zeebrugge Harbour, 300 yards from the end of the Mole, *Thetis* was exposed to heavy fire from the Mole and shore batteries near to the eastern bank of the canal entrance. Bearing the brunt of German shells, she was hit numerous times and was on fire. *Thetis* was holed several times and was listing to starboard. The majority of hits came from guns on the Mole and were sustained on the starboard side of the vessel. Stoker N. McCrory was seconded to *Thetis* from HMAS *Australia* as a stoker. He previously served on the Royal Australian Navy Bridging Train at Suvla Bay, Gallipoli and in the artillery in France. He saw the forward gun receiving a direct hit from enemy gunfire and being blasted overboard along with its crew. He also confirmed that a shell went through *Thetis* from starboard to portside above the engine room. The hole was large enough for three men to walk through abreast.[3]

The 6-inch gun on the forecastle aboard *Thetis* continued to return fire until smoke obstructed the targets. Petty Officer Alfred Messer was in command of this gun, and continued to fire despite the persistent enemy barrage. The gun was silenced when a shell struck, killing Able Seamen Alfred Saunders and Arthur Harris. Able Seaman Charles Jackson was present when these two men were killed.

> *These two men were serving on the 6-inch gun on the forecastle when a shell passed between the conning tower and their gun and took both of them over the side. I was standing against the conning tower at the time, waiting for orders to make smoke and witnessed them knocked over, they must have certainly been killed.*[4]

The Germans concentrated all their firepower upon *Thetis*, which meant that *Intrepid* and *Iphigenia* followed unscathed. *Thetis* also cleared a significant breach that would enable *Intrepid* and *Iphigenia* to pass. At 12.30 a.m. *Intrepid* and *Iphigenia* passed the bows of *Thetis*. With assistance from signals from *Thetis* they were able to locate the entrance piers to the canal, 300 yards from *Thetis*.

As soon as *Iphigenia* passed, a smoke screen was launched by the immobile *Thetis*. In the engine room Boddie and the stokers had no knowledge of what was happening on deck. Boddie was of course concerned for the safety of his men as he tried to contact Sneyd on the bridge by telephone and by sending a runner. Boddie wanted the situation in the engine room reported and he wanted instructions. Ten minutes after he sent the first messenger, he sent another and when he too did not return, Boddie made the decision to abandon ship. He followed his stokers onto the quarterdeck where they found other members of the ship's company, but there was no trace of any officers. Although a smoke screen shielded them they were still being plastered by German shells and machine gun fire. Boddie found Lieutenant George Belben who reported that Sneyd had been wounded and that Lieutenant Francis Lambert, despite being unwounded, was suffering from the effects of gas and could not speak. Boddie also became aware of the damage sustained by *Thetis*. One of the funnels had crashed to the deck after receiving numerous hits. More importantly, one of the two cutters aboard had been shot to pieces rendering it useless for their escape.

The ship was sinking and Sneyd had given the order to abandon ship. There was a lapse in communication, for although Sneyd had already given the order to abandon ship, a seaman found Boddie to deliver a message from Sneyd relayed 15 minutes previously. At that point Engineer Lieutenant Boddie and Chief Petty Officer Frank Gale disregarded Sneyd's later order and returned to the engine room, where he succeeded in getting the starboard engine to operate. This allowed *Thetis* to turn a short distance, while dragging her stern along the bottom of the harbour. Once she was across the dredged channel in front of the canal entrance, Sneyd decided to blow out the bottom of the vessel.

> ... *a seaman found me with a message from Sneyd, saying that he would like the engines to go ahead if possible. Futile as I felt this request to be, nevertheless I returned to the engine room, collecting the E.R.As on the way, shut off the seacocks which were flooding the place, wrestled again with the engines, and to my great astonishment got both engines to move sluggishly ahead, causing the ship to move up the channel for half a mile, where we finally ran aground. It transpired later that Sneyd had issued his order 15 minutes before I received it. When he noticed the ship was moving, he went back to the bridge, but arrived too late to prevent the grounding. It was a remarkable piece of luck, that the ship should steam half a mile up a narrow channel, with no one on the bridge to steer, and finally settle in an advantageous position.*[5]

The entire crew was ordered on deck, before the charges were exploded. The Petty Officer in charge forward was killed and the key to detonate the explosive charges could not be found amidst the chaos and confusion of enemy fire and smoke screens. Therefore the charges were activated at the other end of the vessel, which blew the bottom out of *Thetis*. There were 50 crew members aboard. Ten were killed and five were wounded, including Sneyd and his second in command. Before Sneyd detonated the charges the surviving members of the crew embarked in the single port cutter. The small cutter became very crowded with all crew members, because the starboard cutter had been damaged by a shell and sunk. Sneyd, who was wounded and suffering from the effects of gas, tried to get in the cutter, but fell into the sea. Boddie saw Sneyd fall and helped to pull him into the cutter.

Lambert was sitting in the stern of the cutter and did not observe Sneyd's recovery from the sea. He thought that Sneyd was still aboard *Thetis*. While everyone in the cutter was keen to withdraw and despite being gassed, Lambert displayed great courage by looking for Sneyd. Officer Belben also went back onboard to look for Sneyd. They returned to find Sneyd aboard the cutter.

Under persistent enemy fire, the crew of *Thetis* made their escape. They rowed northward into the harbour, but were unable to rendezvous with the ML designated to pick them up. Rowing under enemy fire for ten minutes they came into contact with Motor Launch 526, commanded by Lieutenant Hugh Littleton. ML 526 followed the blockships and was assigned to rescue their crews. Onboard this overcrowded motor launch was half the crew of *Intrepid*.

According to Boddie, Commander Sneyd was:

HMS *Thetis*, with the White Ensign still flying, sunk in Zeebrugge harbour.

... full of remorse and regret, and took full blame on himself, for the Thetis *not reaching her destination. He said he had underestimated the speed at which we had rounded the end of the Mole, that in consequence he had missed the entrance to the channel, and run into the nets supported by barges to the left of the entrance. Instead of concentrating on his navigation at the vital moment, he was pre-occupied training the 6-inch gun onto the lighthouse at the end of the Mole. He expressed his delight at my having succeeded in getting the engines restarted, but was bitterly disappointed he had left the bridge at that crucial moment.*[6]

While the enemy was pouring heavy fire upon *Thetis*, *Intrepid* managed to sail to the entrance of the Bruges canal sustaining little damage. Although Sneyd failed to ram the canal gates at the entrance to the canal, in leading the blockships he bore the brunt of German shellfire. According to Able Seaman Button the only damage sustained was when a shell carried away a foremast steam pipe, which caused a rush of steam to escape into the sky, revealing their position. On passing *Thetis*, *Intrepid* found the exact sinking position allocated to her in the plan. On arriving at the mouth of the canal Lieutenant Bonham-Carter manoeuvred *Intrepid* across the canal entrance with full steam ahead on the starboard engine and full speed astern with the port helm hard of starboard. Giving the order to abandon ship he awaited for the crews to embark into the boats before scuttling the ship. As the vessel began to come astern, Bonham-Carter was forced to detonate the charges before Engineer Sub Lieutenant Meikle, Engine Room Artificer's Thomas Farrell and Herbert Smith and Stoker Petty Officer Joseph Smith could evacuate the engine room. These four men managed to reach the upper deck and escape. Bonham-Carter detonated the charges successfully, sinking *Intrepid* across the entrance to the canal at 12.45 a.m. The crew abandoned ship and was picked up by ML 282, commanded by Lieutenant Percy Dean. Dean had followed *Iphigenia* as she approached the entrance to the Bruges canal. German shell and machine gun fire was not the only problem facing Dean, for there were 87 men onboard *Intrepid* to evacuate. There was an extra 33 crew among that number and provision for these extra sailors had not been taken into account. It had been the intention that the extra watch of stokers would be removed from *Intrepid* before the attack. It was the reluctance of the 33 surplus crew members to leave the ship, who preferred to take part in the impending fight, that left Dean with more men to evacuate than planned. Some of the crew members escaped in a cutter from *Intrepid* and were picked up by ML 282. One of the cutters had been destroyed by shell fire, forcing others to jump into the mouth of the canal. Bonham-Carter, two officers and four Petty Officers escaped in a Carley raft and they too were picked up by Lieutenant Dean in ML 282. One of those non commissioned officers was Chief ERA Thomas Farrell:

I consider myself lucky to be here alive and well. I was onboard the Intrepid *... and as a matter of fact the last man to leave the engine room. We carried a number of mines, and when the engine room mine blew up I jumped overboard and swam. One of our cutters had already been blown to smithereens and it was with the help of others and some rafts, that we were saved.*[7]

Stoker Petty Officer Harold Palliser, together with Stoker Sidney Nicholls who succumbed to gas poisoning the day after the raid, were the only casualties from *Intrepid*. Married with a wife in London, Harold Palliser was killed by machine gun fire while in ML 282. Chief ERA Farrell witnessed Palliser's last moments. 'He was shot through the head by a German machine gun, after he had done his bit, and had been picked up.'[8]

Able Seaman Button remembered the evacuation, 'Once we were aboard we had to fight our way out, which was a harder task than going in. The smoke and gas were still very strong, and a piece of debris caught me in the left knee.'[9]

Above left: Aerial view of the blockships at Zeebrugge. Q49164: photograph courtesy of the Imperial War Museum.

Above right: Aerial view of *Intrepid* (bottom right) and *Iphigenia* (top left) blocking the Zeebrugge Canal.

HMS *Intrepid* blocking the Bruges Canal, taken from the western bank. The image shows how narrow the canal entrance was and one can appreciate the danger encountered by the crews of the blockships and the motor launches designated to evacuate their crews. For where this photograph was taken there would have been German soldiers and sailors firing rifles at the crews. It is a wonder that so many men were recovered from the sunken ships.

HMS *Iphigenia* blocking the Bruges Canal. The breach caused by HM Submarine C3 can be seen in the background.

This unique image taken from the east bank shows all three blockships, *Intrepid*, *Iphigenia* and *Thetis*. The photograph was taken at low water and shows that it was impossible for any German vessel to pass through the canal entrance. However, the visible high water mark on the sloping quayside to the right of the picture indicates that during high tide there was sufficient draught for a vessel to pass through this narrow channel despite the obstructions.

Where HM Ships *Iphigenia* and *Intrepid* blocked the Bruges Canal, taken from the eastern bank of Zeebrugge sluices in 2004. Although the port has changed significantly since 1918, the slope of the bank is the same.

Iphigenia still had 12 surplus stokers onboard. They also had volunteered to stay onboard to participate in the fight, instead of transferring to another ship. *Iphigenia* passing close to *Thetis* was hit twice by enemy shellfire on her starboard side. One of those shells severed the siren steam-pipes, which resulted in the forward part of the vessel being enveloped in steam. This steam obstructed Lieutenant Billyard-Leakes' vision and he drifted off the correct bearing; *Iphigenia* was heading for the western pier instead of the canal entrance. Billyard-Leake corrected the course on realising his error, bringing the ship in between a dredger and a barge full steam ahead. He then went ahead starboard and forced the barge along the canal. Once the barge was clear, he saw *Intrepid* aground on the western bank of the canal. There was a gap between her bows and the eastern bank. German vessels could still pass through this canal so he brought *Iphigenia* ahead on both engines in an attempt to fill the gap. As he did so, *Iphigenia* collided with the port bow of *Intrepid*. Leading Seaman Edwards was the helmsman aboard *Iphigenia*. He recalled that just before reaching her intended position, *Iphigenia* struck a barge, where four German machine gunners were positioned. The collision took the barge away from her moorings.

Soon after the order for blowing the charges had been given, Engineer Mate Sidney West returned to the engine room to start the engines to ensure that when the charges exploded *Iphigenia* would be in the correct position to block the canal entrance. He did not leave the engine room until he received an order directly from Billyard-Leake. Once the charges were blown, the crew escaped in a single cutter and was rescued by Motor Launch 282. Sub Lieutenant Maurice Lloyd, who was supervising aft, retrieved the White Ensign before leaving *Iphigenia* and boarding the cutter.

Leading Seaman Albert Davis exhibited tremendous devotion to duty. Prior to the operation he was instructed to destroy his gun, and then proceed to the cutter to evacuate the vessel once the mines were blown. Davis did not receive the order to abandon ship and so remained at his post, even when all the crew had abandoned *Iphigenia* in the single cutter. He stayed with his gun until the vessel sank beneath him. At this point he jumped in the water and swam to the rescue boats. On his return home he was awarded the Conspicuous Gallantry Medal.

Once Leading Seaman Edwards had brought *Iphigenia* into position, his job as helmsman was complete, but he was not idle. 'I took up a rifle, pointed it at some figures which I took to be machine gunners on the jetty, and I believe I managed to get two of them.'[10] Edwards then headed for a cutter, but on realising that she was sinking took off his coat and boots and used them to try to plug the hole in the side. This gallant gesture proved futile and he was forced to swim to the other cutter. He was shot in the right arm, but reached the cutter.

Four motor launches were assigned the task of rescuing crews from the blockships, unfortunately ML 110 had been sunk and ML 128 had broken down, which left ML 282 and ML 526. They rescued 166 men in darkness and under hostile enemy fire. ML 526 commanded by Lieutenant Hugh Littleton braved close-range enemy fire to rescue sixty officers and men from *Thetis*. All five stokers from Australia were safely evacuated from *Thetis*. It took ten minutes to get the crew of *Thetis* into the motor launch. ML 526 was holed in three places and despite the overcrowding aboard, Littleton succeeded in evacuating the blockship crews. Littleton's DSO citation records 'It was solely due to his courage and daring that his boat succeeded in making good her escape with the survivors of the "Thetis".'[11]

ML 282 had sustained damage and was taking in water when the skiff carrying the crew of *Iphigenia* approached. They transferred to the damaged ML 282 which was designed to accommodate 50 people. Now it contained 101 men and was attracting enemy fire from the shore. Some men were still in the skiff, so Lieutenant Percy Dean, commanding ML 282, decided to attach the skiff to the stern. Dean had joined the Royal Naval Volunteer Reserve prior to the war so that he could indulge his love of sailing. His 'hobby' made him an accomplished seaman and this helped save many men at Zeebrugge. As they escaped they were hit by heavy machine-gun fire and shrapnel, which caused several casualties, including Sub Lieutenant Maurice Lloyd who was mortally wounded. He still held onto the White Ensign as his life ebbed away, the blood from his wounds staining the flag.

As they increased speed, they attracted further fire and sustained heavy casualties. The enemy fire subsided for a moment when a white flare was ignited in the harbour and attracted the fire. The escape party from *Intrepid* on a Carley float accidentally ignited this flare as they tried desperately to reach ML 282. Lieutenant Bonham-Carter and his party left the craft for the dubious refuge of the water at the canal entrance as enemy fire rained upon them. They swam into the harbour, blackened by thick oil. It was a miracle that the enemy fire did not ignite the oil and incinerate them. Lieutenant Dean had successfully manoeuvred ML 282 away from the harbour when the steering gear onboard jammed and he was forced to use his engines to steer. Dean saw these men stranded in the water, so he bravely turned the vessel around and exposed to heavy fire endeavoured to rescue Bonham-Carter and the crew from *Intrepid*. When Dean was confident that everyone was aboard he put his engines to stern, without knowing that Bonham-Carter was still in the water, holding onto a trailing rope. His arms could not take the strain, so he was forced to let go. As he watched ML 282 speed off he swam for the eastern pier of the canal. A German star shell revealed Bonham-Carter still in the water to Dean, who once again ventured back into the canal entrance to pick him up. As he brought ML 282 close to the Mole to avoid enemy fire his steering gear jammed again. As the heavily laden vessel sailed out of the harbour, many casualties were sustained from enemy machine gun fire from the Mole and coastal batteries. Leading Deck Hand George McKruly aboard ML 282 was killed and his position was taken by Leading Seaman Potter who had been evacuated from *Iphigenia*. McKruly had only recently married. Chief ERA Thomas Farrell remembered 'On one of the motor launches … I saw three men killed outright. The man at the wheel was shot down. Up jumped another to take his place, and he was shot down, and then another, and he was shot too.'[12]

They headed for HMS *Warwick*. Keyes was present when ML 282 came alongside. Both commanding officers from *Intrepid* and *Iphigenia* reported that they had sunk their vessels across the canal entrance. Keyes recalled that Billyard-Leake

Images taken of the blockships from various locations.

... might have stepped straight out of a military tailor's shop, equipped for the trenches, leather coat, shrapnel helmet all complete, very erect and absolutely unperturbed ... Bonham-Carter, bareheaded and dressed in a dirty wet vest and trousers – as he had been swimming in the canal in water covered with oil from the sunken blockships – made a good contrast.[13]

Amongst the wounded that were transferred from ML 282 was Sub Lieutenant Maurice Lloyd. Keyes remembered Lloyd who 'had begged for a place in one of the blockships after I had completed all the appointments.'[14] Fate had provided Lloyd an opportunity when he was appointed after Billyard-Leake replaced Lieutenant Franks, who was forced to withdraw from the operation with appendicitis. Lloyd had done his duty, now he lay dying aboard *Warwick*. Keyes:

Lloyd had the Iphigenia's *white ensign wrapped round his waist, and it was saturated with his blood. I think he knew that his number was up, but was perfectly happy and fearfully proud of having been able to bring away the ensign, which I told him he should keep.*[15]

The ensign still shows the bloodstains of this gallant man and is on display in the Dover Museum. Lloyd was taken to the hospital ship *Liberty* on arriving at Dover and hung on to life for another 24 hours.

Captain Carpenter wrote of the achievement of the blockship crews:

… the finest feat of all was the splendid display of seamanship in the face of extraordinary difficulty. The complete absence of local knowledge, the opposition of the enemy, and the unavoidable lack of practice in sinking vessels under such conditions all combined to make the task appear quite impracticable. Yet all difficulties were surmounted and the object of the operation was achieved.[16]

It is a miracle that anyone from the blockships' crews or the evacuation crews survived that night. To get the blockships and sink them in the intended position was one almighty task, but to safely leave was an achievement of another magnitude. It was Wing Commander Brock's smoke screen that made it possible for anyone to avoid death or capture. Chief Thomas Farrell who returned to his home in Chatham unscathed, knew it: 'It was undoubtedly the smoke screen which helped us wonderfully. The Germans, when once they found us there – for there's no doubt about it we caught them napping – sent up their star shells and then fired, but they could not see us because of the smoke.'[17]

NOTES

1. Imperial War Museum Department of Documents: Engineer Lieutenant Boddie papers IWM 96/47/1.
2. Ibid.
3. Stoker N. McCrory, Royal Australian Navy, HMAS *Australia* AWM Ref: 1 DRL 0429.
4. National Archives ADM 116/1656: Able Seaman Charles Jackson report.
5. Imperial War Museum Department of Documents: Engineer Lieutenant Boddie papers IWM 96/47/1.
6. Ibid.
7. *Chatham, Rochester & Gillingham News*, Saturday 27th April 1918.
8. Ibid.
9. *Halifax Courier*, 4th May 1918.
10. Philip Warner, *The Zeebrugge Raid*, p152: William Kimber, 1978.
11. *The London Gazette* No. 30807, 23rd July 1918.
12. *Chatham, Rochester & Gillingham News*, Saturday 27th April 1918.
13. Sir Roger Keyes, Admiral of the Fleet RN, *The Naval Memoirs 1916-1918*, p291: Thornton Butterworth Ltd, London, 1935.
14. Ibid, p259.
15. Ibid, p291.
16. Captain A F B Carpenter VC RN, *The Blocking of Zeebrugge*, p250: Herbert Jenkins Limited, London, 1925.
17. *Chatham, Rochester & Gillingham News*, Saturday 27th April 1918.

CHAPTER 10

THE RETIREMENT

It was arranged that the storming parties would be given twenty minutes notice of *Vindictive* leaving the Mole. They would be made aware of retirement through a succession of long and short blasts of the ship's siren, sounding the Morse letter K, or if the sirens were disabled the searchlight beams would be directed in a defined manner. As previously described, the upper structure and funnels of *Vindictive* were repeatedly hit by enemy fire as she was rolling and plunging against the Mole. Casualties were increasing rapidly and all the guns that could have fired upon the Mole were put out of action. If *Daffodil* was sunk then *Vindictive* would be unable to remain alongside and would drift uncontrollably from the Mole and the raiders would not be able to embark during the retirement. Since the assault upon the Mole had successfully distracted enemy batteries and the blockships had passed, the decision was taken to signal the withdrawal. The *Vindictive*'s sirens had been shot away during the assault and the port and starboard searchlights had been disabled. Captain Carpenter was compelled to order *Daffodil* to sound the retirement signal at 12.50 a.m. The signal denoting retirement should have been the Morse code letter K, which would have been a series of successive short blasts, but the siren on *Daffodil* was damaged and confusingly sounded long and short blasts. Petty Officer Harry Adams compared the sound of the *Daffodil*'s siren to a 'tin whistle'[1] and was surprised that any of the raiders on the Mole could hear it.

As a result of the fact that *Vindictive* had berthed four hundred yards from the intended position, the fortified zone, including the 4-inch battery at the end of the Mole, had not been captured. Chater and Captain Bamford decided that an attempt must be made to secure this objective. It meant assaulting this strongly defended position across two hundred yards without cover. Captain Bamford assembled the remnants of Nos. 5, 7 and 8 Platoons that were under his command. No. 5 Platoon suffered many casualties as a result of their exposed position. Lieutenant Cooke was shot twice and after losing consciousness was carried back to the ship by Private John Press. As Captain Bamford started to advance along the Mole he must have known that his party of only sixteen men was not an adequate number to take on the position. Major Weller wrote that Bamford's 'disregard of danger showed a magnificent example to his men'.[2] At that moment the emergency recall signal, the Morse letter 'K', was heard. The intended duration of the diversionary assault on the Mole was one hour and a quarter. When the siren was sounded they had only been on the Mole for forty-five minutes and they had not captured the fortified sector. Captain Chater was not convinced that they should withdraw and returned to the conning tower of *Vindictive* to confirm with Captain Carpenter that the signal to retire had been given. Once he had confirmed the withdrawal he returned to the Mole wall to pass on the order. Private Jim Clist:

> I could see a German trawler or destroyer on the other side of the Mole. I should think she was thirty yards away. Some of our chaps were aboard. I think it was Lieutenant Lamplough's men. At times it was as light as day with searchlights, Very lights and star shells showing up all parts of the Mole.

Before the landing we were told that the recall signal would be when the searchlights played up and down the Mole, but apparently the searchlights were all out of action. The ship's siren was sounded and Major Weller told me to tell the men to retire back to the ship. I was on the raised part of the Mole and at different places I stopped and shouted to the men who were about sixteen feet below me. They had to climb rope ladders. They had their bayonets fixed and the man above often got his backside jabbed with the bayonets of the man below.

Captain Bamford, he got the VC and his company of Portsmouth marines were able to come up a gradual incline as they were on the tail end of the Mole. They did not have many casualties compared to Chatham and Plymouth Companies. Most of the Chatham casualties occurred before the landing. Captain Bamford's Company was the first to get back aboard Vindictive.[3]

The men of Captain Bamford's party returned back to *Vindictive* in twos. The gun battery at the end of the Mole was still operational and firing upon the British raiders.

Iris had failed to berth alongside the Mole so Commander Gibbs brought her alongside *Vindictive* in an effort to embark Royal Marines from A Company onto her so that they could land on the Mole. Private Beau Tracey later recalled: 'The Platoon Sergeant saying stand by to jump, jump for it … Well we made the jump for it we were only too eager. Instead of standing still doing nothing we were raring to go. We made the jump, we were on the *Vindictive*.'[4] After a few dozen got aboard, the evacuation siren could be heard and they did not make an attempt to land on the Mole.

Lieutenant Commander Adams ordered the remnants of the naval storming party to withdraw back along the parapet to *Vindictive*. Adams went in the opposite direction towards the Mole end to search for Lieutenant Commander Harrison's body, but was unsuccessful and returned to *Vindictive*. Although the naval landing party had failed to capture the 4.1-inch gun battery at the end of the Mole, their fire upon the position had succeeded in preventing the Germans from firing these guns on the blockships.

Dickinson and the remnants from his demolition team returned to *Vindictive* with unused explosives. This was a hazard to the vessel and the dangerous cargo was ditched into the sea. The wounded were assisted back aboard by the crew while the enemy bombarded the Mole ferociously with shells.

Surgeons Colson and Clegg landed on the Mole to render such medical assistance as they could. Many of the stretcher bearers that accompanied them were killed on the Mole. Able Seaman John Biglin loaded a Stokes mortar on the forecastle at the beginning of the raid. Once *Vindictive* was berthed he landed on the Mole to help in the evacuation of the wounded. Chaplain Charles Peshall carried the wounded from the Mole onto *Vindictive*. He dashed onto the Mole many times during that hour rescuing wounded men and carrying them aboard across the two unstable gangways. Prior to the War, Peshall had been an international rugby player. He had volunteered to accompany the raiding force and Keyes accepted him on the recommendation of Captain A Davidson, the commander of HMS *Hindustan* who considered 'He would be a spiritual force and a fighting force if you will let him'.[5] Peshall's DSO citation mentioned that he 'showed great physical strength and did almost superhuman work in carrying wounded from the Mole over the brows into *Vindictive*'.[6]

Able Seaman Cyril Widdison was one who got back:

The masonry of the Mole was ploughed by our shells and all the time a fierce fire was concentrated on our ship, which represented our only hope of a safe return. Just after one o'clock the retreat was sounded, and those of us who were here ran breathlessly back – ran for our lives amid a hail of shot and shell. Of 14 or 15 landing ladders only two remained and they creaked and bent ominously as 300 or 400 of us scrambled aboard. Some of us were helping the wounded comrades along: and whilst other fellows had to be carried aboard. I found one poor lad lying helplessly on the shore, only a few yards from the gangway, and with a pal's assistance I managed to get him safely on board. The scene both on deck and below was too awful to describe, and I am trying to forget it.[7]

Air Mechanic Gough used his revolver on three Germans who were trying to sabotage the ladders. Afterwards Gough also managed to help wounded men back to the *Vindictive*.

Captain Chater stood on the Mole alongside the *Vindictive*'s berth observing the withdrawal. Some men who passed him thought that he was wounded and tried to transfer him aboard. Captain John Palmer who was promoted to command C Company (Plymouth Company) stayed on the Mole to help the wounded back on board. Major Weller, now in command of the battalion, mentioned Palmer in his report. 'His total disregard of his own safety, was of the greatest assistance during the retirement in helping men to return to the ship. He refused to leave the Mole while any of his men were left there, and it is probably on this account that he is missing.'[8] Private Clist, however, had a different story to tell of Captain Palmer's conduct on the Mole:

A chap who was a Lewis gunner in my section came from Yeovil in Somerset. He was called Taylor. He was trying to get a man on his shoulders who was badly wounded. Someone came along and helped him to carry the man aboard. I was told that he also carried my mate Freeman aboard, but he was dead when he got him aboard. That was the chap who gave me a lock of his hair, which I kept for several months. Most of the men had got back aboard and I was anxiously watching Major Weller hoping he would do the same. He eventually did so. As soon as we were aboard Major Weller told me to find out if Captain Palmer was aboard. I went several places stepping over dead and wounded men making enquiries, but no one had seen him aboard, but someone had seen him on the Mole before they came aboard. I told Major Weller, he said he would go and look for him. He did not ask me to go with him, but I felt under an obligation to do so, also I knew better than the Major, where to find Captain Palmer from the information I got aboard. As soon as we stepped on the Mole I left the Major and made for the place where I was almost sure he would be if still alive. I found him. He was leaning over the raised part of the Mole shining his torch on the rope ladder, which his men were expected to come up. I gave him Major Weller's message. Judging by his speech he had far too much to drink. He said his men were down there and that he would not come without them. That may sound very brave words to some, but to me they were just stupid words coming from a man who had too much to drink and it reminded me of the previous message I gave him when we was training at Deal. He also had too much to drink then. I got back to Major Weller and told him that Captain Palmer had refused to come without his men.[9]

It is recorded in Major Weller's report on the raid that Private William Hopewell (from Plymouth Company) was the last man to retire from the Mole. When the No.1 and No.2 of his machine gun party became casualties on *Vindictive*, Hopewell brought the Lewis gun onto the Mole and continued to fire it throughout the operation until it received a direct hit and was rendered useless. Lieutenant Lamplough reported that to his knowledge his party from the Plymouth Company was the last to leave the Mole. Once Chater could see that no more men were returning he went onboard to report that fact, at which point the *Vindictive* slipped her berth for the journey home. One unidentified Royal Marine officer recalled, 'When we got back on board, the upper deck of *Vindictive* presented a horrible sight. It was absolute chaos. The upper decks were slippery with blood, and all around lay dying and wounded.'[10]

Captain Carpenter was anxious not to leave anyone behind on the Mole and waited for stragglers to get aboard. At 1.05 a.m. Carpenter was informed that no further members of the storming party were boarding. Carpenter waited another five minutes. At 1.10 a.m. Carpenter ordered *Daffodil* to tow her off the Mole. The hawser broke, but *Vindictive* was pulled clear away from the Mole so that she was able to sail off under her own steam. Two seamen were observed by Colour Sergeant Camfield planting the Union Jack on the end of the Mole as *Vindictive* headed home.[11] Though Carpenter denies this in his account.[12] Corporal George Moyse was fortunate to get aboard *Vindictive* as she left the Mole:

> *I nearly got left behind. I jumped for the gangway just as* Vindictive *was shearing off. And it was not until we were half way back to England that I realized that I'd been wounded. That shows what excitement will do.*[13]

NOTES

1. Petty Officer Harry Adams Papers.
2. National Archives ADM 137/3894: Major Weller's Report.
3. Private Jim Clist interview, courtesy David Clist.
4. Private Ernest (Beau) Tracey interview. Courtesy of Richard Davison.
5. Sir Roger Keyes, Admiral of the Fleet RN, *The Naval Memoirs 1916-1918*, p221: Thornton Butterworth Ltd, London, 1935.
6. *The London Gazette*, 23rd July 1918.
7. *Nottingham Journal & Express*, 30th April 1918, Page 3.
8. National Archives ADM 137/3894: Major Weller's Report.
9. Private Jim Clist interview, courtesy David Clist.
10. *Hampshire Telegraph & Post*, Friday 26th April 1918.
11. H.H.R.Camfield's account in *The Zeebrugge Raid*, Philip Warner, p133: William Kimber, 1978.
12. Captain A F B Carpenter VC RN, *The Blocking of Zeebrugge*, p254: Herbert Jenkins Limited, London, 1925.
13. Corporal George Moyse interview. Courtesy Peter White.

CHAPTER 11

PRISONERS OF WAR

There was a fateful moment of confusion on the Mole for Sergeant Wright and his unit when they thought they heard the siren from the *Daffodil*:

> We took it for the signal to retire and commenced doing so when the order was passed that it was not the retire signal and we were ordered back to our posts. We obeyed the order, and very shortly afterwards we had the terrible ordeal of seeing our only means of escape slowly move away. The Vindictive *had left, thinking that everyone was on board! … We were two hundred yards from the ship when she moved off, and in addition there was the twenty-foot wall to climb.*[1]

Sergeant Wright and the remnants of No.10 Platoon had survived this great ordeal only to be abandoned at the last. Shells from German batteries and from Royal Naval Monitors were falling upon the Mole. They lay on the ground where they remained for two hours, pretending to be dead. They were hopeful that someone would realise that they were missing and send a small craft to rescue them. With their swimming belts inflated they were prepared to jump from the Mole into the sea if a motor launch returned to pick them up. During the two hours they waited for rescue, star shells were falling upon them, burning two of the men. Their hopes were dashed when a patrol of German soldiers led by Lieutenant MaBmann searched the Mole.

Lieutenant MaBmann and his Company were staying at the Palasthotel in Zeebrugge that night. Once the alarm was raised, he was ordered to take a boat with sailors to the Mole, and concentrate on the marine aircraft facility. On arriving at the Mole it was discovered that the fuses in the patrol's hand grenades were missing and they had to return to the shore to get them. MaBmann returned to the Mole with two sailors and a naval officer. They could see that the British raiders were in retreat. Searching the wreckage left on the Mole they met many German sailors who had been unharmed during the raid. They then proceeded to search the end of the Mole along the parapet. They found many dead British sailors and Royal Marines. MaBmann met with a patrol sent by Kapitänleutnant Schutte. The patrol approached to shine torches in the faces of the Marines who feigned death. Half an hour later the party returned with bayonets fixed to search the dead bodies; one of the Marines moved and the startled Germans discovered them. It was a very tense and uncertain moment as the Germans, with nerves strained to the breaking point, stepped back pointing their guns towards them: the abandoned Marines were still armed and could still resist. Sergeant Wright:

> What could we do, some of the men wanted to fight it out or to put it in R.M. language one of the men said 'Let's have a bash at the b*****ds. They'll kill us whatever happens. Yes, what could we do, a battery of guns and machine guns behind us, the sea on either side of us and a large force of Germans in front of us, caught like rats in a concrete trap.*[2]

No one pulled a trigger on either side; a German soldier who could speak good English defused the situation, saying 'The game is up lads. Play the game, and we will play the game with you. Lay down your arms and put your hands up. We will not harm you.'[3] The invitation to surrender was accepted and further bloodshed was averted. Sergeant Wright gave the order to put rifles on the ground and as they obeyed his command, the survivors stood to attention as one man. MaBmann took the rifle from Captain Palmer. Sergeant Wright was one of three NCOs who was captured on the Mole together with Captain Palmer, two sergeants, one corporal and ten privates. They all belonged to No. 9 and No. 10 Platoons, C Company from Plymouth. They had been ordered to cover the withdrawal on the Mole to the last, which they had done.

Once they had been searched for weapons and useful documentation for intelligence they were held in a concrete shelter on the Mole. They were guarded by one soldier and held there until further reinforcements arrived. There were two wounded men amongst the prisoners and the Germans ensured that they were taken to hospital to receive medical attention. When reinforcements arrived the dejected prisoners were escorted further along the Mole to the aeroplane sheds. As they were marched along they were ridiculed by a large number of German soldiers and sailors. One German sailor said 'Look, we sink three big English ships in our harbour. Very good German gunfire.'[4] Sergeant Wright wrote,

Looking round we could see our blockships nicely sunk in the entrance of the canal – but not by German gunfire. Their funnels were showing above water; the dredger was also sunk in the fairway. 'Yes, very good German gunfire', we replied, and laughed in turn, but we were soon checked by our guards.[5]

On arriving at the aeroplane shed there was a commotion when British aeroplanes flew over the Mole. These planes were probably on a reconnaissance sortie to assess whether the operation to block the canal entrance had succeeded. There was a further disturbance when angry German soldiers passed through the escort guarding the prisoners and started to berate them. They had found on the Mole a stunning mallet; they knew its brutal purpose and wanted to use it upon the British prisoners in retribution. Fortunately, two German officers arrived to control the situation and the prisoners were unharmed. These officers were most courteous and praised the raiders for their courage. They were hospitable too, bringing hot coffee for them to drink. Sergeant Wright wanted to reciprocate their kindness by offering to detonate the Mills bombs that were lying on the Mole, but they declined his offer, as the Germans had technical knowledge of the workings of these bombs.

At 9 a.m. Sergeant Wright and his fellow prisoners were paraded in front of a camera. The photograph appeared in German newspapers and great propaganda capital was made of it. This photograph appeared in the *Daily Mail* five weeks later. It brought comfort to families at home who discovered that their missing loved ones were not dead. It showed ten prisoners: Sergeant Harry Wright, Sergeant William Taylor, Private Samuel Hopson, Private Ernest Wreford, Private Herbert Hurn, Private Gerald Graham, Private Thomas Middleton, Private Alfred Yeoman, Private Alfred Becquet and Able Seaman Aloysius Smyth. Corporal Harry Sales, Private George Mann and Able Seaman Harold Eves were not in the picture because they were wounded and taken to hospital.

In addition, four sailors were captured in a Carley float while trying to escape after the *North Star* was sunk. They were Engine Room Artificer Robert North, Stoker Frank Johnston, Wireless Petty Officer Leslie Smith and Signalman Kenneth Neville. Smith and Neville were wounded and taken to hospital.

The prisoners were then taken to Zeebrugge. As they were escorted along the Mole they saw the extent of the damage made by C3 upon the viaduct that connected the Mole to the mainland. There was a 30-yard breach where the viaduct once stood. Girders and railway lines were twisted and entangled. A primitive wire bridge had been put in place to cover the gap. As the prisoners walked across this bridge it swayed from side to side. A German motor boat stood by in case someone fell into the sea. As Sergeant Wright waited his turn to cross the bridge a German Captain consoled him. 'I am sorry you are captured now, for we know you had a hard time out there.'[6]

Ten of the 16 men of the assault party who were captured during the Zeebrugge raid. They were to spend the remainder of the war as prisoners of war. Sergeant Wright from No.10 Platoon is standing second from right in the front row. Sergeant William Taylor from No.9 Platoon stands next to Wright. Private Gerald Graham from No.10 Platoon is holding his puttees, third from left. Able Seaman Aloysius Smyth stands second from left, next to the private with his arm in a sling. He was the only sailor from the storming party to be captured. Smyth had served on the battlecruiser HMS *Tiger* from October 1914 until he volunteered for the Zeebrugge raid on 18th February. During his service aboard *Tiger* he had seen action at the Battle of Dogger Bank on 24th January 1915 when the vessel received hits from six German shells, killing ten sailors. He was also present when *Tiger* took part in the Battle of Jutland on 31st May 1916 when fifteen 11-inch shells struck her killing 24 men and 46 wounded casualties. When he was released from the German POW Camp after the war he continued to serve with Royal Navy until May 1923, when he was invalided out due to mental instability. His experiences during the First World War must have been the cause of his mental state and his suffering years after the war had ended. Private Samuel Hopson from No.9 Platoon stands behind Able Seaman Smyth, back row, second left. Hopson would continue to serve in the Royal Marines until June 1935. (Q49204: courtesy of the Imperial War Museum)

This picture of Captain Palmer being brought before Kaiser Wilhelm II featured in the *Daily Mirror* on 21st January 1919 with the headline 'Officer Refuses War Lord's Hand'. Sergeant Wright who was captured along with Captain Palmer described the moment when the Kaiser offered his hand to the prisoner, but Palmer stood rigidly to attention. Kaiser Wilhelm mentioned this meeting in a correspondence to General Ludendorff. He stated that Captain Palmer made an impression on him.

Kaiser Wilhem and Admiral von Schröder inspecting the Mole at Zeebrugge on 23rd April 1918.

Kaiser Wilhelm II and Admiral Von Schröder inspecting the blockships during the morning of 23rd April.

On approaching the town of Zeebrugge the prisoners could see the effects of the explosion caused by C3. Buildings had doors blown in and windows broken. Glass, displaced bricks and masonry littered the streets. At Zeebrugge that they met the two British prisoners ERA Robert North and Stoker Frank Johnston, captured from HMS *North Star*. During the night of the raid Kaiser Wilhelm II was by coincidence near to Zeebrugge. At 11.30 a.m. the Kaiser was in Zeebrugge and during that morning of 23rd April he and his entourage visited the Mole to inspect the damage. During this visit he questioned Captain Palmer. Sergeant Wright:

Field Marshal von Hindenburg and Von Schröder on the Mole after the raid.

The Kaiser came down to Zeebrugge that day, but we did not have a very good view of him. He interviewed the captain who was captured with us, and after complimenting him on the pluck shown by all ranks, gave orders that the men who were captured were to be treated well all the time they were prisoners of war. He then offered to shake hands with the captain, but the officer stood rigidly to attention and ignored the proffered hand. The Kaiser had a strong bodyguard, and on the motor-cars accompanying him machine-guns were mounted.[7]

Despite Captain Palmer's defiance, the Kaiser regarded him with respect. Kaiser Wilhelm mentioned this meeting in a correspondence with General Ludendorff. He said Captain Palmer made an impression on him and when he informed the prisoner of the outcome of the raid, Palmer replied 'I took a sporting chance, but failed. Chance of war.'[8] Captain Palmer was well respected by the NCOs and men that he commanded. He had already received a DSC that had been gazetted on 23rd March 1917 for his part in the landings in Athens in December 1916. During the Zeebrugge raid Palmer refused to leave the Mole until all his men were aboard *Vindictive*. As we have seen, according to Private Jim Clist's testimony Palmer was under the influence of drink. However, no one can deduce from this that Palmer was anything but a brave man. Everyone who made landfall at Zeebrugge was. To be drunk on duty in charge of men cannot be acceptable, but if he was, it was surely Palmer's way to alleviate the stresses and anxieties of leadership in wartime.

At 6 p.m. the POWs were taken to Bruges by boat along the canal. As they were marched through the streets of Bruges their spirits were raised when Belgian civilians waving handkerchiefs greeted them. The Belgians congratulated them with the words 'Well done, England', and 'Brave British heroes'. They were escorted to the German Naval Intelligence Headquarters in Bruges, near to the town square. The Provincial Court near to the Belfry in the town centre was the headquarters of the German Intelligence Staff. Here they were interrogated. The Germans were convinced that a Belgian pilot had guided the *Vindictive* through the German minefields to Zeebrugge and Sergeant Wright was asked for the identity of this person. While being interrogated Wright was unable to pass on the misinformation that they were ordered to pass if they were captured. The chance convincingly to suggest that the Merchant Navy had the technology to detect German submarines within a two-mile radius and that the Royal Navy had captured German U-boats and were using them as decoys never arose during the interrogation.

Despite the Kaiser's orders that the British POWs were to be treated well, while they were incarcerated in Bruges Prison for seven days they received brutal treatment from their captors before being transferred to POW Camps in Germany, where they remained until the Armistice.

It was not until the end of June 1918 that Wright had the opportunity to convey the misleading intelligence that Captain Carpenter had instructed them to pass on if they were captured. The chance arose when he was transferred to Dulman Camp, Germany. During a routine interrogation while at this camp he found the right moment to misinform the enemy, when the German officer said 'Don't worry, our submarines will win the war for us.'

> At that very moment Admiral Keyes's message flashed to my mind. I staggered back to the desk, for I was weak from standing, and said to the Officers:
> 'Your submarines, Sir, will not win the war. We are capturing and sending them back to sea again as 'Decoys', and I also told them about the Merchant Ships. To this day I can visualize their staring eyes and sagging jaws as they looked at me in amazement.
> 'Is this true?' asked the senior officer.
> 'Surely you know about this, Sir', I replied, 'If you don't know your Intelligence Department in Berlin will be well aware of the fact. It was general knowledge, amongst our Naval personnel at Plymouth and Devonport before I left England.'
> 'Thank you very much, sergeant,' said the Senior Officer. They don't know in Berlin but they soon will do,' and looking hard at me for a moment he continued 'You know, Sergeant, a little co-operation from you and you can have preferential treatment during your captivity'. He gave me the loaf of bread and a handful of cigars. Adopting a frightened attitude I said in all humility to the officers 'Perhaps I should not have told you about your submarines. Will you be good enough not to bring my name into this matter please. I don't want to get into trouble when I get home.'
> 'That shall be attended to', said the Officer. 'You have nothing to worry about.'
> 'Thank you very much, Sir,' I replied, mentally adding 'You blasted German swines.'[9]

On their return Sergeant Wright was awarded the Distinguished Service Medal and Captain Palmer received a bar to the Distinguished Service Cross. Owing to undernourishment during captivity Captain John Palmer died shortly after the War.

NOTES

1. Sergeant Wright, Royal Marines Museum Arch 11/12/1(2).
2. Sergeant Wright, Royal Marines Museum Arch 11/12/5(5).
3. Sergeant Wright Royal Marines Museum Arch 10/2/W.
4. Ibid.
5. Ibid.
6. Ibid.
7. Ibid.
8. Bundesarchiv BA-MA, RM 120/275 P22.
9. Sergeant Wright, Royal Marines Museum Arch 11/12/5(5).

CHAPTER 12

THE PASSAGE HOME

The high wall on the Mole had partially protected the three vessels *Vindictive*, *Iris* and *Daffodil* while they were berthed alongside, but as soon as they left the Mole they were bombarded heavily by shellfire before they disappeared into the fog of Brock's smoke screen. Aboard *Iris* Major Charles Eagles commanding A Company from Chatham had given the order 'All Marines below' to clear the deck to ensure that they did not obstruct sailors in their work as they left the Mole. Ordinary Seaman O'Hara:

> Before leaving all hands were ordered below, unfortunately most of the men when they went below stopped on the starboard side; as we were port side to when we turned around the starboard side was exposed to the enemy, we then came under a heavy fire whether from destroyers or shore batteries I do not know, several shots entered the starboard side doing great execution among the densely packed men; half the bridge was shot away and a fire was started near our Stokes gun ammunition, fortunately this fire was soon got under control.[1]

Ten small shells and two large shells struck the *Iris*. It was thought that some of these shells were fired from the Goeben battery situated east of the Bruges canal. An 11-inch shell penetrated the funnel and exploded on the port side of the bridge where everyone became a casualty, including Captain Valentine Gibbs and Major Charles Eagles. Commander Gibbs lost both his legs and was mortally wounded. Lieutenant George Spencer, the navigating officer took command of *Iris*, but soon he too was seriously wounded when his right leg was shattered. Lieutenant Willie Sillitoe, the commander of the machine gun section aboard was killed when he received a machine gun bullet in the head. Acting Sergeant Budd took charge of the section when Sillitoe fell.

Then, a savage, almost unimaginable blow: a second 11-inch shell hit the deck and killed about 50 men and injured scores more. The situation was so desperate that Petty Officer Warrington aged 19 took refuge under the pile of dead and wounded men that lay on the blood-soaked deck. (The Press Bureau the next day gave the number killed by this single shell as 49.)

Lance Corporal George Calverley was obeying Major Eagle's final order to go below decks when the German shells struck with such terrible effect. He recalled this moment in a letter to his granddaughter Vivienne 61 years later:

> I have never been able to describe to your Father or to your Uncle Ron what happened next due to a silly emotional lump which would rise in my throat, but I may be able to write about it. Being a ferryboat there was a wide staircase to the deck below down which we descended, I stood with my back to the ship's side and facing me about 3 ft away and a little to my left was one of my section. Even after 61 years I can remember what I said to him, it was 'Well Cornforth, the worse is over, and now it's a matter of getting home – where are the others?' He opened his lips to answer, gave a gasp and fell forward at my feet. At the same instant I sensed something had come through the ship's side near my left shoulder. I bent down towards him and woke up about 5 yards from where we had

been standing. That is the only way I can describe what happened and I did not know how long I had been 'OUT'. I was on my side and was scared, then happy as I gradually moved my limbs and stood up and as my hearing came back, I could hear moaning and cries of pain and someone yell 'Put that light out', you see we were in darkness except for an occasional electric blue light bulb which gave just a glimmer of light. Finding I could walk I made my way to where I had been standing, stepping over the wounded and at the bottom of the staircase was a heap of dead and dying in a terribly bloody state. I felt a bit sore but went on deck and in the very dim light I found similar conditions there. We were moving very slowly and on looking back I could not see the Mole, nor could I see 'Vindictive' or the 'Daffodil', they were, I hoped, on their way back to England.[2]

Private William Cornforth, the man Calverley was talking to standing three feet away, was killed by the blast.

The shells that hit *Iris* caused a fire amongst the ammunition and bombs; Lieutenant Oscar Henderson with a hose led a fire party to extinguish the flames on the upper deck. Once the fire was put out, Henderson assumed command of *Iris*. While on the deck he saw the considerable damage to the bridge. He dashed to the bridge where he found Gibbs, whom he thought was dead. Petty Officer David Smith had remained at his post on the bridge, despite being dangerously exposed to enemy fire. With him were Commander Valentine Gibbs and Lieutenant George Spencer, both mortally wounded. Gibbs had his legs blown off and Spencer was suffering from a shattered leg. Spencer, despite his wounds, refused to be relieved and remained by the compass conning the ship until Lieutenant Henderson took command. Petty Officer Smith steered the ship with one hand, while using the other to navigate a course by lighting the compass with a torch in the other hand. This physically and mentally challenging feat won for Smith the Conspicuous Gallantry medal.

Ordinary Seaman O'Hara later wrote of the carnage that he saw on the decks of *Iris* as she limped back home to Dover. 'When we were able to strike a light and see the extent of our damage a terrible sight met our eyes, amidships men were piled five and six deep dead on top of the wounded and dying, I believe very few in the starboard side escaped.'[3]

Artificer Engineer William Edgar from the Royal Australian Navy worked for seventeen hours in the hot engine room of *Iris* during the operation. It was Edgar, accompanied by Engine Room Artificer Odam who bravely ventured onto the upper deck to turn on the smoke apparatus to initiate the smoke screen. He was exposed to heavy enemy fire and it was his courageous initiative that allowed *Iris* to escape and return to England under her own steam. Edgar's actions had saved the ship and its crew and his efforts were recognised when he was awarded the Distinguished Service Cross; the only man from the Royal Australian Navy to receive this award.

Able Seaman Ferdinand Lake was another Conspicuous Gallantry recipient who was a member of the Royal Naval landing party. When *Iris* sustained hits from enemy shellfire he was proactive in trying to extinguish the flames under the fore bridge with sand. He was exposed to severe enemy fire and to ensure that Stokes and Mills bombs stored on the deck were not ignited by these flames he picked these extremely hot objects up and threw them overboard. Once the *Iris* had reached the safety of the smoke screen he took the wheel and acted as quartermaster for six hours during the return passage home.

Lieutenant Commander Lionel Chappell commanding Motor Launch 558 assisted *Iris* in her retirement from the Mole by releasing a smoke screen. During this process the Motor Launch was damaged by shellfire. As *Iris* departed the battle the first signal that was sent from her bridge was 'For God's sake send some doctors, I have a shipload of dead and dying.'[4] Surgeon Frank Pocock was attached to the Royal Marines and the majority of his medical team was wiped out. Pocock was left with the daunting task of tending to over a hundred wounded men without assistance. He had to resort to working by candle and torchlight because the dynamo was damaged. Survivors aboard made efforts to help the wounded including Lance Corporal George Calverley: 'Those of us who were able did our best for the wounded, which was very little unfortunately due to the darkness and the severity of the injuries caused by shrapnel.'[5] Pocock worked unaided for several hours before Surgeon A. Green from the Monitor *Erebus* and Surgeon S. Grimwade from the Monitor *Terror*, who had been sent to the *Iris*, supported him. Pocock worked for thirteen hours and was still tending to the wounded when *Iris* arrived in Dover at 2.45 p.m. By his untiring effort he saved many lives and was awarded the Distinguished Service Order.

Signalman Thomas Bryant, known as Tubby, was stationed on the port side of the bridge. He was one of the many casualties caused by the impact of the shell, his legs being shattered. Tubby Bryant laid wounded on the deck of *Iris* as she proceeded towards Dover. He was brought down to the sick bay to receive medical attention, but when it was apparent that he was the only surviving signaller, he insisted on being brought to the top deck so that he could send signals when required. Bryant was suffering considerable pain but he continued to answer signals that were being received. For his devotion to duty he was awarded the Conspicuous Gallantry medal.

As *Warwick* approached *Iris* during the early hours she sent the signal; 'Who are you?' Tubby demanded an officer who was looking at other wounded with a torch to give him the torch. Tubby replied with the signal 'S.O.S. We are the *Iris*'. Then he collapsed and lost consciousness. The next time he opened his eyes he was in hospital. The *Iris* would return to Dover later that morning with 77 dead and 105 wounded onboard.

Private Baker was one lucky fellow for while onboard *Iris* his life was saved in the traditional, usually fictional manner, when a bullet penetrated his left pocket. The bullet was stopped by his cigarette case.

Daffodil ran the gauntlet of German shells as she left the Mole and sailed towards Dover. Petty Officer Cownie had been steering the vessel since 11.00 p.m. and remained at his post until 4.00 a.m. Harry Adams remembered looking to seaward as they headed home and 'every gun the Germans could muster was setting up a murderous "barrage" through which we had to pass – huge mountains of water spurted up everywhere.'[6]

Arrival of HMS *Daffodil IV* and *Iris II* at New Brighton.

Above left: HMS *Iris II*. Shell hole into aft cabin through deck.

Above right: Iris II. Large hole in her side, made by a heavy shell.

Iris II, main deck. The deadliest place to be.

Under the blazing enemy guns, Petty Officer Arnold ventured onto the upper deck to release the valve on the smoke apparatus. Harry Adams stripped off his clothes in case he had to abandon ship following a direct hit. The order was given to dump all ammunition over board. Harry Adams accompanied by Able Seamen Bernard Devlin and Tom Bradley volunteered to go down into the hold to remove the explosives and dump them into the sea. The danger receded once *Daffodil* sailed into the smokescreen and away from Zeebrugge.

Volunteers were sought to go down into the stokehold and relieve the exhausted stokers. Men like Bernard Devlin, who had stormed the Mole and Harry Adams volunteered to go down below to help. There was much work to be done. Water had to be pumped out of the hold, which was previously flooded in order to extinguish a fire that had broken out. As men lay dying on *Daffodil*, Lieutenant Campbell who received a serious wound to his eye refused to leave the bridge until they were safely away from the Mole. Command of the vessel passed to Sub Lieutenant Hegarty, who brought the Mersey ferry boat away from *Vindictive* with the assistance of navigator Lieutenant Rogers.

Able Seaman Devlin described Campbell as 'a man with six hearts'.[7]

> With blood streaming over his face he was at last led below, but gallant fellow that he was he would not give in … I looked in a cabin, where I saw Lieutenant Campbell. Blood trickling down his cheeks and a bandage round his damaged eye and forehead. He was seated at the table and was calmly smoking a cigarette. He smiled at the boy, and then called out, 'And this is an end to a perfect day.'[8]

In comparison to the awful casualties sustained by *Iris*, there were few casualties aboard *Daffodil*: one dead and eight wounded. The body of the only fatal casualty, Able Seaman Ralph Carpenter, aged 17, was apparently sewn in a hammock and a service was read before his body was committed to the sea. However, according to Petty Officer Harry Adams, Campbell the commander did not have the heart to bury the man at sea, so he was brought home for burial.

Deck of the *Iris*, where Lieutenant Henderson led the fire party before assuming command.

As *Vindictive* slipped from the Mole at 16 knots, she took a quarter of a ton of masonry and concrete debris with her as a souvenir of her visit. One large fragment was found lodged between the vessel and a fender. This is now on display at the Imperial War Museum. Leading Seaman Dowell, after assisting his wounded colleagues to safety, had returned to the 6-inch gun on the port side where he and other survivors fired a few rounds. He managed to secure a small piece of the Mole to take home to his wife. Jim Clist was wounded when two pieces of shrapnel penetrated his body above his left lung, before he assaulted the Mole, but performed his duty as Major Weller's runner unaware of his wound. It was not until *Vindictive* left the Mole that he realized that he had been wounded.

> The *Vindictive* was moving, but quite a lot of the ship was still against the Mole when we got aboard. It must have been ten minutes before we got clear. Someone had pointed to my tunic which had several jagged tears and a wet patch near my breast pocket. I took it off and found my shirt was sticking from congealed blood. I remembered ten minutes before the landing when I thought that something the size of a brick had hit me. It was not too bad but I got a pricking sensation near the left collar bone sometimes when I used my left arm.[9]

Lieutenant Dickinson and a party of men frantically discharged the baskets containing the surplus gelignite and fuses into the sea. Dickinson ensured they were thrown overboard before shells hit the explosives and cause further damage. Captain Carpenter described the scene as *Vindictive* left the Mole:

> The enemy cannot have seen much more than the vivid glare of our funnel flames illuminating the upper part of the fog. From all accounts their batteries were far from idle. As the ship sped seaward we had the sensation of the ship jumping at irregular but frequent intervals. This may have been due to the concussion of heavy shell striking the water near the ship. Whether any shell hit us or not during the retirement is unlikely to be known. One could hardly see one's own feet. The ship had already been hit so often that any further damage of the same description would hardly have been noticed. Suffice it to say that no vital damage to the hull was received.[10]

During this time Private Feeney was assisting the wounded from the deck of *Vindictive* to safety below decks. 'When we were at last moving things got worse. A gas-shell burst near me, and I could not find my mask. I fell on a dead man, and put on his. We kept huddled up in little groups on the deck with our dead all around us until the first streaks of dawn.'[11]

As *Vindictive* departed from the Mole the vessel was hit by two shells forward in the canteen and issuing room. Two men were killed outright by the explosions. There were no marks on their bodies, despite their clothes being shredded. One shell devastated the sick bay. Lieutenant Lamplough remembered, 'The ship was a shambles both on the upper deck and below, with doctors and every available individual doing their best to help the wounded.'[12] Leading Seaman Childs found some dressings as they searched the wreckage of the sick bay. 'We then went along the battery and found an old Marine Bugler with his leg smashed, and hanging by the sinew. We could do practically nothing, except for put on a tourniquet above the knee and cut his leg off with a knife. It was a rather unpleasant job – but what else could we do?'[13]

There were at least three casualties in each cabin and the doctors' efforts to tend to their wounds were restricted by lack of space. Engineer Commander William Bury onboard later wrote:

> We had no room to separate out the dead from amongst the living, so thickly were they packed. At daybreak the upper deck was a dreadful sight; truncated remains, sand bags, blackened corpses, represented the howitzer and Stokes gun crews. All but one were blown to bits in the fore top, where they did such good work with their pom-poms.[14]

During the raid, shells had penetrated the fresh water tanks, which made the huge task of tending to the wounded even harder. There were a hundred bottles of water stored onboard and they were given to the wounded. When this supply of the only water onboard was all gone, rum was issued to the wounded and those who needed a drink.

Lieutenant Commander Rosoman continued to act as a lookout and refused medical attention despite being shot through each leg. With the exception of the compass in the conning tower, all other compasses onboard were destroyed. The starboard telegraph was inoperable, although communication to the engine room via telephone was maintained.

During the journey home survivors looked for friends. Leading Seaman Childs tried to look for men from his section, No.1, B Company. He found the wounded McKenzie who was suffering from shrapnel wounds to his back and a smashed right foot. Able Seaman White was suffering from a shrapnel wound to the head, while Able Seaman Thomas Orman had lost an arm during the raid. Leading Seaman Merryweather lost an ear to a bullet. Lieutenant Chamberlain had been killed and Lieutenant Walker had lost an arm. Others were suffering from minor wounds. He could account for everyone in No. 1, 1 Platoon, B Company except for Able Seaman Everest. While he was searching the debris of shrapnel, twisted steel and masonry from the Mole he found the body of Everest, who had been killed by a bullet through the forehead.

Stoker George Smith had worked continuously for eight hours from 8.00 p.m. to 4.00 a.m. that night. Working below decks they could hear the noise of battle taking place above them, but knew nothing of what was happening. At one point it was thought that German gas had penetrated into the stoke hold and respirators were hastily donned. Fortunately this was a false alarm because Brock's smoke screen was being sucked into lower decks by the fans. When Smith and his comrades were relieved, Captain Carpenter greeted them as they came on deck with 'Well done Stokers.'[15] At 5.30 a.m. as *Vindictive* sailed towards Dover she nearly struck a mine. She avoided it by altering course. The mine was exploded by motor launches using rifles.

On their return home, some of the survivors began to question the success of the operation. Those men who assaulted the Mole did not appreciate the significant part they played in the operation. There was a general feeling of dejection and despondency among the survivors from the storming party. Lieutenant Charles Lamplough wrote, 'My impression of the operation was that as far as our objectives were concerned i.e. the capture of the battery at the seaward end of the Mole and the damage to the material on the Mole, the operation was a failure.'[16] Captain Chater and Captain Bamford were disappointed at not achieving any of the objectives assigned to them. Chater later wrote, 'We felt that our part of the operation had been a complete failure. We had lost many good men with what seemed to us no result.'[17] But the objective of the raid on the Mole was diversionary, in order to distract attention of German guns from the approaching blockships. At that point they were unaware that the blockships had succeeded in obstructing the canal entrance. Although the assault on the Mole did not achieve all intended objectives, the storming party did indeed create a substantial diversion, inflicting casualties and damage upon the enemy. And the blockships were sunk. While some of the survivors discussed the operation, others reflected on how fortunate they were to survive and on lost colleagues. Private Alfred Hutchinson put it simply: 'My feelings were that I was lucky to be alive and in one piece; and sorrow for the friends I had lost.'[18]

Three men who replaced the disgraced No.7 Platoon were killed during the raid. They were Corporal Samuel Smith, Private Frank Rolfe and Private Walter Whitley. Private James Feeney who was also a replacement for No.7 Platoon was safely onboard:

Then we saw the cost of our landing, one thing was evident – it cost a great deal of blood. I shall never forget the sight of the mess decks; dead and the dying lying on the decks and tables where, but a few hours before, they ate, drank and played cards. In the light of day it was a shambles … We had all the bodies collected up together at one end of the ship I had a last look at Corporal Smith and Rolfe.[19]

Corporal Frank Regan, Private John Haly, Private James Warburton Taylor, Private Poole and Private Leonard Holding were No.7 Platoon replacements who were wounded.

Once he had confirmation that the blockships had been sunk in the canal entrance Vice Admiral Keyes sent a congratulatory signal, 'Operation successful. Well done, *Vindictive*' as they returned home. *Vindictive*, a mess of tangled metal and debris, arrived at the Prince of Wales Pier, Dover, at 8.00 a.m. on the morning of 23rd April. The horseshoe that was fastened to the funnel of *Vindictive* was still in place. The two black cats that were the ship's mascots also returned from the raid unscathed. These two cats had stowed aboard *Vindictive* and become mascots. They were Mr Thomas and Mrs Tabitha; the officers adopted one, and the crew claimed the other.

The tumultuous welcome received at Dover was quietened when the number of wounded men who were transferred from *Vindictive* to hospitals in Dover became known. Provision had been made for the disembarkation of the 171 wounded men. A Royal Naval ambulance train was awaiting the arrival of the ship. As soon as *Vindictive* secured her moorings the wounded were immediately transferred to the train that was waiting alongside. Priority was given to individuals with serious wounds. 16 wounded men who required urgent operations were dispatched by motor ambulance to the Western Heights Military Hospital, Dover. 130 men with serious wounds were transferred to the ambulance train and were taken to the Royal Naval Hospital, Chatham. A further 25 men with minor wounds were transferred in motor ambulances to the Royal Marine Infirmary at Deal. It took over three hours to disembark the wounded and by 11.20 a.m. all had been removed and were either receiving medical attention or were en route to hospital. Once the wounded had been disembarked, the task of removing 60 dead bodies began. A fleet of lorries took their bodies to the Market Hall Dover, which acted as a temporary mortuary.

During that morning and afternoon other vessels from the raiding force sailed into Dover. *Daffodil* was towed across the Channel by *Trident* and arrived at Dover at 1 p.m. *Iris* arrived at 3 p.m. Keyes was waiting for her to berth and was anxious to go onboard and commiserate with Gibbs for not being able to land the storming party on the Mole. Keyes recalled his feelings as he watched *Iris* berth at Dover:

> It gave me a heartache to see, as she came alongside, rows of dead lying on her poop. I had no idea that Gibbs was dead, but when I saw her young First Lieutenant Oscar Henderson on the bridge, I feared that he must be wounded, and I was shocked to hear that he had died about 9 o'clock that morning, having remained conscious until the last, in spite of his terrible wounds.[20]

Aboard *Iris*, Private Beau Tracey observed Keyes on the quayside at Dover waving a telegram in his hand that informed him of his knighthood. 'He said "You men did the job and I will never forget you," and believe me he never did forget us.'[21]

When *Daffodil* berthed at Dover, each of the crew was presented with a daffodil by members of the YMCA. Those men who survived the carnage were assembled on the Monitor HMS *Sir John Moore* for a roll call. Petty Officer Harry Adams described them: 'A more "motley" crowd, you'd never see in a lifetime. Every man "Ghostly White" – some half clad, some only with shorts and bit of rag round the neck – some still limping with minor wounds but all washed out and "done up".'[22]

The material cost of the Zeebrugge operation amounted to the loss of one destroyer, HMS *North Star* and two motor launches ML 110 and ML 424. The human cost was very much higher. In his report to the Admiralty, Keyes confirmed the casualties as 176 killed, 412 wounded and 49 missing. (14 POWs and 35 killed included in that missing figure). The total casualties reported to the Admiralty amounted to 637 personnel. It is difficult to obtain an exact figure for the number of casualties sustained. I have carried out a study of the casualty figures based on the casualty list in the Public Records Office and my calculation indicates 227 killed, 376 wounded and 18 POWs, a total of 621. (See Appendix 2.)

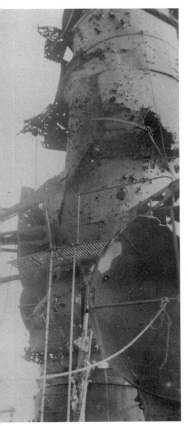

Above: Gangways onboard HMS *Vindictive* before the raid.

Left: The damaged funnel of HMS *Vindictive*.

Below: Deck of *Vindictive* after the raid on the morning of 23rd April 1918. The sailors' faces look drained as they are photographed amongst the debris of the shattered gangways. The funnels are peppered with shell holes.

German losses were surprisingly low, for they had sustained casualties of 10 killed and 16 wounded according to Admiral Jacobsen in his book *Trutzig und Treu*.[23] Captain Karl Shultz also recorded this figure in his account published in 1929. He provided an analysis of the casualties. Zeebrugge Mole Battery; two men killed, one man wounded. Second Destroyer Half Flotilla: five men killed, 11 men wounded. Second Torpedo Half Flotilla: one man killed and one man wounded. Kapitänleutnant Felix Glatzer records eight killed and 16 wounded casualties. Oberleutnant Rodewald, second in command on the Mole lists casualties of eight dead and 16 wounded. Seven German sailors who died on 23rd April are buried in Zeebrugge Churchyard. It has been estimated that there were 200 men based at the Sea Station, 60 men in the Mole Battery and the crews of German destroyers moored on the inner Mole.

It is hard to credit these minimal German casualties, but there are two important factors to consider. Firstly, according to an officer who was based at the sea station on the Mole, many German officers based at Zeebrugge were attending a party at the hotel during the night of the raid. He confided in Keyes after the War that these officers were not expecting an attack that evening. So the officers were not in a position to co-ordinate a defence of the Mole. C3 ensured that they would not get on the Mole while the raid was taking place. If the men were without officers to lead them it is only logical that many would have kept a low profile. The men based in the Air Station were at the western extremity of the Mole, far away from where *Vindictive* landed her raiders. Those German personnel who were located at the end of the Mole were in a dangerous position for they were exposed to German shell fire as well as British fire. It is quite obvious that under these circumstances some German personnel would choose to take cover. Secondly, another explanation as to why there are not many German graves relating to the Zeebrugge raid in Zeebrugge Churchyard could be because some of the German dead may have been buried at home in Germany.

During that day aeroplanes from the 61st Wing bombed the Mole on three sorties. The 61st Wing report records:

> *Several E.A. [enemy aircraft] sighted over Zeebrugge and Ostend. An enemy scout was attacked near Zeebrugge and driven down in a steep glide. A two seater E.A. was attacked over Dixmude. Result indecisive. One of our bombing machines was attacked by 5 Albatros scouts off Ostend, one of which was shot down and probably destroyed.*[24]

Air reconnaissance planes from the 61st Wing flew over Zeebrugge at a height of 50 feet and were able to confirm that the viaduct had been destroyed and a breach had been made in the Mole. A strong German Naval presence was evident off the Belgian coast on St. George's Day. Aerial reconnaissance reported seeing five German torpedo boat destroyers five miles north of Ostend and four patrolling close to the shore at Blankenberge.

Damage and destruction to the defences and harbour facilities upon the Mole had not been entirely effective. However the presence of the raiders for less than an hour had caught the Germans on the hop and helped the blockships pass. The effort to isolate the garrison by destroying the viaduct that connected the Mole to the shore was a complete success, and had prevented further reinforcements getting onto the Mole. Winston Churchill described the raid as 'the finest feat of arms in the Great War, and certainly as an episode unsurpassed in the history of the Royal Navy'.[25] German confidence in the security of their submarine bases was undermined and the British public's faith in the Royal Navy restored after what had been wrongly perceived as their lack of involvement in the early part of the War and the indecisive victory at Jutland. The audacity and daring of this shook the Germans occupying Belgium, to such an extent that officials were preparing to evacuate Bruges in event of an Allied invasion. Fearful of future amphibious operations launched by the Allies upon the Belgian coastline, the Germans brought further reinforcements from the Bight of Heligoland to defend Zeebrugge.

Deck of HMS *Vindictive*, Dover, after the raid.

Able Seaman Henry Groothius landed on the Mole as part of Lieutenant Commander Dickinson's demolition team. He recalled his father's reaction soon after his return from the operation, when he returned to Chatham:

> My father was home from sea and he said to me where have you been son. I said do you never buy a paper, he said no. So I said go and buy one and you will find out. When he found out where I had been he said you mad brave bugger, that was the greeting I got from my Father and he took me across to the local that night.[26]

HMS *Vindictive* in Dover Harbour after the raid looking almost like a hulk.

This photograph was taken soon after the raid at an unidentified naval depot. A roll call is being taken to see who survived and list the missing. This was the grimmest of parades. If there was no answer to a name, then the CSM would ask, did anyone see him, does anyone know what happened to him?

Lance Corporal George Calverley reflected on his own good fortune in surviving the ordeal and on the loss of fallen comrades when he arrived at the Royal Marines barracks in Deal at 4 p.m. that day:

On arrival we went straight to the barrack rooms which we had occupied before the raid. They had remained just as we had left them before the raid, with our kit bags still stacked at one end of the room. We discarded our equipment and took over the beds we had formerly used. Then the reaction set in, there were 24 men in the room originally and now there were only 11. There were no jokes or silly quips in the room that night but on looking around I began to realise how fortunate I had been. After eating my first meal in over 24 hrs and after a good soak in a warm bath, I turned in and in spite of the recent excitement was soon asleep.[27]

Private Harold Aiken from No.9 Platoon was lucky to have survived the raid without a wound. Most of his comrades were killed during the assault. He wrote home to his parents that he was safe and remarked that 'my luck, as usual, was in; I did not get a scratch'.[28]

The raid at Zeebrugge was an important morale boost for the Allies when their fortunes were taking a turn for the worse after the spectacular success of the Kaiser's Offensive launched in March 1918. For the Belgian civilians living under occupation, the raid was enormously encouraging. The aerial intelligence photographs suggested the raid on Zeebrugge was a complete success and that the blockships had effectively obstructed the canal denying the enemy access through it for three weeks. It was reported that it was incredibly dangerous for submarines to pass through the canal entrance for two months. Photographs obtained immediately after the raid on 23rd April showed that 23 torpedo vessels and at least 12 submarines were trapped at Bruges.

The German authorities of course made speedy efforts to open the canal. Keyes never expected to block the canal at Zeebrugge permanently. It was expected that the Germans would try to remove the blockships or find another way to open the canal. In his report to the Admiralty on 9th May 1918, Keyes reported. 'As yet no effective steps seem to have been taken to clear the Zeebrugge entrance to the Bruges ship canal, where the silt is shown to be collecting; although doubtless in time the enemy will succeed in opening a way out.'[29]

Within a week of the submission of Keyes' report to the Admiralty, the Germans dredged the silt for the canal entrance to allow vessels to pass. Sergeant Wright, who had been captured on the Mole after the raid, learned from a German Petty Officer who was in command of a field gun positioned on the sand dunes at Zeebrugge that the sand silted into the entrance of the canal faster than the dredgers could clear it. He also disclosed that 'the German Navy thought highly of our raid and compared it with a German operation of attacking Dover Harbour with units of their fleet.'[30]

Within a day of the raid smaller vessels could use the canal, but the sunken blockships had severely hampered passage from the German Naval Base at Bruges to the sea. Despite the canal becoming partially operational within a month of the raid, Keyes had reduced the German Navy's ability to launch attacks or lay minefields in the Channel. Allied losses had been reduced from 20 to six a month. The Germans could only lay six minefields a month as opposed to 33 a month prior to the raid. Overall, Keyes had given the dragon's tail a 'damned good twist'; he had won a great psychological victory, raising morale at home and raising self-esteem within the Royal Navy.

NOTES

1. Ordinary Seaman William O'Hara Papers.
2. Lance Corporal George Calverley, IWM Ref: 02/30/1.
3. Ordinary Seaman William O'Hara Papers.
4. Petty Officer George Warrington, quoted from *The Zeebrugge Raid*, p104, Philip Warner: William Kimber, 1978.
5. Lance Corporal George Calverley, IWM Ref: 02/30/1.
6. Petty Officer Harry Adams Papers.
7. *The Liverpool Chronicle* 29th April 1918.
8. *Thomson's Weekly News* 4th May 1918.
9. Private Jim Clist interview, courtesy David Clist.
10. Captain A F B Carpenter VC RN, *The Blocking of Zeebrugge*, p203: Herbert Jenkins Limited, 1925.
11. *Globe & Laurel* April 1919.
12. Lieutenant Lamplough Royal Marines Museum ARCH 11/13/79.
13. Leading Seaman Childs, quoted from *The Zeebrugge Raid,* p94, Philip Warner: William Kimber, 1978.
14. Ibid, p49.
15. *The Liverpool Chronicle*, 29th April 1918.
16. Lieutenant Lamplough Royal Marines Museum ARCH 11/13/79.
17. IWM Department of Documents Captain A.R. Chater, RMLI: 74/101/1.
18. Max Arthur, *Lost Voices of the Royal Navy*: Hodder & Stoughton, 2005.
19. *Globe & Laurel* April 1919.
20. Sir Roger Keyes, Admiral of the Fleet RN, *The Naval Memoirs 1916-1918*, p253: Thornton Butterworth Ltd, London, 1935.
21 Private Ernest (Beau) Tracey interview. Courtesy of Richard Davison.
22. Petty Officer Harry Adams Papers.
23. Extracted from *Trutzig und Treu!* By Admiral A.D. Jacobsen, Berlin 1935.
24. National Archives AIR 1/56/15/9/50: 61st Wing report (Daily summaries – Dover Patrol serials 34-112).
25. Winston S Churchill, *The World Crisis 1911–1918*, Volume 2 p1242.
26. University of Leeds Archives Henry Groothius Tape 93.
27. Lance Corporal George Calverley, IWM Ref: 02/30/1.
28. *The Blackpool Times* 27th April 1918.
29. *The London Gazette*, Number 31189, 18th February 1919.
30. Sergeant Wright, Royal Marines Museum Arch 11/12/5(5).

CHAPTER 13

HONOURS AND FUNERALS

Keyes was anxious that the bravery of his Zeebrugge raiders was recognised with honours. As soon as he reported to Admiral Wemyss early in the morning of 23rd April he made requests for decorations to be awarded to two particular officers immediately. He was aware that Wemyss was going directly to Buckingham Palace that morning to provide King George V with an appraisal of the raid and requested that Sub Lieutenant Maurice Lloyd from HMS *Iphigenia* be awarded a bar to his DSC and Lieutenant Keith Wright from ML 282 be awarded a DSC. These two severely wounded officers were not expected to survive that day and Keyes wanted to honour them before they succumbed to their wounds. Keyes received his answer from the King soon after breakfast when he received a telephone call from Weymss confirming the King's approval for Keyes' request to award Lloyd and Wright. Both these men were lying wounded aboard the hospital yacht *Liberty*, which was moored at Dover. Keyes personally told these two men of these awards, he later recalled that 'they were both conscious and fearfully pleased.'[1] Lloyd died later that day, but Keith Wright would make a complete recovery.

King George V also bestowed the honour of Knight Commander of the Bath on Vice Admiral Keyes in recognition of his command of the Zeebrugge operation. The award was announced in *The London Gazette* the following day on 24th April. Keyes was more interested in the bestowal of honours upon the men he commanded. Acting without sanction from higher authority and without confirmation of the success or failure of the operation, Keyes instructed Major Weller to select one officer and one NCO or rank by a ballot for the award of the Victoria Cross. Since all the men who participated displayed outstanding courage to a degree where it was difficult to single out individuals, they were permitted to select amongst themselves who was to receive the most prestigious award for valour. Keyes was implementing Rule 13 of the Victoria Cross Regulations to ensure that two men would be honoured to represent the battalion. Rule 13 states that

> In the event of a gallant and daring act having been performed by a squadron, ship's company, a detached body of seamen and marines, not under 50 in number, or by a brigade, regiment, troop or company, in which the admiral, general, or other officer commanding such forces, may deem that all are equally brave and distinguished, and that no special selection can be made by them, then in such case the admiral, general, or other officer shall be selected by the officers engaged for the decoration; and in like manner one petty officer or non commissioned officer engaged; and two seamen or privates or marines shall be selected by the seamen, private soldiers, or marines engaged respectively for the decoration.

Keyes would use Rule 13 to forward names for the award of the Victoria Cross for King George V to approve, which he did. During the afternoon of 26th April the remnants of the 4th Battalion Royal Marines Light Infantry paraded at Deal. The Adjutant Captain Chater issued them all slips of paper and they were permitted to consult with each other before submitting their slip with the name of the individual they nominated. Half an hour later Captain Bamford was detailed to collect the nominations and count them. To his embarrassment Captain Bamford had received the highest number of nominations for the Victoria Cross and was uncomfortably coy when he presented the result to Major Weller the Commanding Officer. Sergeant Finch received the second highest votes. On 27th April, Admiral Keyes visited the 4th Battalion RMLI at Deal and informed the commanding officer that the battalion would receive an additional Victoria Cross in recognition of their exploits on the Mole at Zeebrugge. Sergeant Finch received the second highest nominations in the ballot and would be the second recipient of the award for the battalion. According to Chater, Bamford was not selected by the officers, but by the ranks to receive the Victoria Cross. The officers thought that Lieutenant Cook was worthy of the award instead of Bamford. 'The officers who discussed the matter before voting, voted for Lieutenant T.F.V. Cooke, who led the assault along the top of the sea wall and was twice wounded.'[2]

A similar ballot was held for the Royal Navy. Captain Carpenter was asked to pick an officer and a rating for the Victoria Cross. Carpenter could not pick two individuals and therefore Keyes implemented Rule 13. Carpenter also refused to participate in the ballot to nominate candidates for the award because he thought that every participant was equally courageous and it was difficult to identify an individual to receive the VC on behalf of the service; but it was Carpenter who received the majority vote to receive the VC on behalf of the officers. He won by a narrow margin; he received one vote more than Lieutenant Campbell, the commander of *Daffodil*. Captain Carpenter also received the Croix de Guerre with Palm, and was made a member of the order of the Legion of Honour. Able Seaman Albert McKenzie won the ballot to receive the award on behalf of the Royal Naval ratings. Lieutenants Percy Dean and Richard Sandford would also be awarded the Victoria Cross.

Ten months later, Keyes recommended that Lieutenant Commanders Arthur Harrison and George Bradford be awarded the Victoria Cross posthumously. It was his opinion that if they had survived they would have been nominated to receive the prestigious award and on 17th March 1919, the awards to both these brave men were announced in *The London Gazette*.

Some of the men who raided Zeebrugge after they were awarded medals for their role at a decoration ceremony in Portsmouth, which took place on 26th September 1918 in the presence of Admiral Sir Stanley Colville. Master at Arms Charles Dunkason is pictured far left after being awarded the Distinguished Service Medal.

A total of eight Victoria Crosses were awarded to Zeebrugge participants. In addition, 17 Distinguished Service Orders, 24 Distinguished Service Crosses, 16 Conspicuous Gallantry medals and 139 Distinguished Service medals were awarded to participants of the Zeebrugge raid.

There was a darkly ironic flaw in the ballot sytem: if a platoon or a unit was decimated, then it was difficult for the remnants of that unit to receive nominations because their dead comrades would not take part in the ballot. No doubt, there are many men who took part in the Zeebrugge Raid who received no award for their role in the raid, but did deeds worthy of the highest military honour. There was one consolation for those who were not recognized because all those men that took part in the Victoria Cross ballot in all participating services had recorded on their service records 'Participated in ballot for V.C. granted for operations against Zeebrugge and Ostend, 22–23 April 1918. London Gazette 28/07/18'. Descendants of those that took part in the raids are very proud that these words are written on their forebear's service records, because they were so close to being a recipient of the greatest award for valour.

After Admiral Keyes visit to Deal on 27th April, the 4th Battalion RMLI was again marched to the railway station where they returned to their divisions. The 4th Battalion was now disbanded and to further honour the courage of the unit at Zeebrugge it was decreed that no other Royal Marine Battalion would be assigned the number 'Fourth Battalion'. The memory of the operation at Zeebrugge would be eternally engraved in the annals of the Royal Marines.

Families of the fallen Zeebrugge raiders were given the option of a military burial at Dover or for their remains to be sent home for a private burial. Those men interred at St. James's Cemetery Dover in a ceremony on Saturday 27th April 1918 were buried by the military. One bereaved mother wrote 'Bury my son with his men. I'm sure it's his wish.'[3]

The first funeral took place two days after the Zeebrugge raid. Captain Henry Halahan who had fallen before *Vindictive* reached the Mole had always expressed a desire for burial at sea and was buried in the English Channel near the Goodwin Sands on 25th April. On 27th April after a funeral procession through Dover, 66 seaman and Royal Marines whose families had requested a military burial with full honours were buried at St. James's Cemetery. With such a large number of deceased it was decided to place the remains of the fallen Zeebrugge raiders in a mass grave at St. James's Cemetery. A funeral procession started from the sea front and marched through the town to the cemetery. Admiral Keyes and Captain Carpenter were among the dignitaries who attended the service that was conducted by eleven clergymen from various denominations. Behind the graves flew the White Ensign that was flown aboard *Vindictive* during the raid.

Many other families chose to bury their loved ones at home and funerals of fallen Zeebrugge raiders were taking place across the country during the following two weeks. National and local newspapers reported these solemn funerals. In Newcastle the funeral of Private David Latimer from No.4 Platoon, A Company, was attended by 20,000 people. Before the war he was a barber in Newcastle and had been a junior champion swimmer. Enlisting in June 1917 aged 17 years and 3 months; he was under-age for the Corps. At the time of his death his father was serving in France on the Western Front. At the funeral the Lord Mayor delivered a brief address to the mourners: 'Private David Latimer set a high value on his own life, but a higher value on honour and the cause to which his country called him. He had died the noblest death a man could die, fighting for truth, love and liberty.'[4]

Private Stanley Jackson's parents, Elizabeth and Walter, had requested that their son be buried at home in York. Their wish was not granted because the body of Private Tom Jackson was sent to Private Stanley Jackson's village of Immingham and Stanley Jackson was mistakenly buried in St. James's Cemetery, Dover. His distraught family's disappointment that their beloved son was not brought home for burial can be felt in Stanley Jackson's epitaph, which states that he was 'from York'.[5] The sister of Tom Jackson had requested that her brother's remains be returned to Singleton.

As funerals of the fallen Zeebrugge raiders were taking place across the country, the wounded were recovering in hospital. King George V and Queen Mary visited the wards at the Royal Naval Hospital at Chatham on 30th April to visit the 15 officers and 242 men who were recovering. The visit was a private affair and they visited 11 wards. In one ward, the King recognised one of the Royal Marines that he had inspected when he visited the Royal Marines Depot at Deal in March 1918. A local newspaper reported their conversation:

> *A sick berth man on the* Iris, *James L Cowgill by name, who had lost three fingers of one hand, besides sustaining other wounds was asked by the King what the operation was like. He replied with a reminiscent grin 'It was very, very bad, sir, but it was well worth it.'*[6]

In another ward Able Seaman Edward Friday was recovering from a head wound sustained while he was aboard the blockship *Iphigenia*. His son never heard his father swear, but his mother recalled an instance while he was recovering from the shrapnel wounds he sustained during the raid. While sitting in bed with his eyes covered by a bandage, Able Seaman Friday was asked 'Does it hurt my good man?' Unbeknown to the blinded Friday the question was asked by King George V. Friday replied with a few choice words, unaware that he had sworn at the King.

Lieutenant Ivan Franks, who had developed appendicitis and was sent to hospital for an operation before the raid, was still recuperating in Chatham Hospital. When King George V visited him, Franks made his bitter disappointment at missing the raid clear.

The families of those men listed as missing were left in a terrible limbo for many months after the raid. They did not know whether their loved ones were prisoners of war, lying in hospital wounded unable to communicate home, or dead. Bessie Cassell was one mother who did not know the fate of her beloved son who fell in the Zeebrugge raid until 18th November, seven months after he had been killed. He was Able Seaman Arthur Cassell of A Company, Royal Naval landing party, a rifle-bomber who assaulted the Mole during that night and he was mentioned in the post-operation report. The last contact she had from Arthur was on 19th April and she knew that he was aboard HMS *Vindictive*. Two letters were written to the Admiralty on the 1st and 6th May 1918 asking for the whereabouts of her son. It must have been an agonising time for her, knowing that the ship had been in action but not hearing from her son since the raid. The Admiralty could not give any precise information, for they did not themselves know the fate of Arthur Cassell when they responded to Bessie Cassell on 10th May. The only response that they could give was MIA. The Admiralty was reluctant to commit in their replies to the letters that were sent by Bessie on a weekly basis. In her letter sent of 8th August, she wrote 'It is a very long time now, no doubt you must know that the suspense is more than I can bear, so if you have any news of him, no doubt you will kindly oblige his mother.'[7]

The Admiralty did make efforts to investigate the fates of those men that were listed as missing after the Zeebrugge raid. They requested information from their comrades to try to find definite confirmation of what happened to them. They sent questionnaires throughout the fleet and comrades were asked to complete a form entitled 'Evidence as to officers or men on Missing List'. Able Seaman Douglas Grey was a comrade of Arthur Cassell and he completed one of these forms for the Admiralty, confirming that Arthur Cassell was killed on the Mole. Grey reported on 15th July: 'I saw Cassell dead on the Mole, his head off, but I am certain of his identity, his tunic being very faded. He was a personal friend of mine.'[8] Grey gave his testimony again, in more formal language, two days later on 17th July: 'I certify that I recognised A.B. Cassell by the colour of his khaki tunic which was noticeably faded. He had just disembarked upon the Mole, with the same landing party as myself when he was instantaneously killed by a shot through the head.'[9] The Admiralty communicated the information provided by Douglas Grey to Bessie in a letter on 13th September:

Albert Edney tried to enlist when he was 14 years old on the outbreak of war. Three years later he succeeded in enlisting in the RMLI on 3rd April 1917. He was aged 17 years and 7 months and was still three months under the age limit. His officers regarded him as being of very good character during his short career with the corps. His brief military career ended when he took part in the Zeebrugge raid as a machine gunner. His funeral cortège leaves Bethnal Green for Ilford Cemetery.

Marines carried the coffin of their comrade, Gunner William Cowley RMA 13151, killed in the Zeebrugge action, to Fulham Cemetery on 1st May 1918. Men of the R.N.V.R. lined the way. Gunner Cowley had served in the Royal Marines Artillery for six years prior to Zeebrugge. During that time he took part in the Battle of Jutland. Three weeks prior to his death he had attended his sister's wedding. He was reported to have been 'hearty and cheery as ever'. His parents had already lost their eldest son two years before, during the battle of the Somme.

Madam – in reply to your letter of 8th instant respecting Arthur Henry Cassell Able Seaman, Official No. J.34572: I have to inform you that as a result of enquiries made by this Department, a statement has been obtained from another member of the expedition who knew your son, to the effect that he was shot in the head immediately after he had disembarked on the Mole at Zeebrugge on the 23rd April 1918 last, and it is believed that he was killed instantaneously. It is feared that little doubt can be entertained that this report is correct, but in view of the fact that it is not yet known for certain that the lists of Prisoners of War captured on this occasion are complete, no definite decision as to your son's fate can yet be arrived at. It is regretted therefore that for the present he must still be regarded as missing.[10]

Only those who have lost a loved one in such a fashion can begin to understand the effect of such a communication. When the War ended in November 1918 the Admiralty had accounted for all POWs and Arthur Cassell was not included on any list. On 18th November the Admiralty confirmed the news that Bessie had been expecting for so long.

With reference to the letter from this department of 13th September last, respecting Arthur Henry Cassell, Official Number J.34572 I deeply regret to have to inform you that his name has not appeared on the lists of Prisoners of War captured by the enemy which are now believed to be complete. Having regard to the statement of one of his comrades communicated to you in the letter referred to, and in view of the length of time which has elapsed since the operation, it is feared that there can be no longer any hope of his safety and it is my painful duty to inform you that in these circumstances the Admiralty has been regretfully constrained to presume that your son was killed in action on 23rd April 1918 – I am your obedient servant – Adjutant General of Navy.[11]

Seven months after Arthur's death, Bessie could now start the process of grieving, but with no body recovered, there was no chance to say goodbye or a grave to visit. Cassell was therefore commemorated on the Portsmouth Naval Memorial.

The mother of Able Seaman John Yeadon was also not aware of her missing son's death. Teresa Yeadon from Hull wrote a letter to the Royal Navy on 8th May, asking for news of her son's fate. She did not know if he was alive, if he was a POW or if he had been killed. John Yeadon was part of the Royal Naval landing party and had been killed aboard *Vindictive* before the assault on the Mole. She did not receive confirmation of his death until 15th August, when she received the following details in a letter from the Accountant General of the Navy:

I have to inform you that among the unidentified bodies landed at Dover following the operations against Zeebrugge, was one, the clothing of which was marked 'E Basten'. As the result, however, of an examination of articles and documents found on this body, there would appear to be now little doubt that it is that of your son. Further, a report has been received from another member of the crew of HMS Renown *who took part in the action, to the effect that he is almost certain that he saw your son lying on the midship ramp of* HMS Vindictive *with a shrapnel wound through his head. In these circumstances, the Admiralty is regretfully constrained to presume that your son was killed in action on the 23rd April last … I have to add that the deceased, together with other Officers and men who lost their lives in the expedition, was accorded a public funeral with full Naval honours in the St. James's Cemetery, Dover, on the 27th April.*[12]

Mrs Teresa Yeadon, bereaved mother of Able Seaman John Yeadon, who was killed at Zeebrugge.

The fact that Yeadon was wearing the coat of another man may have caused the delay. E Basten may have been a sailor or stretcher bearer who tended to the dying Yeadon, and gave him his coat in order to keep him warm. On the first anniversary of the Zeebrugge raid Teresa Yeadon paid this tribute to her late son which featured in the local newspaper, the *Hull Daily Mail*:

In loving memory of John Yeadon of HMS Vindictive, one of the storming party landed at Zeebrugge, who was killed in action April 22-23 1918.

Fierce and strong the battle raged;
Alas, the warrior fell;
His Christian soul was not afraid;
To take its final flight.
He sleeps with British heroes
In the watchful care of God.[13]

The last two lines of Mrs. Yeadon's tribute would be inscribed on John Yeadon's grave in St. James's Cemetery, Dover.

Able Seaman Charles Guenigault was part of the Royal Naval landing party who had also been listed as missing. Forms were sent to his comrades on HMS *Princess Royal* to complete, to confirm what they knew about Guenigault's whereabouts on the Mole at Zeebrugge. Able Seaman Walter Taylor was unsure: 'On the order being given to land, I with Guenigault, and men of No.1 Section of A Company, advanced up the ramp when a shell burst in our vicinity; Guenigault fell and for a second I myself was knocked unconscious, and I am therefore, unable to state definitely whether Guenigault was killed or wounded.'[14]

Taylor's report corresponds with the statement given by Able Seaman Vincent, who saw Guenigault lying dead on the ramps of *Vindictive*. However, the Admiralty received a response from another comrade from HMS *Princess Royal* that did not coincide. Stoker Petty Officer Thomas Haw stated:

I spoke to this man as he started to go up the brow, I watched him get to the top and then throw his hands up and disappear. I then had to go to my station on the forward grappling iron, after which being stretcher party I went to have a look for him but could not find him, he must have fallen between the Mole and the ship.[15]

Guenigault's identity disc and ring were found and removed from his body, which caused the body to be registered as unidentified. It took the Royal Navy nearly a year after the Zeebrugge raid to confirm to Guenigault's father that his son's remains were buried at St. James's Cemetery, Dover. His father received the following letter from the Royal Navy dated 22nd March 1919:

'With reference to your letter of the 10th ultimo, respecting the late Charles William Guenigault, A.B., Official No. J.38286, I have to inform you that from evidence furnished by his shipmates, and reports received when your son's identity disc and ring were forwarded to this Department, it has been ascertained that his body was landed and buried at Dover. It is deeply regretted however that the identity ring and disc were removed from the body on board HMS Vindictive, and consequently on arrival at Dover the remains were buried as unidentified, in the absence of any other means of identification. I have to add that a funeral took place with full Naval Honours on 27th April 1918, when the body of your son was buried in the Zeebrugge grave, St. James's Cemetery, Dover, together with the bodies of other Officers and men killed in these operations. His name has been entered in the official register of burials in St. James's Cemetery, and has been added to the memorial.[16]

Guenigault's name was inscribed on the Cross of Sacrifice near to the Zeebrugge graves.

ST. JAMES'S CEMETERY, DOVER

As mentioned on the previous page, the epitaph on Able Seaman John Yeadon's grave at St. James's Cemetery. Dover reads. 'HE SLEEPS WITH BRITISH HEROES IN THE WATCHFUL CARE OF GOD'. This is a fitting epitaph for all those in the secluded part of the cemetery on the slope of a hill who died at Zeebrugge. It is known as Zeebrugge Corner.

Among the Zeebrugge raiders buried here is 32-year-old John Buckley DSM. Buckley, born in Poplar, London, was a storeboy before he joined the Royal Navy. Captain Carpenter mentioned Buckley in his account of the raid recalling how he remained at his post till the end. He wrote that John Buckley was Yeoman of Signals, who

> … volunteered to take up a position outside the conning tower in readiness to fire illuminating rockets [and] had remained at his post until killed. We found him there at the foot of his rocket tube in the morning, a splendid fellow who had been as helpful in the work of preparation as he was unflinching in the face of almost certain death. All the signalmen except one had been either killed or completely disabled, and almost every soul on the conning tower platform had made the supreme sacrifice.[17]

Sub Lieutenant Maurice Lloyd DSC and bar was severely wounded when he abandoned HMS *Iphigenia* after successfully blocking the canal entrance. Before leaving the vessel he retrieved the White Ensign. He held onto this flag as he bled on the return passage home. As he lay dying, Keyes asked King George V permission to award Lloyd a bar to the DSC he was previously awarded. Keyes request was granted and Keyes personally informed Lloyd of his award onboard the hospital yacht HMS *Liberty*. Lloyd died the following day on Wednesday 24th April, aged 20. His bar to his DSC reads that he 'showed great coolness under heavy fire, and by his bravery and devotion to duty set a fine example to his men. On abandoning ship, after she had sunk, Sub Lieut. Lloyd was severely wounded. This very gallant young officer has since died of wounds.'[18]

Private Henry Conkey who served under Lieutenant Lamplough in No. 9 Platoon is buried in grave P.W.45A. He had served in the RMLI as Henry Campbell for five years. The reason for serving under an alias was probably because when he enlisted at

Above left: Zeebrugge Corner, St. James's Cemetery, Dover.

Above right: Funeral of Zeebrugge raiders at St. James's Cemetery Dover, Saturday 27th April 1918.

17 he was too young to join the RMLI. Born in India on 3rd January 1896 Conkey was a labourer prior to enlistment. After joining the RMLI in Belfast he completed his training and served 242 days as an under-age private. After completing basic training at Deal he was assigned to Plymouth Division. He served on HMS *Challenger* from July to August 1914. From August to October 1917 he served on HMS *Cornwall* in the West Indies. Throughout his early career his commanding officers judged Conkey as being of very good character, but in 1917 he was punished for desertion on three occasions. Conkey would redeem himself at Zeebrugge where he was killed during the fight on the Mole.

Lance Corporal Charles Heffernan was a bugler with No.1 Platoon killed while trying to extinguish a fire aboard *Iris*. Lieutenant Broadwood wrote in his report that 'Heffernan rendered most valuable assistance in helping to put out a fire which had started on board. He removed ammunition from the vicinity of the fire. He was killed whilst doing this.'[19] He is buried in grave P.W.30A.

Private Frank Rolfe who was a replacement for the disgraced No.7 Platoon is buried in grave P.W.1A. When he was killed at Zeebrugge he had only served six months with the Corps. Prior to the raid Rolfe was disciplined on 2nd April for being absent without leave. He was punished with seven days confinement to barracks and loss of two days pay for his misdemeanour. On realising that he might not return from the operation that he was training for, he probably went absent without leave to say goodbye to a loved one.

Sergeant Bertram Sparkes was with No.4 Platoon aboard *Iris* when he was killed. Born during September 1891, he was a butcher from Sheerness before enlisting in 1909. From March 1917 to 10th January 1918 he served with the 3rd Royal Marine Battalion on the Western Front. Sparkes is buried in grave P.W.33A.

Corporal John Jones was born on 5th November 1896 in Pocklington, Yorkshire. He was a seventeen-year-old clerk when he decided to join the RMLI on 14th September 1914. Most of the time he served was spent on HMS *Duncan* from April 1915 to April 1917. For a period this vessel was based at Taranto to reinforce the Italian Fleet in the Adriatic and then in June 1916 she was redeployed to Salonika in the Aegean Sea. From October to December 1917 HMS *Duncan* played a role in the fight against the Greek Royalists. Corporal Jones was awarded the DSM on 13th March 1917 and the Crois de Guerre avec Palme on 14th February 1917. He volunteered to take part in the Zeebrugge raid and during the four days leave that they were given while they were training he married his wife. Jones was with No.4 Platoon. According to Lance Corporal George Calverley he was killed by machine gun tracer fire from the coast. He is buried in Grave P.W.66A.

Private Victor Mayled from Taunton was a farm labourer before he enlisted aged 17 years and 5 months. Assigned to Plymouth Division after training, he served onboard HMS *Berwick* from July to December 1917. Mayled belonged to No.9 Platoon. He rests in Grave P.W.522.

Private David Demery from Swansea was one of the remnants from No.11 Platoon who assaulted the Mole, but was killed while attacking the German destroyer V 69, which was berthed along the inner Mole at Zeebrugge. Demery rests in grave P.W.8A.

When Lord Keyes died during December 1945 he requested that he be buried with the men of the Zeebrugge raid at St. James's Cemetery. His grave is nearest to the Obelisk that commemorates his son Geoffrey Keyes VC, who was killed in North Africa while raiding Rommel's headquarters on the night of the 17th/18th November 1941. Lord Keyes' wife Eva died aged 91 on 30th August 1973 and was buried next to him.

Some victims of German submarine warfare were also buried in this cemetery. Engine Room Artificers George March (0.H.9), Henry Gardiner (L.K.34), Leading Stoker George Hollyer (O.H.10) and Stoker 1st Class John Grice (0.H.11) who were killed aboard HMS *Mohawk* on 1st June 1915 when she hit a mine in the English Channel that was laid by UC-11, all rest in the cemetery.

ZEEBRUGGE CHURCHYARD

Some of the fallen British raiders whose remains were not returned home were buried in Zeebrugge Churchyard. The memorial was dedicated to the Zeebrugge raiders by the British Salvage Section. The memorial inscription reads:

LEST WE FORGET.
TO THE MEMORY OF
OUR COUNTRYMEN WHO FELL
IN THIS PLACE ON ST. GEORGE'S DAY
APRIL 23RD 1918
ERECTED BY THE MEMBERS OF THE
BRITISH SALVAGE SECTION
ST GEORGE'S DAY
1920

Left: Zeebrugge Churchyard. The two headstones in the left corner of the cemetery mark the graves of two unknown Royal Naval Officers who were killed during the raid.

Below: Burial of seven German personnel killed during the raid in Zeebrugge Churchyard. These burials took place soon after the raid and before the remains of British personnel were interred.

Memorial to the Missing, commemorating Wing Commander Frank Brock, Lieutenant Commander Arthur Harrison VC, Lieutenant Hawkings and Mechanic John Rouse, Zeebrugge Churchyard.

The small number of British sailors and Royal Marines are buried at Zeebrugge Church near to the graves of German soldiers and sailors. Captain Charles Tuckey, Corporal George Osborne from the Royal Marines and Petty Officer John Mayers from HMS *Thetis* are buried here. George Osborne was a dairyman from Devon prior to joining the RMLI in May 1914. After his basic training at Deal Depot he served with HMS *Victory* RM Brigade from September to November 1914. Assigned to Plymouth Division he later served on the Dreadnought battleship HMS *Warspite* from April 1915 to February 1918, during which time he was promoted to the rank of corporal and took part in the Battle of Jutland in 1916.

Captain Tuckey, known as Chas, had joined the Royal Marines as a 2nd Lieutenant in 1913. During the initial stages of the war, Tuckey served at Antwerp then later he saw action in Gallipoli. He took part in the landings at Y Beach on 25th April 1915 and was present at X Beach three days later. Tuckey served at Gallipoli until the Allied evacuation on 8th/9th January 1916. On returning to England he trained in gunnery and was then deployed to counter the Sinn Fein Rebellion during 1916. While serving onboard HMS *Erin* from January 1917 to February 1918, Tuckey was promoted to Captain.

There are also several graves bearing the inscription, 'Known unto God'. They include two British naval officers, seven Royal Marines, three British seamen and one stoker. A German report stated that 'none of those who were killed wore identity marks, nor did their uniforms and underclothes bear any indication of their identity'.[20]

There are seven German graves that indicate the date of death as 23rd April 1918. The following men were killed during the defence of the Mole and were buried shortly after the raid: George Rau Artmat, Joseph Miltze OB MTRATI, Eric Hagemann See Offz.anw, Otto Kuhn TMTR, Berthold Schulz TMTR, Otto Bauer TP MATR and Hermann Kunne TMTR.

Among the German sailors buried lies Hermann Kunne, who is reputed to have killed Harrison, but it is also assumed that the officer he killed with a cutlass was Brock. This would be the last recorded instance in history in which a British officer was killed by cutlass. Kunne was honoured during the Second World War with a destroyer named after him.

The cemetery is unique in that it contains the smallest Memorial to the Missing. A small stone, which can be seen on the wall behind the entrance to the cemetery, records the names of three Royal Naval officers, Lieutenant Commander Harrison VC, Wing Commander Brock, Lieutenant Claude Hawking and 2nd Class Mechanic John Rouse.

NOTES

1. Sir Roger Keyes, Admiral of the Fleet RN, *The Naval Memoirs 1916-1918*, p294: Thornton Butterrworth Ltd, London, 1935.
2. Captain Chater's account of the Victoria Cross Ballot, Royal Marines Museum.
3. *Daily Sketch*, 30th April 1918.
4. *The Newcastle Daily Chronicle*, Thursday 2nd May 1918.
5. *Bristol Times & Mirror*, 1st May 1918, Page 4.
6. *Chatham, Rochester & Gillingham News*, Saturday 27th April 1918.
7. National Archives ADM 116/1656: Letter from Bessie Cassell to the Admiralty.
8. National Archives ADM 116/1656: Able Seaman Douglas Grey report.
9. Ibid.
10. National Archives ADM 116/1656: Letter from Admiralty to Bessie Cassell.
11. Ibid.
12. National Archives ADM 116/1656: Letter from Admiralty to Teresa Yeadon.
13. Courtesy Ms Wendy Frew (great niece).
14. National Archives ADM 116/1656: Able Seaman Walter Taylor's report.
15. National Archives ADM 116/1656: Stoker Petty Officer Thomas Haw's report.
16. National Archives ADM 116/1656: Letter from Admiralty to Mr. Guenigault.
17. Captain A F B Carpenter VC RN, *The Blocking of Zeebrugge*, p202: Herbert Jenkins Limited, London, 1925.
18. *The London Gazette*, 23rd July 1918.
19. National Archives: ADM 137/3894: Lieutenant Broadwood's report.
20. Bundesarchiv 270/125 P190.

CHAPTER 14

ASSESSMENT

Great damage was caused as a result of the raid, to the extent that one thousand Belgian civilians were needed to repair the port. But how successful was it in disrupting the U-boat campaign? On 23rd April the German Admiralty communicated a message to the entire German fleet advising them not to return to Zeebrugge because the canal was blocked. (The raid on Ostend had been a complete disaster, because the blockships *Brilliant* and *Sirius* ran aground before reaching the entrance to Ostend Harbour.) Keyes was confident that the Zeebrugge Raid had achieved its objective and successfully blocked the canal. Weather permitting, daily aerial reconnaissance sorties were flown by the RAF over Bruges, Ostend and Zeebrugge, to ascertain whether any of the vessels trapped in Bruges were finding passages to the sea. To confirm, two aeroplanes carried out the operations simultaneously, allowing some rudimentary stereoscopic analysis.

One report on the air reconnaissance recorded:

> *When studying the photos there was great excitement if the numbers of vessels on the photos did not tally with the number of the previous reconnaissance, but numbers remained practically the same up to the Armistice, so that it seemed probable that they had been successfully bottled up, in spite of the fact that Ostend had not been completely blocked; if this was so, it was due to the shallowness and winding nature of the Ostend–Bruges canal.*[1]

Photographs taken on 19th May indicated that large numbers of torpedo craft and submarines were still trapped in this port. 'At least 23 torpedo craft and 12 submarines were sealed up in Bruges.'[2] In a report submitted to the Chief of Naval Staff Admiralty dated 20th May 1918, Keyes wrote:

> *It has been clearly established by aircraft reconnaissance that the Bruges–Ostend canal has not been used by these craft since the blocking of Zeebrugge. Photographs taken on 19th May definitely prove that the large number of Torpedo craft and submarines which were at Bruges on 23rd April are still immobilized there. It can therefore be presumed the Bruges–Ostend canal cannot be used for clearing Bruges of these craft.*[3]

The assumption from aerial reconnaissance that a great number of German vessels were trapped in Bruges suggested to the British authorities that the Zeebrugge operation was a success. However, there were Royal Naval officers who were questioning the effectiveness of the raid. Captain Herbert Grant served as Keyes' Intelligence Officer and played a role during the preparations before the raid. He wrote a very enlightening view of the operations, entitled 'The Immortal Folly of Zeebrugge & Ostend'. The title forewarns the reader of the negative opinion within. Herbert Grant was a contemporary of Roger Keyes at Britannia Royal Naval College where in his own words he 'formed a contempt for him, that time has by no means eradicated.'[4] Grant is venomous in his personal feelings towards Keyes, but his anger at the loss of many good men is valid. The first paragraph of Grant's work describes:

The massacre of Zeebrugge … for no such folly was ever devised by fools as such an operation as that of Zeebrugge. For what were the bravest of the brave massacred? Was it glory?… for sailors to go on shore and attack forts, which Nelson said no sailor but a lunatic would do, is not only silly, but it's murder and it is criminal.[5]

In his work Grant analysed the photographs of the blockships in the canal and looked beyond the propaganda. Surely at high tide the German submarines and torpedo boats of the Flanders Flotilla could pass around the blockships? Keyes confided to Grant after the raid that Admiral Sir William May opined at the Admiralty that the raid 'had no military value'. Grant regretted his involvement with preparations for the raid and wrote that 'nothing is more distasteful to me than thinking or writing of the Zeebrugge attack and often I wish that I had had nothing to do with the affair. The most consummate folly.'[6]

Grant was quite right to question the raid's effectiveness, for the reality was that the operation to block the canal did not affect the capability of the Flanders Flotilla operating out of Bruges. A teleprint message found in the German records at the Bundesarchiv states 'Entrance to locks blocked at low water, partially blocked at high water.'[7] A report from a driver given to Armee–Oberkommando at 3.30 p.m. on 23rd April recorded that 'the mouth is blocked, when low water, hindered, when high water. Clearing seems possible'.[8]
The Bruges canal was reported clear for the passage of submarines and torpedo boats on 24th April.[9] On 25th April UB-16 was the first German submarine to leave the canal. Commanded by Oberleutnant zur See Vicco von der Lühe UB-16 passed east of the blockships to leave the canal and then re-entered the canal. This submarine sailed past the blockships during two later operations. During Operation 86, UB-16 patrolled Hoofden, Lowestoft and Great Yarmouth. Two A Class German Torpedo Boats from the Flanders Flotilla also passed the blockships and left the canal that day according to Admiral Jacobsen, commander of the 1st Marine Division, Marinekorps Flanders.

An effort to open the canal entrance was begun immediately after the raid. By the 25th

Dredging operations in the canal entrance at Zeebrugge [were] proceeding according to plan. The boats of the 2nd Torpedo boat Half Flotilla left the canal through the narrow gap on 24th April without difficulty. Unless anything unforeseen happens, the entrance will be navigable by all torpedo boats and U-boats before long. Meanwhile the large boats will use Ostend.[10]

A German submarine officer later told Lowell Thomas that the raid 'did not have much effect. It did not block the Flanders base. The sunken ships did not cover the entrance thoroughly, and on the day following the raid the U-boats were able to pass in and out at high tide.'[11] Kapitänleutnant Hans Howaldt was commander of UB-107 based at Zeebrugge:

I was one of the first boats after this raid who went in and I could go to Bruges. We took this way only by night so aeroplanes could not see … and so the Admiralty thought Zeebrugge blockaded. We therefore for some weeks or months had a good time because we were not troubled in our way, but it was necessary that nobody could see us, because we did it all by night.[12]

(But see below concerning new orders about night-time passages.) On 25th April UB-109, commanded by Kapitänleutnant Kurt Ramien, was another vessel that passed the blockships when she returned to Zeebrugge. Ramien was an experienced submarine commander who had taken UB-109 on a shake down cruise during which time he sank three Allied merchant vessels.

The Royal Naval raid on Zeebrugge could be considered a limited success because the plan to get three blockships into the mouth of the canal had succeeded. The fact that the entrance to Zeebrugge locks was completely blocked to German vessels at low water is another argument for viewing the operation as a partial success. And the very fact that, as Howaldt explained, the vessels sailed at night to hide the raid's failure, is in itself a restriction of a kind and therefore a strange kind of success!

Despite the restrictions caused by the presence of the blockships, the Flanders Flotilla nevertheless continued to operate from Bruges throughout the remaining months of the War. On 6th May, UB-16 left Bruges for the last time on Operation 87. During this patrol of the North Sea, UB-16 was observed by the Harwich-based British submarine E34. At 6.50 a.m. on 10th May E34 dived to attack. Ten minutes later as the commanding officer of E 34 Lieutenant Richard Pulleyne stalked his prey, all tubes were flooded. At 7.15 a.m. E34 hit UB-16 amidships with two bow torpedoes. Fifteen of the crew was killed as the vessel sank. Vicco von der Luhe was the only survivor and was picked up when E34 surfaced five minutes later. During interrogation he refused to reveal the number of his submarine.[13] He later died as a prisoner of war. Lieutenant Richard Pulleyne was awarded the DSO for sinking UB-16. Pulleyne and E34 were sunk on 20th July 1918 off the Dutch coast.

German records confirm that a signal was communicated after the raid reporting that the western side of the lock channel was clear for ships drawing up to 2.5 metres at all states of the tide, and for ships of greater draught at a correspondingly higher tide. Dredging operations were to start on the eastern side. Ships using the western side of the channel had to keep close to the sterns of the blockships (which were marked by red flags) and keep to the eastward astern of the *Intrepid* so as to clear the sandbank, which extended into the entrance of the lock. Ships had to proceed with caution because of a ridge of stones bordering the western pier of the entrance, which could not be removed.[14]

In the weeks after the operation, the newly established RAF persistently targeted Zeebrugge. The objective was to bomb the two lock gates at the Zeebrugge end of the Bruges canal. The Bruges canal and the German Naval base at Bruges were above sea level. If these *two* gates could be destroyed through bombing, then Bruges harbour and canal would be emptied. The lock gates were damaged, but never at the same time. Major W. E. D. Wardrop was an RNAS observer who took part in sorties carried out by No.7 Squadron to bomb these lock gates.

We had bombed lock gates on many occasions, and we could never understand why although we went down very very low on occasions, and had special commissions we were asked to do, like going down as low as possible to drop 50lb bombs on the gates, and we knew full well we hit, but the photographs were shown the next day and there was no damage. This went on time after time and we were puzzled. A long, long time after we found, of course, that there were two gates. If one was damaged they put the other one out and repaired the other one. That was why we were puzzled about why we never managed to do what we thought we were going to do, smash them up altogether. It was very clever of them, but no good to us.[15]

View of the blockships from a passing German submarine at Zeebrugge at high water. Was the price too high?

Bruges naval base, as well as the surrounding industrial and naval installations, was also heavily bombed. Targets included the Solway works, a facility responsible for repairs and the supply of fuel for German submarines and destroyers. The Brugeoise Works was also targeted, for it was used as a shell and TNT factory. Attention was also given to the docks, floating docks, submarine shelters, cranes and storage sheds during day and night aerial bombings.

Despite the blockships and the air raids there are further examples of submarines accessing the canal from Zeebrugge. UB-74 commanded by Oberleutnant zur See Ernst Steindorff left Zeebrugge on 11th May 1918 on her final passage. During this operation to patrol the English Channel she sank the streamer *John G MacCollough* before being sunk by the British patrol yacht *Lorna* near Lyme Bay, Portland, on 26th May. On 14th May German official records show the German destroyers S-55, S-91, V-71 and V-73 passed through the Zeebrugge locks and past the blockships. These vessels, displacing 950 tons, were the largest vessels based in Bruges.

UB-80 commanded by Kapitänleutnant Max Viebeg carried out three successful operations from Zeebrugge after 23rd April. During Operation 6, from 1st June to 18th June, UB-80 patrolled the Channel and sank the Allied merchant vessels *Axpe Mendi*, *Stryn* and *Boma*. During Operation 7, which began on 27th July and ended on 7th August, she engaged and sank a Q ship on 30th July. UB-80 embarked on her eighth patrol from Zeebrugge on 29th August to patrol the eastern coast of England. During this operation she sank two Allied merchant vessels, the *Audax* and *Taurus*. She returned to Zeebrugge on 10th September. UB-80 finally passed the blockships on 1st October while en route to Wilhelmshaven.

Oberleutnant zur See Rudolf Stier assumed command of UB-30 on 22nd April. Six days after the raid, on 29th April, UB-30 left Zeebrugge but had to return with hull problems. She left Zeebrugge a further four times after the raid. On 6th August she left Zeebrugge for the last time to patrol the eastern coast of England. During the passage she sank the *Madam Renne* off Scarborough. She was then rammed by the trawler *John Gillman* and destroyed by depth charge, killing 26 crew onboard.

By May 1918 the German Fleet based at Bruges comprised 19 destroyers, 16 'A' class torpedo boats, seven motor boats, 24 minesweeping motor boats, four mine laying vessels and two flotillas of submarines, 22 UB and 12 UC boats.

Keyes was a determined individual who wanted to complete the job and achieve all objectives. The second attempt to block Ostend on the night of the 9th/10th May had also failed and Keyes proposed a third operation to be carried out between 6th and 10th June. He proposed the use of *Sappho* and *Swiftsure* as blockships. Keyes' proposal was not sanctioned. It was later deduced from British intelligence reports that there was no real need to block Ostend, because the canal to Bruges was too shallow for German destroyers and submarines to pass.

Throughout the last summer of the War, submarines from the Flanders Flotilla continued to pass the blockships. UC-11, commanded by the 25-year-old Lieutenant Kurt Utke, left Zeebrugge on her last passage on 24th June 1918. The following two days were spent patrolling the coast off Harwich observing shipping routes and assessing positions to lay mines. At 9.45 a.m. on 26th June UC-11 struck a German mine off Harwich. An explosion ripped through the aft part and she sank. Utke had brought his vessel into a German minefield that had been deliberately unswept. UC-11 sank with all hands except for Utke who was in the conning tower at the time of the explosion. The impact knocked Utke unconscious inside the walls of the conning tower. An uprush of water awoke him and he opened the hatch to escape from the sinking vessel. The water rising in the boat had compressed the air sufficiently to enable him to open the hatch of the conning tower. He rose to the surface in an air bubble. Dressed in clothes and boots he swam to a buoy so that he could rest. This buoy could not support him so he had to remain in the water, cold and exhausted for half an hour before being rescued by the lifeboat, *Patrick*. The sole survivor Utke was interrogated and revealed that all vessels could pass the blockships at the entrance to the Bruges canal. The interrogation report recorded that:

All vessels based in Flanders, whether surface or submarine craft, can now pass round the blockships by day or by night at all states of the tide. A passage has been dredged about 10–15 m (33–49 ft.) wide. Prisoner was in Germany at the time of the attack on Zeebrugge. He stated that the whole undertaking was considered by German naval officers to have been very gallant and dashing. He heard that for the first three weeks or so after the attack only the smallest boats could enter the channel, and then only by day.[16]

Kapitänleutnant Kurt Ramien in UB-109 passed the blockships once again at 6 p.m. on 27th July. The intention of this passage was to venture beyond the range of Flanders Flotilla operations that, so far, had reached as far as the Irish Sea and the Bay of Biscay. Ramien took UB-109 to the Azores and Madeira in the Atlantic Ocean. Here his boat preyed upon Allied shipping. During 17th August Ramien pursued SS *Zinal* for four hours before disabling her with a torpedo at 10 p.m. The merchant vessel was boarded and charges were detonated to sink her. On the return passage to Zeebrugge UB-109 sank another two vessels. As she passed through the Dover Barrage at 4.20 a.m. on 29th August UB-109 hit a mine. A violent explosion shook the boat. Some of the crew claimed that there were three to four explosions. Kapitänleutnant Ramien was positioned in the conning tower and was thrown down the periscope well as a result of the explosion. Ramien and seven crewmen escaped from UB-109 as she sank. They were in the sea for fifteen minutes before the trawler D 10 rescued them. The interrogation report of the survivors of UB-109 recorded that 'the survivors were all considerably shaken and suffering from deafness due to the excessive air pressure.'[17] The report also noted that Ramien,

… like several other commanding officers of submarines captured recently … refused to impart any information regarding his career in submarines or of the operations which he carried out while in command; he was extremely guarded in all his remarks, as he feared that he might unconsciously provide us with a 'missing link'. At the same time he was most courteous and expressed his appreciation of the good treatment received at our hands.[18]

Although Ramien was cautious in his answers, much information was gathered from his crew regarding the blockships sunk across the entrance to the Bruges canal and the effect upon operations.

It was stated that submarines are now able to pass on either side of the blockships inside the Zeebrugge Mole from about 3 hours before to 3 hours after high water. Continual dredging takes place to prevent the channels silting up. Recent orders [which had not yet come into effect when UB-109 sailed] lay down that submarines are not to leave Zeebrugge after dark. Owing to the shoal water off the entrance, they almost invariably leave about 2 or 3 hours before high water, so that if they ground it will be on a rising tide.[19]

The Flanders Flotilla continued to operate from Bruges until the end of September. The Allies had broken the Hindenburg Line and the German army was in retreat. On 1st October the Marine Corps based at Flanders was ordered to evacuate. The German evacuation of Belgium had begun and marked the closure of Bruges as a German naval base. Twenty-four torpedo boats and 20 submarines left Bruges, escaped through the canal and the entrance at Zeebrugge to return home to Germany. The evacuation of Bruges and Zeebrugge took place on 19th October. Ostend had ben evacuated the previous day. Before their departure, the Germans destroyed everything that could not be taken back to Germany. Concrete shelters, dock facilities and equipment were sabotaged. Four unseaworthy submarines, UB-10, UB-40, UB-59 and UC-4, together with eight torpedo boats that were considered to be unseaworthy, were scuttled.

The Flanders Flotilla UB-88 in the Panama Canal region photographed in 1919. Note the Flanders eye painted on her bow. This was the emblem of all Flanders Flotilla submarines based at Bruges. It was a means of recognizing friendly submarines when they surfaced. (The painting of eyes on boats of course has an ancient lineage, from the Greeks to the dragon's eyes on a dragon boat that are touched with red to animate the spirit.)

UB-88 was laid down during February 1917 in Hamburg and commissioned into the Imperial German Navy on 26th January 1918. During her ten months of active service UB-88 sank 13 Allied ships, equivalent to 32,333 tons during five patrols. Three of those patrols were launched from Bruges. Commanded by Reinhard von Rabenau, UB-88 arrived at Bruges on 12th June 1918 to join the Flanders Flotilla. A week later she embarked on her first patrol from Bruges towards the north eastern coast of England on 20th June 1918. During this patrol UB0-88 sank the Swedish steamer SS *Avance*.

Encountering a convoy comprising of thirty vessels, she was rammed by one of the ships causing damage to her main periscope. Despite this setback von Rabenau used the secondary periscope to launch a successful torpedo attack on the British merchant ship SS *London*. The ships escorting the convoy retaliated by firing nine depth charges into the sea, but UB-88 escaped. On 25th June UB-88 sank a further two vessels, SS *African Transport* during the morning and SS *Moorlands* during the evening. Surviving a 16-depth-charge attack from the *Moorlands'* protective escorts UB-88, escaped once again. Four days later, von Rabenhau sank two more vessels, SS *Sixth Six* and SS *Florentia*, before returning to Zeebrugge.

The next patrol left Zeebrugge on 29th July and von Rabenhau headed towards the English Channel. Patrolling between the Isle of Wight and Le Havre they encountered two British steamers escorted by a French destroyer. UB-88 fired torpedoes at each of the steamers. One missed its target but the other hit SS *Bayronto* causing some damage. UB-88 was unable to sink her because the French destroyer responded with no fewer than 45 depth charges. Two days later the crew of UB-88 had to endure a depth charge attack that lasted 20 minutes after she made an unsuccessful attack on an American convoy off the coast of Brest. The crew managed to repair the damage to the electrical system that was caused by the explosions of the depth charges and was able to continue the patrol and sink four more Allied vessels before returning to Zeebrugge.

UB-88 sailed on her final patrol from Zeebrugge on 7th September 1918. In order to reach the designated area off the north-western coast of France, UB-88 sailed across the North Sea, around the Orkney Islands passing the Irish west coast. The passage took seven long days. Four Allied steamers were sunk during the patrol. On 28th September she returned to Germany to join the 2nd Submarine Flotilla. After the Armistice, UB-88 surrendered at Harwich on 27th November 1918. She was brought to America where she was dismantled and sunk on 1st November 1920.

When measuring the success of the operation, historians must consider the statistics that show a significant reduction in Allied shipping sunk by German submarines after the operation. The First Lord of the Admiralty Eric Geddes wrote a report, 'Enemy attacks on Merchant Shipping' and presented it to the Cabinet on 17th July. The report analysed German U-boat activity from January to June 1918. It compared the number of German U-boat attacks carried out during the quarter ending 30th June 1918, with the preceding quarter.

> *A comparison of the attacks in the various areas during the two periods shows a marked improvement in the English Channel, the attacks having fallen from 46 per month in the first quarter to 28 per month in the second quarter … There is a reduction in the numbers sunk in all areas except on the East Coast, in which area the losses by Submarine for three months have increased from 25 to 33. The greatest reduction has taken place in the English Channel, the losses in the second quarter being 36 as against 69 in the first three months this year.[20]*

So from April to June 1918 the number of attacks and losses by submarine had been reduced in the English Channel. But as any statistician will tell you, beware of linking cause and effect too readily. The reason for this decrease in German Naval activity in the region was probably a combination of the effect of the raid and the Dover Barrage. The fact that there was an increase in the number of ships sunk off the East Coast of England suggests that Keyes' Dover Patrol Strategy in blocking access to the English Channel was a success. The Flanders Flotilla submarines may have diverted their patrols to the North Sea instead of risking being destroyed by mines in the Dover Barrage or by vessels of the Dover Patrol.

Historians must also look at the statistic quoted by Werner Fürbringer that 83% of Flanders U-boats were sunk during the course of the War. Throughout the War Flanders-based submarines were being lost through Royal Naval anti-submarine measures and one could ask the question, was the attempt to block Bruges really necessary? The catalogue of submarine losses listed in Appendix 4 shows that the Royal Navy was succeeding in countering the U-boat menace around British shores prior to the raid. I think Keyes was a determined individual who wanted to ensure that the submarine threat to Allied shipping and British shipping was dealt with once and for all, but was the Zeebrugge raid in reality sanctioned as a public relations exercise to raise the profile of the Royal Navy during the War and to show that the Senior Service was playing an active role? In his message to the raiders before the operation Keyes wrote of his confidence 'that all ranks will strive to emulate the heroic deeds of our brothers of the Sister Service in France and Flanders'. There is a sense that Keyes wanted to match the efforts of the Army and for the Royal Navy to be seen to be engaging the enemy more prominently. Many of the Zeebrugge raiders had of course played a part in the War before the Zeebrugge operation. Many of the sailors and Royal Marines had served in the engagements at Antwerp, Gallipoli, Jutland and on the Western Front. The Royal Navy and the Royal Marines Light Infantry had been contributing to the war effort since 1914.

The raid on Zeebrugge also raised the morale of those Belgian citizens who had been living under German occupation for four years:

> *Bless the English. During almost four hours they were the masters of the sea at Bruges' Mole. They blocked the harbour with two large ships filled with cement! … We slowly saw them sink, thus preventing any submarines or torpedoes from penetrating into the channel. Our harbour is so beautiful now. It's so pleasant being able to admire these heroic deeds from the bridge, everything was so successful that it may well be considered a miracle, and a major defeat for the Germans.[21]*

Although the Germans managed to dredge a passage through the Zeebrugge canal, the raid was a great accomplishment for all those involved. It was a very grand operation, comprising a series of important objectives. The failure to achieve any one of those objectives would have had catastrophic implications for the entire operation. If the storming force had not succeeded in assaulting the Mole then there would be no diversion for the blockships, which would have been blown out of the water before they even passed the Mole. If the crew of C3 had failed to destroy the viaduct then reinforcements would have poured onto the Mole and could have prevented the escape of *Vindictive*, *Iris* and *Daffodil*. Great navigational skill in reaching the port, together with fortitude and courage in executing this most audacious raid gave the enemy a bloody nose at a time when Allied fortunes were at a low point. It is hard to comprehend how the raiding force even got to Zeebrugge during that night when the Germans had removed all navigational buoys in the region. To accurately navigate the task force to this position in darkness is a remarkable feat.

Although the storming party failed to capture the gun batteries at the end of the Mole they had caused considerable destruction to German sheds and facilities. Their presence had attracted heavy German shellfire from coastal batteries, which helped to destroy parts of the naval facility on the Mole. The operation to isolate and contain the enemy on the Mole was achieved when C3 was exploded beneath the viaduct. The blockships succeeded in penetrating the inner harbour and blocking the entrance to the canal, restricting the passage of German submarines and destroyers temporarily. Three weeks' disruption to the operational capability of the Flanders Flotilla was a genuine setback at such a crucial time in the War. During those three weeks the risk to Allied shipping had been significantly reduced.

When the Allies entered Bruges they captured several German submarines and 21 German destroyers. Why did the German Navy not evacuate these vessels? Perhaps the German Navy had abandoned these vessels in Bruges Harbour because they were too large to pass the sunken blockships at Zeebrugge; another indication of effectiveness. Large submarines and destroyers may have been contained within Bruges harbour and unable to take part in the War. The canal mouth at Zeebrugge was not cleared until 1921 to allow commercial vessels to sail through the canal. *Intrepid* and *Iphigenia* were removed from the canal entrance at Zeebrugge in the mid 1920s.

The men on the Zeebrugge raid were confronting an enemy who had superiority in guns and troops. It is a testament to the planning of Keyes and his staff and the courage of the sailors aboard the support vessels that many men returned home. It was Brock's smoke screen that enabled the raiding armada to approach the Belgian coast without its presence being advertised to the German defenders until the moment of the attack.

Although it was not the intention of Keyes to use the raid as a device to boost morale in England, it certainly did. German submarines were sinking large tonnages of Allied shipping, causing food shortages at home, something that those who were ignorant of the suffering on the Western Front and elsewhere (and there were many) could immediately understand. Those that survived the operation returned home to a hero's welcome from their communities across the country. The Mayor and the people of Blackburn welcomed Petty Officer George Pemberton from *Daffodil* and Air Mechanic John Lomax when they returned; the roads to the station were lined by thousands of people to greet them. In his response to the Mayor's address, Lomax said with great modesty 'It was one hour of hell … I tried to do my duty. I don't think we have done anything great.'[22] Private Jim Clist recalled the warm welcome received from the people of Plymouth as the Zeebrugge raiders returned home to Stonehouse barracks.

> *I remember the great reception we got when we arrived at the Southern Railway Station at Devonport. Thousands of people were lined up at each side of the road between the station and the Royal Marine Barracks at Stonehouse. They had given us gifts of chocolate. I was a bit unlucky as I had my arm in a sling.*[23]

After the war, King George V ordered that the prefix Royal be added to *Iris* and *Daffodil* in honour of their wartime adventure. The New Medway Company bought the the *Royal*

Daffodil in 1933, and she operated between Medway and Southend. In 1937 she briefly operated for the Port of London Authority on dock cruises, prior to being sold for £1,000 for scrapping in April 1938. She was broken up in 1939 in a Belgian shipyard.

For the men who survived the Zeebrugge raid, there were further battles to be fought. Surgeon Frank Pocock MC DSO was transferred to Drake Battalion, Royal Naval Division. He was killed on 29th September 1918 while his unit assaulted the Hindenberg Line weeks before the war ended. Pocock was aged 27 and was buried at Louverval Military Cemetery, Doignies, France. Private Michael Keaveny was another Zeebrugge veteran who died within a month of the war ending. Prior to the war he was a school teacher from Glasgow. Like so many other Royal Marines who took part in the raid he was posted to the Royal Naval base at HMS *Glory III* in Murmansk. He was part of a Royal Marine detachment supporting the Russian White Army during the Civil War. He died on 4th October 1918 from disease and was buried in Murmansk.

Able Seaman Herbert Bambridge who was part of the crew of the blockship HMS *Intrepid* and who was awarded the DSM was another Zeebrugge raider sent to Russia after the First World War. He was serving aboard the destroyer HMS *Vittoria* when she was sunk by the Bolshevik submarine *Pantera* off Seiskari Island, west of Kronstadt. He drowned. His name is commemorated on the Chatham Naval Memorial.

Most who survived the raid and the war tried their best to assimilate back into civvy street. Bert Wells who was specially selected by Lieutenenat Colonel Elliot as a replacement NCO for No.7 Platoon and awarded the DSM, returned to Malvern, where he worked as a postman for twenty years. He died in 1965. Gunner Frederick Jenkins settled on the Isle of Wight where he set up a second-hand bookselling business. Some of these men continued to serve the public, like Corporal John Knell who served as a police constable until his death on 28th January 1924. Private William Warren served for thirty years with the Derbyshire Police Force.

Other Zeebrugge veterans would serve two decades later during the Second World War. Able Seaman Harry Gillard, after serving 22 years in the Royal Navy, was recalled to the service in 1939. He died during an air raid on Plymouth in 1941. Private William Ross from No.9 Platoon was recalled to Plymouth Division as a recruiting sergeant. He too was killed during enemy action on 7th April 1941. Private John Press who carried the severely wounded Lieutenant Cooke back to *Vindictive* would later serve in the Royal Marines, was captured by the Germans on Crete in 1941 and spent the remainder of the war as a POW. Air Mechanic Francis Donovan served as a major with the Royal Engineers and was captured in Tunisia during February 1943. He spent the remainder of the war in a German POW camp.

Vice Admiral Sir Roger Keyes and Sir Douglas Haig received by the Recorder of Dover.

Captain Reginald Dallas Brooks, awarded the DSO for commanding the howitzer aboard HMS *Vindictive,* would play cricket for Hampshire from 1919 to 1924. After retiring from the Royal Marines in 1949 he accepted the role of Governor of the Australian State of Victoria. Serving for eleven years, he was their longest serving Governor.

Many of the Zeebrugge raiders were of course considered too old to rejoin the Royal Navy and Royal Marines during World War Two. Instead some of these men served in the Home Guard, like Captain Alfred Carpenter, Commander Ralph Sneyd, Stoker William Hancock and Private Percy Savage.

That one hour of carnage played an important role in the lives of all who took part. The Zeebrugge Association was established after the war and veterans who took part would return to the Belgian port to remember their fallen comrades. Keyes maintained a close connection with the Zeebrugge Association and was concerned for the welfare of those men who took part in the raid. He was proactive in seeking employment for those searching for work and for those who were disabled he ensured they received the necessary financial and medical support.

The last surviving Royal Marine who took part was Private Alfred Hutchinson, who passed away on 11th June 2002 aged 105. Air Mechanic Sidney Hesse is thought to have been the last surviving Zeebrugge raider, who lived the rest of his days in Auckland, New Zealand until he passed away on 20th November 2002.

NOTES

1. National Archives: AIR 1/2393/249/2, Lecture paper on the blockading operations at Zeebrugge and Ostend.
2. Ibid.
3. National Archives: CAB 45/268, Admiral Sir Roger Keyes' original letters and comments on the Eastern Mediterranean (Dardanelles and Gallipoli), the Ostend and Zeebrugge raid, and the Dover Straits, 1915–1930.
4. Royal Naval Museum RNM, Ad. Lib. MSS 217. Papers of Captain Herbert Grant.
5. Ibid.
6. Ibid.
7. Bundesarchiv RM 120/275 P11.
8. Bundesarchiv RM 120/275 P16.
9. Bundesarchiv RM 120/275 P27.
10. Bundesarchiv RM 120/275 P55.
11. Lowell Thomas, *Raiders of the Deep*: Doubleday, 1928.
12. Imperial War Museum Sound Archives Hans Howaldt 4139.
13. National Archives: ADM 173/1498, Submarine E34 Report.
14. Bundesarchiv RM 120/275 P251.
15. Imperial War Museum Sound Archives Major W E D Wardrop DFM 29.
16. National Archives: ADM 137/3876, UC 11 Prisoner Interrogation Report.
17. National Archives ADM 137/3874, Interrogation Report of Survivors UB-109.
18. Ibid.
19. Ibid.
20. National Archives ADM 116/1601A. (German submarine operations in home waters 1917–18).
21. Nun's account. In Flander's Fields Museum, Ypres.
22. *Blackburn Weekly Telegraph.*
23. Private Jim Clist interview. Courtesy David Clist.

CHAPTER 15

THEY WERE ON THE *VINDICTIVE*

CAPTAIN ALFRED CARPENTER VC RN, HMS *Vindictive*. Alfred Carpenter was born in Barnes on 17th September 1881 into a naval family. He began his naval career in 1896 with training at HMS *Britannia*. Within two years he saw active service as a Midshipman in 1898, in Crete and as a Sub Lieutenant in China during the Boxer rising in 1900. By 1911 Carpenter had attained the rank of Lieutenant Commander. With two other individuals Carpenter received the Bronze Medal of the Royal Society Humane Society for rescuing a sailor who had fallen overboard from HMS *Achilles* at Spithead, Portsmouth. When World War One erupted, Carpenter was serving on the staff of Sir John Jellicoe in an administrative role. He was posted as navigating officer to the battleship HMS *Emperor of India* in November 1915. Two years later as a Commander he joined Admiral Keyes' staff and became involved in the planning for the raid to block Zeebrugge. Commander Carpenter volunteered to command HMS *Vindictive*. He was promoted to Acting Captain for the operation and somehow brought *Vindictive* to the Mole without losing his own life. Able Seaman John Biglin was stationed at a Stokes mortar on the forecastle and later remembered, 'How the Captain of Vindictive escaped seemed to be a miracle, as his clothing was perfectly riddled, but he did not flinch.'[1]

Captain Carpenter VC (officer with arm in sling) with sailors and Royal Marines who took part in the raid on Zeebrugge at Dover. (Q61351: courtesy of the Imperial War Museum)

Carpenter was asked by Keyes to nominate two individuals, one from the ranks and an officer to receive the Victoria Cross on behalf of the Royal Navy for its involvement in the raid. Carpenter declined to participate on the basis that all men were equally brave and it was invidious to identify two candidates. Despite Carpenter's refusal to take part in the ballot he was nominated by his fellow officers to receive the award of the Victoria Cross for his role at Zeebrugge. His citation reads:

This officer was in command of 'Vindictive'. He set a magnificent example to all those under his command by his calm composure when navigating mined waters, bringing his ship alongside the Mole in darkness. When 'Vindictive' was within a few yards of the Mole the enemy started and maintained a heavy fire from batteries, machine guns and rifles onto the bridge. He showed most conspicuous bravery, and did much to encourage similar behaviour on the part of the crew, supervising the landing from 'Vindictive' on to the Mole, and walking round the decks directing operations and encouraging the men in the most dangerous and exposed positions. By his encouragement to those under him, his power of command and personal bearing, he undoubtedly contributed greatly to the success of the operation.[2]

His cap and his binocular case, both damaged during the raid, are on display at the Imperial War Museum alongside his VC. A bullet hole can be seen, where a bullet went through the cap from the back and exited through the front. Carpenter formed part of the Honour Guard for the interment of the Unknown Warrior at Westminster Abbey with other Zeebrugge Raiders on 11th November 1920. He retired from the Royal Navy with the rank of Rear Admiral in 1934. During the Second World War he commanded the 17th Gloucestershire (Wye Valley) Battalion of the Home Guard from 1940. After the Home Guard was disbanded in 1944 he was appointed Director of Shipping at the Admiralty. Carpenter died on 27th December 1955.

STOKER JOHN CONNICK SS115283 RN. John Connick from Ashton under Lyne, Lancashire was aboard HMS *Vindictive*. He was born on 12th February 1895 and his occupation is stated on his service record as leather dresser, before enlistment into the Royal Navy. During the early part of the war he served on the armoured cruiser HMS *Carnarvon* and took part in the Battle of the Falkland Islands on 8th December 1914. He was later transferred to HMS *Lion* and served as a stoker during the Battle of Jutland. Connick returned from the Zeebrugge raid unharmed. One cannot begin to imagine the relief for his parents who had lost another son, Able Seaman William Connick, on 6th June 1915 during at Gallipoli.

ABLE SEAMAN FREDERICK BOWLT J29331, RN. Able Seaman Frederick Bowlt was born in Dover on 30th June 1898. He worked as a paper factory boy until his 18th birthday when he enlisted in the Royal Navy. Volunteering for the Zeebrugge operation he was killed while onboard HMS *Vindictive*. He was buried in St. James's Cemetery Dover (P.W.12.A), where his headstone bears the epitaph 'FOR KING & COUNTRY'.

LIEUTENANT ARTHUR EASTLAKE, ROYAL ENGINEERS. Lieutenant Arthur Lloyd Eastlake was the only son of Arthur Eastlake, the honorary secretary of the Institution of Petroleum Technologists. He held the distinction for being the only representative from the British Army to take part in the Zeebrugge Raid. During the operation he was in charge of the flame-throwers aboard *Vindictive*. Eastlake was an officer serving with the Royal Engineers and had specialist working knowledge of flame-throwers. While attached to the Trench Warfare Research Department he had first-hand experience of the dangers of this new form of warfare. While conducting experiments with flame projector apparatus at the Wembley Experimental Grounds on 18th July 1916, Eastlake suffered severe brain concussion and a broken jaw when a flame gun exploded. He was unconscious for seven and a half hours and his condition was so serious that he had to be admitted to the Hammersmith Military Hospital.[3]

Eastlake recovered and was selected to take part in the Zeebrugge raid on account of his research work. He was involved with preparations for the raid and the construction of a flame-thrower hut aboard HMS *Vindictive*. During the operation he commanded the team operating the flame-throwers from the hut. Heavy shell fire pounded the hut. A shell severed the nozzle of the forward flame-thrower operated by Eastlake, rendering it useless. The oil pipe was burst and the flame-thrower hut was severely damaged by shell fire. The explosion was so powerful that it threw Eastlake from the hut onto the deck below. Eastlake was demobilised from the Army on 3rd June 1919. All Royal Naval and Royal Marines officers that took part in the Zeebrugge raid were eligible to receive special service pay at a rate of six shillings per day. It was Captain Carpenter who wrote a letter of support to the appropriate authorities to ensure that Eastlake received the special service pay. In the letter he wrote 'Lieutenant Eastlake did good work in the fitting up of flame projectors, etc, and carried out his duties in a cool and efficient manner during the attack on Zeebruge Mole.'[4] Eastlake served in Russia towards the end of the war. He died in Chicago on 6th April 1960.

CHIEF PETTY OFFICER CLIFFORD ARMITAGE DSM, F6981 RNAS. Clifford Armitage was born on 10th May 1886 in Birmingham. He worked as a laboratory assistant before he joined the RNAS on 28th July 1915. He climbed the ranks and when he was transferred to Stratford to prepare for the Zeebrugge Raid during January 1918 he was promoted to Chief Petty Officer Mechanic. Armitage was stationed with the large flame-throwers with Wing Commander Brock and Lieutenant Eastlake. Armitage was mentioned in Captain Carpenter's report: 'The foremost flammenwerfer, under the charge of Lieutenant A. L. Eastlake (attached R.E.), was disabled before it could be used. A shell had cut the nozzle completely away, and another had burst the feedpipe from the containers. Through the promptitude of C. P. O. Armitage, in releasing the pressure on the oil containers, the highly inflammable oil was in some measure prevented from spraying and spreading.'[5] Armitage was awarded the Distinguished Service Medal.

The rear of the flame-thrower hut where Lieutenant Eastlake, Chief Petty Officer Clifford Armitage and Air Mechanic John Lomax were positioned during the Zeebrugge raid.

1ST CLASS AIR MECHANIC JOHN LOMAX F12803 RNAS. John Roy Lomax was born in Blackburn, Lancashire on 11th January 1898. Enlisting with the RNAS on 30th March 1916 he spent the early part of his service at the Royal Naval Air Service experimental stations at Stratford and Dover. Aged 20 he volunteered for the Zeebrugge operation. During the raid he was in charge of a flame-thrower, but his apparatus had been destroyed by shellfire. He later recalled his experience on *Vindictive*. 'It was an hour of inferno, not only for us, but for the Germans. I don't know how we did get through. The boat was an absolute shambles.'[6]

PLUMBER ALEXANDER HORNE, 285395 RN. Alexander Horne was born in Edinburgh on 11th May 1878. He joined the Royal Navy aged 19 in 1897. He served for 24 years beginning as a Stoker 2nd Class, then retired as a Master Plumber. During his service he was a keen boxer. On 2nd April 1917 Alexander joined HMS *Intrepid* while she acted as a depot ship in the Russian White Sea. When *Intrepid* returned to Chatham during January 1918 he volunteered for the Zeebrugge Raid. When one of the *Vindictive's* anchors could not be raised, Alexander dived down several times in order to free it. He retired from the Merchant Navy in 1921, but later served in the Second World War. He died of throat cancer on 24th April 1950. He was buried in Warriston Cemetery, Edinburgh and the words 'Rock of Ages Cleft for me' are inscribed on his gravestone.

PETTY OFFICER HERBERT BRITTON, 198651 (CHA) RN.
Petty Officer Herbert Britton had already served 20 years when
he volunteered for the Zeebrugge operation. Although he was
born in Glemsford, Suffolk, on 11th April 1881, the family moved
to Southend. Dissatisfied with his occupation as a domestic
servant Herbert enlisted to serve in the Royal Navy in March
1898. He was trained on HMS *Boscowen* in Falmouth and spent
the first two years of his service there. Prior to the war he served
on vessels that patrolled the China Sea and the Mediterranean.
He also served with the Channel and Home Fleets. When war
broke out he was posted to a minesweeper, then he was drafted
to serve on Q boats. During this posting, Britton had already
played a role in tackling the German U-boat problem prior
to the raid. After serving on a Q ship he was assigned to the
Monitor HMS *General Wolfe* for two years service. During this
time he became familiar with the Flanders coastline, which his
vessel regularly bombarded. Britton later recalled the role he
played as a gunner during the Zeebrugge raid.

*While we were in barracks at Chatham we knew that another stunt was on, and presently volunteers
were asked for. We had two or three tries. We left to start the game at 2 'clock in the afternoon and got
over there when it was dark. We could hear the Monitors bombarding the coast as we closed in towards
the Mole. The Boche put up a nice lot of star shells, just to have a look at us, but I don't think that
they saw us while we were well out. In fact, I fancy we in part surprised them, We closed up to action
station about 10.30 p.m. and all the troops were paraded. I was at my gun, but my orders were not
to open fire until the top had done so. As we approached the Mole the Germans gave us a few rounds
from their batteries, and of course, we retaliated. We then got alongside the wall, with bows nicely on:
and we got astern and tied her up with the help of* Daffodil *and* Iris. *By this time we were getting
pretty well riddled possibly from a German vessel abreast of us on the opposite side; but our pom-poms
in the tops were at the same time giving that destroyer plenty. As we swung in I had the gun on the
port side quarter, and smacked four rounds right into her where her guns were, at point blank range.
Then a shell came and upset our foretop, killing and wounding most of the chaps up there, whilst at
the same time we were getting riddled by machine gun fire. When we got nicely in our lads went over
the Mole, and we saw the block ships pass and shortly after heard a great explosion. We knew that one
of the submarines had blown up the viaduct. Meanwhile scrapping was going on all along the Mole,
and it was getting late. Of course, on account of the water, we had to get away to time. Our lights were
knocked down, so we could not make the prearranged signal: the alternative was the siren, but this we
could not use because the steam pipe had gone. So the* Iris *(or perhaps the* Daffodil*) was ordered to
signal on her siren. Our skipper would not leave until all the boys who were able to get back had done
so; but when this was done we shoved off and started to go ahead. I then closed up my gun screw, ready
for anything we might get – we expected a lot as we came away! But we bumped off at full speed and
were soon lost in the smoke, and it seemed the Germans couldn't find us.*

*When the viaduct blew up the wounded and others cheered, because they knew what was going
on. Our skipper Carpenter is a fine man, there's no doubt about it. And then the doctors, they all did
lots of beautiful work, and stuck at it, but I don't think that I have seen anything about this in the
papers. The action was fought with wonderful spirit and determination, every man doing his job all
right. The weather was not good for our purpose: there was a heavy ground swell, and this of course
kept our ship knocking up against the wall. It must have been about six o'clock in the morning when
we returned to our base. Our ship then looked like a nice old thing. It was of course, a dare-devil
job from start to finish: when we got alongside the wall, I thought 'Well, here we are – in: goodness
knows whether we shall ever get away!'*[7]

LEADING SEAMAN FRED KIMBER J13730 RN. Fred Kimber was born in Pembury on 5th March 1895. He initially worked as a farm labourer, but when he was sixteen, he walked from his home to Chatham to join the Royal Navy as a boy sailor. During his ten years service with the Royal Navy, Kimber served on fifteen ships. He was serving on the cruiser HMS *Yarmouth* when she was involved in the hunt for the SMS *Emden* and the capture of the *Emden* supplier collier in October 1914. He was aboard the armoured cruiser HMS *Shannon* during the Battle of Jutland on 31st May 1916. During 1918 he volunteered for the Zeebrugge operation. After the war he served on the seaplane carrier HMS *Ark Royal* when she transported aircraft from the Royal Air Force to British Somalia with the purpose of suppressing the 'Mad Mullah's' revolt. Fred Kimber left the Royal Navy in 1922. On 5th January 1925 Fred joined the Royal Fleet Reserves. His first job was working for Trinity House as a ship's lighthouse keeper. He would later work as a deep sea diver surveying wrecks for Trinity House. He continued to work as a diver until he was caught in an explosion which ended his diving career. On a visit to Malta he fell in love and married a Maltese woman. In later years he worked as a market gardener for a convent in Staplehurst, Kent and as a farmer in Marden. He had a passion for gardening and took great pleasure in growing prize winning chrysanthemums.

LEADING SEAMAN WILLIAM MARLING, J5690 RN. William Marling was born in Bromley-by-Bow, London on 27th May 1893. Before he joined the Royal Navy in 1909 he worked as a van boy. He was present at the Battle of Jutland while he was serving on the Dreadnought battleship HMS *Hercules*. In 1918 he took part in the Zeebrugge Raid. He continued to serve in the service until April 1926, when he retired with the rank of Petty Officer.

1ST CLASS STOKER FREDERICK POOLEY K29375 RN. Frederick Pooley was born in Deptford, London on 29th November 1896. He worked as a gardener, before enlisting on 22nd November 1915. He was a veteran from Jutland who volunteered for the Zeebrugge operation with twelve other colleagues from the battlecruiser HMS *Inflexible*. He served on the forward gun turret on *Vindictive*. Most of the gun crew became casualties, but Pooley was lucky to escape serious injury with a slight wound to his forehead.

LEADING SEAMAN DANIEL BOWTHORPE J18711 RN. Daniel Allan Bowthorpe was born on 23rd September 1896 in Norwich, Suffolk. He worked as a Printers Feeder before joining the Royal Navy in 1912. He was aged 22 when he took part in the Zeebrugge Raid. Fatally wounded during the action, he clung to life for another day and died in a Dover hospital on 24th April. His body was returned to his family in Norwich where he received a military burial.

STOKER WILLIAM HANCOCK SS111675 RN. William Alfred Hancock was born in Deptford, London on 15th June 1893. He worked as a general labourer before enlisting as a stoker second class in the Royal Navy on 5th January 1912. He began training at HMS *Pembroke* in Chatham. His first sea draft was to the battleship HMS *King Edward VII* from 14th May 1912 until 7th September 1913. He spent a month at HMS *Pembroke*, then he was drafted to HMS *Weymouth*. He served on this cruiser from 15th October 1913 until 18th May 1916. While serving aboard *Weymouth*, Stoker Hancock saw service in the Mediterranean during 1914 and in February 1915 took part in the search for the German Cruiser SMS *Koenigsberg* off the East African coast. He returned to HMS *Pembroke* Chatham for the duration of 1916, and then in March 1917 he was drafted to the battle cruiser HMS *Repulse*. Hancock took part in the second Battle of the Heligoland Bight when *Repulse* engaged the German battleships SMS *Kaiser* and SMS *Kaserin* on 17th November 1917. He volunteered to take part in the Zeebrugge Raid in early 1918 and was drafted as a stoker. He returned home safe. He spent the remainder of the war serving on the cruiser HMS *Yarmouth*. After the war William worked for a paper mill. He tried to re-enlist in the Royal Navy during World War Two, but was considered too old. Determined to do his bit for his country he served in the Home Guard. William Hancock died in June 1977.

Stoker William Hancock, pictured shortly before the Zeebrugge raid while he was serving aboard HMS *Repulse* in 1917.

CHAPLAIN CHARLES PESHALL DSO RN. Charles John Eyre Peshall was born at Alcester, Warwickshire on 13th November 1881. He was the eldest son of the Reverend Samuel Peshall and was known as Jack to his family and friends. Peshall became a pupil at Haileybury College from September 1895 where he excelled at sports, particularly cricket and rugby. Peshall continued his education, studying for a BA degree at Pembroke College, Cambridge and was ordained in 1904. He served as the Curate of Atherston from 1904 to 1907. In 1907 he became the Curate at Tormohun, and then in the following year he enlisted in the Royal Navy. Charles Peshall was an international rugby player prior to the War. On 1st December 1914 he was appointed to serve on HMS *Cornwallis*. Peshall was aboard when this battleship fired the first shot upon the Turkish forts defending the Dardanelles Straits on 19th February 1915. On 26th April 1915, the day after the Allies landed at Gallipoli, Peshall accompanied an engineer party from HMS *Cornwallis* to establish a water supply on V beach at Sedd-el- Bahr. Engineer Commander Crichton was charged to look after Peshall and at one point lost the Chaplain and was forced to search for him on V Beach. Peshall was probably playing a role in assisting the wounded casualties from the landings. On 27th April Peshall went ashore again and from V Beach walked through the ruins of Sedd-el-Bahr. A Staff officer approached him and asked if he could bury some of the dead who were collected near to V beach. When the grave was prepared, Peshall and an army chaplain conducted the burial service. This was a dangerous place to be, as Turkish shells were falling on the beachhead.

In 1917 Peshall and Commander A Stewart wrote a book about the role of the *Cornwallis* and her crew in the Gallipoli campaign entitled *The Immortal Gamble*. The book mentions the burial service that Peshall conducted.

It was a gruesome business, and the stench was awful, as all the bodies had lain in the sun for two days, and some had been in water. In one grave 204 men were buried, and in a smaller, quite close by, five officers. Shells began to fall, and the burial party retired to what cover they could find until comparative peace reigned again. The moon was up as the Chaplain quoted from the Prayer-Book he could not see to read, and the 'Last Post' rang out to an accompaniment of deep guns booming and the crackling of rifles in the distance.[8]

Peshall would return to V beach in a mercy mission to assist the Royal Army Medical Corps in recovering the wounded. Word had reached HMS *Cornwallis* that there was a problem with casualty evacuation and with the permission of Captain Davidson who commanded the battleship, Peshall and Lieutenant Commander Courage organised a volunteer party from the crew to go to the frontline and help bring away the wounded. The small party landed at V beach at seven in the evening and as they ventured two miles to the front line they became the targets for Turkish snipers. During that night they brought in 43 wounded men from the Worcesters, Dublins and Munsters and 35 Frenchmen. Peshall later wrote:

How they got back they hardly knew themselves. It was pouring with rain, and there were only two or three men to each stretcher. The mud in places was knee deep, and the greasy soil squelched under the feet. It was a struggle to go a hundred yards without putting the stretcher down, and in one case it took eight men to lift a stretcher up a bank sleeked with damp clay, which gave no hold at all.[9]

Peshall would visit the hospital ships when it was his turn to act as Chaplain's guard. On one occasion he visited the Cunard liner *Franconia*, which was transformed into a hospital carrier. He recognised the plight of the 1,600 wounded onboard, who were cared for by a small medical team of just three surgeons and 25 orderlies. Every inch of space aboard the ship was occupied by wounded men and all the crew including the Captain assisted the medical staff. Peshall recognised that there was an inadequate number of doctors aboard and asked the senior medical officer to request from Rear Admiral Wemyss that more naval surgeons be sent to the *Franconia* to assist. His request to the Admiral was granted, and each large ship in the fleet sent one surgeon to each of the hospital ships. In his role as Chaplain, Peshall brought comfort to the wounded. They were pleased to receive cigarettes and glad to see someone out of uniform. Peshall also witnessed the evacuation of Suvla Bay, for HMS *Cornwallis* was the last Allied vessel to leave Gallipoli on 20th December 1915.

In 1918 Peshall volunteered to accompany the Zeebrugge raiding force and Keyes permitted him to sail with the armada aboard *Vindictive* on the recommendation of Captain Davidson, who was now the commander of HMS *Hindustan*. Davidson wrote 'He would be a spiritual force and a fighting force if you will let him'[10] Captain Davidson was Peshall's commanding officer aboard HMS *Cornwallis* during the Gallipoli campaign. His recommendation indicates that Peshall, despite been a man of the cloth, may have taken arms and fought during the Gallipoli campaign.

During the days before the Zeebrugge raid, as padre, Peshall endeavoured to to keep up the spirits of the men as they waited in the Swin, isolated from land and from their families. He would organise sporting tournaments, games, hymn practices and distribute comforts such as cigarettes. Petty Officer Harry Adams later wrote:

Just imagine 2,000 men aboard the 'Hindu', stowed, as close as they could possibly be; you will also know that language at any time not being what one would call 'very choice'. But when the Padre appeared – and quite often – it would ease right up. He would 'muck' in with anything that was going ('cept shaking the Dice!). After a chat, he would say 'Any of you lads care to come along to the Cable Locker Flat for a sing-song?' Quite a lot would go. He would offer a wee prayer, then serve out 'Fags and Matches', when we were settled he'd say, 'Rughto! Choose your own Hymns' and we would spend a very happy hour or so that way. He was the ideal Parson for the job – simply couldn't have had a better.[11]

During the raid Peshall was in command of the stretcher bearer parties tasked with evacuating the wounded to the sick bays aboard *Vindictive*. Peshall performed to expectations when he dashed onto the Mole many times during that hour rescuing wounded men and carrying them aboard across the two unstable gangways. For his work at Zeebrugge Peshall was awarded the DSO. He was the only naval chaplain to receive this award during World War One. Peshall's DSO citation mentioned that 'his cheerful encouragement and assistance to the wounded, calm demeanour during the din of battle, strength of character and splendid comradeship were most conspicuous to all with whom he came into contact. He showed great physical strength and did almost superhuman work in carrying wounded from the Mole over the brows into *Vindictive*.'[12]

When King George V visited the wounded Zeebrugge raiders at Chatham hospital, he met Peshall in a corridor. Peshall belittled his part in the operation, declaring that he was not a fighting man. He refrained from revealing the brave deeds he carried out upon the Mole during that night.

After the war, Peshall married Beatrice Docker in 1919. He also continued to serve with the Royal Navy attaining the rank of Chaplain of the Fleet in 1933. This rank was equivalent to Rear Admiral. In 1934 he was appointed Honorary Chaplain to King George V and served in this role until the King's death in 1935. In 1935 he received the CBE (Commander of the Most Excellent Order of the British Empire). Retiring from the service in 1935 he became a parish priest in Deal, Kent. He rejoined the Royal Navy in 1940 and served during World War Two until 1943, when he retired for a second time. Peshall would become Chaplain to the Merchant Taylors Company. Charles Peshall died in 1957 in Westminster, London.

VICTUALLING ASSISTANT PERCY KENWORTHY, M28587 (CHA) RN. Percy Kenworthy was born in Stalybridge, Cheshire on 5th December 1899. The family later moved to Durkenfield where Percy worked as a store keeper. He enlisted in the Royal Navy on 1st January 1918. Within a couple of months he had volunteered for the Zeebrugge operation. Assigned as a Steward's Assistant aboard *Vindictive* his young eyes would witness some horrendous sights. During the operation he performed the role of stretcher bearer.

Although I belonged to the victualling or steward's department, I was for the purpose of the raid actually a stretcher bearer ... The work of the stretcher bearers began amid an inferno of shells and quick firing guns from the land batteries and the Mole. I was with Staff Surgeon McCutcheon, and killed and wounded were lying all over the ship, I saw an injured man being attended to by one of our stretcher parties when a shell killed the whole of them. I helped to fetch the dead and wounded from the upper decks to temporary hospitals below after rendering first aid.[13]

MASTER AT ARMS CHARLES DUNKASON DSM 191301 (PO) RN. Charles George Dunkason was born in Beaulieu, Hampshire on 11th November 1880. He worked as a cow man before enlisting in the Royal Navy as a boy sailor on 23rd November 1896. From June 1898 to December 1901 he served on the cruiser HMS *Marathon*, part of the Naval force that recaptured Peking from the Boxers during August 1900. In 1918, Master at Arms Charles Dunkason led the forward 6-inch turret crew on *Vindictive*. Dunkason suffered severe shell shock as a result of the part he played in the operation; it ended his career with the Royal Navy. After the War, Keyes helped Charles Dunkason to obtain pension entitlements and alleviated financial hardship from a fund that he had established to help distressed sailors whom he had commanded. After being invalided out of the service he worked at Aggie Weston's, a sailor's home in Edinburgh Road, Portsmouth. Charles lived here with his wife Fanny and his children Sydney, Bill and Joan. When some drunken sailors tried to enter their flat, it was Dunkason who laid them out. Being an ex Master at Arms in the Royal Navy he was still able to handle himself in a fight. During the Second World War he moved to Nursling, near Romsey in Hampshire where he served his country for a second time when he joined the Home Guard. The trauma of his experience at Zeebrugge would follow him throughout his life and 48 years later, he was calling out gun laying orders in his sleep, even in the last hours of his life. Charles Dunkason passed away on 27th March 1965.

MAA Charles Dunkason receiving the DSM at Portsmouth after the Zeebrugge Raid.

Harry Bennewith (right) with his brother Walter who served with the 2nd South African Infantry Battalion during the First World War. He fought at Delville Wood during the Somme campaign in 1916 and later in Flanders in 1917 where he suffered severe shrapnel wounds, which necessitated the removal of several ribs. Despite his injuries he served in the Second World War and was nearly captured by the German Afrika Corps during the North African campaign.

ORDINARY SEAMAN HARRY BENNEWITH J51070 RN. Harry Randall Bennewith was born on 28th September 1899 in Uitenhage, Cape of Good Hope, South Africa. His occupation is listed as 'school boy' on his service record. Harry enlisted in the Royal Navy on 12th January 1916 as a boy sailor. He spent the first sixteen days of his naval career aboard the Cape Station flagship HMS *Hyacinth*, before being transferred to HMS *Powerful* on 29th January 1916. Later that year he was drafted to serve on the armoured cruiser HMS *Carnarvon*. He served on this vessel from 23rd August 1916 until 28th February 1918 when she was deployed to the West Indies and North America. During this draft he reached the rank of Ordinary Seaman. At Zeebrugge Harry belonged to the fore gun crew aboard *Vindictive*. It was reported in the *Johannesburg Star* that Harry and the entire gun crew was blown to pieces by German shell fire. Petty Officer Ernest Heathfield was in command of Harry's gun crew: 'Ord. Sea. Bennewith was one of my gun's crew on the fxal deck and at about 12.30 am I witnessed him wounded and had him removed to a sheltered position. From there I believe he was taken below. I do not know to what extent he was wounded but I believe serious.'[14] Harry's wounds were fatal, but not the first injuries. Able Seaman George Gooch was also part of the gun crew and he later testified:

> I was at the same gun as Ord Sea Bennewith and saw him wounded at about 12.30 am on 23rd Apr '18. he was taken from fxal Deck to a sheltered position on a bench below outside the dressing room and I believe he was killed by a shell that exploded in the dressing room as I saw him again at about 6.30 a.m. still outside the dressing room with several others who were dead. I am sure of his identity as he was one of my messmates.[15]

On St. George's Day Harry's mother Ada had a premonition that Harry had died. She was unaware of his involvement in the raid, but she said to other family members 'Harry is gone'. Harry was a long away from his home and family in South Africa and so he was buried in St James's Cemetery, Dover. He is thought to be one of the unknown sailors buried there. His name is commemorated along with 15 other Zeebrugge raiders who were brought home, but whose remains could not be identified, on the Cross of Sacrifice in St. James's Cemetery.

LEADING SEAMAN EDWARD GILKERSON J16397 RN. Edward John Gilkerson was born on 21st January 1895 in Bracknell, Berkshire. He worked as a moulder before enlisting as a boy sailor on 12th March 1912. On completing his training at HMS *Ganges* he was posted to the battleship HMS *Implacable* on 1st July 1912 on which he served until November 1912. He was promoted to the rank of Able Seaman while serving aboard another battleship, HMS *Bulwark*, from August 1913 to June 1914. In June 1914, Edward spent four days at HMS *Excellent*, which suggests that he was training at the Royal Naval Gunnery School at Whale Island, and then from August 1914 until February 1915 his service record states that he served at Woolwich. This period may have been a continuation of his naval gunnery training. Between February and June 1915 he served at HMS *Vernon* which was established as the Admiralty Mining Department during that year. Edward's two elder brothers were both killed within a month of each other during 1915. William Gilkerson was killed on the 26th April 1915 while serving with the Royal Berkshire Regiment at Fleurbaix, near Armentières, in northern France. The eldest brother Stoker 1st Class Archie Gilkerson was killed on 27th May 1915, when his ship HMS *Princess Irene*, exploded at Sheerness when mines were being primed. The cause of the accident was established at an official inquiry as either the inexperience of the personnel priming the mines or tragic error because the mines were being primed in haste.

Edward spent the remainder of the war as a gunner aboard the battleship HMS *King George V* from 24th June 1915 until 28th February 1918. During this draft Edward was present when this battleship took part in the Battle of Jutland in May 1916. On 1st January 1918 Edward was promoted to Leading Seaman and at the end of February volunteered to take part in the raid on Zeebrugge. Before he left for training for the operation his shipmates from HMS King *George V* wrote him the following letter, which was signed by 17 sailors on 24th February 1918. Did any admiral ever receive a more eloquent and heartfelt sendoff?

> *Dear Old Gilky,*
>
> *In every sport, you were our mainstay. At every move you were one of us. At all times have we said, 'Gilky's our man'. We have always counted on you, and never yet have you failed us. Now you are leaving us, and we will hardly yet realize the loss it will mean. In the hazard you are pledged to, you will, we know, play the game as you always have, and the elective Light Party will follow your doings with incessant interest. Go in and win, old mate … with our hearts we wish you God speed and good luck.[16]*

It was probable that Edward Gilkerson was a gunner aboard *Vindictive* and was killed by shell fire. The torpedo party from HMS *King George V* wrote a letter of condolence to his parents:

> *Your son Edward lived and worked, shoulder to shoulder with us, for many months. It was given to a few of us to know him as he really was, and to we few, his intimates, he endeared himself by every word and act. We knew him for a man among men; who took every twist of fortune, standing upright; who faced the world, at all times, unafraid. Truthful sincere and resolute, he hated with a vehement, impassioned abhorrence anything that savoured of dishonour, cowardice, corruption. This last great act of fearless, matchless heroism, proved to the world what we already knew – that through his veins flowed the blood of a thoroughbred.*

We know that by his glorious sacrifice, he passed above_____. We also know this as he entered the portal, Death dipped a saluting wing, courtesy to a gallant gentleman, and the Power that waits all splendid deeds bade him welcome to his place among the noble.

Though his voice is gone from us forever, we still seem to feel him near us. On board, the creaking of oaks in the rowlocks, the boom of the mighty guns, the whirl of destruction's engines, the roar of the restless sea, breathe his prowess. Our shore the music of waiting birds, the whisper of soft breezes … the divine easiness of waking spring, diffuse his love and gentleness. Yes! Dear parents of a noble son, we find him one with all things and at night the stars show us, where a bed is made for him in Heaven.

As long as men's hearts are young and the blood runs warm, Edward Gilkerson's memory will be great. We combine all offering you our deep and heartfelt sympathy and remain his pals The Torpedo Party.[17]

This tribute to Edward was signed by 36 shipmates from *King George V*. Edward was brought home for burial at St. James's Cemetery, Dover. His epitaph reads 'HE GAVE HIS LIFE WILLINGLY'.

Grave of Leading Seaman Edward Gilkerson at St. James's Cemetery, Dover. He was buried with an unknown Royal Marine who was killed during the raid.

Leading Seaman Edward Gilkerson (third from left) Stoker Ernest Thornton (far left) and Able Seaman William Frost (second from left) aboard HMS *King George V*. William Frost was wounded aboard HMS *Iris* and lost his right leg. Stoker Ernest Thornton formed part of the blockship crew aboard HMS *Iphigenia*.

Vindictive after her return from Zeebrugge. The fore top, showing the muzzles of a 1½ pounder Pom-Pom and of three Lewis Guns and two loop hole plates. It was here that Lieutenant Charles Rigby and his crew provided covering fire as the Mole was stormed. All Rigby's party was killed with the exception of Sergeant Norman Finch, who survived to receive the Victoria Cross.

LIEUTENANT CHARLES RIGBY RMA. Charles Rigby was born on 1st May 1894 at the Moat House, Hertingfordbury in Hertfordshire. Educated at Rugby from 1908 to 1912, on completing his studies he worked for a firm of Land Agents and also enlisted in the Honourable Artillery Company. Rigby was an active sportsman and a renowned cricketer. During September 1914 he received his commission in the Royal Marines Artillery. He first saw action in France on the Western Front, serving in Dunkirk with the RMA Brigade from 7th October to 12th October. Rigby was promoted to Lieutenant in March 1915. During that month he was posted to A Howitzer Brigade on 26th March 1915 where he acted as an observation officer for No.3 gun at St. Omer.

Rigby saw action at Gallipoli with A Howitzer Brigade from April 1915 to 6th July 1916. Returning to France he saw further action at Sailly-Au-Bois during the Battle of the Somme in 1916. Rigby was mentioned in dispatches in *The London Gazette* during January 1917. He also served on the Dreadnought HMS *Barham*. During the Zeebrugge raid he commanded the pom-pom gun team in the fighting top aboard *Vindictive*. It was his team that covered the assault by Royal Marine and Royal Naval assault parties and saved many lives. It was here in the fighting top that Rigby was killed, aged 23. Lieutenant Commander Hilton-Young:

I was having a good sit down for a minute on a mushroom head in the battery, when shells began to strike our upper works, the funnels and cowls, which stuck up above the sheltering Mole. German destroyers had seen them from inside the harbour and were shooting at them from a few hundred yards' distance. When the shells struck a cowl or a funnel, a spray of splinters from the thin steel structure dashed down into the battery, causing many casualties there. The top also stuck up above the Mole, just ahead of the funnels; and it was, no doubt, the uproar of its automatic guns that had attracted the attention of the destroyers. But the fire thus directed on them at point-blank range had no effect on Rigby and his stout crew of six marine gunners in the top. While the destroyers' shells were striking our upper works close beside them, one heard their guns still bursting out at regular intervals into mad barking. Then there was a crash there, and a shower of sparks. Silence followed it. They were all gone – I said to myself. But in a minute or two a single gun broke out again, and barked, and barked. Then there was another crash, and the silence of the top became unbroken. Words cannot tell with what a glow of pride and exultation one heard that last gun speak. It seemed impossible that there should be anyone left alive in the top. After the first shell struck it, and when the gun spoke again, it seemed as if the very dead could not be driven from their duty …
the first shell killed all the crew but the Sergeant, who was severely wounded … he managed to get a gun back into action before the second shell struck, wounding him again and putting him out of action. Would that Rigby had lived to know how faithfully his trust was discharged by the last member of the crew that he had trained.[18]

Rigby's commanding officer paid this tribute to him: 'The very best type I have known, beloved by his men and one who had the right qualities of command … the Service has lost a very fine young officer who was much liked by all who had the privilege of knowing him.'[19]

SERGEANT NORMAN FINCH VC RMA 12151. Norman Augustus Finch was born in Handsworth, Birmingham on 26th December 1890. He was educated at Benson Road Board School and Norton Street Council School. On completing his education Finch worked as a tool machinist for a firm in Birmingham. Aged 17 and under the age limit, Finch enlisted in the Royal Marines Artillery on 15th January 1908. Sergeant Finch was second in command of the pom-poms and Lewis guns stationed in the fighting top. He remained at his post despite the entire crew being killed or wounded. Finch maintained covering fire with his Lewis gun for the Royal Marines and Royal Naval storming parties that assaulted the Mole, until a German shell struck the fighting top. He had received shrapnel wounds to his right leg

and right hand. Ordinary Seaman O'Hara aboard *Iris* witnessed Finch in the fighting top. 'He was continually hitting them. The pom-pom in the top was firing short bursts, and we were all lost in admiration when the top was hit severely, at the pom-pom starting again.'[20]

On returning to Eastney Barracks after receiving the Victoria Cross Finch was lifted on the shoulders of his comrades and carried to the Sergeants' mess room where a celebration was held in his honour. His Victoria Cross citation states:

Sergeant Finch was second in command of the pom-poms and Lewis guns in the foretop of 'Vindictive' under Lieutenant Charles N.B. Rigby, R.M.A. At one period the 'Vindictive' was being hit every few seconds, chiefly in the upper works, from which splinters caused many casualties. It was difficult to locate the guns which were doing the most damage, but Lieutenant Rigby, Sergeant Finch and the Marines in the foretop, kept up a continuous fire with pom-poms and Lewis guns, changing rapidly from one target to another, and thus keeping the enemy's fire down to some considerable extent.

Unfortunately two heavy shells made direct hits on the foretop, which was completely exposed to enemy concentration of fire. All in the top were killed or disabled except Sergeant Finch, who was, however, severely wounded; nevertheless he showed consummate bravery, remaining in his battered and exposed position. He once more got a Lewis gun into action, and kept up a continuous fire, harassing the enemy on the Mole, until the foretop received another direct hit, the remainder of the armament being then completely put out of action. Before the top was destroyed Sergeant Finch had done invaluable work, and by his bravery undoubtedly saved many lives.[21]

Sergeant Finch VC (left) and CSM Barker (right) place a wreath in the shape of *Vindictive* in violets at the base of the Zeebrugge Memorial unveiled by King Albert.

In *The Zeebrugge Affair* by Howard Keble, Finch spoke of his Victoria Cross award with great modesty. 'I don't know what I did to get it, and that's a fact. Seems to me if one has the V.C., the whole lot ought to have it.'[22] Being awarded the Victoria Cross meant that he would be saluted by all men in uniform, be addressed as 'Sir' by all officers despite his rank as an NCO, and be piped aboard any Royal Naval vessel. Finch formed part of the Honour Guard for the interment of the Unknown Warrior at Westminster Abbey on 11th November 1920.

Finch continued to serve with the Royal Marines until 1929, when he retired with the rank of Quartermaster Sergeant. As a civilian he lived in Portsmouth where he first worked as a postman then as a bank messenger. Two years later he was back in uniform when in 1931 he was appointed a Yeoman of the Guard for ceremonial duties. He returned to his old job as Quartermaster Sergeant in October 1939 and served with the Royal Marines at home during the War. He retired from the Corps with the rank of Lieutenant in 1943. Finch returned to his duties as bank messenger and Yeoman of the Guard after the War. Finch died on 15 March 1966, aged 76.

GUNNER VINCENT ORMEROD, RMA 14785. Omerod enlisted with the Royal Marines Artillery when he was 18 and had served on HMS *Marlborough* for nineteen months prior to the Zeebrugge operation. Before enlisting he demonstrated his community spirit as Assistant Scoutmaster at St. John Scouts, Birkenhead and being an active member of the YMCA. The *Southport Guardian* mentioned that 'his bright and cheery disposition gained for him many friends'. Ormerod was killed aboard *Vindictive* and was buried in St. James's Cemetery, Dover, (grave P.W. 15A). His epitaph reads:

ONE OF THE BEST
THAT GOD COULD LEND
A FAITHFUL SON & BROTHER
UNTIL THE END

NOTES

1. The *Newcastle Daily Chronicle*, 29th April 1918, Page 4.
2. *The London Gazette*, 23rd July 1918.
3. National Archives: WO 339/58056, re: Lt. A Eastlake.
4. Ibid.
5. National Archives ADM 137/3894: Captain Carpenter's report.
6. *Blackburn Times* 27th April 1918.
7. The *Southend Standard*, 2nd May 1918.
8. Reverend C Peshall and Captain A Stewart, *The Immortal Gamble and the Part Played in it by* HMS *Cornwallis*, p134: A & C Black, 1918
9. Ibid, p137.
10. Sir Roger Keyes, Admiral of the Fleet RN, *The Naval Memoirs 1916-1918*, p219: Thornton Butterworth Ltd, London, 1935.
11. Petty Officer Harry Adams Papers.
12. *The London Gazette*, 23rd July 1918.
13. *The Ashton Reporter*, Saturday 4th May 1918.
14. National Archives ADM 116/1656: Petty Officer Ernest Heathfield testimony.
15. National Archives ADM 116/1656: Able Seaman George Gooch testimony.
16. Leading Seaman Edward Gilkerson papers.
17. Ibid.
18. Lieutenant Commander Hilton-Young, Cornhill, December 1918.
19. *Globe & Laurel*.
20. Ordinary Seaman William O'Hara Papers.
21. *The London Gazette*, 23rd July 1918.
22. Howard Keble, *The Zeebrugge Affair*, p37: George H Doran Co., New York, 1918.

CHAPTER 16

THEY STORMED THE MOLE

COMMANDER PATRICK EDWARDS RNVR, ROYAL NAVAL LANDING PARTY. Patrick Harrington Edwards was born in Wandsworth in 1875. The 1901 census confirms that he was a solicitor living in Earls Court. He was one of those members of the Senior Service who had played a significant role in the War in the trenches alongside the British Army, before taking part in the Zeebrugge raid. He enlisted in the Royal Naval Volunteer Reserve on 1st October 1914 as a Sub Lieutenant. Within months he had attained the rank of Lieutenant and was sent with Howe Battalion, Royal Naval Division, to Gallipoli in April 1915. Lieutenant Edwards and Howe Battalion took part in the Third Battle of Krithia on 4th June 1915. The Battalion along with Hood and Anson battalions from the 2nd Naval Brigade was ordered to launch a frontal assault on Turkish trenches at
midday. Their objective was to capture the two front line trenches and a redoubt. Allied artillery shelled strongly defended Turkish positions at 8.00 and 10.30 a.m., but had no destructive impact. The Turkish soldiers responded by firing back at the lines held by Howe Battalion. As the sun climbed higher in the sky, flies were swarming in the searing heat on the dead casualties that lay on the battlefield. Edwards and his men had to leave their trenches and charge 1,000 yards across No Man's Land towards the Turkish line, in full view of the enemy's guns. To their left advanced the Manchester Brigade and to their right the Anson Battalion.

Despite heavy casualties the Turkish trench was reached and 800 yards of the trench was captured. Edwards was one of the few men that made it across No Man's Land to the trench but was wounded during the action. Edwards was mentioned in Sir Charles Munro's dispatch in *The London Gazette* on 13th April 1916. Douglas Jerrold wrote in his book *The Royal Naval Division* that during the Gallipoli campaign Edwards set 'an inspiring example to Howe Battalion'.[1]

After recovering from his wounds, Edwards was posted to the Western Front in France. During the morning of 13th November 1916 the Howe Battalion took part in the Battle of Ancre, in the final phase of the Somme campaign. The battalion objective was to capture Beaucourt and the lines of three German trenches that lay between the village and the British front line. Despite sustaining heavy casualties the Howe Battalion advanced across No Man's Land and reached the third German line. Edwards was one of those casualties, but despite his wounds he continued to co-ordinate the advance of his company to their designated objective. His service record states that he was admitted to the Duchess of Westminster military hospital at Le Touquet on 16th November with multiple gun shot wounds to his face and right arm and was listed as dangerously ill.

On recovering from the wounds sustained on the Somme, Edwards was assigned to light port duties in Sierra Leone on 3rd April 1917. Within two months he was struck down with rheumatic fever and was invalided out on 25th May. Edwards was still recovering from wounds when Vice Admiral Keyes was searching for volunteers for a dangerous operation on the Belgian Coast during the early months of 1918. Despite his multiple wounds, Edwards was keen to get back into the War. Keyes was aware of Edwards' experience and wanted him to train the Royal Naval landing party that was to assault the Mole. Edwards wrote of his feelings about the operation after being assigned by Keyes.

> When I arrived back in Chatham I was full of it. I thought it was quite hopeless, but, oh my goodness, it was quite gloriously hopeless. It was desperate; but I realized our position and the frightful losses the U-boats were inflicting on our shipping were also desperate. The boats engaged were of no great fighting value; the officers and men? Ah! That was another matter. I went off to my cabin that night, but I could not sleep. How lucky I was to be in it.[2]

As *Vindictive* approached the Mole at Zeebrugge Edwards was standing near to Captain Halahan when Halahan was killed. Edwards fell wounded when he suffered gun shot wounds in both legs. Determined to oversee the Royal Naval landing party assault he ordered his men to carry him ashore onto the Mole. This order was disobeyed to save his life; he was taken below decks to seek medical attention from the surgeon instead. Edwards was mentioned in Keyes' Zeebrugge dispatches in *The London Gazette* after the raid.

Once he had recovered from his Zeebrugge injuries, Edwards was appointed commander of the Russian Allied Naval Brigade in Archangel, from August 1918. The role of the Allied Naval Brigade was to support the Russian White Army in the fight against the Bolsheviks. Edwards was awarded the DSO for his involvement, the citation stating that he did 'very good work under very difficult circumstances'.[3] In February 1919 he was seconded to the British Army with the rank of Lieutenant Colonel working with local forces in North Russia. He was to receive a bar to the DSO for this work.[4]

Edwards was demobilized on 15th June 1920 and returned to the legal profession. He showed compassion and concern for the many disabled First World War veterans who had returned home and who were unable to find employment and rebuild their lives. In 1925 he helped establish the King's Roll Clerk's Association with the aim of helping disabled ex-servicemen to develop administrative skills such as typewriting, clerical work and telephone operating. Edwards also played a role in establishing the 'Society of Our Lady of Good Counsel', the purpose of which was to provide legal aid to persons who could not afford them. Edwards lived in retirement in Hailsham, Sussex where he died aged 69 on 13th September 1945.

LIEUTENANT COMMANDER ARTHUR HARRISON VC RN, ROYAL NAVAL LANDING PARTY. Arthur Harrison was born in Torquay in 1886. Educated at Dover College he joined the Royal Navy as a naval cadet in 1902. By 1908 Harrison had attained the rank of Lieutenant. Prior to the War he excelled as a sportsman. He played rugby for the United Services and Hampshire, where he proved to be a good place kicker. He also played for the Navy and participated in the Navy versus Army match of March 1914. After this match at Queen's he was presented to the King. During that year he represented his country, earning two caps for the England rugby team, playing against Ireland and France.

War interrupted his rugby career and Harrison saw action during the Battles of Heligoland Bight in 1914, Dogger Bank in 1915 and Jutland in 1916. At Jutland Harrison was mentioned in dispatches for being one of three officers who commanded gun turrets aboard HMS *Lion*, which fired 321 rounds during the course of the battle. In 1916 he was promoted to the rank of Lieutenant Commander. In 1918, while serving aboard HMS *Lion* he was seconded to *Vindictive* as second in command of the Royal Naval landing party. A shell fragment struck him on the head knocking him unconscious and breaking his jaw before *Vindictive* berthed alongside the Mole. On regaining consciousness Harrison landed on the Mole and reassumed command of the landing party, where he organized an attack on German machine gun positions on the Mole battery.

He was 32 when he was killed leading a charge on these positions. Able Seaman Eves made a brave attempt to carry Harrison's lifeless body back to *Vindictive*, but he was shot and wounded before reaching the ship. Lieutenant Hilton-Young described Harrison as 'a quiet tower of confidence and security'.[5] Harrison has no known grave and his name is commemorated on the Memorial to the Missing in Zeebrugge Churchyard. He may be one of the two unknown British Royal Naval officers who are buried in this churchyard. A year after the action he was posthumously awarded the Victoria Cross for his role at Zeebrugge. Keyes put his name forward on the basis that had he survived he would have been nominated to receive the award during the ballot. His citation reads:

For most conspicuous gallantry at Zeebrugge on the night of the 22nd–23rd April 1918. This officer was in immediate command of the Naval Storming Parties embarked in 'Vindictive'. Immediately before coming alongside the Mole Lieut.-Commander Harrison was struck on the head by a fragment of shell which broke his jaw and knocked him senseless. Recovering consciousness he proceeded onto the Mole and took over command of his party, who were attacking the seaward end of the Mole. The silencing of the guns on the Mole head was of the first importance, and though in a position fully exposed to the enemy's machine-gun fire Lieut. Commander Harrison gathered his men together and led them to the attack. He was killed at the head of his men, all of whom were either killed or wounded. Lieut.-Commander Harrison, though already severely wounded and undoubtedly in great pain, displayed indomitable resolution of the highest order in pressing his attack, knowing as he did that any delay in silencing the guns might jeopardise the main object of the expedition i.e. the blocking of the Zeebrugge-Bruges canal.[6]

ABLE SEAMAN FREDERICK SUMMERHAYES DSM RN J17594. Frederick Charles Summerhayes was born on 28th February 1897 in Bedminster, Somerset. His father owned a bakery and Fred worked for the family business. It was his father who decided that his son Fred should learn some discipline and forced him to enlist in the Royal Navy. Fred enlisted on 14th May 1912 as a boy sailor. After training at HMS *Impregnable* he was drafted to serve on HMS *Bellerophon* from 7th January 1913. Throughout his life Fred was teetotal and would give up his tot of rum to anyone who would clean his boots. He spent most of the First World War serving aboard this battleship and was present when she took part in the Battle of Jutland in 1916. In February 1918 he was transferred to HMS *Hindustan*, when he began training for the Zeebrugge Raid. He was assigned to B Company aboard *Vindictive*. During the raid he was wounded in the left hand when shrapnel blasted his middle finger after he landed on the Mole. Fred was awarded the DSM. Frederick continued to serve in the Royal Navy and became a Leading Seaman. He was invalided out of the service on 21st May 1919.

In civilian life he married his wife Lilian and fathered six children. Fred rejoined the Royal Naval Volunteer Reserve on 1st January 1923 and by January 1925 attained the rank of Petty Officer. He was discharged again on 30th January 1927. During the Second World War, Fred lost his son Albert. Albert was serving in the Merchant Navy aboard the MV *Bramora* when she was sunk by a Japanese submarine on 14th September 1943.

Fred worked as a beating machine operator at St. Anne's Board Mills in Bristol, a subsidiary of the Imperial Tobacco Company. He retired after 38 years service. During his retirement he took a watchman's job aboard the sea-going dredger *The Severn*, which operated from Avonmouth Docks. When she was at sea he lived at home, but when she was berthed he lived aboard the dredger and was very happy to do so. On 3rd October 1967 Fred was taken ill while aboard *The Severn* and was taken to hospital in Bristol where he died from peritonitis. He was cremated at Canford Lane Crematorium in Bristol. S.C. Brown, the Hon Secretary and Treasurer of the Zeebrugge Association wrote in a letter of condolence to his wife Lilian that 'by his generous and forthright manner he had won the affection of us all, and particularly those who served with him on HMS *Vindictive*'.[7]

ABLE SEAMAN HUBERT HELLIAR J28138 RN. Hubert Helliar was born in Sherborne, Dorset on 16th May 1898, the son of Robert and Grace Helliar from Greenhill Farm, Thornford, Sherborne. Hubert was one of ten children and worked as a farm labourer before joining the Royal Navy as a boy sailor on 14th October 1913. He first served aboard HM Ships *Impregnable* and *Powerful*, and from October 1914 he was drafted to the battleship HMS *Conqueror* where he served throughout World War One. On 27th December 1914 HMS *Conqueror* was involved in a collision with HMS *Monarch* and it took three months for the damage to be repaired. The vessel rejoined the Grand Fleet at Scapa Flow in March 1915. Hubert Helliar was aboard when the ship took part in the Battle of Jutland on 31st May 1916. Having volunteered for the raid he was assigned to the Royal Naval Landing party and was killed while assaulting the Mole. He died within a month of his twentieth birthday. After the raid Hubert was brought home to be buried at Bishops Caundle Church, Dorset.

This unique photograph of the Royal Naval Landing Party was taken during training for the Zeebrugge Raid. Able Seaman William Botley stands far left. Able Seaman Charles Pooley (sixth from left), spent his 21st birthday on the Mole during the raid. Leading Seaman Leonard Ellams is in the front row, seventh from the left. Standing to his right is Able Seaman Walter Taylor. Able Seaman Hubert Helliar stands directly behind Taylor. Able Seaman Edward Tolra is in the front row fourth from left.

ABLE SEAMAN EDWARD TOLRA L10/3516, RNVR. Edward Tolra was born in Highgate on 11th May 1897, the son of Professor A. Tolra. He enlisted in the Royal Naval Volunteer Reserves on 8th August 1914, at the outbreak of War. He was assigned to A Company Drake Battalion. During his service he fought at Antwerp and Gallipoli. On 17th April 1916 he returned to England and was posted to HMS *Pembroke*, Royal Naval Barracks, Chatham. A month later he was assigned to the newly commissioned battleship HMS *Royal Oak* and in that same month took part in the Battle of Jutland. Tolra returned to HMS *Pembroke* on 23rd February 1918 and volunteered for the Zeebrugge raid. Accommodated on HMS *Hindustan* he was chosen to become part of the Royal Naval storming party. He was killed during the landing on the Mole. Schoolchildren from his school followed Tolra's body as he was brought to Highgate Cemetery, London, for burial.

ABLE SEAMAN CHARLES POOLEY J22493 RN. Charles David Pooley was born on St George's Day 1897 in Hackney London. His family moved to Tongwynlais, Wales where he worked as a gardener's boy. He began his service with the Royal Navy as a boy sailor on HMS *Impregnable* from January to August 1913. Pooley was serving on the battleship HMS *Orion* when she took part in the Battle of Jutland in 1916. He was one of the volunteers from *Orion* who took part in the Zeebrugge raid. Pooley was part of the seaman storming party and spent the first hour of his 21st Birthday on the Mole. He was one of the detonator parties aboard *Vindictive* and was one of the first men to get on the Mole. Before *Vindictive* was secured and before the surviving gangways were in place, Pooley and his comrades were eager to get to work, so they jumped onto the Mole. As he landed he slightly injured his ankle. Pooley belonged to a party of four men and they came under heavy machine gun fire from one of the German destroyers that were berthed alongside the inner Mole. Two of Pooley's party was hit as they landed. Pooley later recalled:

> It was safer on the Mole than on the ship. The hottest time we had was when the Germans shelled us with 15 or 17-inch guns as we got away from the Mole. They played havoc on board the Vindictive … When the Vindictive steered off from the Mole we did not wait to take in the grappling hooks, and pulled away with us a large piece of the Mole. I brought home a small piece and some pieces of shrapnel.[8]

Compared with Zeebrugge, Pooley reckoned Jutland was 'a picnic'.[9]

ABLE SEAMAN DUNCAN DRUMMOND J22840 RN. Duncan Glass Drummond was born on 12th September 1897 in Dunoon, Argyleshire. Prior to enlisting as a boy sailor aged 16 years during 1913, Duncan worked as a messenger. He began his training at HMS *Ganges* on 15th February 1913. During October 1914 he joined HMS *Orion*. He served on this Dreadnought Class Battleship until 26th February 1918, when he volunteered for the Zeebrugge operation. Drummond was an Ordinary Seaman when the vessel took part in the Battle of Jutland. In August 1916 he was promoted to Able Seaman. Drummond was killed by a shell as he was returning back to *Vindictive* from the Mole. An investigation was carried out after the raid to determine his fate. 'Leading Seaman Shiner saw Able Seaman Drummond swept over the side of HMS *Iris* and blown to pieces by an exploding shell. He is quite certain of his identity.'[10] Based on George Shiner's testimony, the Royal Navy confirmed in a letter to his father that Drummond's death 'occurred on board HMS *Iris*, and was caused by the explosion of an enemy shell.'[11] The Royal Navy may have misinterpreted Shiner's testimony, because they give the impression that Drummond was aboard *Iris*. It may have been the case that Drummond was withdrawing along the Mole towards the *Vindictive* when the blast of the explosion flung him onto *Iris*. Drummond has no known grave and his name is commemorated on the Plymouth Naval Memorial.

Memorial card dedicated to Able Seaman D. Drummond.

PETTY OFFICER GEORGE ANTELL DSM 232634 RN, A COMPANY, ROYAL NAVAL LANDING PARTY. George Richard Antell was born at Parracombe, Devon on 15th April 1887. He worked as a labourer before enlisting to join the Royal Navy as a boy sailor on 3rd October 1904. He trained at HMS *Pembroke* Chatham and served on several vessels during the first five years of his career. He became an Able Seaman and on 4th June 1912 he was drafted to HMS *Lion*. George would see plenty of action while serving aboard this battle cruiser during World War One. *Lion* was the flagship of Vice Admiral Beatty, 1st Battlecruiser Squadron, Grand Fleet, and during the first month of the war George was present at the Battle of Heligoland Bight, 28th August 1914. During August 1914 George was promoted to Petty Officer.

George Antell later told to his son that there was a lot of grousing aboard HMS *Lion* about the daily rum tots. There should have been one gill of rum and two gills of water, but the rum tots were heavily diluted with more water, much to the distaste of the crew. When Winston Churchill paid a visit to HMS *Lion* as First Lord of the Admiralty he drank a tot of the daily rum ration and confirmed that it was one gill of rum and three parts water. (And he would know.) He arranged for the correct rum measure to be served to the delight of those onboard.

HMS *Lion* participated in the Battle of Dogger Bank on 24th January 1915 and suffered substantial damage, which meant a refit that took until April. The following year George found himself in another major naval engagement when *Lion* took part in the Battle of Jutland. He was lucky to have survived this battle, for 99 of his shipmates were killed and 51 were wounded by German shells. *Lion* was again within range of German guns when she provided part of the escort for the force engaged at the Second Battle of Heligoland Bight on 17th November 1917.

Having volunteered, Antell was assigned to A Company, Royal Naval landing party. Antell was given the task of leading No.1 Section, reporting to Lieutenant Cecil Dickinson. He was wounded in the arm and hand as *Vindictive* berthed. Despite suffering tremendous pain, with dogged determination to do his duty, he led the remnants of his section onto the Mole. Lieutenant Dickinson saw that Antell was leading the way along the parapet with only four men accompanying him. Dickinson sent his team westwards along the Mole parapet. Dickinson observed that Antell 'carried on most gallantly until I sent him away.'[12] Dickinson mentioned Antell in the post-operation report: 'Though wounded onboard and in great pain, [he] came out onto the parapet and did his job very well.'[13] He lost a finger during the operation. Antell returned to *Vindictive*, where he was found later, alive, amongst a heap of dead comrades. He was awarded the DSM. He continued to serve in the Royal Navy until April 1927.

Petty Officer George Antell sitting between his two sisters while convalescing from wounds sustained at Zeebrugge. Note the missing finger from his right hand.

On leaving the Royal Navy, George Antell settled with his wife Margaret in Haddington, East Lothian, where he bought a six-acre market garden. Despite being an Englishman living in Scotland, George Antell became a town councillor after winning local elections and also became a magistrate. Antell was on notice to return to serve with the Royal Navy in 1938, but the notice was cancelled when Neville Chamberlain returned home from Munich to declare 'Peace in our Time'. When this announcement proved inaccurate Antell was recalled once again to the Royal Navy. In 1940 he was drafted to the shore training establishment at HMS *Raleigh* in Devonport with the rank of Chief Petty Officer. While taking a group of trainee recruits to Lowestoft he was tragically killed in a railway accident at Langley, near Slough on 2nd July 1941. Aged 54, he was buried at Langley Marsh (St. Mary) Churchyard.

ABLE SEAMAN HARRY GILLARD 8517, ROYAL AUSTRALIAN NAVY. Harry Gillard was born on 29th January 1890 in New Brighton, Cheshire. As a boy he worked in the printing department of the *North Wales Chronicle*. Harry Gillard was one of four brothers who joined the Royal Navy as boy sailors. His service with the Royal Navy and later with the Royal Australian Navy was eventful. During the Battle of Jutland on 31st May 1916 he was aboard the armoured cruiser HMS *Warrior* when she fired 9.2 inch shells into the German warship *Wiesbaden*. The German fleet responded with 15 heavy projectiles that hit the *Warrior* causing approximately 100 casualties. *Warrior* tried to sail home, but the vessel had to be abandoned by her crew and sank on 1st June. Harry Gillard was transferred to HMS *Engadine* uninjured. Later he transferred to the Royal Australian Navy on loan and served on HMAS *Australia*. (In the photograph he is wearing the cap ribbon of HMAS *Australia*.) He was one of 11 sailors from the Royal Australian Navy who took part in the Zeebrugge operation. He was assigned to No. 4 Section, A Company that belonged to the Royal Naval storming party. Gillard remembered that when they landed on the first step of the Mole, two German soldiers jeered at them to come on. They were soon killed, when one was concussed by the blast from a grenade thrown by Gillard's colleagues. A bayonet thrust killed the other. During the raid he descended a ladder from the parapet onto the Mole, where he and his comrades engaged in hand-to-hand fighting and killed several of the enemy. Gillard described the Zeebrugge raid as 'a tremendous affair' and for him it was a way of avenging the sinking of HMS *Warrior* at Jutland. He said it 'made up for the Jutland fight'. During the bitter fighting that took place on the Mole, his helmet was knocked off and he escaped death when a shell exploding killed a man standing next to him. The post-operation report states that Gillard and Leading Seaman Rudd were among those who clambered down an iron ladder onto the Mole and killed several of the enemy. Gillard was one of thirteen in his party who returned uninjured. He was awarded the Croix de Guerre. When Harry Gillard returned home, the people of Bangor presented him with an inscribed gold watch and war bonds amounting to £35 in appreciation of his brave deeds at Zeebrugge.

Gillard served 22 years in the Royal Navy and was recalled during the outbreak of World War Two in 1939. Harry was killed during a German air raid on Plymouth on 21st April 1941, aged 51. At the time of his death he was with his brother, either coming or going ashore from their ship when the bomb exploded. Harry was standing in the boat and was caught by the blast, while his brother who was sitting down was not affected. Gillard was buried at Plymouth (Weston Mill) Cemetery, Devon. The obituary in the *North Wales Chronicle* paid this tribute to him: 'The memory of Harry will long be treasured in Bangor for his cheerfulness, allied to kindness, which made him very popular among a large circle of friends, who learnt of his death with real grief.'[14] The flags of University College of North Wales were flown at half mast as a mark of respect.

ABLE SEAMAN WALTER TAYLOR J35414 RN. Walter Edward Taylor was born on 10th January 1899 at Furze Field, Shermanbury, Sussex. He joined the Royal Navy as a boy sailor on 29th January 1915. On completing basic training he was drafted to HMS *Argyll*. This armoured cruiser transported an extremely valuable cargo of gold from Devonport to Halifax, Nova Scotia, in May 1915. During the return passage to Rosyth via the Western Hebrides, *Argyll* ran aground in the fog on Bell Rock at 3 a.m. on 28th October 1915. Promoted to Boy 1st Class, Walter Taylor, was posted to HMS *Princess Royal* during February 1916. During this draft Taylor acted as messenger to Captain, later Admiral, Sir Walter Cowan. He was aboard when *Princess Royal* took part in the Battle of Jutland. During the engagement the battlecruiser was struck by thirteen 12-inch shells and one 5.5-inch shell, which killed 22 and wounded 81 men. Taylor was also present when the ship acted as part of a covering force during the second Battle of the Heligoland Bight on 17th November 1917. Taylor was selected as an Able Seaman for special service on 28th February 1918. He was assigned to HMS *Hindustan* at Chatham and allocated to A Company, which was tasked to assault the Mole and destroy the naval installations. He was trained by the 5th Middlesex Regiment while at Chatham. He recounted his experience on the Mole to his son years later. He remembered running towards a pillbox and coming under fire. The man running next to him was killed by a shot in the head. He then took cover behind a wall or some sand bags, which was covered with barbed wire. It was from this position that he opened fire upon the Germans defending the Mole garrison. After the raid, Taylor provided written evidence to an investigation of the fate of his shipmate Able Seaman Charles Guenigault. 'On the order being given to land, I with Guenigault, and men of No.1 Section of A Company, advanced up the ramp when a shell burst in our vicinity; Guenigault fell and a for second I myself was knocked unconscious, and I am therefore unable to state definitely whether Guenigault was killed or wounded.'[15] When the signal was sounded as the recall to *Vindictive*, Walter Taylor remembered running towards the gangplanks and then nothing. He was wounded and lost consciousness. He remembered regaining consciousness, feeling a warm sensation on the left side of his face. He opened his eyes saw someone covering his body with a blanket. The man had presumed that Walter had died. Being thirsty, Walter pulled the cover from his face and called to the man who was kneeling over another wounded sailor. The man tending to the other sailor was startled to see Walter alive. Walter only wanted water, but he was given some rum or brandy. His son remembered his father's scars that he had sustained at Zeebrugge. There was a scar on his left shoulder, one at the front and two deep scars on his back. These wounds sustained during the assault on the Mole would affect him later during his life. During the 1930s pieces of shrapnel were removed from his shoulder. Two decades later, in the 1950s, an x-ray revealed splinters that were still inside him.

Able Seaman Walter Taylor in 1926 on his wedding day.

Despite his wounds, Able Seaman Walter Taylor continued to serve with the Royal Navy. He returned to *Princess Royal* during February 1919 and six months later he was transferred to HMS *Research* at Portland, Dorset. Volunteering to crew a destroyer that was being transported to Australia as a gift from Britain, Taylor would serve two years with the Royal Australian Navy from 1920. Returning to the UK in 1922 he joined HMS *Vernon*, where he qualified as a torpedo man. He was then posted to P 38 at Portland during that same year. Two years later he volunteered for the Asdic Qualifying Course and joined HMV *Osprey*. Throughout his naval career he endeavoured to develop his skills and in June 1931 qualified as a Submarine Detector Instructor. A year later he was awarded a Long Service Good Conduct Medal. Walter Taylor continued to serve in the Royal Navy until 9th January 1939 when he retired as Chief Petty Officer.

One day after retiring he joined HM Anti-Submarine Experimental Establishment as a laboratory assistant, on 10th January 1939. When World War Two broke out he was transferred to Newcastle upon Tyne where he was involved in ship fitting duties, converting corvettes, frigates, drifters and trawlers for anti-submarine roles. For his wartime work Taylor was awarded the British Empire Medal. After the war he was appointed as Senior Assistant to the Royal Naval Scientific Service during January 1947. He retired in 1963 and passed away four years later on 23rd January 1967 in Portland.

ABLE SEAMAN FREDERICK BERRY J36264 RN. Frederick John Matthew Berry was born in Abingdon, Oxfordshire on 31st August 1899. He was known as Fred and worked as a laundry boy before joining the Royal Navy on 15th March 1915. He began his naval career as a boy sailor and he would say in later life 'There is no better life than the Navy for a young man.' After completing his training he was drafted to serve on the cruiser HMS *New Zealand* on 25th June 1915. Fred Berry was aboard when *New Zealand* took part in the Battle of

Jutland. He was promoted to Ordinary Seaman on 31st August 1917 and Able Seaman on 24th February 1918. Within weeks of his promotion to Able Seaman, Berry volunteered for the Zeebrugge raid and was drafted to the depot ship HMS *Hindustan*. He was part of No.4 Section, A Company, Royal Naval landing party and was wounded during the raid. His certificate of wounds confirms that he was 'wounded on 23rd April 1918 by the bursting of an enemy shell. He sustained punctured wound of left scapula region, abrasion of right arm.'[16]

He continued to serve in the Royal Navy for two decades and received his discharge from the Royal Fleet Reserve on 30th August 1939. Fred was the father of four sons. His son Maurice followed his father's example and enlisted in the Royal Navy. He was due to serve aboard the battleship HMS *Hood*, but was taken ashore to recover from the mumps, two days before she embarked on her final voyage. Fred Berry worked at the famous MG Motor factory in Abingdon, Oxfordshire after leaving the Royal Navy. Fred was known as 'Sailor' by his work colleagues at MG. He worked there until his sixties and died on 12th December 1969. His ashes rest in Abingdon Cemetery.

Telegrams:-"Navy Accounts, London."

IN REPLY PLEASE QUOTE
No. 9 H.P./Cas.

Admiralty,

25th April 1918.

AND ADDRESS LETTER TO:—
THE ACCOUNTANT-GENERAL OF THE NAVY,
ADMIRALTY, LONDON, S.W. 1.

Madam,

I regret to have to inform you that telegraphic information has reached this Department that

Frederick John Matthew Berry,   Ordinary Seaman.

Official Number   J. 36264.   , belonging to

H.M.S.   "VINDICTIVE"   was slightly wounded in action on

the   23rd instant   , and is now in the Royal Marine Infirmary, Deal.   He is stated to have sustained wound to to his back and his condition is reported to be satisfactory.

Further Information ~~as to the nature of his wounds, present~~ respecting him ~~condition and disposal~~ may be obtained from the Hon.

Secretary, Royal Naval Medical Information Bureau. Royal Marine Barracks, Deal.

I am, Madam,
Your obedient Servant,

Mrs. Harriett Berry,
5, Turnagain Lane,
Bridge Street,
ABINGDON.

Accountant-General
of the Navy.

Telegram sent to Fred's mother, Mrs Harriett Berry, informing that her son was wounded aboard HMS *Vindictive*.

ABLE SEAMAN FREDERICK LARBY DSM, J27317 RN. Frederick James Larby was born in Farnham, Surrey on 17th March 1897. He worked as a brickworker before enlisting as a boy sailor on 24th September 1913. As the first year of war drew to a close in December 1914, Larby was drafted to HMS *Caroline*. During this posting he was promoted to Ordinary Seaman. Larby was posted to the Dreadnought Battleship HMS *Canada* on 15th September 1915 and saw action at Jutland in 1916. HMS *Canada* was undamaged during the battle. Four days before the Battle of Jutland Larby was promoted to Able Seaman.

Throughout his career with the Royal Navy Fred Larby was an enthusiastic boxer and was victorious in many service tournaments. He was highly respected and regarded as a gentleman boxer. He won the Lonsdale Belt twice. If he had won it a third time he would have been allowed to keep the belt, but the story told is that the Navy ensured he was unavailable to fight for the third time for the belt, for some unexplained reason. Larby won about 50 trophies, but only a dozen remain in the Royal Naval Trophy Store in Portsmouth today. The remainder was destroyed in a German bombing raid during the Second World War.

In February 1918 while serving aboard HMS *Canada*, he and fellow shipmate Leading Seaman Leonard Ellams volunteered for special duties. They were assigned to A Company. Being a champion boxer and physically fit ensured that Fred Larby was selected for the operation. Larby's role during the raid was hand bomber. Lieutenant Commander Adams recorded, 'Hand-bombers all showed great gallantry in advancing with me. More especially Larby and Staples, who are most strongly recommended; they were very useful in helping the wounded on board *Vindictive*, when returning and formed part of S 1 gun's crew.'[17]

Able Seaman Fred Larby pictured with boxing trophies that he won in Royal Naval boxing tournaments

Larby, who was wounded, was awarded the Distinguished Service Medal. He continued to serve with the Royal Navy until March 1927. After the tragic death of his wife and child, Larby emigrated to New Zealand where he remarried. He settled in Bluff on the South Island where he worked for the Bluff Harbour Board. He continued his association with boxing by giving coaching lessons to local boys. Fred Larby suffered a heart attack and died on 7th August 1945, aged 48.

LEADING SEAMAN LEONARD ELLAMS J37173 RN. Leonard Ellams was born on 1st June 1896 in Frodsham, Cheshire. He worked as a labourer before enlisting on 15th April 1915. Ellams served aboard the battleship HMS *Canada* from August 1915 to February 1918. The ship fought at Jutland. In March 1918 he was transferred to HMS *Hindustan* to prepare for the Zeebrugge operation. He was killed during the raid. The family requested that his remains be brought home to be buried at Frodsham, St. Lawrence Church, Cheshire.

ABLE SEAMAN WILLIAM BOTLEY J12351 RN. William Botley was born at Colmore Green, near Bridgnorth, Shropshire on 11th April 1895. He was known by his family as Billy and was educated at Worfield School. He worked as a farm labourer before enlistment in the Royal Navy. When he was 16 Billy began his naval career as a boy sailor aboard HMS *Impregnable* in May 1911. On 22nd November 1912 he was drafted to serve on the cruiser HMS *New Zealand*. Botley served five years on this vessel until February 1918 and sailed around the world. He was promoted to Ordinary Seaman on 11th April 1913 and by 5th September 1914 he was Able Seaman and torpedo man, after passing the examinations with flying colours. During this posting he was present when *New Zealand* fought in several of the major naval engagements of the War. On 28th August 1914 *New Zealand* fought in the first naval battle of the war at the Heligoland Bight. On 28th January 1915 she fought in the Battle of Dogger Bank.

The ship collided with HMAS *Australia* on 22nd April 1916. After her repair she was back in action at the Battle of Jutland in May 1916. During this epic naval engagement she fired 420 12-inch shells, which was the most number of shells fired by any ship in the British fleet during that day. The German Fleet hit her with one 11-inch shell, which penetrated her works.

Botley again saw action on 17th November 1917 when HMS *New Zealand* took part in the Second Battle of Heligoland Bight. He was one of six sailors from *New Zealand* selected to take part in the Zeebrugge raid. He was transferred to HMS *Hindustan* on 1st February. Botley was one of the men who landed on the Mole for detonating purposes. His service record states that he was slightly wounded, but he returned home safely from the raid.

Botley was transferred back to HMS *New Zealand* on 1st July 1918 and served on her until October 1919. He continued to serve with the Royal Navy until 1926 retiring as an Able Seaman. After his service with the Royal Navy he joined Shropshire Police Force as a police officer. He served until 1934, leaving the force to work in agriculture. Botley joined the wartime police force during the Second World War. After the war he resumed his work in agriculture. Billy Botley died in January 1960 and was buried in Adderley Parish Church in Shropshire.

ABLE SEAMAN FRANCIS KELLAND DSM J30116 RN. Francis Henry Kelland was born on 31st December 1898 in Exeter, Devon. He worked as an errand boy before enlisting in the Royal Navy as a Boy sailor on 2nd March 1914. He began his naval career on the training ship HMS *Impregnable*, based in Devonport. After completing his training during October 1914, he was posted to HMS *Conqueror*. Francis spent most of the war serving aboard this battleship and he was there when she rammed *Monarch* in December 1914 and when she took part in the Battle of Jutland. He was assigned to D Company, Royal Naval landing party.

Official records state that D Company went to Zeebrugge aboard HMS *Daffodil*, but Francis Kelland went to Zeebrugge aboard *Vindictive*. He wore a *Vindictive* cap ribbon and a telegram sent to his mother from the Accountant-General of the Navy, confirming that he was slightly wounded, confirms Francis belonged to *Vindictive*. Francis received a shell wound to his right hand. He was awarded the Distinguished Service Medal.

After recovering from his wound he continued to serve in the Royal Navy and reached the rank of Chief Petty Officer. After serving 22 years he retired from the service on 30th December 1938. His retirement only lasted for a few months. On 31st December 1939 Francis was recalled with the rank of CPO (GM) at the Gunnery School HMS *Drake* based at Devonport, where he served as an instructor. In May 1940 he was drafted to HMS *Defiance* (*Centurion*), the Royal Naval Torpedo School, another shore base near Devonport. He spent seven months at HMS *Britannia*, before returning to HMS *Drake*. On 26th November 1941 Francis was promoted to temporary Warrant Officer. During the following month he was drafted to serve on the armed merchant carrier HMS *Pretoria Castle* as a gunnery officer. She was one of many merchant vessels requisitioned by the Royal Navy and equipped with guns and naval personnel for military operations. Her role was to protect convoys. *Pretoria Castle* was converted into a carrier and was used as a training carrier in the Atlantic from 1940 until 1942. Francis served aboard her from 18th December 1941 until 28th August 1948. She was a participant in the Battle of the Atlantic. Francis was posted to HMS *Cormorant*, a shore base at Gibraltar and served there from December 1942 until May 1945. After the War he returned to England and served at Royal Naval shore establishments until retiring on 1st September 1947.

Above left: Francis Kelland pictured left with walking stick recovering after the Zeebrugge raid at a convalescent home at Harting. The other two unidentified men may have been wounded at Zeebrugge. The sailor on the right has lost his right arm from the elbow.

Above right: Francis Kelland before the Zeebrugge raid. He is pictured with fellow Zeebrugge raiders (from left to right) Able Seamen Beare, Ahern and Matthews.

On leaving the Royal Navy for a second time he was employed in the Master Riggers Department at HM Dockyard Devonport. He worked here from October 1947 until retiring in December 1963. He spent his few retirement years gardening and sailing his 24-foot half-decked skiff on Plymouth Sound and the River Tamar. Francis Kelland died on 29th September 1969 and was buried in the cemetery at Higher St. Budeaux Parish Church, Plymouth.

WING COMMANDER FRANK BROCK OBE RNAS. Frank Arthur Brock was born in Surrey St Horwood, Croydon in 1885. His family formed Brock's fireworks. It is not surprising that he was nicknamed 'Fireworks'. In 1914, while posing as an American tourist he attended a Zeppelin demonstration in Germany in 1914. As a result of this spying trip Brock developed the anti-Zeppelin dart that could ignite and explode after penetrating the double layered fabric and bring the Zeppelin crashing to the ground. Once successful tests had been completed an order was made to produce 500,000 of Brock's bullets in May 1916. Brock's bullet shot down several German Zeppelins during the summer of 1916. Two more were brought down in September and October 1916, shot down near Potters Bar and Cuffley using Brock's bullet. Brock's invention was superseded in early 1917 by a Royal Flying Corps invention, but it was still used by the RNAS in anti-Zeppelin operations over the North Sea. The tracer bullet was a further development from Brock's invention and is still used today.

Leaving the family business at the outbreak of the War, Brock enlisted in the Royal Horse Artillery but was soon transferred to the Royal Naval Air Service for special work. He trained as a pilot and in 1916 he was promoted to Flight Commander, and during April 1917 received special promotion to Acting Wing Commander as recognition for 'very valuable services performed for naval & military air services'.[18]

He was the founder of the Royal Naval Experimental Station at Stratford and was responsible for developing Very pistols, signal flares and floating flares that illuminated vast areas on contact with water. For his scientific work Brock was made an OBE. A confidential report written on 14th January 1918 wrote of Brock's 'exceptional talent for devising and knowledge of perfecting new devices for use during war' and that he was a 'very capable, hardworking and zealous officer [with a] good command of men'.[19]

A friend commented 'He was without fear, during recent air raids he dashed about in a car to the spots where bombs had dropped, intent on discovering all he could of the explosives employed by the Huns.'[20]

Brock's greatest achievement was the invention of the flameless smoke screen, which was a fundamental element in the planning for the raid on Zeebrugge. Keyes wrote that 'the value of Brock's contribution to the undertaking was simply incalculable.'[21] Brock demonstrated his commitment and dedication to the operation, by working 36 hours continuously without rest on one occasion, as the deadline loomed.

As well as producing smoke to conceal the raiding armada as it approached Zeebrugge, Brock also used light buoys to define the course and flame-throwers that would fire flames of burning oil upon the Mole as *Vindictive* secured alongside. Keyes agreed with great reluctance to permit Brock to take part in the actual operation, but his hand was forced by Brock's insistence and the fact that he was the only person who understood the scientific principles behind the application of the smoke apparatus. Brock also wanted to examine what was thought to be a German device used for sound ranging for shore batteries on the Mole. 'Brock's one plea, which I would have preferred to have refused – as his genius for inventions was so valuable – was that he should be allowed to get on to the Mole, in order to try and find out the German method of sound ranging, so I reluctantly consented to his going on *Vindictive*.'[22]

HMS *Daffodil IV* demonstration of patent fog producing apparatus.

German personnel stand next to a searchlight and one of the metal tubes on the Mole at Zeebrugge which so intrigued Brock.

Wing Commander Brock assaulted the Mole with Lieutenant Commander Adam's first wave and some reports state that he was dressed in khaki uniform and armed with two revolvers and a cutlass. Once on the Mole he ran along the parapet towards the lighthouse. There was an observation shelter with a range finder above it. Once bombs had been thrown inside the shelter to clear any enemy, Brock inspected the range finder. This was where Lieutenant Commander Adams saw him for the last time. Air Mechanic Roland Entwisle assaulted the Mole with Brock as his gun bearer. He witnessed Brock fall near to an enemy machine gun emplacement.

> At 11 pm I proceeded with Commander Brock to our gun station on the aft flammenwerfer. At first we were able to get no pressure, and he tried several times, but could get no juice. He then left the flammenwerfer, and told me what to do, and I handed the speaking tube to him. Just as we bumped against the Mole, the juice came through, but the port fires were dying out. I lit two boxes of matches and finally got the flammenwerfer alight. I then left the flammenwerfer and joined Commander Brock outside. At that moment Oxenbury was hit. I followed Commander Brock on to the Mole; we had not gone far when a machine gun opened fire on us. I dropped down behind some gear; just at that moment it was very dark and smoky, and I saw Commander Brock either fall forward or commence to run, I could not say which. When the firing had stopped, I crawled round to see where I had last seen Commander Brock, but there was no sign of him.[23]

A German Marine Officer spoke of an officer 'who seemed to be entirely devoid of fear':

> He was without arms, but he did not seem to mind anything. He rushed straight at the first gun, and with his fists he struck out at the gunners, knocking down four of them and putting the rest to flight. The men at the other gun positions tried their hardest to get into action before this attack reached them, but it was all to no purpose. The brave British officer and his men were on top of us, and had overpowered our gunners before they could do anything. I saw clearly that it was this daring officer

who was our greatest danger, and I ordered my men to fire on him. It is true there was some danger of hitting our own men, but it was most important to knock out the brave British officer, and if that end was achieved I did not care about anything else.[24]

This was almost certainly Brock. An unidentified member of the Mole storming party related his experience to the *Northern Daily Mail*:

We were one of the earliest crowds to go over and Commander Brock went ahead. It was a fearful job getting over the brow, but the Commander dropped down on to the Mole, a distance of at least ten feet. 'Come on you boys' he shouted, and one by one we followed him. There were Huns near us in a nest surrounded by barbed wire, but we stormed that and reached one of the guns on the Mole. Commander Brock single handed, attacked the gun's crew and we captured the gun and put it out of action. Then we went further along the Mole, and in the light of the star shells, I saw the officer fighting the crew of another gun. The last time I saw him he was removing one of the locks of the gun. He shouted to us to go on, and said he was coming too, but I never saw him again. Another man says that just before we went back to the ship he saw Commander Brock wounded, and being held up against the side of the Mole by two marines, who refused to leave him.[25]

There were 12 Royal Marines from C Company from Plymouth who were captured on the Mole and these two men, who helped the dying Brock, were probably amongst them.

When the *Vindictive* returned to Dover there was hope in some quarters that Brock was alive. Commander Osborne commented to a journalist at Dover 'I don't think he is dead. He is like a cat with nine lives, and I should not be surprised to hear he is a prisoner. Although we all know, he was at any rate severely wounded.'[26]

Officers and men from the ranks respected Brock. Another journalist reported that 'Whilst in the wards yesterday one of the Chief Stewards was giving a little brandy to one of the patients. The man in the next cot, with a smile said "Give me a drop of that please." Looking at him the steward remarked "You don't want this." The patient replied "I only want it to celebrate for Brock's benefit."'[27]

Two British Zeebrugge Raiders lie dead on the Mole, pictured after the raid. The body nearest to the camera could be Wing Commander Brock.

Despite the hopes of his family and those that knew him, Brock was killed and his body was not found. In a tribute in *The Times* an old friend of the Wing Commander described him as

> … *a big, powerful, broad-shouldered, typical Englishman – a good all round sportsman, excelling in football and boxing, and a good rifle and games shot. He was the sort of man who would never dream of going back. I can imagine him being on the Mole at Zeebrugge, and if he lost his revolver, fighting on with his fists.*[28]

If it was not for Brock's smoke screen the author does not think anyone would have returned home from the raid. The German batteries along the Belgium coast would have sunk the entire flotilla and the raiders would either have been killed or taken prisoner. He had certainly prevented a massive disaster for the Royal Navy and Royal Marines. Stoker Petty Officer Pointer from the *Daffodil* knew how important Brock's contribution had been. 'The smoke screens were what helped us; they hid us going in, and they hid us coming out, but none of us expected to get back. Yes I escaped without a scratch, but I never expected it.'[29]

LEADING MECHANIC JOHN WILKINSON F12815 RNAS. John Frederick Wilkinson was born on 10th June 1897 in Oldham, Lancashire. His mother died when he was two years old. His father who was a mill owner sent John to Blackpool to be raised by his aunts. In 1908 he joined the Scouts and was associated with this organization throughout his long life. Educated at Arnold School in Blackpool, he continued his education at the University of Manchester where he read Chemistry from 1913. When War broke out Wilkinson wanted to enlist. Since he was a chemistry undergraduate he was exempt from military service; the decision to allow Wilkinson to enlist rested with his tutor professor at the University, who always refused his request. Wilkinson and several other fellow students were able to enlist during March 1916 when the professor went on a three-month lecture tour of New Zealand. Wilkinson enlisted in the Royal Naval Air Service on 30th March 1916. One of his first research projects was to see if sea lions could detect submarines and defuse bombs. The project was a dismal failure because after the sea lions were trained, when they were released into the sea they would, unsurprisingly, say thanks for the fish and swim away. Wilkinson was attached to the large flammenwerfen, smoke and rocket parties aboard *Vindictive* according to the official post-operation report by Lieutenant Hewitt. During the Zeebrugge Raid he was responsible for the lighting of flares and although designated to stay aboard *Vindictive* he assaulted the Mole, armed with cutlass and pistol. During an after-dinner speech he later recounted that while on the Mole he stopped a comrade from shooting a German soldier. Years later, when Wilkinson was a distinguished physician, he met the German soldier he saved when he visited the Paris Medical School. That German soldier also became a physician after the war and recognized Dr Wilkinson as the man who saved his life.

After the War Wilkinson resumed his studies at Manchester University, graduating in 1920 with a first class degree and was awarded his MSc a year later. In 1923 he became a Fellow of the Royal Institute of Chemistry. He directed his studies towards medicine and in 1931 became a member of the Royal College of Physicians. During his long and productive life he was one of the founders of the British Haematology Society and became the Vice-President of the International Society and the European Society. He was the author of numerous articles for medical journals throughout his 70-year medical career. Retiring as a doctor with the National Health Service in 1963, he continued to act as a medical consultant. He was also the director of Chester Zoo. John Wilkinson died during his 101st year on 31st August 1998.

AIR MECHANIC FRANCIS DONOVAN F19971 RNAS. Francis Donovan was born in Bow, London on 31st July 1897. His service record states that before enlisting in the Royal Naval Air Service he was a science student. His scientific education helped him to become Air Mechanic First Class within a year. During the early part of his service career he worked at Wing Commander Brock's experimental station at Stratford. He was involved in chemical work for the RNAS developing flame-throwers and smoke screens that would be later used in the raid.

Donovan was assigned to HMS *Vindictive* where he manned the flame-thrower hut adjacent to the navigation bridge. His orders were to sweep the Mole with flames of burning oil, before the Royal Marine and Naval force ascended the gang planks and went ashore. Donovan was twenty years old and this would quite literally be his baptism of fire. He recalled his first action, when the Mole battery opened fire. 'My, what a din, it was shattering! Although Captain Carpenter put the *Vindictive* full speed ahead to run her alongside the Mole, I think we suffered more casualties running the gauntlet of the Mole battery than in the rest of the action.'[30]

The flame-thrower hut received heavy shellfire. The flame-thrower equipment was riddled with bullets and rendered inoperable. He did however have a portable flame-thrower to hand, but before he could use it he had to find some way of getting ashore. Donovan and a couple of comrades tried to slide a third gangway onto the Mole. As he carried the portable flame-thrower up the gangway a bullet shot away the nozzle.

I dropped it and ran onto the Mole – and the only weapon I had was a rather blunt cutlass. All I could see through the drizzling rain and under the glare of the star shells, was blazing gun-fire and barbed wire entanglements on the Mole, and the parties of our men and Germans firing at each other.[31]

He safely reached *Vindictive* when the evacuation signal was sounded. 'It was not until I went along the deck during the return voyage and I saw the awful mess of splintered steel, blood, oil and shattered bodies that I realized the horror of it.'[32]

After the war Francis Donovan served as the Chairman of the Zeebrugge Association. When World War Two broke out Donovan was recalled. He was commissioned in the Royal Engineers as a Major. He was captured at Thala, Tunisia on 21st February 1943. As a POW he was incarcerated in Oflag IXA in Germany. Liberated by the 7th US Armored Division during March 1945, Major Donovan worked for the Displaced Persons Centre at Lollar, Landkreis Giessen. He spent the rest of his life in Australia.

FIRST CLASS MECHANIC WILLIAM GOUGH F19842 RNAS. William Henry Gough was born on 25th July 1897 in Mile End, London. He was a student when the War began. He enlisted in the RNAS on 15th August 1916. Gough volunteered for the Zeebrugge raid in early 1918. An RNAS man was attached to each of the Royal Marine and Royal Naval landing parties to provide covering support with a flame-thrower. Gough was assigned to Lieutenant Lamplough and No.9 Platoon. Before the raid, he wrote to his mother, 'Dear Mater, Going into Action tonight'.[33] Gough was exposed to the ferocity of German shellfire as he waited on the deck of *Vindictive*, armed with a flame-thrower containing fuel oil and petrol. Had a bullet or shell penetrated this weapon, he and the marines that he supported would have been engulfed in flames.

With one terrible crash every gun on board spoke, and pandemonium reigned. Six-inch naval guns, howitzers, pom-poms, machine guns and trench mortars [Stokes] added their quota to the general noise. Of course, the Germans located us then quite easily and shells of every description and calibre rained on us. The situation for the landing party was terrible. There we were, lying on the deck being shelled and unable to defend ourselves. The few minutes [(about 15 minutes] between the first shell and the time when we actually landed were in my opinion the worst of the whole business. We lay there hardly daring to move even to help the wounded down below, because we did not know at what moment we were due to commence our part in the affair.[34]

It was miraculous that Gough survived, for most of No.9 platoon had been wiped out before *Vindictive* reached the Mole. 'Our casualties during this bombardment were fearful. Out of the platoon to which I was attached – over 40 men – not more than 8 to 10 got up to land when the signal was given. The remainder were either dead or wounded.'[35]

On surviving the deadly German barrage, Gough's priority was to scramble across one of two remaining gangways and land on the Mole, heavily laden with a flame-thrower.

It was a nerve-trying experience – walking along narrow gangways with a hand rail one side only, encumbered by decidedly heavy equipment and being shelled the while by heavy guns at close range – not more than 100 yards. Some of the shells were actually sweeping the deck, clearing the wall of the Mole and the gangways by a few inches only. The noise of course was terrible.[36]

Once on the Mole Gough's objective was to support Lieutenant Lamplough and the remnants of No.9 platoon by engulfing in flames any opposition they encountered. Gough experienced difficulty in keeping pace with Lamplough and the remnants of his platoon, burdened as he was. He had slung this weapon over his right shoulder and had to descend 20 feet by rope and scaling ladder from the Mole parapet to the ground. During this time he lost contact with Lamplough. Gough did reach his objective, which was a shed on the Mole, which he was to destroy. When he arrived he found that the shed had already been destroyed, with two dead Germans lying amongst the wreckage. On leaving the shed Gough observed a party of armed German sailors who were on the deck in the process of disembarking from the destroyer V 69 which was berthed along the inner Mole.

Pressing on, found myself up against an iron handrail at the water's edge; and in front of me, a German destroyer with her guns going and most of her crew on deck. I therefore turned my flammenwerfer on them and swept the whole deck with flames. I must have killed the lot of them. I tried to reach the bridge, from which someone was potting at me with a revolver, but the range was too great, and my flame-thrower played out. Then, as the bullets from a machine-gun from further up the Mole got too close to be safe, I left my now useless weapon and took cover behind a low wall. From this position I saw my weapon smashed to pieces by machine-gun fire.[37]

Kapitänleutnant Benecke, the commander of V 69, may have been the person who was shooting at Gough from the bridge. Once his flame-thrower was destroyed, Gough made his way back to the *Vindictive*. This journey was doubly perilous as he had to run the gauntlet of enemy and friendly fire.

While crossing the open part of the Mole, absolutely regardless of danger from machine guns (all sense of personal danger is lost on occasions like this) I again became aware that I was being fired at, and turning, saw three men break from the cover of a wrecked locomotive, and run towards our scaling ladders. Two fell almost immediately, but the third kept running, firing a pistol as he went. I returned his fire with my revolver and he then seemed to single me out as his particular enemy. Then followed a revolver duel at a gradually decreasing range – we began at about 30 yards – until when we were absolutely in contact, he went down with a bullet in the throat.[38]

Gough survived the Zeebruge raid without a wound. He regarded the operation 'as a great adventure. One, which – having emerged safely – I would not have missed for a fortune, but which I should not care to undergo again.'[39]

Gough continued to serve in the RNAS until demobilization on 6th February 1919. After the War William Gough worked as an analytical chemist and lived in Croydon. He would serve his country once more during World War Two, as an ARP. His helmet bore the letters 'GIO', which indicated that he was a Gas Identification Officer. Gough was issued with a special type of gas mask, superior to the gas masks issued to civilians. He was issued with a telephone installed in his home for his work, an unusual mark of importance. His son Philip recalled that outside their Croydon home there was a small board covered with a special surface, which would react to any spots of mustard gas with which it might come into contact.

ABLE SEAMAN ALBERT MCKENZIE VC J31736 RN B COMPANY, ROYAL NAVAL LANDING PARTY. Able Seaman Albert McKenzie was born on 23rd October 1898 in Bermondsey, London. He began his service with the Royal Navy as a boy sailor at HMS *Ganges* in 1914 and later served on the battleship HMS *Neptune*. McKenzie belonged to B Company, Royal Naval landing party. He supported Lieutenant Commander Harrison in an assault upon German positions and was one of the few survivors. Severely wounded, he crawled back aboard *Vindictive*.

McKenzie was selected by the men of *Vindictive*, *Iris*, *Daffodil* and the naval assault force to receive the Victoria Cross. He was the first London sailor to receive this award.

After succumbing to septic poisoning from his injury to his foot McKenzie died from influenza on 3rd November 1918. Aged 20, he was buried at Camberwell (Forest Hill) Cemetery, London. His Victoria Cross citation reads:

The Mayor of Southwark escorting Able Seaman Albert McKenzie to his home off the Old Kent Road on his return from Buckingham Palace, where he received the VC from King George V.

On the night of the operation he landed on the Mole with his machine-gun in the face of great difficulties, and did very good work, using his gun to the utmost advantage. He advanced down the Mole with Lieut. Comdr. Harrison, who with most of his party was killed, and accounted for several of the enemy running from a shelter to a destroyer alongside the Mole. This very gallant seaman was severely wounded whilst working his gun in an exposed position.[40]

SERGEANT MAJOR CHARLES THATCHER DSC 4TH BATTALION RMLI. Charles John Thatcher was born on 7th May 1882. He joined the Royal Marines Light Infantry on 2nd July 1900, aged 18. During his initial years he served in Somaliland and received the African Service Medal 1908–10. In his service record Brigadier-General C. Trotman wrote that Thatcher was 'very zealous, smart and quite satisfactory … very energetic and has tack … a superb warrant officer.'[41] It was Sergeant Major Charles Thatcher who heard the rumour in the sergeants' mess that No.7 Platoon failed to parade during training and reported this serious breach of discipline to Captain Chater, Battalion Adjutant. This resulted in numerous courts of enquiry being held and No.7 Platoon sent back to Portsmouth in disgrace.

During the raid Thatcher played his part by ensuring that the scaling ladders were brought from *Vindictive* onto the Mole. Under dangerous enemy fire he organised the securing of the ladders from the Mole parapet so that assault parties could reach the ground level. His citation for the Distinguished Service Cross says he was 'mainly instrumental in conveying the heavy scaling ladders from the ship to the Mole, and throughout the operation displayed great coolness and devotion to duty'.[42]

Thatcher was badly wounded, receiving a penetrating wound in the right thigh. His wound was so severe that when he was admitted to the Royal Naval Hospital Chatham his right leg was amputated. Retired from the Royal Marines Light Infantry on medical orders on 23rd July 1922, he returned to his home on Jersey. He died aged 46 on 14th March 1928 as a result of the wounds that he sustained during the Zeebrugge Raid.

The Fight on the Mole, 23rd April 1918, by D. Macpherson.

CAPTAIN ARTHUR CHATER DSO, 4TH BATTALION RMLI.

Arthur Chater was born in Kensington, London on 7th February 1896. His father was a clergyman from Devon and Arthur was one of eleven children. He was educated at Aldenham School, Hertfordshire and as a young adolescent had aspirations to join the Royal Navy. On completing his education he failed the medical examination to enter the Navy. Chater, unperturbed, enlisted in the Royal Marines Light Infantry with the rank of 2nd Lieutenant on 1st October 1913. His military training began at the Royal Naval College at Greenwich. Towards the end of July 1914 he was given the option of choosing a Royal Marine Depot to serve with. The Commandant at Deal Depot gave him the choice of Chatham, Portsmouth and Plymouth Depots. With the War drawing closer, Chater chose the Chatham Depot because it was nearer to the enemy. Within a year of enlisting Chater was promoted to Lieutenant, on 9th September 1914, and was assigned to the Royal Marine Brigade, Chatham Battalion. This Battalion was shipped to Dunkirk on 20th September 1914. Chater was transferred with his battalion to Antwerp on London buses on 3rd October. On the march from the buses towards the front line, Chater was greeted by Winston Churchill, First Lord of the Admiralty. Chater experienced action for the first time during the defence of Antwerp. He fought in the battle at Lierre in Belgium on 4th October and helped to delay the German advance for a short period. This delay enabled the British Army to fall back and consolidate their defensive positions. At Lierre Chater was wounded when a German shell exploded on a nearby parapet on 5th October. Chater received shell splinter wounds to his face; the blast decapitated a fellow soldier.

Chater recovered from his wounds in time to join the Chatham Battalion in the landing at Gaba Tape and Cape Helles at Gallipoli on 28th April 1915. He was active in the consolidation and defence of the southern sector. Chater was part of the assault force on Razor Back on 3rd May. On 4th May Chater was appointed Adjutant for Chatham Battalion. The Battalion was defending the positions of Pope's Hill and Quinn's Post from 4th May until 12th May. On 7th June Chater took part in the attack on Turkish trenches. He remained Adjutant until 27th July 1915. During his time in Gallipoli Chater received a shrapnel wound to his back. After Gallipoli Chater was posted to the light cruiser HMS *Courageous* serving with the Grand Fleet from November 1915. He was promoted to Captain on 17th September 1917. After participating in the second Battle of the Heligoland Bight he was awarded the Croix de Guerre.

In February Chater was appointed Adjutant to the 4th Battalion Royal Marines Light Infantry. He played a prominent role in the organisation of the raid. During March 1918 he had to deal with the mutinous indiscretions of No.7 Platoon and escort them back to Portsmouth in disgrace.

Chater was standing between Lieutenant Colonel Elliot and Major Cordner when they were both killed by an exploding shell on the bridge of *Vindictive* as she approached the Mole. During the raid Chater landed on the Mole three times, actively coordinating the storming party. He received 15 votes to receive the Victoria Cross in the ballot. Instead he was awarded the DSO. His citation reads:

> [He] was of the greatest assistance in keeping up communication between the various units of the battalion, and carried out his duties in a calm manner, which greatly contributed to the success of the operations. Gave great assistance in the preparation of the plan for the assault.[43]

After Zeebrugge, Chater was appointed Adjutant of the Depot, Royal Marines at Deal, an appointment he held until February 1921. He was then seconded to the Egyptian Army and Sudan Defence Force until February 1931, when he resumed duties with the Royal Marines

Corps, being assigned to Portsmouth Division in May 1931. During June 1931 he was posted to HMS *Effingham* and served in the East Indies. While serving aboard this ship he was promoted to Major in October 1931. He later served on HM Ships *Enterprise* and *Hawkins* before returning to Portsmouth Division in June 1933.

Selected for Staff training at the Royal Naval Staff College during 1934 he was awarded the King George V scholarship. Chater returned to the sea the following year, serving on the battleship HMS *Nelson* from June 1935 until June 1936. During this draft he was promoted to Brevet Lieutenant Colonel in December 1935.

Chater was seconded as Officer Commanding Somaliland Camel Corps and was responsible for organising the defence of British interests in the country. During the years spent in this British colony, Chater was promoted to Lieutenant Colonel in 1939, followed by Acting Colonel in 1940. During 1940 Chater was appointed Commander of the Somaliland force and organised operations against the Italians at Ras Hafun and Cape Guardafui in the Horn of Africa.

Chater returned to the Royal Marines as Commandant of Portsmouth Division in 1943. Promoted to Acting Major-General in May 1944, Chater was appointed to 231st Brigade LCT(H). Chater held the particular distinction of landing at Gallipoli, Zeebrugge and then on 6th June 1944, King Sector, Gold Beach, Normandy with the 231st Brigade. Appointed to Director of Combined Operations, India and South Asia from October 1944 he served aboard HMS *Braganza*. It was from this vessel that he coordinated the operations off the Arakan Coast during 1944/45. Major General Chater retired from the Corps on 7th April 1948. Ron Moyse, the cousin of Zeebrugge Raider George Moyse, served under Chater when he was Major General in Chatham and remembered Chater as being 'a small man with a big heart'. Chater died in 1979.

CAPTAIN EDWARD BAMFORD VC DSO CO NO.7 PLATOON, 4TH BATTALION RMLI. Edward Bamford had already distinguished himself in battle prior to the Zeebrugge raid. On 31st May 1916 he was aboard HMS *Chester* commanding the Royal Marine Light Infantry contingent at Jutland. During this epic clash of British and German naval power Bamford was positioned aft where he commanded the port and starboard No. 3 guns. German shells from four German vessels poured onto the *Chester* disabling most of her guns and causing fifty per cent casualties amongst the personnel manning them. (Among them was Boy First Class John Cornwall, who was a member of a gun crew on the foc'sle. He was mortally wounded at the outset of battle and remained at his post for further orders despite his wounds. His bravery and devotion to duty was recognised by being awarded posthumously the Victoria Cross. At 16 he was the youngest recipient to receive this award.) Bamford was forced to abandon the aft control room when it was blasted by shell fire. Suffering wounds to his leg and face he assisted the surviving remnants of the starboard gun crew in firing their rounds. Bamford was awarded a DSO for his role at Jutland. Vice Admiral Sir David Beatty wrote the following citation:

In after control when it was blown to pieces by a shell burst. Slightly burnt in face and slightly wounded in leg. Then assisted to work one gun with a much reduced crew, and controlled another gun. Assisted in extinguishing a fire, and in general showed great coolness, power of command, judgement and courage, when exposed to heavy fire.[44]

The Friedrichsort Leitstand on the Mole after the raid.

Zeebrugge Mole, on the morning of 23rd April, hours after the raid.

During 1918 he was appointed commander of No.7 Platoon, after the breach of discipline that occurred in this platoon during the early stages of training for the raid. Bamford led his platoon onto the Mole during the raid. One Royal Marine who was blinded by a shell burst just as *Vindictive* approached the Mole heard Bamford cry 'Come on lads, let's get at them ashore'. While on the Mole he coordinated the remnants of the storming party. His Victoria Cross citation reads:

> *This officer landed on the Mole from 'Vindictive' with numbers 5, 7 and 8 platoons of the marine storming force, in the face of great difficulties. When on the Mole and under heavy fire, he displayed the greatest initiative in the command of his company, and by his total disregard of danger showed a magnificent example to his men. He first established a strong point on the right of the disembarkation, and, when satisfied that that was safe, led an assault on a battery to the left with the utmost coolness and valour.*[45]

During the afternoon of 26th April, the survivors of 4th RMLI Battalion took part in the ballot to vote for who should be the representative from the Battalion to receive the Victoria Cross. Bamford received the most votes, 64. Adjutant Captain Chater later wrote:

> *I explained what was to be done, slips of paper were issued, the troops were then told to break off for a few minutes to consult each other before writing a name on their paper and handing it in. While this was being done, the CO and I went to the office to complete the report, leaving Captain Bamford in charge to collect the voting slips and add up the result. Half an hour later he arrived at the office looking rather sheepish. He handed to the CO a list showing himself as having received the greatest number of votes.*[46]

Bamford continued to serve with the Royal Marines Light Infantry after the war. In March 1928 he was promoted to Major; however he became ill while at the Chinese naval base at Wei Hai Wei. He required immediate medical attention and was taken to Hong Kong aboard HMS *Cumberland*. During this passage he succumbed to this mysterious illness and died before reaching Hong Kong on 28 September 1928.

LIEUTENANT THEODORE COOKE DSO, CO NO.5 PLATOON 4TH BATTALION RMLI. Theodore Frederic Vernon Cooke was born on 22nd June 1896 in Putney. London. His father John had served with the Indian Police Force in Bombay. Theodore was educated at Bedford School and enlisted with the RMLI at the outbreak of war on 22nd August 1914. Assigned to the Portsmouth Division he served on HMS *Suffolk* patrolling the West Indies and the North American coast. He also served on the Aegean Islands with the 3rd Royal Marine Battalion from 17th January 1917 to 10th January 1918. On his return to England he volunteered for the Zeebrugge operation and was transferred to the 4th Battalion.

Cooke played a prominent role in leading the first party of Marines, No.5 Platoon from B Company, onto the Mole. Cooke sustained a gun shot wound fracturing his skull. He carried on the attack until he received a second wound. Private John Press, who was also wounded, carried him back to *Vindictive*. Cooke's bravery is mentioned in the 4th Battalion RMLI report written for the Admiralty by Captain Chater. His actions in any other engagement would probably have earned the Victoria Cross. During the ballot for the Victoria Cross, he received five votes from his colleagues. Instead, Cooke was awarded the DSO and promoted to Brevet Major in recognition of his contribution. His citation reads:

> *By his personal bravery under fire set a magnificent example to his men, and led them forward with the greatest courage and dash in spite of being wounded. He was wounded a second time whilst endeavouring to carry a wounded man back to the ship.*[47]

It was Chater's view that Cooke should have received the Victoria Cross. Chater later recalled that during the ballot 'The officers who discussed the matter before voting, voted for Lieutenant T. F. V. Cooke, who led the assault along the top of the sea wall and was twice wounded.'[48] Cooke was also awarded the Croix de Guerre. Cooke's head wound was so severe that he required three operations. Royal Naval surgeons refused to carry out the final operation to remove some remaining shrapnel that was causing pressure on his brain. Cooke had to seek private medical assistance to perform the operation at a personal cost of £250. The Admiralty declined to reimburse Cooke, but after some time they relented. As a result of his head wound Cooke had to wear a silver plated head brace, covered by a black skull cap, to protect his brain. Cooke retired from the RMLI in 1922 and lived on the island of Jersey, where he became involved in the local community. He endured five years of German occupation during World War Two. During that period Cooke served as an Air Raid Protection Warden and as a Sergeant in the St. John's Ambulance Brigade. During the War, a group of Russian Prisoners of War escaped on Jersey. These POWs were being used by the Nazis as slave labour to build German defences that would form part of Hitler's Atlantic Wall. One of those escaped prisoners was harboured by Cooke for the duration. At

Lieutenant Theodore Cooke and No. 5 Platoon RMLI.

great personal risk to himself and his family Cooke sheltered the prisoner in his loft while the German occupiers searched the island. Had the German authorities discovered the Russian POW in Cooke's home, his life and the lives of his family would have been in great danger. They could have either been shot or sent to a concentration camp. This was Cooke's way of contributing to the fight against the German invaders. He displayed great courage at Zeebrugge in 1918 and demonstrated it again during World War Two. In 1945 Cooke was responsible for coordinating the distribution of Red Cross Parcels on the island. Cooke was a public-spirited individual and continued his duties with the St. John's Ambulance Brigade after the War. He maintained his interest in the organization up to the months before his death. He died on 30th December 1958 aged 62. A colleague from the St. John's Ambulance Brigade paid this tribute: 'He was a man who never failed in his duty: he was always willing and whenever there was a public duty to perform he would volunteer.'[49]

PRIVATE ARTHUR BURNELL, PO 18773, NO.6 PLATOON, B COMPANY, 4TH BATTALION RMLI. Arthur Burnell was born in Scunthorpe, Lincolnshire on 23 July 1899. His service record states that he enlisted with the RMLI on his eighteenth birthday, on 23rd July 1915, in a Nottingham recruitment office listing his occupation as a labourer. But Arthur was sixteen when he enlisted. His younger brother Thomas remembered that Arthur was patriotic as a boy and always spoke about serving and fighting for his country in one of the armed services. When Arthur was sixteen, Britain had been fighting the war with Germany for two years. He was under the permitted age to serve and contrary to his mother's wishes he enlisted. Most of his service was spent serving aboard the battleship HMS *Emperor of India* from June 1916 to December 1917. In 1918 he was selected to take part in the Zeebrugge raid and was assigned to No.6 Platoon, B Company. Arthur Burnell sailed aboard *Vindictive*; his role was bomb thrower. Arthur and his mate Private Jack Finney from No.9 Platoon were runners who reported to Lieutenant Bloxham. Arthur never got onto the Mole because he received a fatal wound as *Vindictive* approached. Jack Finney wrote a letter to Arthur's sister, saying, 'It was the last thing that I ever thought, that Arthur would get hit, because we used to talk about what a good time we would have when it was over. Arthur did not say much when he got hit, he seemed like as if he was asleep, because he had his eyes shut.'[50] In a letter to the the Burnell family, he wrote:

Far left: Private Arthur Burnell. As a bomb thrower aboard the *Vindictive*, Arthur would have had little need of his rifle if he had made it onto the Mole – except perhaps the bayonet.

Left: Private Arthur Burnell's grave in Scunthorpe Cemetery.

Below: Private Arthur Burnell, is on the left.

We were all layed down at that time you know, and when Lieut. Bloxham shouted 'come along' orders to 9 Platoon, also shouting for Burnell and Smith, see, of course I said to Arthur, come on Arthur he's shouting at us and Arthur never spoke. So I says, 'Arthur you are not hit are you, and then he said quietly, 'yes'. 'Where are you hit?' I said, he then said, 'in the head'. So I said come on down to the sick bay, I thought … he could have walked with me … So I got hold of him to lift him and then he said … ' leave me alone'. So I then shouted for stretcher bearers, but there were none about. So I then got two fellows to give me a lift with him and they did do, to the sick bay. I did not know them two fellows, in fact I never thought to look who they were, when we were carrying him down, Arthur said two or three times 'Oh do leave me alone' and they were the last words he said to me. When we got him down to the sick bay, some ambulance fellows took him off us and then I said to Arthur, you will soon be alright Arthur now, and with that I left him, and these other two fellows were just going on up the steps before me to follow the lads that had gone on the Mole.[51]

Arthur clung on to life as *Vindictive* headed home from the Zeebrugge raid. On arriving at Dover, he underwent an emergency surgical operation. Arthur continued to fight for life for another day, but he succumbed to his wounds, passing away on the 24th. Arthur's grieving family wanted him to be brought home for burial. His father Thomas paid for Arthur's body to be returned. Arthur Burnell was buried in Scunthorpe Cemetery and received a military funeral. A Union Jack was draped over his coffin and three volleys were fired over his grave. His mother was unable to attend Arthur's funeral because she had given birth to another son, George on the 25th April. The death of Arthur Burnell was mourned by his shipmates aboard HMS *Emperor of India* who paid for his gravestone. The headstone reads: 'To the memory of Private Arthur Burnell who died of wounds received at Zeebrugge on 23rd April 1918. Aged 19 years. This stone was erected as a token of respect and esteem by his shipmates of HMS *Emperor of India*. He gave his life for his friend and country.'

PRIVATE WILLIAM GLOVER WARREN 2115 (S) NO.8 PLATOON, B COMPANY, 4TH BATTALION RMLI. William Glover Warren was born on 11th April 1898 in Castle Donnington, Loughborough. He worked as a farm hand before enlisting in the Royal Marines Light Infantry on 20th March 1917. Private Warren was assigned to No.8 Platoon, B Company. He landed on the Mole and formed part of the small force assembled by Captain Bamford to attack the 4-inch battery. He was initially reported missing, presumed killed soon after the raid. For a week his mother was devastated after receiving the news, before the mistake was rectified. One explanation which was passed down through the family was that William placed his greatcoat over a wounded mate and left it there. When his mate passed away he was mistakenly identified as Private Warren, because of the coat. Warren was not killed, but wounded in the foot. He was awarded a specially minted badge awarded by King George V to Zeebrugge survivors. Discharged from the RMLI during March 1919 he later joined the Derbyshire Police Force, serving from February 1922 until 1952, when he retired with the rank of Sergeant. He was commended on twelve occasions for outstanding police work during his thirty years service. After the war he married Ann Renshaw, the widow of Edward Yarwood who had been killed at Arras leaving two children, aged three and four. William Warren and Ann had another child, Mary, born in 1925.

PRIVATE WILLIAM GALLIN PLY 15290 NO.9 PLATOON, C COMPANY, 4TH BATTALION RMLI. William George Gallin was born on 27th November 1893 in Heavitree, Exeter. He worked as an errand boy before enlisting to join the Royal Marines Light Infantry on 10th January 1911 in Exeter. William served aboard HMS *Colossus* from 14th February 1913 until 1st January 1918. He was aboard *Colossus* when she took part in the Battle of Jutland in 1916. He stormed the Mole with No.9 Platoon. After the war he married his wife Linda and served as a Royal Marines MP in Plymouth Dockyard. William Gallin died in Plymouth in March 1985.

PRIVATE FRANK KENDALL NARRACOTT PLY 2508 (S), NO.9 PLATOON, C COMPANY, 4TH BATTALION RMLI. Born in Manor Park, London, Frank Narracott (pictured left) came to Southend in 1908. Educated at the London Road School and Southend Technical School he was first employed in munitions work. He was permitted to continue to work in a munitions factory after attesting under Lord Derby's scheme. In September 1917, aged 32, he was called up and he joined the Royal Marines Light Infantry. He was assigned to Lieutenant Lamplough's No.9 Platoon. Frank Narracott was injured during training. On 30th March a Court of Inquiry, comprising Major Eagles, Captain Tuckey and Lieutenant Underhill was convened to investigate and report upon the circumstances surrounding his injury. During the raid he was reported to have been pulled out of the water, which suggests that he fell into the sea either while he was going onto the Mole or during the retirement. Corporal Hewitt from No.8 Platoon organised the rescue of a man who had fallen into the sea between *Vindictive* and the Mole, which may have been Frank. He was brought to Deal Hospital where he recovered from a strained right arm. From 21st May 1918 to 9th July 1919 Narracott served at HMS *Glory* in Russia. In 1919 he was awarded the MSM (Meritorious Service Medal). He was demobbed on 10th September 1919.

No. 9 Platoon, C Company, 4th Battalion Royal Marine Light Infantry photographed at Deal prior to the raid. Lieutenant Lamplough is seated, second row, seventh from left. Lamplough was a veteran from the Gallipoli campaign and was highly respected by the men he commanded. He was awarded the Distinguished Service Cross for his role. His citation states that 'He covered the retirement with great resource'. Bugler Frederick Greenway is seated directly in front of him. Private Frank Kendall Narracott is in the back row, sixth from left.

PRIVATE WILLIAM HOPEWELL CGM PLY 15995, NO.9 PLATOON, C COMPANY 4TH BATTALION RMLI. William Hopewell was born in Kimberly, Nottingham on 11th February 1894. He was the son of Henry and Alice Hopewell and had five brothers and six sisters. He worked as a lace threader at Carey's Lace Factory in Southwell before enlisting to join the Royal Marines Light Infantry on 7th January 1913. His older brothers Albert and John Hopewell also enlisted, joining the Sherwood Foresters. Both his brothers served in the 1st/8th Battalion and both were killed within three months of each other in 1915 on the Western Front near Ypres. Albert was killed on 15th April and John was killed on 30th July. John may have been killed during the battle for Hooge. Soon after the deaths of his two brothers William wrote to his aunt and vowed 'I'll get my own back for what they did to Albert and John.' The opportunity to avenge the death of his brothers came in early 1918, when volunteers were sought for the Zeebrugge raid. In an interview after the raid William told a journalist 'I volunteered for this particular job, because I lost two brothers at the front in six months, and I wanted to get my own back.'[52] William was assigned to No.9 Platoon, C Company, commanded by Lieutenant Lamplough. When two of the men from his Lewis gun crew became casualties aboard *Vindictive*, it was William Hopewell who carried the gun onto the Mole, where he continued to fire at the enemy. William was awarded the Conspicuous Gallantry medal and his citation confirms that he was the last man to leave the Mole. *The London Gazette*:

> After the No.1 and No.2 of his Lewis gun section had become casualties in the ship in which Private Hopewell was serving, he took the Lewis gun ashore and brought it into action. He continued to fire the gun throughout the operation, and was almost the last man to retire, bringing his gun out of action with him, until it was rendered useless by a direct hit by a shell.[53]

William's daughter Betty remembered that her father was a very reserved and unassuming fellow. When her father returned home immediately after the raid the town band with local dignitaries and press was waiting for him, to welcome him home. Observing the crowds waiting for his arrival, he jumped out of the train and went home across the fields.

When the War ended William married Beatrice Hancock on 13th December 1919. They had three sons and three daughters. William served in RMLI until 1922. After leaving the Corps he returned to Southwell to work at Carey's Lace Factory. He would also work as a stoker at the local gasworks and as a gardener at the local workhouse. When the Second World War broke out William tried to enlist, but was considered too old to serve. Instead, William joined the Home Guard and served with them throughout the War. William would later become a member of the Dragon Lodge, Southwell, The Royal and Ancient Order of Buffalos. William Hopewell died on 9th May 1973.

PRIVATE SAMUEL HOPSON PLY 16725 NO.9 PLATOON, C COMPANY, 4TH BATTALION RMLI. Samuel Houston Hopson was born on 1st July 1893. He was one of the Royal Marines captured on Zeebrugge Mole. He served with the Corps until June 1935.

PRIVATE ARCHIBALD WILLIAM TOACH, PLY 2494(S), NO.9 PLATOON, C COMPANY, 4TH BATTALION RMLI. Archibald William Toach was born in Leicester on 2nd September 1899. Archie enlisted to join the RMLI on 11th September 1917 when he was aged 17 and under age. His nephew Gordon recalled: 'Throughout my life, at the mention of his name, there was a feeling of quiet respect, for like many more teenagers, he responded to the call of duty much earlier than necessary through volunteering at 17 years of age.' He was assigned to No.9 Platoon, C Company and was under the command of Lieutenant Lamplough. He assaulted the Mole at Zeebrugge from *Vindictive* and received a gun shot wound under the side of his right arm. Archie died a bachelor on 10th July 1928 and was buried at Belgrave Cemetery, Leicester.

BUGLER FREDERICK GREENWAY PLY 15955, NO.9 PLATOON, C COMPANY, 4TH BATTALION RMLI. Frederick Greenway was born on 13th March 1898 at St. Aubyn, Devonport. He worked as a baker's boy before enlisting on 22nd January 1913, aged 14 years and 10 months. When World War One broke out he served as a bugler aboard HMS *Cumberland*. In September 1914 this county-class armoured cruiser captured 10 German merchant vessels off the Cameroon coast. While serving in this region Bugler Greenway caught malaria and the bouts of fever would reoccur throughout his life. During December 1914 he transferred to HMS *Challenger*, where he served for three years. This cruiser patrolled the West African Coast and took part in the blockading of Dar es Salaam during 1916. He assaulted the Mole with No.9 Platoon. He was one of the few from that platoon to return. Greenway continued to serve with the Royal Marines until March 1937 when he retired with the rank of Bugler Major. He tried to rejoin the service at the outbreak of World War Two, but was considered too old. Instead he served in the Home Guard. Frederick Greenway passed away in 1956.

The guns and crew quarters of the Hafenkopf Battery on Zeebrugge Mole. Ten men from this battery were sent by Schütte to confront the British raiders.

PRIVATE TOMMY KEEGAN PLY 17921 NO.10 PLATOON, C COMPANY, RMLI. Tommy Keegan was born in Toxteth, Liverpool on 11th December 1896. After schooling he worked as a tram car cleaner for Tramways. At the outbreak of war Tommy was keen to play his part and wanted to follow other family members to join up. His service record states that he enlisted on 20th January 1915 aged 18 years. However, his great nephew remembers that Tommy enlisted aged 16 and that his mother went to the recruiting office to secure Tommy's release, because he was too young to serve. Her efforts to get her son released failed and Private Tommy Keegan was sent to Deal Depot to train as a Royal Marine. On completing his training during July 1915 he was assigned to Plymouth Division. Five months later he was given his first taste of sea life when in December 1915 he was drafted to serve aboard HMS *Erin*. He took part in the Battle of Jutland in May 1916. He continued to serve aboard this Dreadnought Class battleship until January 1918 when he left to begin training for the Zeebrugge raid. Private Keegan was assigned to No.10 Platoon commanded by Lieutenant Stanton. It was initially planned that No.10 Platoon together with No.9 Platoon would have been the first units to ascend the Mole. Only a few men from No. 9 and No.10 Platoon landed on the Mole, because both platoons sustained many casualties from shellfire as *Vindictive* approached. Sergeant Wright from No.10 Platoon estimated that only 12 men from each platoon landed. Other sources give the combined complement of the two platoons as only 14 men. Tommy continued to serve with the RMLI after the war serving on HMS *Orion* during 1920 and on HMS *Glorious* during the following year. He was discharged on 22nd February 1923 and returned to working on the Tramways as a conductor.

PRIVATE THOMAS JACKSON PLY 17316, NO.10 PLATOON, C COMPANY RMLI. Thomas Herbert Jackson was born in Singleton, Lancashire on 3rd July 1897. Before the war he worked as a blacksmith. When war broke out he was the first to volunteer from his village, but was turned away by the army for being too young. Determined to answer Kitchener's call for volunteers he lied about his age and enlisted in the Royal Marines Light Infantry on 17th September 1914. Throughout his service he was judged by his superiors to be of very good character. Most of his service – from June 1915 to December 1917 – was served on board the Dreadnought HMS *Marlborough*. Jackson was at Jutland in 1916 when she was torpedoed during the battle. During the Zeebrugge raid, as *Vindictive* approached the Mole a shell fired from the Mole battery exploded directly over the deck killing 30 men from No.10 Platoon. There were originally 44 men in the Platoon. The 20-year-old Jackson may have been one of those initial casualties. His sister Ivy Jackson had received a telegram asking if she wished her brother Tom to receive a naval burial at Dover or to be brought home for private burial in Singleton. It was Ivy's wish that Tom would be brought home to Singleton, however that wish was not fulfilled because of an administrative error. Private Tom Jackson's remains were mistaken for Private Stanley Jackson's and were accidentally sent to Stanley's village of Immingham in Lincolnshire for burial. Tom was buried in Immingham, Stanley was buried in Dover. This terrible error would accentuate the grief of the two bereaved families.

SERGEANT HARRY WRIGHT DSM, PLY 14423, NO.10 PLATOON, C COMPANY RMLI. Harry Wright was born in 1889 at Red Hill Worcester. On leaving school, Harry worked as a farm labourer. Enlisting in the RMLI in February 1908 aged 18, Wright was mentioned in dispatches on 28th August 1915. In early 1918 he volunteered for the Zeebrugge operation while serving on HMS *Powerful*. When Lieutenant Stanton was mortally wounded, it was Harry Wright who led the remnants of No. 10 Platoon onto the Mole. When *Vindictive* left the Mole Wright and his men were left stranded and had no option but to surrender. He passed the last months of the war as a POW. During his time in captivity, Wright made efforts to forward information of military value to England. On his release and repatriation to England he was awarded the Distinguished Service Medal for his role in the Zeebrugge operation. He continued to serve with the RMLI until August 1925. He rejoined the corps during World War Two and served as a gunner on defensively armed merchant ships.

No.10 Platoon with Major Weller, seated front row, fifth from right, and Lieutenant Robert Stanton to his right.

PRIVATE WILLIAM BUSHELL, PLY 16431 NO.11 PLATOON, C COMPANY, RMLI. William Bushell was born on 15th September 1895 at St. Peter's Walsall, Staffordshire. Before the War he worked at the Oak Tanning Company. He enlisted in the Royal Marines Light Infantry during August 1913. Throughout his war service he had served on the battlecruiser HMS *Lion* and experienced battle on three occasions. Four days after joining HMS *Lion* the ship was engaged in the failed attempt to prevent German battlecruisers from bombarding the eastern coast of England, on 16th December 1914. A month later the vessel was involved in the Battle of Dogger Bank on 24th January 1915. Bushell was present during the Battle of Jutland when HMS *Lion* was hit by 13 twelve inch shells and one 5.9 inch shell. Bushell was lucky to survive, for over 100 casualties were sustained aboard during the battle. During the Zeebrugge raid he was seriously wounded in the right arm, back and thigh.

PRIVATE ERNEST RHIND, SERVICE NUMBER PLY 2153(S), NO.11 PLATOON, C COMPANY, 4TH BATTALION RMLI. Ernest Hesketh Rhind was born on 25th June 1891 in Moss Side, Manchester. He enlisted to join the Royal Marines Light Infantry on 28th April 1917. A year after enlisting he was assigned to the 4th Battalion RMLI to prepare for the Zeebrugge Raid. Assigned to No.11 Platoon he assaulted the Mole from HMS *Vindictive*. He received a shell wound to his left shoulder and was discharged from the Corps during September 1918. The family still possesses the piece of shrapnel that wounded Ernest. Ernest died on 12th July 1966.

CORPORAL GEORGE MOYSE, PLY 12098 NO.11 PLATOON, C COMPANY, 4TH BATTALION RMLI. George James Moyse was born on the 17th September 1889 at St Matthew's, Stonehouse, Devon. His father John Moyse was a Colour Sergeant in the Royal Marines light Infantry. George left his job as a machine boy to join his father as a bugle boy with the RMLI in 1902. In 1912, while serving aboard HMS *Cambrian* George Moyse was sent to New Zealand and then onto the Antarctic to search for the ill-fated Scott expedition. When World War One broke out Private Moyse and his father were dispatched to Ostend with the Plymouth Division to aid Belgium in her defence against the German invasion. Transported aboard the battleship HMS *Goliath*, they landed at Ostend on 25th August 1914. George's service record indicates that he served on HMS *Goliath* throughout 1914 until the end of June 1915. During this time the battleship was involved in the blockade of the SMS *Konigsberg* during October and November 1914. The vessel took part in the attack on Dar-es-Salaam on 28th and 30th November 1914. During April 1915 HMS *Goliath* was deployed to the Dardanelles and supported the Gallipoli landings on 25th April. George was a gunlayer aboard when HMS *Goliath* was sunk by the Turkish torpedo boat *Muvenet-i-Milet* on 13th May 1915. When he went overboard his foot got caught on something on deck and contused his hip, obliging him to swim without the use of his legs.

On 11th March 1916, George was posted to the cruiser HMS *Diana* which was patrolling Chinese waters. He served on this cruiser until December 1917, during which time he was promoted to Corporal. During January 1918 Corporal Moyse was drafted to the 4th Battalion RMLI and was selected for Zeebrugge. He was assigned to No.11 Platoon, which was to lead the assault on the Mole from *Vindictive*. He recalled:

I was with the storming parties, formed up below deck. A shell burst among us and wiped out almost all the men standing on my right. But when we got alongside every able man dashed through the inferno on the deck and climbed the gangways up to the parapet of the Mole. By that time most of the gangways had been shot away. I had a bag of 40 bombs and a pair of insulated wire cutters. As a Corporal of the Marines, I was supposed to lead a party of twelve men, but only two of us got there – and then it seemed like a nightmare, didn't it? The worst of it was that the Vindictive *moored on the outside – the seaward side – of the breakwater, we had to climb down from the parapet where we landed, to the floor of the Mole. That was 16 feet, and they had machine guns under us. Eventually I ran into a concrete shelter and chucked bombs at a German destroyer moored against the Mole, which was shelling* Vindictive.[54]*

After they had attacked the destroyer V 69, the recall was sounded and George Moyse was nearly left behind, jumping onto *Vindictive* just as it was leaving the Mole. It was during the passage home that he realised that he had been wounded. He received further wounds when serving in Russia during 1919. He was medically discharged from the Corps on the 25th August 1919 and embarked on a career with the Civil Service. For 25 years George Moyse worked tirelessly for the Zeebrugge 1918 Association and took a great interest in the welfare of its members. His commitment was recognised on 1st January 1963 when he was awarded the MBE by the HM Queen Elizabeth II.

CORPORAL ALFRED GUMM, PLY 15119, NO.11 PLATOON, C COMPANY 4TH BATTALION RMLI. Alfred Percival Gumm was born in December 1894 in Ilfracombe, Devon, one of five sons born to James and Annie Gumm. Percy worked as a postman before enlisting to join the Royal Marines Light Infantry on 18th October 1910 in Exeter. His service record states that he was born on 11th September 1893, contrary to his birth certificate, which says December 1894. So Percy was probably yet another under-age volunteer. When World War One broke out Percy Gumm was serving aboard the battleship HMS *Ocean*. He began his service on this vessel on 29th July 1914 and he was to experience an eventful beginning to the War. On 21st August 1914 HMS *Ocean* was sent to Queenstown, New Zealand as a guard ship. A month later she was deployed to the East Indies Station in support of cruisers on convoy duty. HMS *Ocean* protected a convoy to Bahrain in October 1914. This battleship became the senior ship that coordinated the capture of Basra. This was an important strategic strike, in that it secured oilfields that would supply the Royal Navy. During December 1914 *Ocean* was sent to Suez to defend the Canal. She was ordered to sail to the Dardanelles during late February 1915. Percy Gumm witnessed the opening shots fired in the Gallipoli campaign, as HMS *Ocean* with other Royal Naval vessels bombarded Turkish forts guarding the Dardanelles Straits. On 1st March *Ocean* was damaged as her guns bombarded the Turkish positions. Four days later the battleship provided covering fire as Royal Marines landed in an attempt to destroy Fort Dardanus. The attack failed after Turkish guns positioned on both sides of the straits repulsed them. On 18th March 1915 during another bombardment of the Turkish coast, *Ocean* struck a mine and sank. Percy was one of the survivors rescued after abandoning ship. One day after being rescued, Percy Gumm was transferred to the sea-plane tender HMS *Ark Royal*, the second Royal Naval vessel to bear this distinguished name. The role of the tender was to act as a base for eight Short 184 seaplanes that performed reconnaissance and aerial observation duties in support of the Gallipoli landings and campaign during 1915. Percy Gumm served aboard *Ark Royal* for only a month, from 19th March until 19th April 1915.

Percy was transferred to the torpedo gunboat HMS *Hussar* from 20th April to 8th August 1915 and remained in the Dardanelles. He spent the next two and half years posted at the Royal Naval Depot at Port Said. During February 1918 he was selected to take part in the raid on Zeebrugge. By that time he had reached the rank of corporal. He was assigned to No.11 Platoon, C Company. Before *Vindictive* berthed at the Mole many of the men from Percy's platoon had succumbed to shell fire. Percy received a shrapnel wound to his right hand. He survived the ordeal of Zeebrugge and the War. He continued to serve with the RMLI and was commissioned 2nd Lieutenant on 8th October 1920.

Percy married Marion Grice in 1924 and had one son Peter, who would follow his father and join the Royal Marines as a Commando. Percy Gumm would serve in the Royal Marines right up to and during World War Two. He was finally deemed too old to serve and was retired on 11th September 1943, but was later recalled. On 1st January 1946 he was appointed Recruiting Staff Officer, RN and RM, Liverpool, and served until September 1953, when he retired from the Corps with the rank of Major. Percy died in 1984.

PRIVATE JOHN EDGE PLY 18308 NO.11 PLATOON, C COMPANY, 4TH BATTALION RMLI. John Edge was a labourer from Blackburn when he entered the Manchester recruiting office on 1st November 1915. Aged 17 years and 5 months he was seven months under the age limit for joining the Corps. Private John Edge was 19 when he took part in the Zeebrugge Raid. He was part of No.11 platoon RMLI, who were intended to lead the assault upon the Mole. This platoon was decimated before they reached the target. During the operation Private Edge received injuries to his neck and was sent to Chatham Hospital to recover.

PRIVATE WILLIAM CUTHBERT PLY 17129, NO.12 PLATOON, C COMPANY, 4TH BATTALION RMLI. William Robert Hutton Cuthbert was born on 11th October 1897 in Clydebank. William enlisted to join the RMLI on 3rd September 1914 in Glasgow. According to his discharge papers his date of birth is given as 11th October 1896 and he was aged 17 years and 11 months, which was close to the legal required age limit to serve. William was actually close to 16 years of age, too young to join the RMLI when he enlisted and therefore he altered his date of birth. He did most of his service during the War aboard HMS *Diana* from April 1915 to November 1917. During 1915 the cruiser was sent to the Far East and was part of the China Station. During early 1918, William was assigned to the 4th Battalion RMLI to train for the Zeebrugge raid. William Cuthbert landed on the Mole with No.12 Platoon from HMS *Vindictive*. He returned home unharmed and would serve aboard HMS *Cornwall* and HMS *Impregnable*.

No.12 Platoon pictured before the raid at Deal. Major Weller is seated in the front row fifth from right. Lieutenant Underhill is seated to his right. Underhill, who was a veteran of the Gallipoli landings, was awarded the Distinguished Service Cross for the part he played in the Raid. His citation stated that he 'showed great coolness and courage. At a critical time he organised and led reinforcements with the greatest dash and contempt of danger. His action was of the utmost value to the success of the operation'. Bugler Rogers is seated front row, 2nd from right. Private Caffrey is seated on the floor to the right.

On 28th January 1919 he married Elsie and they would raise two children, William and Dorothy. Elsie died in 1934. William was discharged from the RMLI on 28th February 1920 and returned home to Clydebank. He worked temporarily in the Singer sewing machine factory. William would spend most of his working life as a charge-hand at the large oil depots on Clydeside. William married Mary in 1938 and they adopted a daughter, Patricia. During World War Two William was working in the oil depots and played a prominent role in fighting the fires during the Clydebank blitz in 1941. William retired aged 67 and received a long service medal. He continued to live in retirement in Clydebank until he passed away on 8th January 1975.

CAPTAIN CHARLES CONYBEARE MACHINE GUN COMPANY 4TH BATTALION RMLI. Conybeare had seen action during the opening weeks of the War. From 26th September to 15th October 1914 he participated in operations at Dunkirk and Antwerp. He served with the Royal Marine Brigade in Gallipoli the following year, landing at Y Beach on 28th April 1915. He received a wound during the next day. He was hospitilised for a period and then he returned to the peninsula on 20th May. He spent most of the year fighting the disastrous Gallipoli campaign. His role was Machine Gun Officer for 2nd Brigade. He was mentioned in dispatches in September 1915. During December 1915 he  was promoted to Captain. Conybeare remained in Gallipoli until the evacuation on the night of the 8th/9th June 1916. On his return to the UK he was posted to Plymouth Division from 15th February 1916. Conybeare served aboard the battlecruiser HMS *Glorious* with the Grand Fleet from 13th October 1916 to 26th November 1917. During this posting he took part in the Second Battle of the Heligoland Bight on 17th November 1917. Volunteering for the Zeebrugge raid during February 1918, he was appointed Commander of the Machine Gun Company. During the raid he received a wound to his leg.

PRIVATE JOHN KEMBER CH 15357, MACHINE GUN SECTION, 4TH BATTALION RMLI. John East Kember was born at St. Clements, Sandwich, Kent on 17th July 1888 from Ramsgate. He worked as a seaman before joining the RMLI in January 1906. He was serving aboard HMS *Victorious* when war broke out. He spent most of the war serving aboard the submarine depot ship HMS *Bonaventure* from March 1915 until October 1917. He was a machine gunner aboard *Vindictive*. He referred to the experience as 'that veritable death trap ordeal.'[55] He was wounded as *Vindictive* approached the Mole. He later recalled:

The full history of Zeebrugge will rank amongst the foremost ever related in connection with the Royal Navy. I was severely wounded early in the action, sustaining a shell wound on the chin two inches long, which clearly shows the jaw-bone, and also a shrapnel wound in the right forefinger, which has practically destroyed the nerve. It was a terrible time that we all had; the sight of the dead and dying upon the decks of my ship and the agonised voices of the wounded who laid for hours helpless, and their continual enquiry of our chaplain to know if we had succeeded in our operations, will never be forgotten. Our heroic Captain took the ship alongside the Mole amidst a tornado of shells and machine gun fire, calmly giving his orders from the open bridge. He came along the mess deck on our journey back to Dover and showed us his uniform cap, which had bullet holes in it round the peak, but after being so exposed he only received a wound in the arm.

He handled the ship as though it was but a picket boat. Some of our stokers, who had been for eight hours or more down below, had complained of the gas that descended into the stokehold while laying alongside the Mole, and had to come up and put their gas masks on. It was a fine sight to see the flames shooting up feet high from the funnels on leaving the Mole. I should think our boilers were almost at exploding point in getting speed out of them under such conditions. The greatest marvel was, however, how we managed to reach Dover the next morning in such a ship, battered and perforated as she was.[56]

PRIVATE LEWIS STODDART PLY 1879(S) MACHINE GUN SECTION 4TH BATTALION RMLI. Lewis Stoddart was born on 28th July 1895 in Darlington. Prior to the First World War he worked as a pianist at cinemas in his local town of Ashington, Northumberland. He began his first job at 14, when he worked for ten hours each day. Aged 16, Lewis became the resident pianist at the Buffalo Cinema in Ashington. Two years later he was appointed musical director of the Pavilion. On 8th January 1917, aged 21 years and five months, he enlisted in the Royal Marines Light Infantry at the Newcastle recruiting office.

During the Zeebrugge operation Private Lewis Stoddart served with Machine Gun Section, 4th RMLI Battalion. As they landed on the Mole Lewis later recalled to his son that an officer (or NCO), who came from Alnmouth, Northumberland 'just threw his life away by jumping on to the Mole and encouraging his men on, was just cut down by enemy fire'.[57] As he was about to ascend the scaling ladders onto the Mole Lewis heard a voice urging him 'Run Louie, head down, and hope for the best.'[58]

Lewis Stoddart landed on the Mole and responded to the recall, but as he returned to the *Vindictive*, a shell penetrated the top deck and exploded below deck, causing chaos and carnage. During the raid his company of 56 men suffered heavy casualties; only seven returned home and four of the survivors were wounded. Stoddart was one of the three men from his company who came out of the ordeal unscathed.

After Zeebrugge, Stoddart served at HMS *Glory*, Russia from May 1918 to June 1919. Lewis Stoddart survived the war and resumed his career in music. Returning to his old job at the Pavilion and then onto the Wallow, Lewis entertained the people of Ashington. Among the famous people he accompanied on the piano were Gracie Fields, George Formby and Flanagan and Allen. (He had little regard for the celebrated Gracie. During one performance she made a personal remark about Lewis in front of the audience. He took great offence, walked off the stage and only returned when she apologised to him.)

As a consequence of his experience at Zeebrugge there was one song that he refused to play on the piano, 'The Roses of Picardy'. Lewis Stoddard explained that 'One of the lads who was horribly wounded tried to sing it. It was his favourite tune. But the lad died. I've never forgotten that night.'[59] Playing the piano was a great passion for this Zeebrugge veteran and Lewis worked until he was aged 70 before retiring. He passed away in February 1981, aged 85 years.

PRIVATE MAURICE FRENCH CH 15811 MACHINE GUN SECTION, 4TH BATTALION RMLI. Maurice French was born in Kibworth, Leicester on 26th April 1890. He worked as a printer before enlisting in the Royal Marines Light Infantry on 21st May 1907, under age. Maurice was attached to the printers shop from 5th October 1912 until January 1914. He was then assigned as Admiral's printer from 3rd January 1914 until 25th September 1916. Maurice may have made some kind of an error, for his service record states 'not recommended for further employment as a printer'. Maurice served aboard battleship HMS *King Edward VII* from 3rd January 1914 until she was sunk by a mine off Cape Wrath on 6th January 1916. The engine rooms flooded and
this battleship sank twelve hours later. Maurice ingested oil, which would affect his health. On 2nd June 1917 Maurice was promoted to Corporal while serving with Chatham Division. On 23rd April 1918 Maurice French took part in the Zeebrugge raid while attached to the Machine Gun Section of the 4th Battalion RMLI. Maurice died in 1923 from a lung disorder, which was probably caused when he was sunk aboard HMS *King Edward VII*.

PRIVATE JOHN WEAVER, PLY 1895(S) MACHINE GUN SECTION, 4TH BATTALION RMLI. Private John Henry Weaver was born on 24th October 1897 in Welshpool. He worked at the BSA Works as a wood cutting machinist before enlisting in the Royal Marines Light Infantry in a Birmingham recruitment office on 19th January 1917. During the Zeebrugge raid he formed part of the Machine Gun Section. He landed on the Mole and returned home unharmed.

PRIVATE VICTOR LOXLEY PO 1921(S) MACHINE GUN SECTION, 4TH BATTALION RMLI. Victor Loxley enlisted 18 months before the Zeebrugge raid. Tall and strongly built, he was an ideal candidate for the Royal Marines Light Infantry. Designated to the Machine Gun Section of the RMLI Private Loxley was part of the storming party aboard HMS *Vindictive*. His death at Zeebrugge was an immense tragedy for his parents, for Victor was their only son. His grief-stricken comrades who survived the turmoil of Zeebrugge sent a letter of sympathy to his parents, who lived in Oswaldtwistle, Lancashire. They wrote:

It will be a great blow to you and may God give you strength to bear it. As it is it is very hard for us to realise the truth. We cannot tell you how great his cheery disposition and kindness of heart is missed by us, without doubt he was the favourite of our party. We have been together for the past 15 months and we are heavy at heart for his absence. He died a hero's death in one of the most brave and glorious actions in the history of the world … We shall never forget him, he was a real and noble British lad.[60]

The community of Oswaldtwistle thronged the streets to express their sympathy. As a mark of respect, all schools were closed along the route of Loxley's funeral cortege. The students lined the streets, bareheaded with hand held at the salute. He was buried in Immanuel Church, Oswaldtwistle. A volley was fired over the open grave and The Last Post sounded.

PRIVATE PERCY FREDERICK SAVAGE CH 21057, MACHINE GUN SECTION, 4TH BATTALION RMLI. Born 13th July 1898 at St. John's Woking, Surrey, Private Savage served aboard *Vindictive* during the Zeebrugge raid. After Zeebrugge he served in Russia for 18 months. On his return home he caught typhoid fever and was hospitilised for some time. After the war he delivered bank notes from paper mills to the Bank of England. He was later employed by Southern Railways. During the Second World War he served with the rank of Corporal in the South Railways Home Guard. He died in June 1976.

Percy Savage continued to serve his country during World War Two when he enlisted with South Railway Home Guard. Corporal Savage is seated second from right. The sign reads '21st (4th South Railway) Battalion, Shooting Championship, No.2 Section, No.1 Platoon, D Company, Basingstoke, Winners 1942'.

PRIVATE ROBERT QUARRINGTON CH 2392(S) MACHINE GUN SECTION, 4TH BATTALION RMLI. Robert Edward Quarrington was born at St. Mary's Chatham on 12th August 1891. He served with the Royal Marines Light Infantry from 11th July 1907 until 1911. He found work as a labourer, and then re-enlisted to return to the RMLI on 23rd April 1917. Selected to take part in the Zeebrugge raid during early 1918, Robert Quarrington was assigned to the Machine Gun Section. During the raid he landed on the Mole, but when he returned to *Vindictive* he was blown from one deck to another. As the ship's Chaplain Peshall was performing the last rites, he noticed that Robert's lips were moving as he tried to ask for a drink of water. After the raid it took nearly a year for Robert to recover from the wounds he sustained at Zeebrugge. After being de-mobbed on 7th June 1919 he found

employment at Chatham Dockyard as a rigger. Robert would later become the Master of the tug *Tyke*, a position he held for thirty years. The *Tyke* was the largest tug working the three basins in Chatham Dockyard. Her role included towing HM ships after refit or repair down the River Medway to the Thames Estuary. He enjoyed his life as a Master. He would have five children, two boys and three girls. His daughter Joan remembered him as a 'wonderful person and father'. His son James would follow his father and joined the Royal Marines. He took part in many of the landings during the Second World War, including Dieppe, Salerno, Rimini, the Dalmation Islands. He fought in the Mediterranean, North Africa, Sicily and Southern France. Robert Quarrington passed away in January 1946. Sixty years after his passing his children still lay flowers at his grave.

NOTES

1. Douglas Jerrold, *The Royal Naval Division*, p151: Naval & Military Press.
2. Sir Roger Keyes, Admiral of the Fleet RN, *The Naval Memoirs 1916-1918*, p222: Thornton Butterworth Ltd, London, 1935.
3. National Archives: ADM 337/127 P298 P.H.Harrington Service Record.
4. *The London Gazette*, 3rd February 1920.
5. Edward Hilton-Young MP, *By Sea and Land, Some Naval Doings*, p277: T.C. & E.C. Jack Ltd, London & Edinburgh, 1920.
6. *The London Gazette*, 17th March 1919.
7. Able Seaman Frederick Summerhayes papers.
8. *South Wales Daily News*, 27th April 1918.
9. Ibid.
10. National Archives ADM 116/1656, Operations against Zeebrugge casualties 25th April 1918.
11. Ibid.
12. National Archives ADM 137/3894, Reports on Zeebrugge and Ostend operations April May 1918.
13. Ibid.
14. *North Wales Chronicle*, 2nd May 1941.
15. National Archives ADM 116/1656: Able Seaman Walter Taylor report.
16 Able Seaman Frederick Berry DSM papers.
17. National Archives: ADM 137/3894: Lieutenant Commander Adams report.

18. National Archives ADM 273 Vol. 4/35: Lieutenant Commander Brock's service record.
19. Ibid.
20. *Daily Mail*, 24th April 1918.
21. Sir Roger Keyes, Admiral of the Fleet RN, *The Naval Memoirs 1916-1918*, p240: Thornton Butterworth Ltd, London, 1935.
22. Ibid.
23. National Archives: ADM 137/3894: Air Mechanic Roland Entwisle report.
24. *Thomsons Weekly News*, 4th May 1918.
25. *Northern Daily Mail*, 27th April 1918.
26. *Hampshire Telegraph & Post*, Friday 26th April 1918.
27. Ibid.
28. *The Times*, April 1918.
29. *Chatham, Rochester & Gillingham News*, Saturday 27th April 1918.
30. Air Mechanic Francis Donovan recollection, courtesy Peter White.
31. Ibid.
32. Ibid.
33. Acting 1st Class Mechanic W.H. Gough, courtesy Philip Gough.
34. Imperial War Museum Department of Documents: Acting 1st Class Mechanic W.H. Gough IWM Reference: 91/11/1, courtesy Philip Gough.
35. Ibid.
36. Ibid.
37. Ibid.
38. Ibid.
39. Ibid.
40. *The London Gazette*, 23rd July 1918.
41. National Archives ADM 196/ P247-8: Sergeant Major Charles Thatcher's service record.
42. *The London Gazette*, 23rd July 1918.
43. Ibid.
44. *The London Gazette*, 6 September 1916.
45. *The London Gazette*, 23rd July 1918.
46. IWM Department of Documents Captain A.R. Chater, RMLI: 74/101/1.
47. *The London Gazette*, 23rd July 1918.
48. Captain Chater's account of the Victoria Cross Ballot. Royal Marines Museum.
49. *Jersey Weekly Post*, 10th January 1959.
50. Private Arthur Burnell papers: Letter dated 26th May 1918 from Private J Finney 2492(S): Courtesy of the Burnell family.
51. Ibid.
52. *Hampshire Telegraph & Post*, 26th April 1918.
53. *The London Gazette*, 23rd July 1918.
54. Corporal George Moyse recollection, courtesy Peter White.
55. *Thanet Times*, 3rd May 1918.
56. Ibid.
57. Private Lewis Stoddart papers. Courtesy Mr. Bryan Stoddart.
58. Ibid.
59. *The Newcastle Journal*, September 29th 1975. (Courtesy of NJC Media.)
60. *Accrington Observer & Times*, 4th May 1918.

CHAPTER 17

THEY WERE ON THE BLOCKSHIPS

COMMANDER RALPH SNEYD DSO RN, HMS THETIS. Ralph Stuart Sneyd was born at Bray in the parish of Morval, East Cornwall on 25th September 1882. Ralph was the second child and eldest son of George and Elizabeth Sneyd. His father died in January 1894, when Ralph was aged eleven. Three years after the death of his father Ralph enlisted to join the Royal Navy as a cadet. He began his career on the training ship *Britannia* berthed on the River Dart. He first experienced life at sea aged fifteen when he was posted to serve aboard the battleship HMS *Magnificent*. His early service career took him to the East Indies in 1899, and China in 1904 and 1909/10. While he was serving aboard the cruiser HMS *Cumberland* in 1913, Ralph Sneyd acted as naval tutor to Cadet HRH Prince Albert, who would later become King George VI.

Commander Ralph Sneyd aboard HMS *Thetis* on 18th April 1918.

While serving aboard HMS *Cumberland*, Commander Ralph Sneyd distinguished himself during the early part of the War when he took part in operations to remove the German presence in Cameroon, West Africa. It was here that he was awarded the DSO for his involvement in operations. His citation published in *The London Gazette* on 1 January 1916 citation states:

> *For his services during operations in the Cameroons. Commander Sneyd has commanded several successful operations on the coast and up the rivers, notably on the Dibamba River on 19th Sept. 1914, when he engaged and sank a large enemy launch, drove the enemy out of their post at Piti, and captured important defence plans.*[1]

During early 1918, when Vice Admiral Roger Keyes was planning the raid on Zeebrugge, it was Captain Fuller, Keyes' liaison officer at the Admiralty, who recommended Sneyd for command of *Thetis*. Sneyd was very inquisitive during his interview with Keyes. He was a man of great experience and asked numerous pertinent questions pertaining to the raid. Keyes misinterpreted Sneyd's concerns as negativity and was not prepared to appoint him, but Sneyd was adamant that no one else was going to command *Thetis* and he allayed Keyes' fears. Keyes later wrote that he 'had every reason to be thankful for the choice'.

Sneyd brought *Thetis* past the Mole and into Zeebrugge harbour. Although he did not succeed in either ramming the gates of the entrance to the Bruges canal or in scuttling his blockship across the canal entrance, it was his vessel that ran the gauntlet of German shells. Being the lead blockship, *Thetis* attracted the German guns and diverted attention from *Intrepid* and *Iphigenia* that followed behind, enabling these blockships to be scuttled in the canal entrance as planned. Sneyd was wounded and after the raid taken to the hospital ship, *Liberty*, berthed at Dover. He evinced little pride in the Zeebrugge operation, because of the terrible loss of life and because the objective of blocking the port was not achieved, the

German vessels passing through the canal soon after. The Belgian and French governments recognised Sneyd's role in the raid, awarding him the Order of Leopold of Belgium, the Croix de Guerre and making him an Officer of the Legion of Honour. Keyes mentioned him in dispatches, but he was not decorated with any British medals. He later explained to his daughter-in-law that they must have run out of by the time they got to him, so he was given an early promotion to Captain instead. This early promotion at 35 did not accelerate his career in the Royal Navy in the long term. When he was looking for further promotion in 1929, he was competing against more experienced officers. He received promotion to Rear Admiral on the day he retired and was promoted to Vice Admiral on the retirement list.

In 1920 Ralph married Harriet Fursdon in June 1920. At that time he was 'on the beach', living on half pay. In 1921 he was appointed to command the cruiser HMS *Caroline* on the East Indies station, based at Trincomalee in Ceylon. A year later he was commander of HMS *Comus*, which escorted the return passage of the Prince of Wales after his tour of Africa, Australia and New Zealand in 1922. In June 1922, his son Roger was born. The Wykes-Sneyd family has a strong connection with the Royal Navy. Roger would follow his father and enlist in the service. He trained at Britannia Royal Naval College, Dartmouth in 1935 and retired as a Captain in 1973. He commanded various warships and ended his career as Commodore Hong Kong. Roger's son Ralph, named after his grandfather, would also serve in the Royal Navy. He began training as a seaman officer, specializing as a pilot at Britannia Royal Naval College in 1964. Like his grandfather, he held Royal responsibilities, being Prince Andrew's commanding officer while serving with No.820 Squadron aboard HMS *Invincible*. Commander Ralph Sneyd was awarded the Air Force Cross for operations during the Falklands War in 1982.

During 1923, Ralph Sneyd was seconded on loan to the Royal Australian Navy for two years. He first commanded the Flinders Naval Depot, located 40 miles east of Melbourne, and was later appointed commander of the cruiser HMAS *Brisbane*. In 1925 he and his family returned to England where he was appointed to 'Victory' and Sheerness as a Senior Officer, before taking command of the cruiser HMS *Berwick*.

After retiring in 1929 with the rank of Vice Admiral, Ralph became a countryman. He was a man who was concerned with the community and the welfare of others, to the extent that he employed more people than he could afford to provide incomes in an area where there was little employment opportunities. He also provided funds for recreational facilities within his local community. His grandson Ralph considered him to be 'a modest man of great integrity who would do the right thing in any circumstances even if it was to his disadvantage. He was full of interesting tales delivered in a quiet voice that was often difficult to hear. He was a strict officer of very high standards, but his bark was worse than his bite'.

When the Second World War began, Ralph immediately set off to London with the intention of offering his services to the Admiralty. At that time he was in poor health and never reached the Admiralty. He wrote several letters, but the Admiralty never accepted him. His daughter Elizabeth recalled that he 'always regretted not visiting the Admiralty and told me just before he died, that if they had accepted him, he would not have lasted three months, but it would have been better.' He was suffering from a massive stomach ulcer and underwent an operation which saved his life.

Captain Ralph Wykes-Sneyd when ADC to King George V.

Despite his ill health Ralph continued to serve his country by establishing a Local Defence Volunteers Company from the Tamar to the Fowey and north to the A30. When the LDV evolved to become the Home Guard, Sneyd commanded the western half of this area. His daughter Elizabeth recalled a night when there was a German invasion alert. 'I have a memory of waking up one fine moonlight night in summer 1940 and looking out of the window to see him pacing up and down outside the front door with his shotgun under his arm! No doubt his revolver was in his pocket.' He was proud of the 20,000 men from Cornwall that served in the Home Guard and strongly believed that he and his men could give the Germans a bloody nose if they ever attempted an invasion. Ralph died in November 1951.

ENGINEER LIEUTENANT RONALD BODDIE DSO RN, HMS THETIS. Ronald Charles Boddie was born in Belfast in 1886. He was educated at the Model School in Coleraine, Ulster. At the age of eight, Boddie was awarded a scholarship to attend the Coleraine Academical Institution, then the newly opened Technical School in Coleraine where he received private tuition from the headmaster. This was fortunate for Boddie, because this was a time when sciences were hardly taught in Coleraine and without this tuition he would have failed the entrance exam for the Royal Navy, which he sat in 1902 in Dublin. Boddie began his naval career as an Engineer Cadet at the Royal Naval Engineering College at Keyham, Plymouth. Here he enjoyed playing rugby and for two years held the Lightweight Championship in the college boxing  tournaments. On graduating from Keyham he spent his final year of training at the Royal Naval College, Greenwich, which he completed in 1906. His first posting was as an Engineer Officer aboard the battleship HMS *Ocean* in July 1907. He served aboard the small battleship HMS *Goliath* from February 1908 to April 1909. Boddie was recommended for his actions whilst on watch. Boddie recalled in his diary:

> *Whilst alone on watch during a full power trial it was reported to me that the bottom of the hull was pulsating up and down under the propeller shaft as the propeller turned. I quickly reduced speed of the starboard engine to dead slow and informed the bridge. The Chief Engineer quickly came down followed by the Captain and it was decided to stop the engine. It was then possible to see that the bent shaft had a three feet longitudinal crack with a quarter inch gap in one place. It was generally agreed that if the shaft had broken at full power it might have knocked a hole in the bottom of the ship, the engine would have raced and smashed itself to pieces with possible loss of life.*[2]

He would serve on the Torpedo Boat Destroyer Leader HMS *Skirmisher* (1909–1910), the battleship HMS *Vanguard* (1910–1912) and the cruiser HMS *Dublin* (1912–1914). In June 1914 Boddie was seconded to the Royal Australian Navy on engineering staff at the Naval College at Geelong, which was 40 miles from Melbourne. Boddie then served at the new Naval College built at Jervis bay, located 200 miles from Sydney. When the First World War began, Boddie wrote to the Australian Navy Board to ask if he could be released from his secondment to return to Europe to fight the War. To his great disappointment he was told that he had to serve the two years of his appointment.

During April 1916, Boddie was recalled to England and appointed to the battleship HMS *Hercules*. In February 1918 Boddie volunteered to take part in the Zeebrugge raid and was appointed Engineer Officer of the blockship *Thetis*. Chief ERA Frank Gale was keen to volunteer, but Boddie had problems in persuading six stokers to volunteer for the operation. 'To my astonishment, the secret nature of the venture discouraged the men from volunteering, and I had great difficulty in persuading six eligible but rather indifferent stokers to accompany me.'[3]

Boddie later recalled the feeling of vulnerability as *Thetis* approached the Mole. 'My first reaction was a sensation of nakedness and a feeling of certainty we should be immediately fired at from the shore batteries'.[4] Boddie and Chief ERA Frank Gale each took control of an engine room. The main engines were disabled as they could not rotate, because the propellers were entangled in the underwater net of the boom. When the order to abandon ship had been given, it was Boddie who returned to the engine room and managed to get the both engines to go ahead. This enabled *Thetis* to proceed a further half a mile towards the entrance to the Bruges canal with no one on the bridge.

The two Thetis *main engines instantly went from full speed to stop. Gale and I subjected those poor reciprocating engines to the most violent treatment they can ever have experienced but nothing would persuade them to move an inch. After about 10 minutes of this futile effort I felt defeated and to complicate matters we were being plastered by gunfire from the battery adjacent to the Mole light house, 400 yards away. I tried to phone the bridge for instructions but there was no response, so I sent a stoker with a message to find the captain if he was still alive. He did not return. I then sent another stoker who also did not return so I feared the worst and decided to abandon ship on my own authority. I sent all the stokers up to their shelter station, then the engine room artificers opened the sea cocks to start flooding the engine rooms. I then betook myself to the quarter deck where I learnt we had fouled the boom at the entrance to the channel which led to the canal and realised that both propellers were locked in the entanglement net beneath the boom. A few minutes later a seaman found me with a message from the Captain saying that he would like the engines to go ahead if possible. Futile as I thought the request to be, I returned to the engine rooms collecting the ERA's on the way, shut off the seacocks to stop the flooding, wrestled again with the engines and to my astonishment got both engines to move sluggishly ahead for half a mile until we ran aground with no one on the bridge.[5]*

The Captain and crew abandoned *Thetis* in a cutter within range of German machine gun fire and proceeded to pull out of the canal entrance where they were recovered by Lieutenant Hugh Littleton, RNVR in ML.526. Boddie was awarded the DSO and two years accelerated seniority with the rank of Lieutenant Commander for his role during the raid, and continued to serve in the Royal Navy after the war. In 1920 he was appointed to the Naval Inter-Allied Control Commission in Berlin and was involved in the destruction of German war materials. In 1922 Boddie worked for the Engineer-in-Chief's Department at the Admiralty and returned to the sea in 1924 when he was appointed Engineer Commander of HMY *Victoria and Albert*. He served on the Royal Yacht until 1932. King George V presented Boddie with a CVO in 1930. He was appointed Engineer Captain in Command of the RN Engineering College at Keyham, Devonport from 1933 until 1936 when he was promoted to Engineer Rear Admiral and placed on the retired list. In 1936 he acted as Aide de Camp to the King.

Retired from the Royal Navy, Boddie became the Superintending Engineer & Constructor of Shipping to the War Department. To his regret this role prevented his recall to the Royal Navy during World War Two. From the summer of 1943 Boddie served as an Air Raid Warden. Engineer Rear Admiral RC Boddie CVO DSO died in 1967 in Campbeltown, Argyll.

CHIEF ENGINEER ROOM ARTIFICER FRANK GALE 272503 (CHA) RN, CGM, HMS THETIS. Chief Engineer Room Artificer Frank Marsden Gale from Beatley in Norfolk was one of the engineers who assisted Engineer Lieutenant Boddie in the engine room of *Thetis*. He was born in Dereham Norfolk on 8th August 1886. He enlisted in the Royal Navy during October 1907. Gale patrolled the Mediterranean during 1916 while serving on the cruiser HMS *Lowestoft*. Awarded the Conspicuous Gallantry Medal for his part in the Zeebrugge Raid, his citation reads: 'After both engines of *Thetis* had been disabled, and when the ship was in a sinking condition, this Chief Petty Officer returned to the engine-room, with an Engineer Officer, and succeeded in re-starting the starboard engine, thereby enabling the ship to be turned more into the fairway before she sank.' Gale also received the French Croix de Guerre for his role at Zeebrugge. Gale later recalled:

I could not see so much of what was going on as others on the deck until we got the order to abandon ship. They started firing at us as soon as we came round the lighthouse, but all we got in the engine room was splinters, smoke and gas. We put our gas masks on for a little while, but as they hampered our movements we took them off again. Although we were under heavy fire neither our engines or our lighting apparatus were damaged. The first intimation I had that anything was wrong was when the port engine started labouring and pulling up. I thought we were aground, but it appeared that we had picked up some wire. The telegraphs were still showing 'Full speed ahead' and we tried to keep her going. All this time we could hear the crashing and banging of the shells overhead. We got the engines going again, and then the other set got trouble. What was happening on deck all this time I could only surmise. The telegraph went ' stop'. We did not see that there was much more we could do, so we went on deck. On looking round I could see that we were in the harbour, and were getting it hot, being fired at from three directions, and the air was full of everything from machine gun bullets to heavy stuff, and shells of all shapes and sizes were bursting around us. I walked over to the starboard side to the boat to which I had been allotted in the water, but found it smashed up and hanging in the water. I then went to the only other boat we had left on the port side. There was a little group round it, and they were all quite cool and trying to get a wounded man in. Finally we all got into the boat by slipping down ropes' ends that had been previously prepared. We then found that the boat was leaking pretty badly, but we had not gone more than a hundred yards when we came across a motor launch. We scrambled on board and crouched down. We were a bit crowded, as we found they had half the crew of another ship on board and in consequence she was a little top heavy. She put on full speed and kept a smoke screen going to cover our tracks, but they put up star shells and bombarded us for forty minutes from the great land batteries. In this launch we came right across to Dover and sat on deck and watched the dawn break. On the way back an incident occurred which shows the guts of these little motor boat people have. We were just beyond the shell fire when a great ship loomed up near us and our captain banged the challenge flash signal into her. Luckily it was one of our big Monitors ... we looked nice objects when we arrived at Dover for we were all as black as the ace of spades. The funnel of the Thetis *had been hit, and the soot had all showered over us in the engine room. They gave us a splendid reception, and cheered us through the streets. Any one was lucky to get out of that lot without being hit, and I might say the Germans were a jolly sight more scared than we were. We succeeded in sinking our vessel in the fairway and she was a wreck before we left her and the Germans were still firing at her.*[6]

Gale formed part of the Honour Guard for the interment of the Unknown Warrior at Westminster Abbey with other Zeebrugge raiders on 11th November 1920.

LEADING STOKER WILLIAM BOURKE, SERVICE NO. 2237 RAN HMS THETIS. William John Bourke was born in Perth, Western Australia on 7th December 1891. He was one of eleven volunteers from the Royal Australian Navy who participated in the Zeebrugge Raid. He was a stoker aboard the blockship HMS *Thetis*.

Above: HMS *Thetis* sunk at Zeebrugge. To the right of the Mole lighthouse the wreck of SS *Brussels* is visible. *Brussels* was the steamship commanded by Captain Fryatt who was executed by the Germans for ramming a German submarine. After being captured by the Germans the *Brussels* was used as accommodation by German personnel on the Mole. The vessel was scuttled when the Germans evacuated the port in October 1918.

PETTY OFFICER ALFRED MESSER DSM 228561 RN, HMS THETIS. Alfred John Messer was born on 8th April 1888 at Popham near Basingstoke. He worked as a carter before enlisting to serve in the Royal Navy on 7th April 1905. He began his naval career as a boy sailor and by June 1915 had reached the rank of Petty Officer. He had served on many vessels throughout his naval career. During the First World War he served on the battleship HMS *Hindustan* from 20th March 1915 to 31st May 1915. During this draft he spent over two months on a gunnery training course at HMS *Excellent* at Whale Island Portsmouth. Petty Officer Messer was one of the volunteers from HMS *Hindustan* to be selected to take part in the raid on Zeebrugge. He was assigned to the blockship *Thetis* and was in command of the 6-inch gun crew on the forecastle. As *Thetis* passed the Mole and was

heading for the entrance to the Bruges canal a shell exploded near the gun turret killing two of the gun crew members, Able Seamen Alfred Saunders and Arthur Harris. One moment they were manning the gun, the next they were vapourised. Messer confirmed in a report that they were 'blown to pieces'. Despite receiving a wound above the eye Alfred remained at his post until he was given the order to abandon ship. His steadfastness in manning the gun under a hail of shells won him the Distinguished Service Medal.

Alfred retired from the Royal Navy on 2nd October 1938 with the rank of Chief Petty Officer. He was employed by Colonel M. Courage to carry out maintenance work on the Preston House estate, near Preston Candover. During the Second World War Alfred Messer returned to the Royal Navy to serve as a gunnery instructor at HMS *King Alfred* at Lancing, Shoreham. During his retirement he enjoyed gardening and was a regular visitor at horticultural shows in the area. Alfred died aged 74 on 20th August 1962 in the Royal County Hospital, Winchester.

ABLE SEAMAN WILLIAM STINGEMORE J19505 RN, HMS THETIS. William Stingemore was born in Edmonton, London on 7th May 1895. He was the son of Pharoah and Charlotte Stingemore. William had five brothers and three sisters. His father was a Metropolitan Policeman who moved the family to Tottenham. William enlisted to join the Royal Navy as a boy sailor on 23rd August 1912. At the outbreak of War William had become an Able Seaman and was serving aboard the cruiser HMS *Andromache*. During 1914 this vessel had mine laying duties based at Dover. William served in the Dardanelles aboard the cruiser HMS *Blenheim* from April until October 1915. This cruiser served as a depot ship supporting destroyers. He went to HMS *Pembroke* in Chatham for three months before returning to HMS *Blenheim* from January 1916 until July 1917.

From 8th March 1918 he was drafted to the Depot ship HMS *Hecla* (*Mosquito*), based in Belfast. William volunteered for the Zeebrugge raid after he had been drafted to this depot ship. He is pictured wearing the *Mosquito* ribbon in the photo taken in Tottenham, which suggests that it was taken weeks before the Zeebrugge raid. He was assigned to the blockship HMS *Thetis* and was killed during the raid. A shipmate confirmed that he was gassed near to some smoke boxes that he was attending to. He has no known grave and his name is commemorated on the Royal Naval Memorial, Chatham.

LIEUTENANT STUART BONHAM-CARTER DSO RN, COMMANDING OFFICER HMS INTREPID. Lieutenant Stuart Bonham-Carter was the commander of the blockship HMS *Intrepid* who had the daunting task of sinking this obsolete cruiser across the entrance of the Bruges canal. When he died in 1972 *The Times* described him in his obituary as 'of jovial appearance … He was always good company and in spite of a slight stammer, an excellent raconteur. He was universally popular with officers and men alike, and had all the qualities of a well loved leader.'[7]

Bonham-Carter was born in Portsmouth on 9th July 1889. Joining the Royal Navy in 1904 he began his training as a naval cadet at *Britannia*. By September 1908 he attained the rank of Acting Sub Lieutenant by September 1908. In 1918 he was appointed commander of HMS *Intrepid* and given the task of blocking the entrance to the Bruges canal. He was awarded the Distinguished Service Order for this brave deed. His citation states that he 'handled his ship with great skill and coolness in a position of considerable danger under heavy fire. Great credit is due to him for his success in sinking 'Intrepid' in the Bruges canal'.[8]

Lieutenant Percy Dean rescued the crew of the *Intrepid* in ML 282, wihtout realising that Bonham-Carter was still in the water. Bonham-Carter briefly held onto a trailing rope attached to ML 282 until his arms could take the strain no more. Stranded in the water he swam for the eastern pier. Dean noticed that he left someone in the water when a star shell burst. Dean turned ML 282 to rescue the abandoned Bonham-Carter.

Bonham-Carter continued his naval career after Zeebrugge by taking command of the destroyer HMS *Shark* until January 1919. A keen cricketer, he represented the Royal Navy in tournaments in 1925/6. By the time the Second World War broke out he had reached the rank of Commodore and was Naval Secretary to the First Lord of the Admiralty. He had been in this office role since May 1939 and working from a desk did not appeal. A brief illness forced him to resign from this position. Once he was recovered he was posted to a sea command, where he was most content. Promoted to Vice Admiral in October 1939 he served as Commander of 3rd Battle Squadron based in Halifax from January 1940 to February 1941. Bonham-Carter had command of all British warships in Canadian waters. During the autumn of 1940 he received the fifty US destroyers

Vice Admiral Stuart Bonham-Carter DSO pictured during World War Two.

transferred from the American World War One Reserve Fleet to the Royal Navy as part of the Lend Lease agreement. These vessels commissioned into the Royal Navy under Bonham-Carter's command in Canada were loaned by the US in exchange for use of British ports around the world, and in an effort to aid Britain during the dark early days of the Second World War. In January 1942 Bonham-Carter was appointed as Commander of the 18th Cruiser Squadron, Home Fleet where he served until August 1942. During this command he supervised the efforts to protect the Russian convoys and his flagship was torpedoed twice by German submarines.

Bonham-Carter's career would take him to Malta, where he served as Flag Officer in-Charge from December 1942. He became a a KCB in 1943. Ill health would force Bonham-Carter to relinquish his command at Malta. Later that year on 31st December Bonham-Carter was placed on the retired list, however during 1944 and 1945 he served in the Royal Naval Reserve as Commodore of Convoys. Sir Stuart Bonham-Carter died aged 83 in Petersfield on 5th September 1972. He was buried in Buriton Church, near Petersfield.

SUB LIEUTENANT EDGAR MEIKLE, ROYAL NAVY, HMS INTREPID. Edgar Meikle was the Engineer officer aboard. During the first attempt to block Zeebrugge on 12th April he spent twelve continuous hours in the engine room when the fire and bilge pumps were broken. He only reported these problems to Lieutenant Bonham-Carter on their arrival at Dover. Bonham-Carter was forced to detonate the charges before Engineer Sub Lieutenant Meikle, ERAs Tom Farrell and Herbert Smith, and Stoker Petty Officer Joseph Smith could evacuate the engine room. These four men managed to reach the upper deck and escape in a cutter. Rowing past the scuttled *Thetis*, they were picked up by a motor launch.

STOKER BENJAMIN EAGLETON K10049 RN HMS INTREPID. Benjamin Eagleton was born into a large family of six brothers on 26th April 1891 at Leigh-on-Sea, Essex. His father was a fisherman and by 1918 worked for Southend Corporation. Benjamin worked as a fisherman before enlisting in the Royal Navy on 30th January 1911. After completion of basic training at Chatham he was drafted to HMS *Africa*. He was on board when she took part in the great review at Spithead in 1911. He sailed for some time in the Indian Ocean, then in the Persian Gulf. When war broke out he was deployed to Mesopotamia and for two years served at the Tigris Force depot in Basra. Among his more unusual duties was to make ice for the local hospital. He returned home for leave during January 1917 then after spending three months at Chatham barracks he was posted to HMS *Albacore*, escorting merchant convoys between Norway and Britain. On 14th March 1918 Stoker Eagleton was posted to HMS *Intrepid*. He later described the scuttling:

We then lined up for the attack on Zeebrugge. I was with the other stokers below and stuck there until the gong sounded to clear ship before blowing her up. Then we got overside into the cutters and had no sooner done this than we saw her scuttle: as a fact, we were still on board when the mines exploded, and she was settling down before we left her. As we got away we could see the Germans running about on the Mole with machine guns, and as they shot our fellows they got into the khaki, so that you couldn't tell one from the other. Of course all the time they were firing from the land guns, and shells fell into the water everywhere: there were so many of them, that they made the sea like a volcano, and the water boiled all round, the shells being, many of them, filled with poison gas. We stood by until the motor launches took the cutters in tow; but whilst ours was tugging us she got a salvo of 8-inch right through her, and went up in the air, so we had to row the cutter through the blaze of shells. However we got enough fellows to pull through the water pretty quick and after a tough job, at about 5.30 a.m. on Tuesday, we were picked up by a destroyer. We got into Dover about 11.30 that morning, and then we saw the Vindictive *up against the wall with her funnels pierced and other parts pretty well riddled with shrapnel. We had a great reception at Dover, and passed the day and night there, being taken round to find billets: I went to the Salvation Army Rooms, and was treated well by all there, and slept there. In the morning we went aboard the* Arrogant *to breakfast, and then got to the train for Chatham. At the station at Dover, Admiral Keyes came to see us off, and when we reached Chatham all the barracks turned out to cheer us and the bands were out to give us a good reception. Admiral Sturdee read to us the King's message of thanks to all who shared in the operation.[9]*

On each Zeebrugge raider's service record the following stamp can be found: 'Participated in ballot for VC granted for operations against Zeebruge & Ostend 23 April 1918 (*London Gazette* 23/7/18)'. Eagleton's service record does not have the stamp, probably because he was one of the individuals designated as part of the stoker's crew who would work in getting the *Intrepid* to the Belgian Coast, and were then meant to have disembarked from the blockship before she entered the canal. It is highly probable that Eagleton had refused to disembark.

ENGINE ROOM ARTIFICER JOHN FERGUSON DSM M12154, HMS INTREPID. John Ferguson was born in Glasgow on 11th January 1884. He joined the Royal Navy on the 16th July 1915. His service record states that he was an engine fitter prior to enlistment and it was only natural for him to serve as an Engine Room Artificer in the Royal Navy. He trained at Chatham and served on various vessels during the war. Assigned to HMS *Intrepid* he formed part of the blockship crew working in the engine room. His service record does not give any indication that he took part in the

Zeebrugge raid, but the reason for this may lie in the fact that he was only meant to be part of the crew that took the vessel to the Belgian coast and was not intended to be aboard the blockship when she was scuttled in the canal entrance at Zeebrugge. When the blockships were close to the Belgian coast and the boat came alongside to take off the crew members who were not meant to take part in the complete operation, the majority of these men hid below decks, because they wanted to see the operation through to the end. John Ferguson may have been one of these men. He was aboard this blockship when she was sunk in the canal entrance and returned home safely without being wounded. After the raid he was awarded the Distinguished Service Medal. After World War One, John Ferguson worked for the Isle of Man Steam Packet Company. John Ferguson would see action once again during World War Two. He was mentioned in dispatches for his role as Third Engineer aboard HM Transport *Manxman*, helping the Allied army evacuate from the Dunkirk beaches in 1940. When the war ended he returned to work for the Isle of Man Steam Packet Company, until a serious accident forced him to retire early. John Ferguson passed away in 1951.

STOKER SIDNEY NICHOLLS K33101 RN HMS INTREPID. Sidney Alfred Thomas Nicholls was born in Herne Bay on 6th June 1897. He was the son of James and Martha Nicholls. James belonged to the Coastguard Service and together with Martha raised a large family of six sons and three daughters. James had already served in the Royal Navy prior to joining the Coastguard Service, so when World War One broke out he was recalled to rejoin the Royal Navy. Sidney's brother, John, known as Ernest, had joined the Royal Navy as a boy sailor before the war. He was killed on 15th October 1914 when HMS *Hawke* was attacked in the North Sea. Sidney's other brother James (Junior) also served in the Royal Navy on submarines. During the early years of the War Sidney was too young to enlist. He worked on a farm near Herne Bay in Kent. Sidney enlisted to join the Royal Navy on 11th May 1916 as a stoker and began training at HMS *Pembroke* in Chatham. After completing his training in August 1916 he was posted to Gibraltar, where he served until January 1917. Sidney then served aboard the battleship HMS *Monarch*. He was assigned as a stoker aboard the blockship HMS *Intrepid*. During the raid he was afflicted by gas poisoning. He was brought back to England but died on 24th April 1918. He was buried at Herne Bay Cemetery.

SUB LIEUTENANT ALAN CORY-WRIGHT DSC RN, HMS INTREPID. Alan Cory-Wright was born on 6th March 1896. He trained at Dartmouth College from 1909 until 1913. He first served as a Midshipman on the battleship HMS *Hibernia* from 16th September 1913 until November 1915. During World War One he worked for a time in observation balloon work. He later described to his son Godfrey how he performed a parachute jump from a balloon, explaining that the actual parachute canopy was in a leather sleeve under the balloon basket.

While serving aboard the destroyer HMS *Broke* as a Sub Lieutenant, Cory-Wright took part in the Battle of Jutland on 31st May 1916. HMS *Broke* fired one torpedo which struck a German vessel, however this hit was claimed by other vessels in the vicinity. Cory-Wright was in command of four guns in the forecastle during the battle. Between 11 p.m. and midnight on 31st May HMS *Broke* found herself within five hundred yards of the German Battlecruiser *Westfalen*. High explosive 12-inch shells from the *Westfalen* poured into HMS *Broke* during a three-minute engagement which killed 47 and wounded 36 onboard. All men in the forecastle were killed with the exception of Cory-Wright. He was saved when the bodies fell onto him and protected him from enemy shell fire and shrapnel. However Cory-Wight was seriously wounded when a piece of shrapnel grazed his left leg just above the ankle and passed through his right leg.

Rowland Lishman, a friend of Cory-Wright, described him as 'only a kid, tho' he's pretty tall, but he's a man from top to bottom, and a gentleman every inch. He wouldn't allow his wounds to be touched until every man with a blue collar had been attended to'.[10] HMS *Broke* was severely damaged by her encounter with the *Westfalen* and limped back home at a speed of 5 knots. It took three days to reach the Tyne.

While serving aboard HMS *Ramilies* in early 1918 Cory-Wright volunteered for Zeebrugge. It was when he arrived aboard HMS *Hindustan* moored in the Thames estuary that he was told of his role in the operation. In a letter to his father he wrote: 'I am not really appointed to the *Hindustan* at all. I am First Lieutenant of the *Intrepid* which is a capital appointment. I am very pleased with the appointment which may mean a great deal to me.'[11]

During the raid Cory-Wright was in the aft control position aboard *Intrepid*. All communication between the aft control and the conning tower, where Bonham-Carter was commanding the ship, had been destroyed in the approach to Zeebrugge harbour. Cory-Wright thought that Lieutenant Bonham-Carter was killed as they entered the entrance to the Bruges canal and assumed command of the vessel. He gave the order to the steering engine to hard-a-starboard just as Bonham-Carter gave the same command, as the blockship was manoeuvred into her planned scuttling position. Cory-Wright discovered that his Commanding Officer was alive when he abandoned the blockship in a Carley float with Bonham-Carter, Sub Lieutenant Babb and four Petty Officers. The flares had not been removed from the Carley float, which ignited on contact with water and made them an illuminated target for the Germans to focus upon. They were picked up by ML 282. As they escaped from the harbour a fire broke out aboard the motor launch. Cory-Wright was gassed as he tried to extinguish the fire. In a letter to his mother dated 28th April 1918 he wrote, 'I unfortunately got gassed by our own smoke after we had escaped. This smoke is not really poisonous, but very painful to one's lungs and throat.'[12]

Lieutenant Bonham-Carter wrote that Cory-Wright was 'a most capable, very keen and gallant officer'.[13] Cory-Wright was awarded the Distinguished Service Cross. His *London Gazette* citation posted on 23rd July 1918 states that he 'showed great coolness during the action, and by his bravery and cheerfulness throughout set a fine example to his men'.[14] He also received, interestingly enough, 16 pounds, 7 shillings and 6 pence from the Admiralty in compensation for loss of personal effects during the Zeebrugge raid.

Cory-Wright was very disappointed to have been posted to HMS *Malaya* after the raid. Throughout his career he had served on larger Royal Naval vessels. In a letter to his father dated 1ˢᵗ August 1918 he wrote: 'It is very annoying to go from one big ship to another. I wanted to go to Coastal Motor Boats, still hope to before long.'[15]

Cory-Wright was never given the opportunity to serve in Coastal Motor Boats and left the Royal Navy at the end of 1920. On leaving he worked for HA & D Taylors (Maltsters) until he was called up for the Second World War. He served as an instructor at HMS *Ganges*, Shotley, Ipswich, 1939 to 1940. He was constantly agitating for a more active role. He left the service during May 1941 and commanded the local Home Guard until the end of the War. He returned to Taylors to become Managing Director. He retired in 1961 and died in 1964. The local newspaper recorded an estimated 700 mourners attended his memorial service.

PETTY OFFICER PERCY INGE DSM J1840 HMS INTREPID. Percy Stanley Inge was born on 4ᵗʰ May 1892 in Faversham, Kent. He worked as a farm labourer before enlisting to join the Royal Navy on 27ᵗʰ July 1908. According to an interview he gave to a Kent newspaper Bonham-Carter gave Inge the order to scuttle the blockship. Bonham-Carter and Inge were the last to leave the blockship.

STOKER PETTY OFFICER HAROLD LANGSTON PALLISER 226201 RN HMS INTREPID. Harold Langston Palliser was born 1887 in Portsmouth. He worked as a labourer before enlisting as a boy sailor on 13ᵗʰ May 1903. He began his naval service training at HMS *Ganges*. Throughout his service he served as a Stoker. When he volunteered for the Zeebrugge Raid he was promoted to the rank of Acting Stoker Petty Officer and assigned to the blockship HMS *Intrepid*. When selecting personnel for the raid Admiral Keyes specified that he wanted unmarried men to take part in the operation. Palliser had married Kate Gutteridge in 1915, so he may have removed his wedding ring from his finger when he volunteered for the operation. Palliser was killed by machine gun fire while in the motor launch ML 282. Chief ERA Farrell confirmed after the raid that Palliser was killed by machine gun fire. Harold Palliser's remains were brought to London where he was buried at St. Pancras Cemetery.

MATE (E) SIDNEY WEST DSC, OBE. RN, HMS IPHIGENIA. Sidney Greville West was born in Toddington, Bedfordshire on 3ʳᵈ February 1890. On completing his education at St. Olave's Boys Grammar School and with a glowing reference from his headmaster, he joined the Royal Navy as a boy sailor on 14ᵗʰ July 1905. By the time the First World War broke out, West was Engine Room Artificer. He had been serving on the Dreadnought HMS *Neptune* and would serve on this vessel until August 1917. During his time aboard U-29 unsuccessfully tried to sink *Neptune* on 18ᵗʰ March 1915. A year later, West was aboard when *Neptune* took part in the Battle of Jutland where she fired 28 rounds of 12½ inch shells and received

no damage. West was commissioned in August 1917. Six months later he volunteered for the Zeebrugge raid and was assigned to the blockship HMS *Iphigenia*. He was responsible for setting the time bomb that blew the *Iphigenia* when she was in position across the entrance to the Bruges canal. Admiral Keyes recognized Sidney West's contribution by mentioning him in dispatches: 'Mate (E) West has throughout the operation and preparations worked his department in an admirable manner.'[16] Lieutenant Billyard-Leake also noted West's involvement in his report: 'He returned to the engine room after the alarm bell had been rung in order to put the engines ahead, and finally left at my order.'[17]

During his naval career West served on HMS *Achilles*, *Neptune*, *Benbow*, *Hawkins* and *Ramilies*. West was Chief Officer when he served on HMS *Berwick*. West was renowned for producing Gilbert & Sullivan operettas on board the ships he served. He retired from the Royal Navy with the rank of Captain. Sidney never married and always believed that he was married to the sea. He lived in retirement in a house on the cliffs at Boleze, overlooking Portland Harbour.

STOKER PETTY OFFICER FRANK LUCAS K4460 (CHA) RN, HMS IPHIGENIA. Frank Lucas was born on 10th April 1890 in Wanstead, East London. He first worked as a clerk, and at the age of 19 during October 1909 he joined the Royal Navy. He was wounded during the battle of Heligoland Bight. He was assigned to the blockship *Iphigenia*. He had served on this cruiser before from 11th October 1916 to 1st December 1916 and 2nd March 1917 to 17th January 1918. Lucas died from gas poisoning during the raid and was buried in Wanstead. Lucas had only been married for one month when he was killed.

Stoker Petty Officer Frank Lucas pictured with his wife.

STOKER 1ST CLASS GEORGE SOUTH K29760 RN HMS IPHIGENIA. George Reuben South was born in Southminster, Essex on 8th September 1896. His father was a Farm Bailiff and moved his family to Southend, where the 15-year-old George developed an attraction for the sea. He enlisted in the Royal Navy in November 1915. On completing his basic training at Chatham he spent four months in Gibraltar, and then served seven months aboard HMS *Kestrel*. He later spent a year serving on board HMS *Iphigenia* in the White Sea and off the Russian coast. He later recounted his Zeebrugge experience.

I went back to Chatham and waited for this little lot to come along. Yes, being a stoker, I was of course, below a great deal, and know very little of what took place, over and above what I tell you. I left the Iphigenia *and got into the boat I was detailed for: this went under and thirty of us scrambled for another boat which was all right. That went under, and we swam from there to a German drifter and hung on to her for a quarter of an hour. Then some of us were at the side of the pier, at Zeebrugge, and again hung on. Whilst I was there a rowing boat came along and I shouted for help and got taken off. It was a very warm business all the time, with plenty stuff flying about in all directions. I ought to have told you that before I left the ship a shell came in at one side of the stoke hole and carried away the main steam pipe: it went out of the other side. I got into Dover all right, with a lot of the others, and had a good reception all round, and I don't think that I am much the worse for my share in this job.*[18]

After the war, he worked for the Southend Corporation. Too old for war service during World War Two he played his part as an Air Raid Protection Warden.

Above left: HMS *Iphigenia* in Russia, before the Zeebrugge operation.

Above right: Scuttled blockships HMS *Iphigenia* and HMS *Intrepid*.

 STOKER JOHN CLEAL SS114982 RN, HMS IPHIGENIA. John Cleal was born in Cardiff on 28th November 1893. He was aged 24 when he volunteered for the Zeebrugge operation and had served six years in the Royal Navy. Prior to his enlistment on 10th October 1913 he worked as a labourer in Cardiff dockyard. When war broke out, Cleal was serving as a stoker aboard HMS *Marlborough*. He was still serving on this vessel when she took part in the Battle of Jutland during 1916. During the Zeebrugge raid he was drafted as a stoker onboard HMS *Iphigenia*. Wounded during this action he was evacuated back to Dover, but he died of his wounds while aboard the hospital yacht HMS *Liberty*, moored at Dover, on 24th April. Cleal's parents expressed the wish for the body of John Cleal to be brought home for burial in Cardiff. The epitaph on his headstone reads 'Died doing his duty to God and man'. He had been engaged to be married to May Price; their wedding was postponed so that he could take part in the Zeebrugge raid.

 STOKER ANDREW MARSHALL SS110978 RN, HMS IPHIGENIA. Andrew Marshall was born on 2nd February 1893 in Killinchy, County Down. Selena Marshall was a single mother. When he reached the age of eighteen he decided he wanted to do something with his life and decided to join the Royal Navy. He walked a distance of 24 miles to enlist in Belfast for 12 years service as a Stoker. When the First World War broke out, Andrew was serving aboard the cruiser HMS *Minotaur* based at the China Station. In 1915 he returned to home waters when *Minotaur* was attached to the 2nd Cruiser Squadron and patrolled the North Sea. A year later, Andrew would see action when *Minotaur* took part in the Battle of Jutland on 31st May 1916. While serving aboard *Minotaur*, Andrew was promoted to Stoker First Class. During November 1916 he was drafted to serve on the battleship HMS *King George V*. In February 1918 Andrew volunteered to take part in the Zeebrugge raid. He was sent to the depot ship HMS *Hindustan* to prepare for the raid. He returned home to Ireland from the war unscathed and to a hero's welcome from the people of Comber and Killinchy. His name was inscribed on the war memorial at Comber. After the War he worked in the Harland & Wolff shipyard. Andrew Marshall died aged 69 in 1962 and was buried at Roselawn Cemetery, Belfast. His son Tom recalled that 'he was a lovely man and loved by all his family and friends'.

STOKER ERNEST THORNTON K35837 RN, HMS IPHIGENIA.
Ernest Thornton was born in Manchester on 25th July 1898. He
worked as a carter before enlisting to join the Royal Naval
Volunteer Reserve in 1915. He began his naval career as a
galley boy. His first experience of war came when his ship
assisted the evacuation of Australian soldiers from Gallipoli
from December 1915 to January 1916. He was part of a shore
party sent to the beaches to retrieve equipment, where he was
lightly wounded on barbed wire. In May 1916 Ernest took part
in the Battle of Jutland.

He was transferred to the Royal Navy on 16th August 1916
as a stoker. Ernest was posted to Gibraltar from 27th November
1916 until 12th September 1917. He served on HMS *King George
V*. While serving aboard this battleship he received promotion
to Stoker First Class and volunteered to take part in the Zeebrugge Raid. Ernest was only
meant to be part of the stoker party that brought *Iphigenia* to Zeebrugge. He was not a
part of the skeleton crew designated to bring the blockship into her scuttling position at
the entrance to the Bruges canal. Immediately before the raid, Ernest and many others hid
below decks when a picket boat came alongside to take them off before the final approach.
He was determined to see the operation through to the end, despite being ordered to leave
the ship. Ernest later recalled to his family that he believed that the reason the blockships
were spotted was because one of the ships had become entangled upon something and a
torch was shone upon it to see if it could be freed. He could have been referring to the *Thetis*
becoming entangled on the boom nets as she passed the inner Mole. He also mentioned that
there was a popular rumour amongst the sailors who took part that someone lit a cigarette
on the approach to the scuttling position, which alerted the German defenders.

Fortunately, Ernest returned safely home to England unharmed. After Zeebrugge he
returned to serve on HMS *King George V* until he was de-mobbed in February 1919. He
adapted to civilian life quite quickly after the war. He married his sweetheart Lily Bolton
(nee Williams). Lily was a widower after her first husband was killed, leaving her to look
after two children. Ernest became the step father to Lily's two children from her first
marriage and they added four more children to their family. On leaving the Royal Navy he
worked as a gravedigger for Manchester Borough Council. During the next few years Ernest
worked his way up to gardener and Head gardener at Manchester Piccadilly Gardens
where he was employed until the outbreak of World War Two. Ernest was determined to
serve once again. He made four attempts to rejoin the Royal Navy, but was refused because
he was considered too old to serve. He was so determined he altered his age in order to be
accepted, only to be found out by an attesting officer who knew him from the First World
War. Resigned to the fact that he was too old to enlist, he worked at a Manchester Munitions
factory by day and during the night he was part of the local district Mortuary Squad who
searched for civilians who were killed during German bombing raids. One night he had to
retrieve the body of his sister-in-law Emily Williams who was killed when a bomb landed
and exploded outside her house.

Ernest was shocked when his sons Frederick and Ernest joined the Royal Navy in World
War Two. Ernest Senior did not want them to enlist, but they had the same spirit that their
father had. They too wanted to serve their country and both sons would follow their valiant
father's footsteps. Ernie Junior served as a stoker and Rick served on the second HMS *King
George V*. Ernie was killed on 9th October 1943 when a JU87 attacked and sunk HMS *Panther*
near the island of Kos in the Aegean Sea. Ernest Senior's bereavement was made much
worse because there was no funeral for his son. He went down with the *Panther* as she sank
and his name is commemorated on the Portsmouth War Memorial.

After the war Ernest returned to his job at Piccadilly Gardens, but within a few years his health declined and he was forced to retire in 1948. Ernest died just before Christmas 1953. He was buried in Manchester's Southern Cemetery.

NOTES

1. *The London Gazette,* 1 January 1916.
2. Engineer Lieutenant Boddie papers, courtesy of Commander R.G.Boddie.
3. Ibid.
4. Ibid.
5. Ibid.
6. *Downham Market Gazette*, 4th May 1918.
7. *The Times*, 7th September 1972.
8. *The London Gazette*, 23rd July 1918.
9. *Southend Standard*, 2nd May 1918.
10. Lieutenant Cory-Wright papers, courtesy of Godfrey Cory-Wright.
11. Ibid.
12. Ibid..
13. Ibid.
14. *The London Gazette*, 23rd July 1918.
15. Lieutenant Cory-Wright papers, courtesy of Godfrey Cory-Wright.
16. Keyes Dispatch. *The London Gazette*, 19th February 1919.
17. National Archives: ADM 137 / 3894: Lieutenant Billyard-Leake report.
18. *The Southend Standard*, 2nd May 1918.

CHAPTER 18

THEY WERE ON THE *DAFFODIL*

LIEUTENANT HAROLD CAMPBELL DSO RN, HMS DAFFODIL. Harold George Campbell was born on 6th April 1888. He was the fifth son of Henry and Ivy Campbell who lived in Norfolk. He was educated at Cheam School, Sutton in Surrey from 1897. On completing his schooling, Campbell enlisted to join the Royal Navy as a Naval Cadet in February 1903 and began his training at HMS *Britannia*. His first sea posting was aboard the cruiser HMS *Ariadne*, as a naval cadet. He was later promoted to Midshipman from 15th September 1904 and served at this rank until 11th July 1905. Campbell's commanding officer wrote that he conducted himself 'with sobriety and to my satisfaction. A smart and promising young officer'.[1] Campbell married Violet Stephens in 1912 and they had two daughters. When War broke out, Campbell was serving as First Lieutenant aboard the destroyer HMS *Lurcher*, with the Harwich Force. On 28th September 1914 Lurcher took part in the Battle of Heligoland Bight. It was during this engagement that Roger Keyes, who was aboard *Lurcher* as a Commodore

first encountered Campbell. Keyes was impressed by the First Lieutenant: 'I formed a high opinion of him on that occasion.'[2] Commander Wilfred Tomkinson, commanding officer of HMS *Lurcher*, wrote that Campbell was 'a very capable and zealous officer'.[3]

During October 1914 Lieutenant Campbell was transferred to the battleship HMS *Emperor of India*, before being commissioned to the Grand Fleet. Campbell spent most of the war at Scapa Flow while serving aboard this vessel. When the Battle of Jutland took place in May 1916, HMS *Emperor of India* was in refit at Invergordon. Captain Charles Royds wrote that Campbell was 'a most able and efficient officer. Zealous, most reliable and loyal'.[4] While serving aboard *Emperor of India*, Campbell learned of the death of his elder brother Lieutenant Colonel Claude Campbell. He was commanding officer of the 1st/4th Battalion Seaforth Highlanders who had earned the DSO for his service on the Western Front. On 14th March 1916 Claude was killed in France near Arras.

Despite Keyes' request for unmarried men to take part in the Zeebrugge operation, Campbell, who was a married man and father to two small daughters, stepped forward. He was appointed commander of HMS *Daffodil* and Keyes gave him the task of pushing the cruiser *Vindictive* alongside the Mole while the diversionary assault force went ashore.

As decribed earlier, during the first two attempts to raid Zeebrugge, on some vessels the men over-consumed the rum ration. Campbell had faith in his men and trusted them to know their own limitations regarding the consumption of rum before battle. He said before returning to the bridge 'Well men, there's the rum. It's your lives, and you know what is expected of you.'[5] Nineteen years later Campbell confided to Petty Officer Adams that only a small amount of rum had been consumed by the men aboard *Daffodil* during that evening.

As *Daffodil* pushed *Vindictive* onto the Mole, Campbell received a shrapnel wound above one eye and was unable to see through this eye. Despite suffering pain from his wound, he continued to command. Keyes wrote: 'That she was maintained in position alongside and able to land and re-embark her storming party was entirely due to the skill and determination with which Commander Campbell handled the *Daffodil* under a tremendous fire for an hour, during the greater part of the time he was suffering from a painful wound which temporarily blinded one eye.'[6]

After the order to withdraw was given, command of the *Daffodil* passed to Sub Lieutenant Hegarty, who brought the Mersey Ferry Boat away from *Vindictive* with the assistance of navigator Lieutenant Rogers. Campbell was taken below deck to receive medical attention to his wound. Able Seaman Bernard Devlin:

> With blood streaming over his face he was at last led below, but gallant fellow that he was he would not give in … I looked in a cabin, where I saw Lieutenant Campbell. Blood trickling down his cheeks and a bandage round his damaged eye and forehead. He was seated at the table and was calmly smoking a cigarette. He smiled at the boy, and then called out, 'And this is an end to a perfect day'.[7]

Lieutenant Harold Campbell was a very popular and highly respected officer. Lieutenant Harold Rogers:

> I was aide de camp to a great hero, our Captain Lt. Campbell RN. A typical clean cut naval officer. He was an inspiration to all of us. Wounded at the Mole in the eye with shell splinters, he still carried on refusing to have his eye bandaged until he saw his little ship safely away and then although he was suffering excruciating agony refusing morphia; and when he was coming into Dover declined to wear his bandage because he felt it looked too much like swank!!![8]

Vice Admiral Sir William Nicholson regarded Campbell as 'a most exceptionally fine officer, possessing a high sense of duty. Strict, but tactful, and the men always liked him. Fearless but not rash. Full of energy and common sense. Quickly grasps a situation. Forms a sound opinion and does not hesitate before acting. An extremely nice officer to work with.'[9] Able Seaman Bernard Devlin described Campbell as 'a man with six hearts'.[10] Harry Adams also shared similar sentiments:

> One respects an 'Officer', respects his uniform even; because of discipline etc., but on such an occasion, you respect, (and I say it with all reverence) 'The Man', for his flesh and blood – like you – and you either love him, or detest him. We all loved Commander Campbell, and mighty pleased we were to see him come through – although wounded for he brought the 'Daffodil' and us back.[11]

After the raid Keyes sent a telegram to Campbell's family confirming that 'Harold is quite fit, very slightly wounded and has done simply splendidly.'[12] In the Victoria Cross ballot, Captain Carpenter of the cruiser *Vindictive* received one vote more than Campbell and so Carpenter was the officer elected to receive the prestigious award. Campbell was awarded the Distinguished Service Order. The French and Belgian governments also recognised his bravery and awarded him the Croix de Guerre with Palm and Chevalier of the Order of Leopold. The Mayor of Wallasey presented Campbell with an engraved gold cigarette case in honour of his role in the raid.

Many years after the war, Campbell attended a luncheon and by chance sat next to a stranger who happened to be the Chairman of Messrs. R. Stephenson and Co. Ltd, the company that built the *Daffodil*. He offered to build Campbell a model of the *Daffodil*. When the model eventually arrived in a mahogany and glass case, Campbell wanted to display the model in his study. However, his wife Violet had never fully recovered from her distress and horror that he had volunteered for an almost certain 'suicide mission', which might well have left her to bring up their two small daughters by herself. She would not have the ship on display. Campbell sadly stored the model of the *Daffodil* in his cellar. Years later his grandson, Michael Anson, found the abandoned model under a thick layer of coal dust. He had it carefully restored and placed it in a special room in his house – which became known as 'The *Daffodil* Room'. This gesture gave Harold Campbell a lot of pleasure in his later years. Michael was later able to add the *Daffodil*'s very own ship's bell and one of the special medallions struck to commemorate 'The Glorious Deeds of the British Navy on St. George's Day 1918', to his collection of his grandfather's Zeebrugge memorabilia.

After the raid Campbell was promoted to the rank of Lieutenant Commander and was appointed commander of HMS *Sikh* with the Dover Patrol. In 1922 the Royal Navy encouraged officers who had private incomes to leave the navy, to enable those officers who only had their naval pay to live on to remain on the active list and continue serving. Campbell held the rank of Commander at that time and reluctantly retired from the Royal Navy at his own request in October 1922.

Campbell met King George VI (the then Duke of York) when they served together in the Royal Navy. In 1930 Campbell was asked to become his Assistant Private Secretary and Equerry. He later served as his Private Secretary and Equerry from 1933 until 1936, when he was appointed Deputy Comptroller and Equerry. After the Duke of York was crowned King George VI, Campbell was appointed to his Household as Groom of the Robes in 1937. For his services to the Royal Family Campbell was made a CVO (Commander of the Royal Victorian Order) in 1935. He was later promoted to KCVO (Knight Commander of the Royal Victorian Order) in 1943. On VE Day on 8th May 1945 Princess Elizabeth and Princess Margaret wanted to take part in the celebrations that marked the end of the War in Europe. They were eager to wander amongst the jubilant crowds who were celebrating in the London streets. They were allowed to go onto the streets incognito and join the celebrations on the proviso that an escort accompanied them. Sir Harold Campbell was designated. However, the two young princesses were determined to participate independently and gave him the slip! Campbell had to return to Buckingham Palace without the princesses that evening.

King George VI and Sir Harold Campbell spent much time together and enjoyed shooting and fishing at both Sandringham and Balmoral. When George VI died in 1952, Campbell continued to serve as Groom of the Robes until 1954. In 1953 he was made a GCVO (Knight Grand Cross of the Royal Victorian Order). From 1954 until his death Campbell served as Extra Equerry to Queen Elizabeth II. He would keep himself active in later life. At the age of eighty he found relaxation at his home in Kent in ploughing a five-acre field and planting potatoes. Sir Harold Campbell died in 1969.

CHIEF ARTIFICER ENGINEER WILLIAM SUTTON DSC 269564 RN. William Sutton was born in Kingswear Devon on 4th January 1878 He was listed as a fitter on his service record when he enlisted into the Royal Navy on 11th January 1899. After 18 years service he was promoted to Artificer Engineer on 14th April 1917. During the Zeebrugge Raid it was doubtful as to whether the boilers could maintain enough steam to enable *Daffodil* to carry out her role during the operation. Chief Artificer Engineer William Sutton worked tirelessly during the raid to ensure that *Daffodil* had sufficient steam in her boilers. Lieutenant Harold Campbell recorded in his report:

Mr. Sutton's untiring exertions, his initiative and resource generally, enabled these difficulties … to be overcome. Throughout the pushing operation he managed to maintain 160 lbs of steam, a pressure which would have seemed quite impossible in view of previous experience. The engine room was holed and 2 compartments flooded. These were immediately and efficiently dealt with by Mr. Sutton. He was ubiquitous in handling every emergency that arose, and his energies, example, and inspiration to all in the engine and boiler rooms were beyond all praise.[13]

For his work at Zeebrugge he was awarded the Distinguished Service Cross.

PETTY OFFICER GEORGE PEMBERTON DSM F13706 RNAS. Petty Officer George Pemberton was born in Blackburn on 29th July 1896. He joined the Royal Naval Air Service in May 1916. During the Zeebrugge raid, Pemberton was in charge of the five-man RNAS contingent on HMS *Daffodil*. They were responsible for the flammenwerfers and phosphorus grenades onboard.

Unscathed, Pemberton returned to his home town of Blackburn to a hero's welcome. Thousands of local people congregated around Blackburn Station and waited for his arrival. Accompanying him was 1st Class Air Mechanic John Lomax, who was part of the RNAS party aboard *Vindictive*. Both these men came from Blackburn and attended the local technical school where they excelled in chemistry. They were welcomed by the local Mayor who told the people of Blackburn that 'they had only done what the soldiers were doing every day in France. Their work had for its object the keeping of the submarines from attacking our food ships, and that had been done'. Pemberton added that it was well worth sacrificing his life 'to save the people of England'.[14] He was awarded the Distinguished Service Medal.

ABLE SEAMAN TOM BRADLEY J62159 RN HMS DAFFODIL. Tom Bradley was born on 27th July 1898 in Houghton Le Springs, County Durham. His father was a miner and during Tom's early years the family moved to Wallsend. He later became a Fitter's Apprentice (Ships) in Tyneside in the shipbuilding yard. On 16th November 1916 he enlisted in the Royal Navy. Two years later he volunteered for the Zeebrugge Raid and joined HMS *Daffodil* on 12th March 1918.

Tom was a member of the Seaman Storming Party armed with bandoliers, cutlasses and revolvers. He had a lucky escape when equipment that he was wearing prevented a piece of shrapnel from tearing into his body. A piece of shrapnel passed through his body belt and grazed him:

A chap who was standing next to me amidst the turmoil remarked that he had two brothers killed in the war. 'I am the last one in the family,' he added 'and I don't think I will ever see England again'. 'The words had no sooner left his lips than a shell burst overhead; a fragment tore through his lifebelt and bandolier and penetrated his body just below his heart. The lad dropped at my feet.

Then I felt something strike me. My hand rushed to my side, and honestly I thought that I had received my death wound. It amazed me that I was still on my feet. I looked at my lifebelt and saw that a hole had been torn in it. My bandolier was also torn, and when I felt my jersey I saw another hole. I pushed my hand next to my skin, and my fingers rested on something hard. I pulled my fingers out, and with it a large piece of shrapnel, which by some wonderful luck had merely grazed the flesh after having been driven through my equipment and then through my clothing, where it had stopped a few inches beneath my heart. I shook hands with myself at my escape.[15]

Wallsend Council presented him with a gold watch when he returned home. After the War Tom became a motor mechanic and then a bus driver. He drove buses throughout the Second World War until the mid 1950s. He worked as a labourer with his son, who was maintenance fitter for British Ropes, until he died aged 60 in 1958.

PETTY OFFICER JAMES COWNIE DSM 239385 (DEV) RN. Petty Officer James Holroyd Cownie was born in Birmingham on 11th September 1891. The family later moved to Cathay, Cardiff. On leaving school he enlisted in the Royal Navy on his eighteenth birthday in 1909. During the Zeebrugge raid Cownie was the coxswain onboard HMS *Daffodil*. Lieutenant Campbell, commanding *Daffodil*, wrote that Cownie 'remained continuously at the wheel from 11.00 p.m. till about 4.00 a.m. During this period he carried out his responsible duties with marked efficiency and coolness, at times under heavy shell fire.'[16] After the raid Cownie recounted:

When we emerged from the smoke cloud we found ourselves right outside the Mole, and star shells illuminated the place like daylight. I was at the wheel, and could see what was going on. Our duty was to put the Vindictive *alongside the Mole, and we had to get our bows underneath her fore bridge. The first orders I heard after we had done this were from the* Vindictive, *'Campbell [Lieutenant Campbell] shove the* Vindictive *to the Mole', and of course we did so.*

Then the storming parties and the demolition parties landed, and we heard the explosion. The sound was overwhelming. Just at that time we noticed the submarine full of explosives, passing us to go and blow up the viaduct. We saw the big red flame and heard a huge explosion. Then a great cheer went up from every ship in praise of one of the submarines for a fine exploit. Shortly afterwards we saw the blockade ships proceeding under very heavy shell fire, and surrounded by star shells. We could see them passing the end of the Mole until they were again lost in the smoke and fog clouds. After all the work had been done we were given orders to blow the 'K' signal to recall those who had landed on the Mole. I sounded it on one siren, and a signalman on the other. We sounded it a dozen times, and we imagined everybody living and able to get away had left, when the captain of the Vindictive *told our captain to pick up his tow rope and tow him from the Mole. We did so, but a shell came and carried away the tow rope.*

During this time the captain of the Daffodil *was hit with a piece of shrapnel, and he sent up to me and said, 'Cownie, steer north and steam hard,' but when he found that the tow rope had parted he wanted to go back and see if the* Vindictive *was off the Mole or not. In half an hour we were clear of shell fire, and next morning saw the* Iris *steaming all right, and it was only then that we knew what the whole facts were.*

… I remember on one occasion receiving a severe thump on the back, which knocked me against the wheel. A piece of shrapnel crashed through, and according to the condition of my coat and lifebelt I should think hit me in the back. It was not until morning though that I noticed it, when the captain came on the bridge and pointed out the holes in my coat, saying 'You have had a narrow escape.'[17]

HMS *Daffodil*, flying the White Ensign.

Daffodil after the Zeebrugge raid (photographed by J H Mumford, New Brighton)

NOTES

1.Campbell papers courtesy Michael Anson.
2. Ibid.
3. Ibid.
4. Ibid.
5. Petty Officer Harry Adams Papers.
6. Campbell papers courtesy Michael Anson.
7. *Thomson's Weekly News*, 4th May 1918.
8. Letter from Lieutenant Harold Rogers to the Mayor of Wallasey. Campbell papers courtesy Michael Anson.
9. Campbell papers courtesy Michael Anson.
10. *The Liverpool Chronicle*, 29th April 1918.
11. Petty Officer Harry Adams Papers.
12.Campbell papers courtesy Michael Anson.
13. National Archives: ADM 137/3894: Lieutenant Harold Campbell's report.
14. *Blackburn Weekly Telegraph*, April 27th 1918.
15. *Thomson's Weekly News*, 4th May 1918.
16. National Archives: PRO Ref: ADM 137/3894: Lieutenant Harold Campbell's report.
17. *South Wales Daily News*, 29th April 1918.

CHAPTER 19

THEY WERE ON THE *IRIS*

LIEUTENANT OSCAR HENDERSON DSO RN. Oscar Henderson was born on 2nd October 1891 at the family home at Windsor Park, Belfast. He was one of five sons born to Sir James Henderson, who was proprietor of the *Belfast News Letter* and who later served as Lord Mayor of Belfast and First High Sheriff of the City. Oscar Henderson was educated at Bradfield College, Berkshire and he joined the Royal Navy as a Midshipman in 1909. He trained at the Royal Naval Colleges at Osborne and at Dartmouth. For the raid he was appointed second in command of HMS *Iris*. After the withdrawal from the Mole Henderson assumed command of *Iris* and with many dead and wounded crewmen as well as a damaged ship, navigated back to Dover. Commander Gibbs was mortally wounded as the ship headed home. For his role during this raid, Henderson was awarded the DSO and Croix de Guerre. His DSO citation states: 'When a shell carried away the port side of the bridge of his ship and caused a serious fire amongst the ammunition and bombs, he led a volunteer party with a hose on to the upper deck to quench the fire.'[1]

After the war he married Molly Henry of Strandtown, Belfast on 4th August 1921 and had two sons. On leaving the Royal Navy he was appointed Private Secretary and Comptroller to the first Governor of Northern Ireland, His Grace the Duke of Abercorn, 1923–1946. His role as Private Secretary to the Governor of Northern Ireland made Henderson ineligible for Royal Naval service during the Second World War. However, Henderson played his part by serving in the Ulster Home Guard. In 1946 Henderson joined the family business as a Managing Director of the *Belfast News Letter*. This newspaper was established in 1737 and still exists as the oldest surviving daily newspaper in the world. Henderson was involved with the establishment of Ulster Television Limited in 1958 and in 1963 he played an active role in the establishment of the *Sunday News*, which was the first Sunday newspaper in Northern Ireland. He was made a CVO and a CBE in later life. Oscar Henderson died on 3rd August 1969, aged 79, at his home in Glenburn House, Dunmurry, County Antrim.

HMS *Iris* at Dover after the Zeebrugge Raid.

MAJOR CHARLES EAGLES DSO, COMMANDING OFFICER, A COMPANY RMLI. Charles Eagles was born on 16th November 1883. Educated at Marlborough, he enlisted in the RMLI during September 1901 and was gazetted as a 2nd Lieutenant during that year. When War broke out he had attained the rank of Captain. In 1915 he served in Gallipoli and on 1st January 1917 he was awarded the DSO. Eagles was promoted to Major in early 1917. He commanded B Company, 2nd Battalion RMLI during the defence of Gavrelle Windmill during April 1917. For three days he and 37 men fought off several German attacks on the windmill. He married his wife Esme in July 1917. Volunteering for the Zeebrugge operation in early 1918 he was commander of A Company. Eagles was killed when a shell struck *Iris*. He was brought home to be buried at Coughton Church Cemetery, Warwickshire.

ORDINARY SEAMAN HENRY HOLLIS J56456 RN. Thomas Henry Hollis was born at Appleford Farm, Godshill on the Isle of Wight, on 24th March 1897. His father was a farmer and when he died aged 52 in 1905, his mother took Henry and the family to live with relatives in Australia. The family returned to the Isle of Wight because the climate was not agreeable. They returned to Littlestone Farm where Henry Hollis worked as a farmer. He enlisted in the Royal Navy and from August 1916 to May 1917 Hollis served aboard the Q Ship HMS *Cullist*. A German U-boat sank *Cullist* on 11th February 1918 in the Irish Sea. Hollis survived and three weeks later on 1st March he was assigned to HMS *Iris*. He was killed during the Zeebrugge raid on HMS *Iris* and was buried in St. James's Cemetery. His inscription reads:

THEIRS NOT TO REASON WHY
THEIRS BUT TO DO AND DIE

ABLE SEAMAN JOHN AHERN J22332 RN. John Ahern was born in Listowel, Kerry on 11th June 1896. He worked as a farm labourer before joining the Royal Navy as a boy sailor on 15th February 1913. When War broke out he was an Ordinary Seaman. He served on HMS *Orion* from September 1916 until he volunteered for the raid in 1918. While aboard HMS *Iris* he was wounded during the raid and his left leg had to be amputated at the thigh.

SURGEON FRANK POCOCK MC DSO RN. Frank Pearce Pocock was born in Hendon, London on 15th May 1891. He joined the Royal Naval Division as a temporary Surgeon Lieutenant on 28th August 1915. He was assigned to the Medical Unit at the Royal Naval Division Camp at Blandford. On 5th December 1915 he embarked on a ship that would take him to his first foreign role attached to the Royal Naval Division Mediterranean Medical Unit in Alexandria and later Imbros. On 2nd February 1916 he was assigned to Drake Battalion and during May 1916 Pocock and the battalion were sent to France. Drake Battalion took part in the final phase of the Somme Campaign at the Battle of Ancre in November 1916. During this battle Pocock earned the Military Cross for his efforts to recover and attend to the wounded. His service record states that he was 'Awarded M.C. in connection with recent operations North of the Ancre. Awarded Military Cross for gallantry and devotion to duty.'[2] During April 1917, Pocock provided medical support when Drake battalion took part in the Battle of Gavrelle.

Grave of Surgeon Frank Pocock, Lourval Military Cemetery, France.

Surgeon Frank Pocock served with the Navy, but during the raid was attached to the 4th Battalion Royal Marines Light Infantry. He worked tirelessly to aid the wounded onboard *Iris*. Lieutenant Oscar Henderson wrote that 'immediately the shelling commenced he set to tend the wounded. He had all the work to do himself, as all his staff were killed. His work certainly saved many lives.'[3]

With all his medical staff wiped out Pocock was solely responsible for tending to the wounded until two surgeons from other vessels were brought aboard to assist him. Pocock worked continuously for 13 hours and was awarded the DSO for his efforts. His citation reads: 'By his devotion to duty, he undoubtedly saved many lives. When *Iris* was hit he at once commenced tending the wounded, and as all the sick-berth staff were killed, had all the work to do alone. After the dynamo was damaged, he had to work by candle and torchlight.'[4]

Pocock was transferred to Drake Battalion Royal Naval Division on 9th August 1918. He was wounded near the Escault Canal on 29th September 1918 while tending to the wounded as Drake Battalion assaulted the Hindenberg Line. Pocock was taken to 149th Royal Naval Field Ambulance where he died from his wounds. Pocock, aged 27, was buried at Louverval Military Cemetery, Doignies, France. On 5th November 1918, Pocock was awarded a Bar to his Military Cross for his conduct in the final stages of the war. His citation states:

He attended to the wounded under very heavy fire and most adverse circumstances during operations lasting several days. His courage and self sacrificing devotion to duty were a splendid example to his stretcher-bearers and his skill was instrumental in saving the lives of many wounded men.[5]

LIEUTENANT COMMANDER GEORGE BRADFORD VC RN, C COMPANY, ROYAL NAVAL LANDING PARTY. Lieutenant Commander George Bradford was one of four brothers from Durham who fought during World War One. The family moved to Darlington when he was very young. Bradford was educated at Darlington Grammar School, before attending Royal Naval Academies in Hampshire. In 1902 he joined HMS *Britannia* as a Cadet. During World War One he served on HMS *Orion* and took part in the Battle of Jutland. He was a keen athlete and for some years was Royal Navy lightweight champion boxer.

By the time he began preparing for the Zeebrugge raid he had lost two of his younger brothers. His brother 2nd Lieutenant James Bradford MC was killed while serving with the Durham Light Infantry on 14th May 1917. Aged 27, he died of wounds sustained near Arras. His youngest brother Brigadier General Roland Bradford VC had been killed at Cambrai on 30th November 1917. He had won the Victoria Cross at the Somme during 1916 while serving with the Durham Light Infantry. The Bradford brothers are the only brothers to be awarded the Victoria Cross during the First World War. When Roland was appointed Commander of the 186th Infantry Brigade on 10th November 1917 at the age of 25, he may have been the youngest person in the army ever to achieve that rank.

Lieutenant Commander George Bradford continued the family tradition for courage when he was appointed Commander of D Company, the Royal Naval storming force onboard *Iris*. He was killed by enemy fire while attempting to secure *Iris* alongside the Mole. Ordinary Seaman O'Hara witnessed Bradford's courageous act, which would win him the Victoria Cross:

> *I heard a cheer and looking up saw our section commander, Lt Comdr Bradford climbing up our derrick which was trained over the Mole; he was successful in reaching the Mole and immediately made fast our grapnel; unfortunately as he finished he stood up, and therefore became a target for enemy snipers, he was shot and fell between the ship and the Mole; we managed to get a line to him which he grasped but as he was badly wounded he did not have the strength to hold on and be pulled up; a ladder was procured and placed over the side but unfortunately just as a volunteer was descending to his aid a rather heavy swell dashed* Iris *against the Mole and he was crushed between.*[6]

In a letter of condolence to his sole surviving brother, Captain Carpenter wrote that 'His supreme contempt for danger and his unforgettable self-sacrifice were typical, not only of those whose deeds gave birth to our traditions, but of himself. George Bradford was not only a great fighter but a great gentleman, a great friend and a great sportsman. His was a most lovable nature. Both in everyday life and in the manner of his death he has set the rest of us an example of incalculable benefit.'[7]. His citation for the Victoria Cross reads:

Grave of Lieutenant Commander George Bradford VC.

Great difficulty was experienced in placing the parapet anchors owing to the motion of the ship. An attempt was made to land by the scaling ladders before the ship was secured. Lieutenant Claude E. K. Hawkings managed to get one ladder in position and actually reached the parapet, the ladder being crashed to pieces just as he stepped off it. This very gallant young officer was last seen defending himself with his revolver. He was killed on the parapet. Though securing the ship was not part of his duties, Lieut–Commander Bradford climbed up the derrick, which carried a large parapet anchor and was rigged out over the port side; during the climb the ship was surging up and down and the derrick crashing on the Mole; waiting his opportunity he jumped with the parapet anchor on to the Mole and placed it in position. Immediately after hooking on the parapet anchor Lieut–Commander Bradford was riddled with bullets from machine guns and fell into the sea between the Mole and the ship. Attempts to recover his body failed. Lieut–Commander Bradford's action was one of absolute self sacrifice; without a moment's hesitation he went to certain death, recognising that in such action lay the only possible chance of securing 'Iris II' and enabling her storming parties to land.[8]

Bradford's remains were recovered and he was buried in Blankenberge Town Cemetery.

AIR MECHANIC FIRST CLASS GEORGE WARRINGTON F26702 RNAS. George Warrington was born on 7th July 1898, the son of a farmer in Shotwick Chester, Cheshire. He was a student at Manchester University studying to become an analytical chemist. He interrupted his studies when he enlisted to join the Royal Naval Air Service on 13th March 1917. He spent the first day of his service at Crystal Palace, and then he was sent for training at the RNAS Experimental Station at Stratford. In September 1917 he was promoted to Air Mechanic First Class. Within a year of enlisting
George Warrington volunteered to take part in the Zeebrugge raid. He was assigned to HMS *Iris*, given the rank of Petty Officer and was in command of the Forward Mole Flammenwerfer position, which was to protect the landing party with jets of burning oil. Before they set off for Zeebrugge on 22nd April 1918, George Warrington recalled that Lieutenant Henderson ordered him and his men to cover the top with sand to soak up the blood of the dead and wounded. As German shells hit the deck of *Iris*, George Warrington was saved as he sheltered under a pile of dead and wounded men. He returned home safely and was de-mobbed from the RNAS on 31st March 1919. George did not return to Manchester University to complete his studies. Instead he joined the family farming business. George Warrington continued to serve his country during the Second World War when he became an active member of the Home Guard. He was a public spirited individual within the community where he lived and continued the family tradition of being a parish councillor.

ABLE SEAMAN WILLIAM FROST J15029 RN. William Frederick Frost was born in Cardiff on 18th April 1895. He served in the Merchant Navy Service as a cook's boy and travelled around the world. On his sixteenth birthday he joined the Royal Navy, volunteering to serve for 12 years. He served for many years on the Dreadnought Class Battleship HMS *George V* as a gunner. William was aboard this vessel as an Able Seaman during the Battle of Jutland.
During the raid William Frost served aboard HMS *Iris*. He received shell splinter wounds in his right ankle joint and left thigh. Prostrate on the deck of *Iris* he remembered that he lay 'with a dead marine for a pillow'. When gangrene set in it was necessary to amputate a third of his right lower leg to save his life. Throughout the rest of his life William Frost suffered from the injuries that he received at Zeebrugge. He was always in poor health and he died of tuberculosis on the 12th February 1944.

LIEUTENANT GEORGE SPENCER DSC RNR. Lieutenant George Spencer enlisted in the Merchant Navy at the age of 15 and at the same time joined the Royal Naval Reserve. During the First World War he was commander of a destroyer serving off the China coast. The following year he returned to Europe and served in the English Channel escorting Allied shipping. In 1917 he was awarded the Distinguished Service Cross for 'action with submarines'. Two months prior to the Zeebrugge raid Spencer was serving aboard the Q ship HMS *Cullist* when she was torpedoed by a German submarine in the Irish Sea. An explosion ripped through the middle of the vessel after midday on 11th February 1918. Water began to fill the vessel immediately. Hannah Spencer recalled her brother's experience in a letter to a relative:

They had been assured several times that the ship was so built that it was impossible for it to sink quickly and it would keep afloat for 3 or 4 hours. George said no one quite believed that, but they thought that she would float for half an hour perhaps, accordingly every one went to his appointed place and those poor fellows whose duty took them down below were drowned without any chance of escape, because the ship went down in three minutes. First it tipped over to one side, and George had to jump off into the sea. He clutched hold of a lifeboat in doing so, hoping it would float, but the men hadn't had time to release it properly so it was dragged down with the ship, and George found himself underneath it for a little while and quite thought he was being drowned. However, as he says, he kept on kicking and presently found himself up on the top of the water. By this time the ship was up and on one end … The lifeboats were dragged down with her and except for a few spars, the only thing left floating was a raft that George himself had had made. He managed to get on to it, and they picked up a few more, including the Capt. whose shoulder was dislocated by being knocked down when the explosion came. Then the submarine came up closer to have a look at them, and the brutes trained their gun on the raft, and George says they thought they were all going to be shot. However the Germans evidently changed their minds and did not shoot. They picked one man up out of the water and made off.[9]

HMS *Cullist* had a crew of 75 men. Thirty survivors including Lieutenant Spencer found refuge on the raft on which they drifted for five hours until they were rescued by a trawler. After ten days leave Spencer was immediately transferred to the Zeebrugge operation and was assigned navigating officer onboard *Iris*. After the ordeal of being sunk by a German submarine he must have been keen to take part in an operation devised to block this menace at Zeebrugge. When Commander Valentine Gibbs was wounded during the operation, Lieutenant Spencer took command of *Iris*. Moments later Spencer was severely wounded when his right leg was shattered by one of the numerous explosions that were pounding the vulnerable Mersey ferry. Lieutenant Henderson wrote that Spencer 'Though seriously wounded remained by the compass, conning the ship until relieved by myself'.[10] On arrival at Dover, the mortally wounded George Spencer was transferred to Gillingham Naval Hospital where he passed away later that day, on 23rd April. He had been married for over two years and his wife Grace Spencer was expecting their child. A month and a day after he died, Grace gave birth to a daughter whom she named Iris.

George Spencer's body was brought to Brondesbury in north London, where he received a funeral with full military honours. Borne on a gun carriage, with his coffin draped with the Union Jack and bearing his naval sword he was taken to Hampstead Cemetery, where three volleys were fired and the Last Post sounded. He was listed as being mentioned in dispatches in *The London Gazette* of 23rd July 1918.

Above left: Mersey ferry *Iris* after Zeebrugge.

Above right: 'HMS *Iris*, Bridge and fore-deck wrecked, Bridge End.' Where Commander Valentine Gibbs and Lieutenant Spencer received their mortal wounds.

ARTIFICER ENGINEER WILLIAM HENRY VAUGHAN EDGAR DSC, ROYAL AUSTRALIAN NAVY. William Henry Vaughan Edgar was a Warrant Officer Artificer Engineer serving with the Royal Australian Navy on HMAS *Australia* when he volunteered for the operation in early 1918. He was appointed engineer on HMS *Iris* and during the Zeebrugge raid he worked unceasingly to keep the ship going while under heavy fire. After the bridge was shot away he showed great bravery in coming onto the upper deck to turn on the smoke apparatus, so that *Iris* had a chance to withdraw without further loss of life. For his part in the raid Edgar was recommended for special promotion to Lieutenant and was awarded the Distinguished Service Cross, the only member of the Royal Australian Navy to receive this award during World War 1. His DSC citation states:

It was due to this officer that the ship was kept going during the action under very heavy fire, and though holed several times, succeeded in returning to base under her own steam. He did invaluable work in the engine-room and boiler-room throughout the operation for a period of seventeen hours without rest. He showed great bravery when the ship was under heavy fire, by coming up onto the upper deck, and with the help of an engine room artificer turned on the smoke apparatus.[11]

This last action allowed the *Iris* to make a successful escape. *Iris* limped back to Dover burning fiercely. Edgar was immediately commissioned as a lieutenant as a consequence of his bravery. He was promoted to Lieutenant Commander on 23 April 1926.

STOKER PETTY OFFICER HENRY MABB DSM RN K1043. Henry Mabb was born in 1890 in Maidstone, Kent. He worked as an agricultural labourer, and then in July 1908 he enlisted in the Royal Navy as a Stoker. By the time that War broke out, Henry Mabb had attained the rank of Petty Officer and was serving aboard the cruiser HMS *Lowestoft*. He was drafted to this vessel in April 1914 and served on her until 31st December 1917. Henry Mabb was aboard when HMS *Lowestoft* sank a German merchant vessel in August 1914 and when she took part in the Battle of Heligoland Bight on
28th August 1914. Henry Mabb saw action once again on 24th January 1915 during the Battle of Dogger Bank. During 1916 HMS *Lowestoft* was sent to the Mediterranean. On 1st January 1918 Henry Mabb was in Chatham and posted to HMS *Pembroke*. He then volunteered and was assigned as a stoker aboard HMS *Iris*. During the raid he worked below decks in the engine room and for his role he was awarded the Distinguished Service Medal. After the raid he continued to serve in the Royal Navy until November 1928. On leaving the Royal Navy Henry returned to Kent where he resumed working in agriculture as a tractor driver in Barming, Kent. He married Alice Capewell and had one son named John. Henry continued to work in agriculture until retirement. He passed away on 21st March 1965 aged 75.

PRIVATE ERNEST TRACEY CH 21150 NO.1 PLATOON, A COMPANY 4TH BATTALION RMLI. Ernest Frederick Tracey was born in Richmond on 31st December 1899. He was known as Beau Tracey and was a garage cleaner before he enlisted to join the Royal Marines Light Infantry on 31st January 1917. At the time of enlistment he was 17 years old and under age to serve. He volunteered for the Zeebrugge raid and was assigned to No.1 Platoon aboard HMS *Iris*. He was one of the few marines from *Iris* to jump onto *Vindictive*; however, the withdrawal siren was sounded before they got

onto the Mole. 'I can remember very clearly the Platoon Sergeant saying stand by to jump, jump for it. Well we made the jump for it, we were only too eager, we were raring to go. Instead of standing still doing nothing.[12] A few dozen got aboard the *Vindictive* before they heard the evacuation siren.

After the Zeebrugge raid he was sent to HMS *Glory* to serve in Russia from 21st May 1918 until 23rd June 1919. He continued to serve with the Corps attaining the rank of Colour Sergeant during June 1938. During World War Two he served with the Royal Marine Reserve Regiment from 1st January 1940 until 20th July 1946. He emigrated to Victoria, British Columbia, Canada and died on 29th November 1988.

No.1 Platoon, A Company, 4th Royal Marine Light Infantry Battalion, RM Museum Archive 2/10/15(9). Major Charles Eagles is seated front row, fifth from left. Captain Ralph Del Strother is seated fourth from left, front row. Del Strother was wounded during the raid. Lieutenant Sydney Inskip is seated first row, sixth from left. Private Ernest Tracey was very complimentary about these three officers in Philip Warner's book *The Zeebrugge Raid*. He wrote that 'they were of the very best … they bought mouth organs for use on the march, and they made themselves interested in a man with his affairs at home etc. On parade, it was On Parade, but even so at times when on the march the officers would move along the unit and come out with a cheery 'Everybody happy' or something like it … I would say every man was 100% content within his unit, and would not want to leave that high degree of contentment.'

PRIVATE HAROLD MERCER CH 2055(S), NO.1 PLATOON, A COMPANY 4TH RMLI BATTALION. Private Harold Mercer was born in Burnley, Lancashire on 29th September 1897. He worked as a labourer before enlisting in the Royal Marines Light Infantry at the Liverpool recruiting office on 2nd January 1917. He was killed aboard *Iris* during the raid and was buried in Burnley Cemetery.

PRIVATE GEORGE LAMING CH 19816, NO.1 PLATOON, A COMPANY, RMLI 4TH RMLI BATTALION. George Robert Laming was born on 24th March 1898, Ringwould, Deal, Kent. He had worked as a farm labourer before enlisting to join the RMLI on 24th March 1915. Laming had taken part in the Battle of Jutland. Serving aboard HMS *Iris* with No. 1 Platoon, he was lucky to come away from the Zeebrugge raid unharmed. He continued to serve with the Corps until December 1945.

PRIVATE GEORGE PARKS CH 21276, NO.1 PLATOON, A COMPANY, 4TH RMLI BATTALION. George Parks was a resident of Folkestone who took part in the operation. Born on 30th May 1898, George Parks was a student at the Black Bull Council School and was an enthusiastic member of the Folkestone Troop of Boy Scouts. As a scout during the early part of the war he carried out useful work along the south coast. On leaving school he worked as a plumber until he enlisted in the Royal Marines Light Infantry on 11th April 1917. He saw considerable service in the North Sea before being killed in action during the Zeebrugge raid. Private George Parks was buried in Folkestone Old Cemetery.

PRIVATE PERCY LINKIN CH 17284 NO. 1 PLATOON A COMPANY, 4TH BATTALION RMLI. Percy Linkin was born in Faversham, Kent on 26th March 1892. His family came to live in Folkestone when he was five. He attended the Sidney Street School and worked for the plumbers and decorators Messers Crouch & Son for four and a half years. His next employment took him to Saxeilby, Lincolnshire, where he worked for an engineering works. Looking for a life of adventure he enlisted with the Royal Marines Light Infantry on 12th January 1912. On completing his training at Deal he was assigned to serve on the cruiser HMS *Lowestoft*. He spent the early part of the war patrolling the North Sea. He took part in the Battle of Heligoland Bight in August 1914 and was present when HMS *Hogue*, *Aboukir* and *Cressy* were sunk during September 1914. He also took part in the Battle of Dogger Bank in January 1915. From 1916 the ship patrolled the Persian Gulf and Mediterranean for two years. When he returned to England in early 1918 he was granted a month's leave, during which time on 28th January he married his wife May. When he returned to duty he volunteered for the Zeebrugge raid. His involvement in the operation is listed in the casualty list and on his service record, but for some unknown reason he is not listed on the 4th Battalion Royal Marines Light Infantry muster list. Linkin is pictured in the group picture of No.1 Platoon (opposite) taken at Deal during March 1918. He was assigned to HMS *Iris* and was seen by one of his mates Leading Stoker Henry Baker trying to ascend the Mole. Baker, also from Folkestone, had attended the same Sydney Street School and was working on the deck of *Vindictive* during the raid when he saw his pal. 'I saw young Larkin going over the top from the *Iris*. He looked very merry and bright. That was the last I saw of him.'[13] Linkin was so badly wounded that he died from his wounds. His body was brought to the home of his widow May Linkin in Upper Holloway, North London. The funeral service was performed in the church where three months previously he had married and he was buried in Islington Cemetery.

LIEUTENANT SYDNEY HOPE ELSDALE INSKIP, NO.1 PLATOON, A COMPANY 4TH BATTALION RMLI. Sydney Inskip was born on 25th September 1895 in Sydney, New South Wales, Australia. Known to his family as Hope, he was born into an affluent family. His mother Gertrude originated from a prominent and wealthy Australian family, while his father Herbert was a Captain serving on the Orient Line. When Herbert retired from the Orient Line he served as Harbour Master at Ramsgate where Hope was brought up.

Hope enlisted in the Royal Marines Light Infantry when War broke out and after completing his training was appointed to the Royal Marine Brigade, Chatham Division. Hope landed at Gallipoli on 27th April 1915. At that time he had recently been promoted to 1st Lieutenant and in a letter home to his mother Gertrude he wrote:

It was quite dark and as we neared the beach we could see all the Australian bivouac fires, also heard the crackle of rifle fire and the screech of shrapnel. It was very weird and impressive, and as the majority of us were all going in to action for the first time, we got our first taste of the reality of things when some stray bullets came on to our deck and wounded one or two of the fellows.[14]

Once Inskip had landed at Anzac Beach he and his men reassembled at the rendezvous point in Shrapnel Valley, from where they headed off to the support trenches two miles away. As they proceeded towards the lines they were vulnerable to further bullets and shrapnel. On arriving at the trenches they relieved soldiers from the Australian Infantry force who had been fighting since 25th April. Inskip was involved in another landing on 29th April at Cape Helles.

At 8.30 the following morning we steamed up … and lay off there for a few hours in which time we heard we were going to land. The shelling started at 8 and went on for about 4 hours in which several poor fellows were blown to atoms … after having to read a Burial Service over one, I nearly collapsed. Everyone's nerves went to pot, and it's not surprising either. However after a tot of rum and good night's rest we felt better.[15]

Hope Inskip's service record indicates that he took part in the defence of the southern sector of the Gallipoli peninsula from 29th April to 12th May 1915. A year later, Hope was involved in quelling the Irish Rebellion from 26th April to 15th May 1916. On 30th January 1917 Hope was appointed to the battleship HMS *Hindustan*. He served on this ship until 4th April 1917 as physical training instructor. During February 1918 he was assigned to No.1 Platoon, Chatham Company, 4th Battalion Royal Marines Light Infantry to begin training for the Zeebrugge raid. Hope was concerned with the welfare of the men that he led and in return he was a respected and well liked officer. Private Tracey wrote that 'Off parade, it was Off Parade; Lieutenant Inskip would often come out with something like: "How are you today, are you short in any way, can I help you at all?"'[16]

Hope and No.1 Platoon were assigned to the *Iris*. During the raid Hope was unable to land on the Mole. As *Iris* left the Mole Hope went to the wardroom to get a packet of cigarettes from his greatcoat to give to his men who were suffering on the deck. A shell struck the wardroom at that moment and killed Hope. His mother, who was grieving for the loss of her husband from the previous year, requested that Hope's body be brought home for burial. Hope was buried next to his father in the City of London Cemetery at Ilford.

Charles Allbones, centre, with his brothers Joseph (left) and George (right).

PRIVATE CHARLES ALLBONES CH 19467, NO. 2 PLATOON, A COMPANY, 4TH BATTALION RMLI. Charles Allbones was born in Barnsley, Yorkshire on 5th January 1897. When he enlisted to join the RMLI in a Nottingham recruitment office on 24th November 1914 he was aged 17 years and 10 months and was under age to serve. He was drafted to HMS *Lowestoft* from 12th July 1915 until 15th January 1918 and spent most of that time serving in the Mediterranean. During February 1918 he was selected to take part in the Zeebrugge raid. He was assigned to No.2 Platoon, A Company. His son confirmed that his father Charles Allbones went to Zeebrugge aboard *Vindictive*. He must have been for some unknown reason separated from his mates in No.2

Platoon on the *Iris* and transferred to other duties aboard *Vindictive*. Or he could have been one of the few marines who transferred from *Iris* to get onto the Mole via *Vindictive*. Charles received a wound in the shoulder and was left for dead. However, he managed to make a noise to get some medical attention. Charles was discharged from the RMLI on 27th February 1920.

PRIVATE ALEXANDER GORDON CH 20545, NO.2 PLATOON, A COMPANY, 4TH BATTALION RMLI. Alexander Robert Gordon was born in St. Pancras, London on 27th August 1896. He enlisted in the RMLI on 3rd April 1916. After training at Deal he was assigned to serve on HMS *Inflexible* based at Scapa Flow. This battlecruiser performed convoy duties in the North Sea while he was aboard. During the Zeebrugge raid Alexander Gordon was part of No.2 Platoon aboard *Iris*. A shell struck the deck where he and 55 other marines were waiting. The shell killed about 50 men and Alexander was among the seven that were wounded. His wounds necessitated the amputation of the left leg below the knee. His right ankle was also shattered, but after several operations the leg was saved by the surgeon. Alexander spent two years recovering from the injuries he sustained at Zeebrugge. He had to wear a metal artificial leg and visited Roehampton on many occasions for fittings. He was discharged from the RMLI on 3rd May 1919.

After being invalided from the RMLI Alexander worked for a picture framers and would cycle to work. Despite losing a leg, he was able to lead a full life. He married Bessie Roberts on 7th April 1928 in Eastbourne, Sussex. They had two children, Sheila and Roger. His son was named after Admiral Keyes. It was through Admiral Keyes' efforts that he was able to secure a position of work at the Howard Pneumatic Engineering Company in Eastbourne. Alexander worked there for 22 years. On the fiftieth anniversary of the Zeebrugge raid on 23rd April 1968 his wife Bessie wrote of her husband in her journal. 'Although, often in pain he has led a full life at work and in the home. Throughout his life everyone said of him: – "HE NEVER COMPLAINED".'[17] His grandson Kevin remembered his grandfather to be 'always a friendly and happy man'. He asked him about his service in the Royal Marines Light Infantry on a couple of occasions, but was hushed by his grandmother because she said it would upset him. He also remembered Alexander playing the spoons against his metal leg. He was a member of the Royal British Legion and enjoyed playing snooker. Alexander Gordon passed away on 15th April 1978 aged 81 and was buried in Ocklynge Cemetery, Eastbourne, Sussex.

LANCE CORPORAL GEORGE CALVERLEY CH 19805, NO.2 PLATOON, A COMPANY, 4TH BATTALION RMLI. George Calverley was born on 20th July 1898 in Armley, Leeds. He was aged 16 when the War broke out. Despite being under age to join up, George and his older friends Jack Hamilton and Tom Arms tried to enlist in the Royal Field Artillery by adding a year to their real ages. The strict recruiting sergeant was not fooled and turned them away saying 'Thanks for trying lads, but try again in a few months'. The boys made a further attempt when they tried to enlist by answering Kitchener's call for volunteers a few weeks later in September 1914. George was turned away a second time for being under aged to serve, however his mates Jack and Tom successfully enlisted in the Army.

While his mates were training for war, Calverley worked as a solicitor's clerk in Leeds. One of his duties included serving County Court writs to debtors. On one occasion in March 1915 he was returning from issuing a writ to a debtor, Calverley passed the Royal Navy and Royal Marines recruiting office in Leeds. To serve as a sea soldier was more appealing to George and so he decided to enlist in the Royal Marines Light Infantry, and at 16 years and 7 months he was still under the age limit. He passed the height requirements by raising himself on his toes. The recruiting sergeant who either did not notice or turned a blind eye, instructed Calverley to report back to the recruiting office the following day and bring with him his birth certificate to prove his age. The following day Calverley returned to the office and was sent with five other lads by train to the main recruiting office in York where he was given a medical examination. Once again, he passed the height test by standing on his toes and when he was asked for his birth certificate, he told the recruiting officer that it was lost. Although the officer did not believe Calverley, he was accepted and sent to the Royal Marine Light Infantry barracks at Deal. On 15th March 1915 he swore the oath to the King. He spent four months in basic training – marching, physical training and bayonet training. During his training Calverley and his fellow recruits were granted four days leave. During this time he received the tragic news that his mates Jack and Tom had been killed on the Western Front in France.

Calverley was assigned to Chatham barracks and completed further training in gunnery, musketry and field training. On serving one year after enlistment George had hoped to be on active service, but instead he was drafted to serve aboard HMS *Prince George* on 15th March 1916. This battleship acted as a Thames guard ship until September 1916 when she was paid off. Calverley was then drafted to serve on HMS *Hibernia* which was based at Sheerness and patrolled the North Sea.

In February 1918 Calverley was assigned to A Company, 4th Battalion RMLI and began training for the Zeebrugge raid. During this training 4th Battalion Headquarters Staff made the decision that there should be a second in command of each section. Calverley was the youngest member of his section and to his surprise he was appointed the second in command and promoted to Lance Corporal. King George V visited Deal barracks on 7th May 1918 and inspected 4th Battalion RMLI. The King was unaware that the men from the battalion were preparing for the raid on Zeebrugge. Calverley later remembered:

I was standing in the supernumerary rank two paces behind my section. He had a very gruff voice. He looked at me for a couple of seconds and as he passed on I heard him remark to the accompanying General about someone being very young and I assumed that it was me he was referring to.[18]

Calverley belonged to A Company, assigned to *Iris*. He described the action of the night as being like 'Dante's Inferno'. As they passed HMS *Vindictive* he recalled, 'All hell seemed to be let loose, her troops were climbing the wooden scaling ladders onto the Mole and flame-throwers were shooting flames across the Mole.'[19] During the raid *Iris* was unable to land Calverley and A Company onto the Mole. When the order for *Iris* to withdraw was given, Major Eagles commanding A Company ordered 'All Marines below' to ensure that the deck was clear to enable the sailors to work as the ship returned to Dover. Calverley was obeying Major Eagle's final order to go below decks when the German shells struck *Iris*. He later recalled this moment, and his final words to a shipmate, in a letter to his granddaughter Vivienne, 61 years later:

Even after 61 years I can remember what I said to him, it was 'Well Cornforth, the worse is over, and now it's a matter of getting home – where are the others?' He opened his lips to answer, gave a gasp and fell forward at my feet. At the same instant I sensed something had come through the ship's side near my left shoulder. I bent down towards him and woke up about 5 yards from where we had been standing. That is the only way I can describe what happened and I did not know how long I had been 'OUT'. I was on my side and was scared, then happy as I gradually moved my limbs and stood up and as my hearing came back, I could hear moaning and cries of pain and someone yell 'Put that light out' you see we were in darkness except for an occasional electric blue light bulb which gave just a glimmer of light. Finding I could walk I made my way to where I had been standing, stepping over the wounded and at the bottom of the staircase was a heap of dead and dying in a terribly bloody state. I felt a bit sore but went on deck and in the very dim light I found similar conditions there.[20]

Calverley was incredibly fortunate to have survived the explosion. Private William Cornforth, from Coxwold, Yorkshire, not three feet away, was killed by the blast.

As *Iris* sailed back across the English Channel, Calverley and the remaining members of his company set about establishing defensive positions aboard the Mersey ferry boat as a precaution against German vessels en route. They were alone in the English Channel and they found eight Lewis machine guns amongst the wreckage and debris, which enabled them to organise a defensive position 'Our next task was to sort out the dead out by laying them alongside each other in lines along the deck and then bring those up from below to add to them.'[21] It was not until he returned to his barracks at Deal in the afternoon that the enormity of the loss of fallen comrades struck him.

On arrival we went straight to the barrack rooms which we had occupied before the raid. They had remained just as we had left them before the raid, with our kit bags still stacked at one end of the room. We discarded our equipment and took over the beds we had formerly used. Then the reaction set in, there were 24 men in the room originally and now there were only 11. There were no jokes or silly quips in the room that night but on looking around I began to realise how fortunate I had been. After eating my first meal in over 24 hrs and after a good soak in a warm bath, I turned in and in spite of the recent excitement was soon asleep.[22]

When Calverley paraded for Muster the following morning on 24th April he discovered that he was one of three survivors from a Section which had comprised thirteen men. Once the roll call was completed Calverley and the remnants of 4th Battalion RMLI took part in the ballot to award the two Victoria Crosses. After the roll call Calverley prepared to return to his barracks in Chatham. He changed from his blood-stained uniform and collected his belongings, which included a revolver and a sailor's cutlass that he retrieved from the wreckage aboard HMS *Iris*. It was a heartbreaking moment for them on arriving at Chatham Station. 'There was a band waiting at the station to march us to the barracks, but as we were detraining and before we could fall in relatives of the men in our force were among us, asking about their menfolk. It was distressing both for them and us.'[23]

Survivors of the raid at Chatham barracks. This photograph was amongst Lance Corporal George Calverley's possessions.

At Chatham barracks A Company was inspected by a General, and a group photograph was taken. They were then granted seven days leave. Calverley returned home to Leeds. As he waited for his train at Kings Cross he took a walk along the Pentonville Road. It was during this walk that he met May, his future wife, although it was an unusual and frightening introduction for a young lady.

> *After a few minutes we almost bumped into two girls coming towards us at which I whipped out the revolver and held them up. Perhaps I was suffering from 'shell shock' after all. After chatting for a few minutes they returned with us to the station and waved us good-bye as our train left, but not before I had obtained the address of the prettier of the two girls, her name was May.[24]*

Calverley married May a year later on 22nd June 1919 at St. Philips Church, Islington.

It was standard practice that any man who was promoted on detached service would revert back to his original rank on returning to his barracks. But on his return from leave, Calverley was permitted to retain his stripe and the rank of Lance Corporal. During May and June 1918 he was in command of a firing party for funerals of the men who fell at Zeebrugge. He attended funerals every three or four days during this period.

Calverley continued to serve with the Royal Marines Light Infantry and by June 1932 he had attained the rank of Company Sergeant Major. He retired from the Royal Marines on 20th July 1936, on his 38th birthday. When World War Two broke out he volunteered and rejoined the Royal Marines for a further six years service. Since there were not enough vacancies as Company Sergeant Major, he served at the reduced rank of Colour Sergeant at Browndown Small Arms School. He was eager to play his part and was later promoted to Regimental Sergeant Major. Calverley served with fellow Zeebrugge raider Sergeant Finch in 1941.

After the Second World War, George Calverley settled into civilian life as a lock keeper in Roydon in Hertfordshire. He later moved his family to Lindford in Hampshire where he worked as a civilian armourer in Bordon Army Camp. His grandson Nigel recalled his grandfather to be 'a very genial man who loved his garden and grew his own tobacco'. In 1952 he gained the Meritorious Service Record. George Calverley passed away aged 84 in the King Edward VII hospital in Midhurst in 1983.

F. W. HOATH.

ROLL OF FAME

H.M.S. PHAETON.
The DARDANELLES, Mar. 18, 1915.
Zeppelin L 7, May 4, 1916.
Battle of JUTLAND, May 31, 1916.

PRIVATE FREDERICK WILLIAM HOATH CH 18302, NO. 3 PLATOON, A COMPANY, 4TH BATTALION RMLI. Frederick William Hoath was born in Westerham, Kent on 29th October 1894. He worked as a carpenter before enlisting to join the RMLI. Fred enlisted in a London recruitment office on 6th January 1914. During the First World War, Fred served aboard HMS *Phaeton* from 9th February 1915 until 25th November 1917. While serving aboard this light cruiser he took part in the Dardanelles campaign, when she was deployed to support the Gallipoli landings from February to September 1915. During 1916 HMS *Phaeton* was transferred to the 1st Light Cruiser Squadron of the Grand Fleet. Private Fred Hoath was aboard when *Phaeton* and HMS *Galatea* shot down Zeppelin L7 on 4th May 1916. Later that month Fred was present when *Phaeton* took part in the Battle of Jutland. Assigned to No.3 Platoon, A Company he went to Zeebrugge on HMS *Iris*. He was mentioned in dispatches for his role in the operation. After the raid he served in Russia with the RMLI from 21st May 1918 until 16th July 1919. The harsh Russian climate caused Fred to be ill with asthma. Fred should have been brought out of the line, returned home and discharged from the Corps. Since he was the battalion's only carpenter, his commanding officer kept him in the line despite his illness. It was not until he returned home on 19th November 1919 that he was invalided out of the RMLI. His son Neville recalled that his father was so furious at the callous decision made by his commanding officer in Russia that he showed his son his discharge papers then poured paraffin on them before setting light to them. After the war he resumed his occupation as a carpenter. In 1933 he bought the license of the Fox & Hounds public house in Toys Hill. He continued to work as a carpenter as well as manage the pub as landlord. During the Second World War he worked as the Assistant Clerk of Works at Woolwich and was involved in the construction of gun emplacements that were built in Eltham and the south east of London. These gun emplacements were used to defend London during the Battle of Britain, the Blitz and throughout the war. Fred Hoath continued to run the pub until his death in February 1958. He died as result of the asthma exacerbated by his exposure to the cold climate in Russia.

Private Fred Hoath (seated) with fellow Zeebrugge raider Private Stanley Hobbins. This photograph was taken on Fred's wedding day when Private Hobbins acted as his best man.

PRIVATE STANLEY HOBBINS CH 14962, NO.4 PLATOON, A COMPANY, 4TH BATTALION RMLI. Stanley Howard Hobbins was born on 24th November 1890 in Wapping, London. He enlisted to join the RMLI straight from grammar school on 19th September 1906. His service record indicates when he enlisted he was not of legal age and was in fact an extraordinary three years and six days under the age limit. He did not receive a pension for the time served while under age. He spent most of his time during World War One serving aboard HMS *Euryalus* from 15th July 1914 until 29th August 1917. Stanley was aboard when this cruiser landed men from the 1st Lancashire Fusiliers on W Beach during the Gallipoli landings on 25th April 1915. He was aboard HMS *Iris* during the Zeebrugge raid. Stanley was invalided out from the RMLI on 16th June 1926. He died on 17th June 1970.

PRIVATE PAROWMAS HARRIS CH 18113, NO. 2 PLATOON, A COMPANY, 4TH BATTALION RMLI. Parowmas Harris was born at Little Barstead, Billericay, Essex on 16th January 1896. He worked as a farm labourer before enlisting to join the Royal Marines Light Infantry on 1st August 1913. While serving aboard the cruiser HMS *Shannon* he took part in the Battle of Jutland in May 1916.

During January 1917, Parowmas made an attempt to change his christian name from Parowmas to Robert. In order to effect the change of name so that it would be written on his service certificates he had to advertise the change of name in two newspapers, local to his place of residence and provide cuttings to the RMLI as evidence. In his service documents, after January 1917 he was still referred to as Parowmas, which means he did not advertise the change in name in local newspapers in Billericay. When he returned home from the war he was known as Bob Harris. His name is given as Robert Harris on his daughter's birth certificate.

He was drafted to serve on another cruiser HMS *Drake* from 10th August 1917, but this draft was for a short period, because she was sunk by the German submarine U-79 near to the Northern Ireland coast. During the Zeebrugge raid he belonged to No.2 Platoon aboard HMS *Iris*. He was seriously wounded by a shell and his left leg had to be amputated above the knee. After the raid Parowmas was sent to Queen Mary's Hospital, Roehampton, where many amputees received medical attention. It was here that he was fitted with an artificial limb and on 9th November 1918 he was examined and passed as medically

Private Parowmas Harris is standing alongside Thomas Attridge. Both men enlisted together and would become future brothers-in-law, when Thomas married Parowmas' sister. They trained together and served together, but Thomas did not take part in the Zeebrugge raid.

unfit for further service with the RMLI. He was sent to his home in Billericay, Essex pending discharge. He was discharged during December 1918 from the RMLI.

On 11th October 1919 Parowmas married Emily Read. In 1920 the newly married couple moved to Hull where Parowmas worked as a steam engine driver in a timber yard. During this time the first of four daughters was born. Later that year Parowmas and his family returned to live at his parent's home in Billericay, where he worked as a steam engine driver for the local council until his retirement.

He suffered from the wounds he sustained at Zeebrugge for the rest of his life. In 1936, Parowmas and his entire family were afflicted with jaundice. He was very poorly with the condition and was admitted to St. John's Hospital, Chelmsford. When he was suffering from an infection, a doctor wanted to amputate Parowmas's good leg in order to save his life. Doctor Shakleton and Doctor Bowseman were two local doctors who resisted this course of action. They decided to discharge him into their care and they nursed him back to health at his home. The doctors both slept in the garden overnight as they monitored his condition. As a result of their care, they saved his leg and he recovered from his illness. Parowmas died on 27th July 1963. The name Parowmas Harris is inscribed on his tombstone.

PRIVATE GEORGE JONES, CH 20137 NO.2 PLATOON, A COMPANY, 4TH BATTALION RMLI. George Jones was the second eldest son of eleven children born to John and Ada Jones of Bromley-by-Bow, London. John worked as a cabman and groom while Ada looked after the family and worked in the general store which they owned. George attended Marner Street School. He enlisted to join the Royal Marines Light Infantry. The 4th Battalion muster list confirms that George was assigned to No.2 Platoon during the raid. This would have meant that he would have sailed to Zeebrugge aboard HMS *Iris*. However, a

newspaper reporting his funeral stated that he was part of the Mole landing party from HMS *Vindictive*. Private George Jones was aged 20 when he was killed during the operation and his body was brought home. The people of the East End of London solemnly lined the streets to pay their respects to George and a pal Private George West, who also died at Zeebrugge, as they were brought to City of London & Tower Hamlets Cemetery for burial.

SERGEANT ARTHUR TRIM, CH 16152, NO. 3 PLATOON, A COMPANY, 4TH BATTALION RMLI. Arthur Trim was born on 1st September 1891 at St. Georges, Deal. He enlisted to join the RMLI on 16th May 1908 while under age. His service record lists his occupation as a hotel servant. Trim served aboard the cruiser HMS *Natal* until she exploded in the Cromarty Firth on 30th December 1915. He then served with Chatham Division until 13th November 1916, when he was drafted to the cruiser HMS *Intrepid*. He spent a year aboard *Intrepid* patrolling the freezing Northern Russian coast.

Trim spent three months with Chatham Division between December 1916 and February 1917. Drafted to serve on the cruiser HMS *Bacchante* he spent a year patrolling the western coast of Africa. This must have been a welcome draft after the awful climate in northern Russia. In April 1918 Trim took part in the raid on Zeebrugge. He was assigned to No.3 Platoon and went to Zeebrugge aboard HMS *Iris*. After Zeebrugge he returned to Russia and was posted to serve at HMS *Glory* from May 1918 until 5th June 1919. After the war Trim served in the Black & Tans and then the B Specials in Ireland, an armed unit that policed Northern Ireland from 1920. He married and settled down in Ireland, but according to family accounts he had to leave Ireland for reasons unknown in 1928. He joined the Royal Marine Military Police during that year and served in Rosyth, Scotland. His wife and son left Ireland and joined him by 1933. Trim served with the Royal Marines Police throughout the Second World War and was discharged from the service on 31st August 1946. He died in the mid 1950s.

CORPORAL LEONARD PICKERING CH 17025, NO.3 PLATOON, A COMPANY, 4TH BATTALION RMLI. Leonard Pickering was born in Warrington on 19th April 1894. He worked as a clerk before enlisting to join the Royal Marines on 24th April 1911. He served most of the First World War aboard the Monitor HMS *Prince Rupert*, which was attached to the Dover Patrol. He survived the Zeebrugge operation aboard *Iris*.

PRIVATE FRED SWAN CH 19349 NO.4 PLATOON, 4TH BATTALION RMLI. Fred Swan from Wolverhampton was only 16 years old when he enlisted to join the RMLI in 1914. He was yet another under-age soldier that passed through the recruiting officers who were keen to recruit as many men as possible. During the War he served on HMS *Implacable* from June 1915 to March 1916. While Swan served on board, this Formidable Class Battleship supported the Italian Navy in patrolling the Adriatic and during November 1915 blockaded

Greece. From November 1915 until March 1916 the *Implacable* patrolled the Suez Canal. In March 1916 Swan transferred to the armoured cruiser HMS *Euryalus*, where he served patrolling the East Indies until August 1917. Fred Swan had lost his brother Corporal W. Swan when he was killed on 28th July 1917, while serving with the Royal Engineers. During the Zeebrugge operation Private Swan belonged to No.4 Platoon, Chatham Company and was killed while aboard *Iris*. After returning to Dover, Private Swan was buried at St. James's Cemetery. The epitaph on his headstone reads 'LOVED BY ALL'.

PRIVATE HAROLD PRANGNELL CH 19762 NO.4 PLATOON, A COMPANY, 4TH BATTALION RMLI. Private Harold Prangnell from Chatham, Kent was a riveter before he joined the RMLI. According to a newspaper article in the *Chatham News* published after the raid, Harold Prangnell landed on the Mole from *Iris* and attacked German gun positions, turning the guns on the enemy. No.4 Platoon sailed to Zeebrugge on *Iris* and he may have been one of the few Royal Marines from this platoon who clambered aboard *Vindictive* and assaulted the Mole. The newspaper report also mentions that he was killed by a shell that killed 47 other men out of 57 that were on the deck at that time. His father who served in the Royal Naval Reserve was told that Harold was aboard the *Vindictive* and that he was manning the forward gun after the original crew had been killed, and was killed in turn. This photograph was found on the deck of *Iris* and sent to his father after the operation. An undelivered letter that he had written to his fiancée was also found, in which he wrote, 'My dearest Girlie, Just a short letter to let you know I am still alive and well. Will write a long letter later on, when I know where we are. Good night. With Fondest Love.'[25] Harold was buried in Chatham Cemetery, Kent.

LIEUTENANT WILLIE SILLITOE CO MACHINE GUN SECTION, 4TH BATTALION RMLI. William Sillitoe was born on 12th November 1895 in Eastry, near Walmer in Kent. His father was Colour Sergeant T. G. Sillitoe serving with the RMLI and the young Willie was brought up with the Corps. Willie was educated at the Depot Royal Marine School in Deal and joined the Corps in October 1910 as a Bugler. He was a good cricketer and while serving as bugler at RMLI Headquarters he was frequently selected to play for the officer's cricket team. He was to first taste life at sea when he was posted to the battleship HMS *Queen* in 1912. When he entered the ranks he went back to the RMLI Depot at Deal for training in March 1914 and returned to headquarters at the outbreak of War. He served for fourteen months with the drifter patrol, and then was transferred to the battleship HMS *Hibernia*. It was during this posting that Willie got his first experience of active service, in the Mediterranean. During October 1915 he was promoted to Corporal. He was transferred to the Monitor HMS *Abercrombie* and served for a short period with the Salonika Field Force. He was recommended for a commission and trained in gunnery at Whale Island, Portsmouth. Willie was a very studious individual. On successfully passing his exams he was commissioned as 2nd Lieutenant. He served with Portsmouth Division from 17th August 1917 to 22nd April 1918. On his officer record Sillitoe is described as 'hardworking, smart, [with] good manners'.[26]

He was assigned commanding officer of the machine gun section when he volunteered for the Zeebrugge operation. He returned to Deal depot for training during February 1918. Sillitoe was killed while manning a machine gun aboard *Iris*. He was shot through the head. His body was brought home to be buried in Deal Cemetery. He was buried next to Private John Bostock, who was also killed aboard *Iris*, on Saturday 27th April. His father had retired from the Corps in 1905, only to be recalled to serve with the Corps at the outbreak of the War. When Willie was killed at Zeebrugge he was serving at RN Division headquarters. He was proud of his son and his achievement in rising from the ranks to officer status. The inscription on Willie's headstone, which consists of a stone cross and an officer's ceremonial sword, reads:

SACRED
TO THE MEMORY
OF
OUR BELOVED SON
WILLIE ERNEST SILLITOE
LIEUTENANT ROYAL MARINES
BORN 12TH NOV 1895
KILLED IN ACTION AT ZEEBRUGGE
23RD APRIL 1918
SERVING IN HMS IRIS

PRIVATE JOHN BOSTOCK CH 19897 NO. 4 PLATOON, A COMPANY, 4TH BATTALION RMLI. Private John Bostock was born in Stretton, Warrington on 31st March 1894. He worked as a farm labourer before enlisting with the South Lancashire Regiment at the outbreak of the War. He saw active service in France with the regiment, and then transferred to the RMLI on 10th May 1915 aged 21. He served aboard the cruiser HMS *Intrepid* between March 1916 and January 1918. *Intrepid* was based in Russia and patrolled the White Sea. When *Intrepid* returned to England,  Bostock volunteered for the Zeebrugge raid. During the training, Bostock was disciplined on two occasions for going absent without leave. He was confined to barracks for ten days and forfeited two days pay on 30th March. While serving this punishment he broke out of the barracks a second time on 8th April. Maybe he was reconciled with the thought that he may not return from this operation and absconded to spend precious last moments with his wife Dorothy, who lived nearby in Duke Street, Deal. He had married Dorothy in 1916 and during those two years he had spent most of the time patrolling the Russian coast. While acting as a machine gunner on *Iris*, Bostock was killed by a shell. His remains were buried next to Lieutenant Willie Sillitoe, bearing a Commonwealth War Grave headstone in Deal Cemetery.

CORPORAL WILLIAM MITCHELL CH 17448, NO.4 PLATOON, A COMPANY, 4TH BATTALION RMLI. At the outbreak of war the Mitchell family answered Lord Kitchener's call to arms. William (standing right in the picture overleaf) had served 18 months in the RMLI. His brother Victor standing left joined the Royal Field Artillery and would later be awarded the MM. Harry enlisted as a drummer for the South Staffordshire Regiment, while Fred joined the Lancashire Fusiliers. Their father, Stanley Mitchell, despite being 54 years old, served with the Worcestershire Regiment and saw action in France.

Mitchell had originally enlisted in the Royal Marines Light Infantry at a recruitment office in Birmingham in 1912. Seventeen at the time of enlistment William Mitchell was under age. After his real age was discovered he was forced to resign from the regiment on 10th December 1912, but was able to re-enlist on the following day because it was his 18th birthday.

At the onset of the War, Mitchell was serving aboard HMS *Russell*. In November this Duncan Class Battleship was assigned to the Channel Fleet. Mitchell was aboard when the vessel bombarded Zeebrugge on 23rd November 1914. Mitchell's service aboard *Russell* ended in January 1915. In June 1915 he was promoted to Lance Corporal. In that same month he was transferred to HMS *Conquest*. During his service aboard this vessel he took part in the sinking of the German Mine Layer *Meteor* on 9th August 1915. Mitchell and his fellow crewmen received a prize bounty for this action.

Top: The Mitchell family under arms.

Above: The shell-shattered deck of the *Iris* photographed by J H Mumford, New Brighton.

William Mitchell served on HMS *Conquest* until January 1918 when he was transferred to Chatham Barracks, where he received promotion to Corporal. During the Zeebrugge raid Mitchell served with No.4 Platoon, Chatham Company and with his mate Private Frederick Swan went to Zeebrugge aboard the *Iris*. Both these men from No.4 Platoon were waiting with 54 fellow marines to embark on the Mole. Mitchell told his daughter years after the raid that the scaling ladders that they were given were too short to scale the Mole. *Iris* could not berth and a shell wiped out 49 marines that were waiting on deck. Miraculously, Mitchell received no wounds and was one of seven survivors who returned home unscathed. His friend Frederick Swan was killed.

After Zeebrugge, Corporal Mitchell served in Murmansk with the Royal Marines Light Infantry. He continued to serve with the Royal Marines in the reserves until 1934. At the age of 40 he drove a bus, and then in later life he and his wife owned and managed a shop each. According to his daughter Jean, William Mitchell was a very quiet, shy man who would rarely talk about his experiences during the Great War. He passed away aged 70 in 1964.

GUNNER FREDERICK JENKINS RMA 10248. Frederick Jenkins was born in Bristol on 10th February 1885 in Bitton. He worked as a postman before enlisting in the Royal Marines Artillery on 24th September 1902. Aged 17 on enlistment he was too young and when his real age was discovered he was posted to the RMA Depot for 139 days until he reached 18. Jenkins served on various sea drafts from 1904 to the outbreak of World War One. During February 1912 he was posted to HMS *Hibernia* and served on this Edward VII Class Battleship until February 1916. While aboard Jenkins saw service in the Dardanelles.

From April 1916 Jenkins served on HMS *Hindustan*, which was part of the 3rd Battle Squadron based in Sheerness under the Nore command. While on this draft he married his wife May Lillian on 26th October 1916. Being a married man did not prevent his participation in the Zeebrugge raid. Gunner Jenkins was assigned to *Iris* where he manned one of the Stokes Trench mortars under the command of Lieutenant Broadwood. He was lucky to be one of eight RMA personnel who were uninjured. Jenkins was posted to the battleship HMS *Britannia* during July 1918. As the war drew to a close Jenkins signed on to serve a further five years with the RMA. He was involved in another drama during the last days of the war. Two days before the Armistice was signed, *Britannia* was sunk by a torpedo fired from UB-50 off Cape Trafalgar while sailing towards Gibraltar. UB-50 was based in Pola and patrolled the Mediterranean. Her commander, Heinrich Kukat had fired two torpedoes at *Britannia* on 9th November 1918, but they missed their target. The third torpedo struck *Britannia* amidships. It took three hours for the vessel to sink with forty crewmen aboard. Jenkins survived the last sinking of a British warship of the war. The reduction of service personnel, known as the Geddes Axe, meant that Jenkins retired from the RMA earlier in 1922.

Jenkins settled on the Isle of Wight where he established a second-hand bookselling business from his home. He was recalled to serve in the Royal Marines on 25th August 1939. During the first year of the War he served as a gunner on merchant vessels sailing down the Western Approaches into the Bay of Biscay and into the Mediterranean. Later during the war he was posted to Northern Ireland where he became a gunnery instructor. He attained the rank of Temporary Sergeant. De-mobbed on 11th May 1945 he returned to his bookselling business on the Isle of Wight. He died in on 3rd October 1957 aged 73.

NOTES

1. *The London Gazette*, 23rd July 1918.
2. National Archive: ADM 339/3: Surgeon Frank Pocock service record.
3. National Archives: ADM 137/3894: Lieutenant Oscar Henderon's report.
4. *The London Gazette*, 23rd July 1918.
5. *The London Gazette,* 11th January 1919.
6. Ordinary Seaman William O'Hara Papers.
7. Lieutenant Commander Bradford papers courtesy of Mr. Jonathan L Bradford Cremer.
8. VC Citation: *The London Gazette*, 17th March 1919.
9. Lieutenant Spencer papers. Courtesy the late Hannah Spencer, Iris Mary Spencer Latour and Catherine Latour.
10. National Archives: ADM 137/3894: Lieutenant Oscar Henderson's report.
11. *The London Gazette*, 23rd July 1918.
12. Private Ernest (Beau) Tracey interview. Courtesy of Richard Davison.
13. *Folkestone, Hythe, Sandgate & Cheriton Herald*, 4th May 1918.
14. Lieutenant Hope Inskip papers, courtesy Dave Eastman.
15. Ibid.
16. Private Ernest Tracey, quoted from *The Zeebrugge Raid*, p137, Philip Warner: William Kimber, 1978.
17. Private Alexander Gordon papers, courtesy of Kevin Gordon.
18. Imperial War Museum Department of Documents: Lance Corporal George Calverley, IWM Ref: 02/30/1: Courtesy Nigel Calverley.
19. Ibid.
20. Ibid.
21. Ibid.
22. Ibid.
23. Ibid.
24. Ibid.
25. Private Harold Prangnell papers, courtesy Sheila Kitchener.
26. National Archives: ADM 196/98 P103: Lieutenant Willie Sillitoe's service record.

CHAPTER 20

THEY WERE ON THE SUPPORT VESSELS

LEADING DECKHAND JAMES SMITH DA12271 RNR MOTOR LAUNCH. James Smith was born in Burnley, Lancashire on 1st February 1887. Before the war he worked as a baker in the Stoneyholme district of Burnley. He was a member of Burnley Swimming Club and worshipped at Stoneyholme Wesleyan Church, where he was secretary of the young men's class. He enlisted in the Royal Navy on 21st July 1916. He was then drafted to serve with the Special Trawler Reserve on 2nd October. When he volunteered for the Zeebrugge operation he had served eighteen months at sea. During the Zeebrugge raid he served aboard a Motor Launch performing the vital smoke screening operation. He returned from the action unharmed:

We remained with the Vindictive, *the* Iris *and the* Daffodil, *and then passed through the smoke screen. When about half a mile from the shore the first star shells were observed and the heavy guns opened fire. The first large shell burst about six yards on our port hand. From the other side of the screen we observed the searchlights from the Mole, and for a short time we lost sight of* Vindictive. *I heard a yell which signified that the* Vindictive's *men had landed on the Mole, but a big explosion at this moment prevented us from recognising exactly what was going on. We [were] confined sailing about in the fog and mist outside the harbour for two hours and then returned. Shells burst all round us, but our boat had a miraculous escape and was never touched. One particular thing we observed as we were leaving Zeebrugge was that not a gun on the Mole was firing. We left in perfect quiet. From what I have heard the engagement was a complete success, and we achieved what we set out to do. On arrival at our base we had a wonderful reception. The working parties at the piers were standing on the piles, and as the boast passed the officers and men cheered for all they were worth, and the inhabitants lined up on the shore swelled the great chorus accompanied by the sound of ships' hooters and bells.*[1]

ABLE SEAMAN NORMAN BROWN J64618, RN HMS NORTH STAR. Norman Clapham Brown was born in Skipton, Yorkshire on 26th August 1895. His father was a farmer who owned land on the north east Lancashire and Yorkshire border. Norman attended Nelson Secondary School before following the family tradition and becoming a farmer. He joined the Royal Navy during January 1917. After completing his training at HMS *Vivid*, he was posted as an Ordinary Seaman to the destroyer HMS *North Star* on 3rd March 1917. By October 1917 he had been promoted to Able Seaman. During the Zeebrugge raid, before *North Star* was sunk, Norman Brown was accidentally knocked overboard.
Fortunately he fell into a motor launch. During the ordeal, Brown exchanged farewell notes with a mate from Bradford. They both pledged to pass on these notes to parents if the other did not survive. Brown believed that his pal was lost during the operation. Brown returned home unscathed after the Zeebrugge affair.

ABLE SEAMAN HENRY UNDEY J39762 RN HMS PHOEBE. Henry George Undey was born on 16th April 1898 in Fulham, London. He was serving aboard HMS *Nonsuch* during the Battle of Jutland in 1916.

After the war he worked for the Great Western Railway Company as a checker at Paddington Goods Station. When World War Two broke out, Henry Undey continued to serve his country with Civil Defence work as an auxiliary fireman at Paddington Station. In later life he was an active member of the Zeebrugge Association Committee.

MIDSHIPMAN DAVID RAY MORRIS, RNR, CMB 22. David Ray Morris was born in 1902 in Leigh. He was educated at Atherton Higher Grade School and Leigh Grammar School. Morris had decided on a career at sea at an early age. During January 1916, when he was aged fourteen, Morris left home to attend the school HMS *Conway*, to be taught seamanship. He appears in letters sent to his parents to be happy while at HMS *Conway*. On 11th June 1916 he was confirmed with 67 other cadets by Bishop Chavasse, the Bishop of Liverpool. Bishop Chavasse was the father of Noel Chavasse, the double Victoria Cross recipient. When Morris graduated from HMS *Conway* in February 1918 he was awarded a certificate that allowed him to bypass the examination for Second Mate after serving three years at sea instead of four years. His education at HMS *Conway* enabled him to enlist in the Royal Naval Reserve. In a letter to his parents dated 10th February 1918, he wrote of his enthusiasm to put the skills that he had

learnt into practice. 'I shall be well equipped to start on "active service". I can assure you I have looked forward to this time since I first joined.'[2] On leaving *Conway* he was assigned to Coastal Motor Boat 22. His desire to see active service would be fulfilled within a couple of months when he took part in the Zeebrugge raid. The objective of CMB 22 was to establish a smoke screen around the Light House and the Battery at the end of the Mole. It was a dangerous task, but the smoke screening carried out by this CMB assisted in concealing *Vindictive* as she approached the Mole. In a letter home to his parents dated 25th April 1918 he wrote of his experience at Zeebrugge:

I am glad to say that I am quite safe, except for a wound in my left arm. However it is not serious. We had a terrible fight, but quite enjoyed it, and of course we won. I got two Lewis Gun bullets into my left arm, just as we got to Zeebrugge Mole, but managed to keep on firing until all was over. When we arrived outside Zeebrugge 15-inch shells were flying about and we got it pretty hot. We sighted the 'Vindictive' and as she was getting badly hit, and no smoke screen to shield her, we decided to set our screens going. We then went between her and the Mole, which was 160 yards away. The result was that the enemy could not see the 'Vindictive' and she was able to put her men ashore. In a few minutes we were all hit. After firing one machine gun we left for ___ where we rested an hour. Our officers were wounded – one of them having 14 bullets through his chest – and I helped to bring the boat back. We had been 35 hours without sleep, and had hardly any food, so you can guess we were pretty exhausted.[3]

Midshipman Morris continued to serve in the Royal Navy and spent most of his life at sea with the Merchant Navy. He died aged 42 from heat apoplexy with acute cardiac failure, while serving as a Second Officer aboard the merchant vessel SS *City of Agra* on 29th June 1944. He was buried at sea.

LEADING DECKHAND JAMES DANIELS SD 3147 DSM, RNR, ML 110. James Daniels was born on 10th December 1894 in Chatham. His childhood was spent in Dartford and he was educated at the Greenhithe National School. Daniels enlisted in the Royal Naval Reserve on 8th November 1915. He was awarded the Distinguished Service Medal for actions off the Belgian coast during June 1917. Aged 23 years he volunteered for the Zeebrugge Raid in early 1918. Assigned to ML 110 Daniels was killed at the helm when a shell struck the motor launch. Lieutenant Bowen described the last moments of Daniels in a letter of condolence to his mother:

> *He was in no pain: his death was instantaneous. He was at the wheel at the time, as cool and collected as though we were just off for a refit. In fact, it was on account of his coolness and reliability that he was at the helm on this occasion. Suddenly a shell hit the bridge, just at your son's elbow, and of course, it was all over with him in a second. He was a splendid chap. If ever I wanted a job done well I could always give it into his hands and leave it, knowing that there would be nothing more to worry about. We were shipmates for over a year, and after his family there is probably no one who will miss him more than his surviving messmates and myself.*[4]

LIEUTENANT COMMANDER JAMES DAWBARN YOUNG ML 110. James Dawbarn Young was born on 2nd August 1877 and educated at St Albans Grammar School from 1887 to 1893. His social conscience and concern for others was demonstrated when he was a schoolboy in St Albans. It was James who established the 'Children's Circle'. This was a scheme which he devised to help the poor children in St Albans by providing them with a free breakfast. The simple motto of the scheme was 'Help others' and James would often be by a fire stirring porridge for the cause.

On completing his education at the London University James chose the profession of surveyor as a career. He became a Fellow of the Surveyors' Institution. As he worked as a Surveyor he became interested in law and later qualified to be a barrister. He was called to the Bar at Gray's Inn during 1906 and became an Honorary Examiner in law to the Surveyors' Institution. He would also write several legal books. James established a successful law practice specializing in compensation cases.

James continued to show great public spirit when he assisted the Reverend Newlands to establish the Claremont Central Mission. James wrote to the Reverend Newlands to offer his help in 1902. Newlands later recalled:

> *He was a splendid comrade and did a great deal to commence and foster the work of the Sunday School mission service, boy's brigade, and men's gymnasium, gathering around him a large company of young people. The lads and men will never forget his genial leadership. He and his brothers were always ready to lend a hand in any enterprise. I was very much struck with the indomitable perseverance of this man of versatile ability.*[5]

James would give Bible classes at Clarement Central Mission and a colleague at the Mission later recalled that 'Jim was so gallant and brave, so sweet of soul, and with those high attributes which go to make the English gentleman, that he was regarded with something like hero-worship by the lads whom he taught and helped at Claremont.'[6]

His main recreational pursuit was yachting and as soon as war broke out in 1914 James Young enlisted in the Royal Naval Reserve as a Sub Lieutenant. James Young was involved with minesweeping in the North Sea and spent some time with the Grand Fleet. He received promotion to Lieutenant and was transferred to the Royal Naval Volunteer Reserves during 1915. Lieutenant Young was given command of the Motor Launch ML 12 from 25th October 1915 and attached to the Dover Patrol. On 7th May 1916 he assumed command of ML 110. During his command of ML 110 Young took part in the bombardment of Zeebrugge on the nights of 11th/12th May 1917, and 4th/5th June 1917. He was mentioned in dispatches and his name entered in *The London Gazette* on 20th July 1917. On 11th July 1917 Young was promoted to Lieutenant Commander.

When Keyes was looking for volunteers to raid Zeebrugge he was one of the first to volunteer in early 1918. Lieutenant Commander Young was ordered to take ML 110 to Zeebrugge to moor calcium buoys off the Mole to mark a path for the blockships to follow into the harbour. Once this was accomplished he was ordered to rescue the crews of the blockships. One of the men who served under him also came from St Albans. In the *St Albans and District Congregational Magazine* of June 1918 one of the men who served under James Dawbarn Young's command wrote 'He was one of the finest officers we ever had, and was loved by all the men. He volunteered for his job with the full knowledge that he had very little chance of returning alive.'[7] On the evening before the raid he attended a church service with Lieutenant Gordon Stanley Maxwell:

> It was a Sunday evening, and about six o'clock, your son came along to my boat and asked me if I would go to Church with him. Owing to a mistake in the time we arrived we entered there rather late, and I remember the verse of the hymn that was being sung as we opened the door – it was: 'Run the straight race through God's good grace' – and I have often thought since how appropriate it was, for no one in this world ever ran a straighter race than your son, and we all respected him for it. To us, who served under him, he was the soul of fairness, and would never ask anyone to do a job he was not equally willing to do himself if need be. After Church we went for a long walk together, and he spoke, more than he had ever done before to me, of his people and private affairs. I have always liked the way he spoke of his 'Little Mother' … Later on in the evening we went back to his boat for supper, and it was nearly twelve o'clock before we left him. His last words to me that night have stuck in my memory. We both knew, of course, what we had to go through the next day, and as we shook hands at parting he said to me: 'Well, good-bye old chap, we have both got to go through hell tomorrow, and if one of us is fated never to return, I hope it will be me, for I am single and you have a wife and child.' It was a remark worthy of him – unselfish to the end.[8]

As ML 110 approached the entrance to Zeebrugge harbour she was hit by three shells, which caused casualties amongst half of the crew and damaged the engines. James Dawbarn Young received three wounds from machine gun fire that would prove to be fatal, but remained at his post. He gave the order to abandon ship, then collapsed. The man who served under him from St Albans remembered his last words: 'When he was caught by the enemy machine gun fire and put out of action, he said 'Never mind me, carry on.'[9]

A barrister friend wrote a letter of condolence to his bereaved father:

> The last time I saw him – a few months ago – he told me that, though he had sacrificed his career at the Bar, he would not have changed his life in the Navy for anything; he was absolutely wrapped up in the idea of duty and patriotism, and had not even a sneer for his younger contemporaries who had stayed behind and profited by the self-sacrifice of others. I knew that he would be in the naval battle: he was a successful officer and was certain to be chosen. Had he not been chosen, I knew him well enough to know that he would have fought to be sent.[10]

Lieutenant Commander James Dawbarn Young's funeral took place on 27th April 1918. He was buried at Saunderton Church, Princes Risborough.

DECKHAND WILLIAM FRANCIS ON 13899 DSM RNR ML 526. William Francis was born in Shropshire in 1891. He was living at The Fields Farm in Tybroughton, when the First World War began. He enlisted in the Royal Naval Reserve and during the Zeebrugge raid served aboard ML 526 and was involved in the evacuation of the crews from HMS *Thetis* and *Intrepid*. Francis' commanding officer, Lieutenant Hugh Littleton, confirmed that it took ten minutes to recover 65 men from the blockships. During that time they were exposed to heavy enemy gunfire at close range. William Francis was awarded the Distinguished Service Medal for his role in the Zeebrugge raid. After the war he returned to Shropshire, where he became gardener to the family of Commander Alfred Godsal at Iscoyd Park, Whitchurch. Godsal was killed during the Ostend raid in May 1918 and his family provided William Francis with employment and a home. Francis lived a long life, but apart from his war experiences he never ventured far from his home in Shropshire. He died aged 91 in 1982 and was buried at Whitewell Church.

AIR MECHANIC 2ND CLASS SIDNEY HESSE F47738 RNAS HMS PHOEBE. Sidney Hesse was born in Bermondsey, London on 15th December 1899. His mother died when he was five years old. His father remarried and Sidney later had three half brothers. On leaving school aged fifteen he worked for a photographer's assistant. During the war there was high demand from servicemen for photos for their loved ones and it was Sidney's job to wash the prints. The working day was very long. On one night he saw two Zeppelins that were on a bombing raid over London shot down. Towards the end of 1917 Sidney enrolled for evening art classes at a county council school in London. As he was approaching his eighteenth birthday he was conscious of the fact that he would be of an age where he would be expected to enlist and fight for his country. During January 1918 he decided to enlist in the Army. He declared his intention one evening to his art school teacher. The teacher said 'Don't join the army, join the Royal Naval Air Service, I'm in the Royal Naval Air Service.' Sidney was intrigued by his teacher's admission and asked 'How can you be in the Royal Naval Air Service when you're a teacher here?' The teacher replied 'It's a special unit. There's about a thousand of us doing experimental work on all sorts of things like that.'[11] The teacher further explained that the RNAS comprised of chemists from university and doctors with specialist knowledge. Sidney was not confident that he would be accepted into the RNAS because he did not have a similar academic background. The teacher encouraged him to join the RNAS and gave him the names of useful contacts that could assist him in his application. Sidney successfully enlisted in the RNAS on 24th January 1918. His service record states that his occupation was gas fitter and he may have been advised by his teacher to employ this fabrication in order to be accepted.

He began his training as a 2nd Class Air Mechanic at the RNAS Experimental Station in Stratford, East London. After completing basic training he volunteered for various jobs in an effort to escape from London. He volunteered to work in Dover on installing smoke screen apparatus on destroyers. On occasions Sidney would get the opportunity to sail on night patrols with these destroyers and was only required when the commanding officer wanted to produce a smoke screen. He had difficulty adjusting to life at sea and during these passages experienced sea sickness. During April 1918 Sidney Hesse volunteered to take part in the Zeebrugge raid.

I must have been mad! We were all volunteers for that job. They told us beforehand that a lot of us wouldn't come back. They said that if we hadn't given our parents a photo, then we should get one because we probably wouldn't get another chance! At the last minute they gave us a chance to pull out: I volunteered so I'll go. I'm not sorry I went, although I didn't like it at the time![12]

During the first attempt to raid Zeebrugge on the night of the 11th/12th April, Sidney Hesse was aboard HMS *Mansfield*, which towed the submarines C3 and C4 across the English Channel. During the attempt on 23rd April 1918 he was aboard HMS *Phoebe* which was designated the task of ensuring that there was a smoke screen as the patrolled near to the Mole during the operation. During the passage to Zeebrugge Sidney was too frightened to be seasick.

The RNAS personnel. The photogrpah was taken at the RNAS Experimental Station at Stratford, but does not feature Sidney Hesse and several other participants because they were granted leave immediately after the raid. Hesse was given this photograph when he returned from leave. The shield includes a piece of the shrapnel-riddled funnel from HMS *Vindictive*.

We didn't go inside the harbour. We were just on the outside. It was all light, with star shells and searchlights. The smoke that I was putting up was all dispersed then, as the wind again changed direction just as the attack began, and blew all the smoke away. It was all bright. We were right up close to the German guns on the Mole. You could see them loading up their guns. They couldn't miss us.

I had to stay on deck all the time, with no shelter at all, because I had to be alongside the funnel. They never gave me any proper protection, I mean, they gave me a cutlass! I could hardly handle the thing, and couldn't pull it out of its sheath in one go. This cutlass was in case the Germans tried to board us. When I was standing there on the deck and all this water was seething up like a boiling pot from the gunfire, I thought, 'Well, I can't see anybody getting out of this lot!' You wouldn't think you could put your hand out without it being hit. It was amazing.[13]

As the destroyer *North Star* was sinking, HMS *Phoebe* went alongside to evacuate her crew. German shells were pouring into *North Star* as the rescue operation was taking place. Sidney was nearly killed at this moment during the raid.

I was talking to three fellows – they were stokers who came up from a manhole down below and asked how the battle was going. I'd never been in action before, and I said that it didn't look too good to me. Just then a shell hit the funnel where I was standing and blew bits all over the place. It knocked me senseless, and killed these three fellows that I was talking to.[14]

The three men that Sidney was talking before they were killed were Stoker Arthur Ada, Able Seaman Charles Howes and Able Seaman Alfred Matthews. Sidney was knocked unconscious. His life was saved by his lifebelt when a piece of funnel that would have torn into Sidney was deflected by it. Sidney's sea sickness recurred during the return to Dover.

After the war Sidney emigrated to New Zealand. He settled in Auckland and worked for the Waitemaa Electric Power Board. During the Second World War Sidney served in the New Zealand Home Guard. Sid retired in 1960 to enjoy his garden. It is believed that Sidney Hesse was the last survivor of the Zeebrugge Raid; he died in Auckland on 20th November 2002.

NOTES

1. *The Burnley News*, 1ˢᵗ May 1918, Page 4.
2. Midshipman David Ray Morris papers. Author's collection.
3. Ibid.
4. *Dartford Chronicle & District Times*, 10ᵗʰ May 1918.
5. *The British Weekly*, 2ⁿᵈ May 1918.
6. Letter of condolence to James father sent by secretary of Central Mission, 25ᵗʰ April 1918. Young papers (Author's collection).
7. *St. Albans & District Congregational Magazine*. Young papers (Author's collection).
8. Letter from Lieutenant Gordon Stanley Maxwell to Young's parents dated 22ⁿᵈ May 1918. Young papers (Author's collection).
9. Young papers (Author's collection).
10. Ibid.
11. Peter Chapman interview in *Cross & Cockade*.
12. Ibid.
13. Ibid.
14. Ibid.

CHAPTER 21

THE MONUMENTS

The Zeebrugge Memorial, which stands in Admiral Keyesplein, Zeebrugge, consists of two pieces of concrete from the original Mole. The inscription reads:

THE BRONZE FLORAL SPRAY NOW MOUNTED ON A SECTION
OF THE ORIGINAL ZEEBRUGGE MOLE WAS PRESENTED TO
VICE ADMIRAL ROGER KEYES BY THE CITY OF BRUGES IN 1918
AND RETURNED BY HIS SON
LORD KEYES OF ZEEBRUGGE AND OF DOVER
WHO UNVEILED THIS MEMORIAL ON SAINT GEORGE'S DAY
APRIL 23RD 1998, THE 80TH ANNIVERSARY OF THE FAMOUS
ZEEBRUGGE RAID

Seven years after the raid the Belgian King Albert unveiled a memorial comprising a 70-foot-high column with a statue of St. George slaying the dragon. This memorial was destroyed in 1942 during the German occupation. The current memorial, dedicated on 23rd April 1983, stands at the landward entrance to the Mole. Stones from the original memorial and plaques that marked the site where *Vindictive* moored alongside the Mole and where C3 caused a breach in the viaduct are incorporated in the memorial.

The bow of HMS *Vindictive* is preserved as a permanent memorial to the raids at Zeebrugge and at Ostend on 10th May. The masts of the blockships HMS *Intrepid* and *Thetis* stand behind the bow of *Vindictive*, however the upper mast from *Thetis* succumbed to wood rot and was replaced. HMS *Vindictive* was scuttled in Ostend Harbour on the night of the 9th/10th May 1918 in the second unsuccessful attempt to block the Ostend canal that led to the German submarine base at Bruges. The following words are inscribed on the rear of the bow section:

IN MEMORIAM
23-IV-1918
10-V-1918

In a specially constructed belfry at Dover Town Hall hangs the bell that was used by the Germans to warn of approaching ships and aircraft at the Zeebrugge Mole. It was cast in Antwerp, according to the inscription around the top of the bell. The bell was presented to the Corporation of Dover as a gift from a grateful Belgian nation and commemorates the raid at Zeebrugge. The tablet beneath the bell bears the date 23rd April 1918.

This bell is rung eight times each St. George's Day, by the Mayor of Dover, before the annual Zeebrugge commemoration service which takes place at St. James's Cemetery. A grappling iron that was used by British Sailors and Royal Marines to hold HMS *Vindictive* against the Mole during the Zeebrugge raid was unveiled as a memorial near to Dover Town Hall on 23rd April 2003. It still bears the scars that it received during the raid.

Left: The Zeebrugge Memorial, Admiral Keyesplein.

Below, left and right: The 1925 Zeebrugge Memorial and the memorial dedicated on 23rd April 1983 at the landward entrance to the Mole.

Bottom: The bow of *Vindictive* is preserved as a memorial to the raids at Zeebrugge on 23rd April and at Ostend on 10th May.

Opposite, top and middle: The bows of HMS *Vindictive*, Ostend.

Opposite, bottom left: Zeebrugge Bell, Dover Town Hall.

Opposite, bottom right: Grappling Iron Memorial, Dover.

APPENDIX 1

NAVAL FORCE COMPOSITION

From	Monitors	Light Cruisers	Leaders	Torpedo Boat Destroyer	Motor Launches	Coastal Motor Boats	Picket Boats	Parent Ships	Blocking Ships	Submarines	Minesweepers	Auxiliary Craft	Total Ships	Officers	Men
Grand Fleet (Excluding Royal Marines)														27	365
Harwich Force – Covering Squadron		7	2	14									23		
Harwich Force – For Operations			1	6									7		
Dover Patrol	8	1	4	17	36	12						1	79		
Portsmouth					10	12		2	1	2		1	28	9	41
The Nore					12		1	1	4			1	19	7	469
Plymouth														2	8
Royal Australian Navy														1	10
French Navy				8	4								12		
Dover Experimental Base														4	87
Royal Marine Artillery														2	58
Royal Marine Light Infantry														30	660
Total	8	8	7	45	62	24	1	3	5	2	1	2	168	82	1698

MAIN NAVAL FORCE COMPOSITION & ROLES

Please note that this list of vessels only consists of the principal assault force and does not contain the covering force.

UNIT	VESSEL DEPARTURE	DESIGNATED DUTY	UNIT COMMANDER	PORT OF DEPARTURE
A	CMB 24A, 17A	Central smoke screen	Lt. A. Welman	Dover
B	CMB 15A	Western flank smoke screen	Lt. A. Welman	Dover
C	CMB 16A	Blankenberge smoke floats	Lt. A. Welman	Dover
D	CMB 35A	Western smoke screen	Lt. A. Welman	Dover
E	CMB 28A	Eastern smoke screen	Lt. A. Welman	Dover
F	HMS Myngs,	Eastern guard patrol	Captain W. Tomkinson	Dover
	HMS Whirlwind			Dover
G	ML 121, 258, 280, 314, 397, 420, 525, 549, 562.	Western smoke screen	Captain R. Collins	Dover
H	CMB 5,7	1st torpedo attack inside Mole	Lt. A. Welman	Dover
I	ML 223, 239, 241, 272, 308, 416, 422,513, 533.	Eastern smoke scree	Captain R. Collins	Dover
J	CMB 21B, 26B, 25B.	Stokes mortar attacks on Mole parapet	Lt. A. Welman	Dover
K	Picket boat, HM Submarines C1, C3.	Demolition of Mole viaduct	Lt-Commander F Sandford (Picket boat) Tomkinson.	Dover
L	HMS North Star, HMS Phoebe	Patrol off Zeebrugge Mole	Captain W. Tomkinson	Dover
M	HMS Mansfield, HMS Trident	Submarine tugs for C1 & C3, Western guard patrol	Captain W. Tomkinson	Dover
N	HMS Vindictive, Iris II & Daffodil	Assault ships transporting Royal Marine and Royal Naval storming parties	Captain Alfred Carpenter Captain Halahan	The Swin
O	ML 265, 424, 552, 558.	Escort boats for assault ships	Captain R. Collins	Dover
P	CMB 30B	Reserve smoke screen vessels	Lt. A. Welman	Dover
Q	ML 110, 128	Moor calcium buoys off Mole and canal. Rescue blockship crews	Captain R. Collins	Dover
R	HMS Melpomene, HMS Moorson, HMS Morris, HMS Velox	Outer guard patrol	Captain W. Tomkinson	Dover
S	HMS Iphegenia, HMS Intrepid, HMS Thetis	Zeebrugge blockships	Commander F. Sneyd	The Swin
T	ML 282, 526	Rescue blockship crews	Captain R. Collins	Dover
U	ML 79, 257, 345, 555, 557, 560, 561	Reserve smoke screen vessels	Captain R. Collins	Dover
V	CMB 22B, 23B	Smoke screens Mole and Lighthouse	Lt. A. Welman	Dover
W	HMS Brilliant, HMS Sirius	Ostend blockships	Commander A. Godsal	The Swin
X	HMS Tetrarch, HMS Tempest	Destroyer escort for Ostend blockships	Captain W. Tomkinson then Commodore Ostend	Dover
Y	CMB 29A, 34A	CMB. escort for Ostend Blockships	Lt. A. Welman	Dover
Z	CMB 32A, 27A	2nd torpedo attacks inside Mole	Lt. A. Welman	Dover

APPENDIX 2

ROLL OF HONOUR

ROYAL NAVAL PERSONNEL KILLED DURING RAID ON ZEEBRUGGE 23RD APRIL 1918

NAME	RANK	SERVICE NO.	SHIP/UNIT	AGE	CEMETERY/GRAVE
Ada, Arthur	Sto.1	K36864 (Cha) RN	HMS Phoebe	34	Maidenhead Cemetery, Berks (B.F.14)
Ashley, Joseph	O Sea.	SS7786 (Cha) RN	HMS North Star	19	Blankenberge Town Cem. (A, 3)
Aylott, Henry	A.B.	Lon Z/4690 RNVR	HMS Vindictive	20	Dover, St. James's Cemetery (P.W.35A)
Barnes, George	A.B.	J7603 (PO) RN	HMS Hindustan	23	Enfield (Lavender Hill) Cem. (U.C.923)
Baty, Andrew	A.B.	J55493 (PO) RN	HMS North Star	21	Dover, St. James's Cemetery (P.W.6A)
Baxter, Joseph	Dk. Hd.	13667DA RNR	ML 424	31	Flushing (Vlissingen) North. Cem. (II.2.3.)
Beckett, Joseph	A.B.	J27536 (Cha)	HMS Vindictive	20	Long Crendon (St. Mary) Ch, Bucks.
Beer, Leonard	E.A.3.	M2714 RN	HMS Lightfoot	29	Belfast City Cemetery. Northern Ireland.
Bennewith, Harry	O Sea.	J51070	HMS Vindictive	18	Dover, St. James's Cemetery (P.W.60A)
Best, Harold	A.B.	207332 (Cha)	HMS North Star	34	Chatham Naval Mem. (Panel 28, NKG)
Bingley, John	A.B.	J25408 (Dev)	HMS Vindictive	21	Liverpool (Toxteth Park) Cem. (O.C.E.557)
Bowlt, Frederick	A.B.	J29331 (Po)	HMS Vindictive	19	Dover, St. James's Cemetery (P.W.12A)
Bowthorpe, Daniel i)	L. Sea.	J18711 (Cha)	HMS Vindictive	22	Norwich Cemetery, Norfolk.
Bradford, George	Lt-Cdr		HMS Iris II	31	Blankenberge Town Cem. (A.5)
Bray, Henry	A.B.	J9935 (Po)	HMS Vindictive	23	Portsmouth (Kingston) Cem. (Perkin's 4.44)
Brock, Frank	Wing Cdr	RNAS		34	Zeebrugge Memorial (NKG)
Buckley, John DSM	Yeo.Sig	212203 (Cha)	HMS Vindictive	32	Dover, St. James's Cemetery (P.W.45A)
Bult, Reginald	A.B.	J22432 (Po)	HMS Iris II	21	Nunhead (All Saints) Cem. London
Caine, John	A.B.	J12591 (Po)	HMS Vindictive	22	Dover, St. James's Cemetery (P.W.62A)
Calvert, Jonathan	A.B	J2021 (Cha)	HMS North Star	26	Chatham Naval Mem. (Panel 28, NKG)
Carpenter, Ralph	A.B	J36355 (Po)	HMS Daffodil IV	17	Whitchurch (All Hallows) Ch. Cem. Hants.
Cassell, Arthur	A.B.	J34572 (Po)	HMS Vindictive	21	Portsmouth Naval Mem. (Panel 29 NKG)
Chamberlain, Arthur	Lt.		HMS Neptune	28	Dover, St. James's Cemetery (P.W.4A)
Clark, Edward	Sto.	6084S RNR	HMS Iphigenia	18	Chatham Naval Memorial (NKG)
Cleal, John ii.)	Sto. 1	SS114982	HMS Iphigenia	24	Cardiff (Cathays) Cem. Glamorganshire
Cochran, Thomas	Shpt.1	M6437	HMS Vindictive	19	Gillingham (Woodlands) Cem. Kent.
Cowley, Emmanuel	A.B.	J14282	HMS Vindictive	26	Dover, St. James's Cemetery (P.W.59A)
Cox, Percy	L.Cks Mt	M10666 (Cha)	HMS North Star	35	Chatham Naval Mem. (Panel 29, NKG)
Coxhedge, John	Sto.1	K35770 (Cha)	HMS North Star	28	Faversham Borough Cem. Kent
Culmer, Jesse iii.)	A.B.	J3816 (Cha)	HMS Vindictive	25	Gillingham (Woodlands) Cem. Kent.
Daniels, James DSM	L.Dk.Hd	3147.SD	ML 110	22	Chatham Naval Memorial (Panel 30) (NKG)
Dibben, William	A.B.	214950	HMS Iris II	31	Dover, St. James's Cemetery (P.W.57A)
Digby, Sydney	A.B.	J36259	HMS Vindictive	19	Dover, St. James's Cemetery (P.W.58A)
Drummond, Duncan	A.B.	J22840	HMS Vindictive	20	Plymouth Naval Mem. (Panel 27 NKG)
Dunmow, Edwin	A.B.	J4405	HMS Vindictive	24	Dover, St. James's Cemetery (P.W.13A)

Ellams, Leonard	A.B.	J37173	HMS Canada	21	Frodsham (St.Lawrence) Ch. Cheshire
Everest, Reginald	A.B.	J15780	HMS Vindictive	22	Brighton (Lewes Rd) Borough Cem. Sussex
Fearn, Fred	Ld.Dd.	13714.DA RNR	HMML 424	29	Chatham Naval Memorial (Panel 30) (NKG)
Fountain, F.C iv.)	A.B.	J42566	HMS North Star	19	Edmonton Cemetery, Middlesex, England
Gibbs, Valentine	Cdr.		HMS Iris II	37	Kingswear Cemetery, Devon (304)
Gilkerson, Edward	L.Sea.	J16397 (Po)	HMS Vindictive	23	Dover, St. James's Cemetery (P.W.43A)
Gilmour, Joseph	A.B.	J30454 (Dev)	HMS Vindictive	21	Stevenston (New St) Cem. Ayrshire
Guenigault, Charles	A.B.	J38286	HMS Vindictive	19	Dover, St. James's Cemetery (P.W.63A)
Halahan, Henry	Capt.		HMS President	34	Chatham Naval Memorial (Panel 27) (NKG)
Hallihan, Michael	P.O.	238198 (Dev)	HMS Vindictive	28	Dover, St. James's Cemetery (P.W.48A)
Handford, Frederick	A.B.	J22457	HMS Vindictive	21	Dover, St. James's Cemetery (P.W.51A)
Henniker, Ernest.	L.Sea.	183726 (Cha)	HMS North Star	38	Flushing (Vlissingen) North. Cem. (II.1.1.)
Hannon, John	A.B.	222623 (Dev)	HMS Vindictive	32	Gillingham (Woodlands) Cem,. Kent.
Harland, William	Sto.1	303027 (Cha)	HMS North Star	33	Chatham Naval Mem. (Panel 29 NKG)
Harris, Arthur	A.B.	J926	HMS Thetis	26	Chatham Naval Mem. (Panel 28, NKG)
Harrison, Arthur	Lt-Cdr.		HMS Vindictive	32	Zeebrugge Memorial (NKG)
Hawkings, Claude	Lt.		HMS Erin	22	Zeebrugge Memorial (NKG)
Helliar, Hubert	A.B.	J28138	HMS Conqueror	19	Bishops Caundle Church, Dorset
Hick, Alexander v.)	L.Sea.	J11442	HMS Iphigenia	24	Scarborough (Dean Rd) Cem. Yorkshire
Hillier, George	A.B.	194434 (Cha)	HMS North Star	37	Oostende New Communal Cem. (B.2)
Hollis. Henry	A.B.	J56456 (Po)	HMS Iris II	21	Dover, St. James's Cemetery (P.W.65A)
Howes, Charles	A.B.	SS4089 (Cha)	HMS Phoebe	24	Wandsworth (Earlsfield) Cem. London
Hughes, Jonathan	Sto.1	K32304 (Cha)	HMS Vindictive	19	Woodgrange Park Cem. East Ham, London.
Jarrett, Charles	A.B.	J48074	HMS Vindictive	18	Portsmouth Naval Mem. (Panel 29, NKG)
Jones, Harold vi.)	A.B.	J35564 (Dev)	HMS Iphigenia	19	Dover, St. James's Cemetery (P.W.49A)
Lee, Ralph	A.B.	T/Z10482	HMS North Star	U	Cement House Cem. Langemark (XX.A25)
Lloyd, M vii.)	Sub-Lt.		HMS Hindustan	20	Dover, St. James's Cemetery (N.V.18A)
Lucas, Frank viii.)	Sto.P.O.	K4460 (Cha)	HMS Iphigenia	38	Wanstead (St. Mary Ch) Essex.
Lyons, George	A.B.	212050 (Dev)	HMS Vindictive	33	Dover, St. James's Cemetery (P.W.39A)
MacDougall, Stewart	Sig.	Clyde Z2087 RNVR	HMS Iris II	21	Cathcart Cemetery, Renfrewshire.
McElhatton, James	Sto.1	K20216	HMS Iphigenia	23	Plymouth Naval Mem. (Panel, 28, NKG)
MacIntyre, Angus ix.)	Dk.Hd.	1677SD RNR	HMML 282	24	Gillingham (Woodlands) Cem. Kent
McKruly, George	L.Dk.Hd.	T1930SD RNR	ML 282	28	South Shields (Harton) Cemetery, Durham
McNicol, Ernest	A.M.2	F29069 RNAS	HMS North Star	21	Blankenberge Town Cemetery (A.2)
McShane, Thomas	A.B.	SS4230 (Cha)	HMS Vindictive	24	Dover, St. James's Cemetery (P.W.7A)
Martin, Ernest	A.B.	J12137 (Cha)	HMS Iphigenia	30	Buckhurst Hill (St.John the Bapt. Ch) Essex
Matthews Alfred	A.B.	189716 (Po)	HMS Phoebe	38	Bristol Greenbank Cemetery, Glous (NKG?)
Mayers, John	P.O.	181106	HMS Thetis	30	Zeebrugge Churchyard (Grave 163)
Miller, Herbert	P.O.	210224	HMS Vindictive	34	Mitcham (Church Rd) Burial Grd. Surrey
Mills, George	A.B.	J25150	HMS Vindictive	22	Dover, St. James's Cemetery (P.W.64A)
Napper, Alan	A.B.	J71949	HMS North Star	28	Chatham Naval Memorial (Panel 28, NKG)
Nicholls, Sidney x.)	Sto.1	K33101 (Cha)	HMS Intrepid	20	Herne Bay Cemetery, Kent.
Palliser, Harold	Sto.P.O.	226201 (Cha)	HMS Intrepid	30	St. Pancraes Cemetery, Middlesex (12.U.72)
Payne, Reginald	A.B.	J57260 (Cha)	HMS North Star	22	Oostende New Communal Cem. (B.1)
Paynter, Charles	Lt.		HMS North Star	22	Chatham Naval Memorial (Panel 28, NKG)
Pearson, Charles	P.O.	220920	HMS Thetis	32	Chatham Naval Memorial (Panel 28, NKG)
Pool, Ernest	A.M.1.	F12787 RNAS	HMS President	20	Nottingham (New Basford) Cemetery, Notts
Pratt, Stanley	A.B.	J31231 (Po)	HMS Vindictive	19	Portsmouth (Kingston) Cemetery Hampshire
Richards, Frederick	A.B.	J32880 (Po)	HMS Vindictive	18	Portsmouth Naval Mem. (Panel 29, NKG)
Rouse, John	A.M.2	F50269	HMS Myng	18	Zeebrugge Memorial (NKG)
Robinson, Oswald	Lt.		HMML 424	29	Plymouth Naval Memorial (Panel 29, NKG)

Saunders, Alfred	A.B.	J32337	HMS Thetis	19	Chatham Naval Mem. (Panel 28, NKG)
Scott, Frederick	A.B.	J16005	HMS Vindictive	21	Wimbledon (Gap Rd) Cem. Surrey
Schoolcraft, Oliver	Wmm.2	M22964 (Po)	HMS North Star	24	Portsmouth Naval Mem. (Panel 30, NKG)
Smith, Albert	A.B.	J25472	HMS Vindictive	20	Chatham Naval Mem. (Panel 28, NKG)
Smith, William	A.B.	J25311	HMS Vindictive	19	Dover, St. James's Cemetery (P.W.61A)
Smy, Noah	L.Sto.	K17913	HMS Intrepid	26	Clopton (St. Mary) Churchyard, Suffolk.
Sutherland, William	A.B.	J33465 (Cha)	HMS Vindictive	19	Sunderland (Mere Knolls) Cem. Durham
Spencer, George	Lt.	RNR	HMS Iris II	31	Hampstead Cemetery London
Stevenson, Albert	A.B.	J24003 (Cha)	HMS North Star	22	Blankenberge Town Cemetery (A.1)
Stingemore, William	A.B.	J19505	HMS Thetis	22	Chatham Naval Mem. (Panel 28, NKG)
Stone, Thomas	A.B.	J26466	HMS Vindictive	20	Dover, St. James's Cemetery (P.W.31A)
Taylor, Alfred xi)	A.B.	SS4751 (Cha)	HMS Vindictive	23	Gillingham (Woodlands) Cem. Kent.
Taylor, William xii.)	A.B.	J22888	HMS Vivid	21	Leicester (Welford Rd) Cem. Leicester.
Tolra, Eduardo	A.B.	Lon 10/3516 RNVR	HMS Vindictive	20	Highgate Cemetery London
Trees, Bertrand	A.B.	J27231 (Dev)	HMS Vindictive	20	Bootle Cemetery, Lancashire.
Watson, Harold xiii.)	A.B.	SS5035	HMS Iris II	22	Dover, St. James's Cemetery (L.V.11)
Weeks, Reginald xiv.)	A.B.	J18219 (Cha)	HMS Vindictive	22	Bradford (Scholemoor) Cem. Yorkshire.
Wilkinson, Cedric	A.M.2.	F26703 RNAS	HMS Iris II	20	Leeds (Lawn Wood) Cemetery, Yorkshire.
Willmore, George xv.)	A.B.	J30159 (Dev)	HMS Vindictive	20	Gillingham (Woodlands) Cem. Kent
Wilson, Albert	Ch.Sto.	287554 (Cha)	HMS North Star	38	Les Baraques Mil. Cem. Sangatte (IV.A.9A)
Wood, John	Sto.1	K12661 (Cha)	HMS Iphigenia	26	Dover, St. James's Cemetery (P.W.41A)
Woods, Guy	Sig.	J37108 (Cha)	HMS Vindictive	19	Dover, St. James's Cemetery (P.W.37A)
Yeadon, John	A.B.	J30413	HMS Vindictive	20	Dover, St. James's Cemetery (P.W.19A)
Young, James	Lt. Cdr	RNVR	ML 110	40	Saunderton (SS Mary & Nicholas Ch) Bucks

ROYAL NAVAL PERSONNEL WOUNDED DURING RAID ON ZEEBRUGGE 23RD APRIL 1918

NAME	RANK	SERVICE NO.	SHIP/UNIT	NAME	RANK	SERVICE NO.	SHIP/UNIT
Ahern., J.	A.B.	J22332 (Dev)	RN	Burton, A.J.G.	ERA.3	M7269 (Cha)	RN
Annesley, J.C.	Lt.		RN	Bury, W.A.	Eng. Cdr.		RN
Antell, G.R.	P.O.	232634 (Dev)	RN	Bush. V.R.	Sto.I	K23345 (Dev)	RN
Bailey, W	A.B.	J71740 (Cha)	RN	Byron, G.H.	Sto. P.O.	307590 (Cha)	RN
Baker, A.D.	A.B.	SS.6089 (Cha)	RN	Callf, A.E.	A.B.	J4780 (Cha)	RN
Bassett, J.K.	A.B.	J2164 (Cha)	RN	Calvert, J.	A.B.	J2021 (Cha)	RN
Bendall, H.C.	Sto.1	K5343 (Po)	RN	Campbell, H.G.	Lt.		RN
Berry, F.J.M.	O.Sea.	J36264 (Po)	RN	Campbell, T.	A.B.	C/Z6290	RNVR
Berry, P.	Dk. Hd.	12986.DA	RNR	Carnochan, A.	A.B.	J32306 (Cha)	RN
Billyard-Leake, E.W.	Lt.		RN	Carpenter, A.F.B.	Capt.		RN
Blades, E.A.	A.B.	J20958 (Dev)	RN	Casey, D.	L.Sto.	K19359 (Dev)	RN
Bodley, E.R.	Midn.		RNR	Chalkley, F.	O.Sea.	J63837 (Cha)	RN
Bonsor, F.	A.B.	221734 (Cha)	RN	Clark, W.	A.B.	C31495	RNVR
Bramble, F.G.	Lt-Cdr		RN	Clinch, H.A.S.	Sig.	J34097 (Cha)	RN
Brayfield, F.F.	Lt.		RNVR	Coates, S.	Sto.1	312345 (Dev)	RN
Briskham, A.J.	A.B.	J36296	RN	Cochrane, J.	A.B.	218409 (Cha)	RN
Brooker, P.R.	Art.Eng		RN	Cockburn, R.	P.O.	J4132 (Cha)	RN
Brooks, A.F.	Dk.Hd.	16116.DA	RNR	Connolly, J.J.	Dk. Hd.	13590 DA	RNR
Brown, L.J.	Sig.	J30561 (Cha)	RN	Cook, D.A.	P.O.	J722 (Cha)	RN
Bryant, T.C.	Sig.	215297 (Cha)	RN	Cory-Wright, A.	Lt.		RN

Cowgill, J.M.	Snr. R.A.	M8848 (Cha)	RN	Johnson, A.V.	A.B.	J24734 (Po)	RN
Cox, L.R.	A.M.I.	F19790	RNAS	Johnson, E.S.G.J.	CERA.2	271752 (Cha)	RN
Crabb, G.F.	A.B.	J32766 (Cha)	RN	Joy, W.E.	L.Sto.	K12668	RN
Cribben, E.G.V.	Sto.2	K33067 (Cha)	RN	Joyce, F.	P.O.	J522 (Po)	RN
Critcher, J.F.	O.Sea.	J38839 (Po)	RN	Keith-Wright, J.C.	Lt.		RNVR
Cross, W.A.E.	Sto.1	K29177 (Cha)	RN	Kelland, F.H.	A.B.	J30116 (Dev)	RN
Cunningham, D.	A.B.	J4130 (Cha)	RN	King, L.J.	A.B.	J41060 (Cha)	RN
Curtis, F.W.	Sto.1	K19904 (Cha)	RN	Lambkin, A.J.	Shpt.1	M6342 (Cha)	RN
Cuthbert, F.E.	A.B.	J23500 (Cha)	RN	Larrett, W.	A.B.	J28133 (Po)	RN
Davies, A.O.	A.B.	189243 (Cha)	RN	Lee, L.J.	Lt.		RNVR
Deighton, D.	A.M.I.	F19791	RNAS	Lepper, A.J.G.	A.B.	J3624 (Po)	RN
O'Donnel, J.	Sea.	8202.A.	RNR	Lewis, T.H.	CERA.1	268023 (Cha)	RN
Divers, T.F.	L.Stok.	K9197 (Cha)	RN	Louch, F.G.	A.B.	J38271(Cha)	RN
Dunn, A.W.	O.Sea.	J61960 (Cha)	RN	McBean, R.H.	Lt.		RN
Edwards, P.H.	Cdr.		RNVR	McCorquodale, R.H.	ERA.4	M20108 (Cha)	RN
Edwards, W.H.	L.Sea.	238481 (Cha)	RN	McKenzie, Albert VC	A.B.	J31736 (Cha)	RN
Eldred, G.P.	A.M.2	F47354	RNAS	MacAlister, D.	Dk.Hd.	1973.SD	RNR
Ellis, C.	A.B.	J3334 (Cha)	RN	Mead, H.W.	A.B.	240071 (Cha)	RN
Evans, A.W.	Armr.	M7148 (Cha)	RN	Mepham, A.P.	A.B.	J36139	RN
Evans, D.	A.B.	J52471 (Cha)	RN	Mereweather, W. T.	L.Sea	J9073 (Dev)	RN
Fairweather, R.R.	L.Sea.	J27503 (Cha)	RN	Merritt, A.G.	A.B.	233495 (Po)	RN
Field, E.A.G.	A.B.	J4139 (Cha)	RN	Milroy, J.	A.B.	J56386 (Po)	RN
Fields, J.	A.B,	J563 (Po)	RN	Morley, N.E.	Midn.		RNR
Frew, R.J.	A.M.2	F39638	RNAS	Nash, H.C.	A.B.	J19150 (Po)	RN
Friday, E.	A.B.	188057 (Cha)	RN	Northcott, R.	P.O.Tel.	J10672	RN
Frost, W.F.	A.B,	J15029 (Po)	RN	Omans, A.W.	Sto.1	K25561 (Cha)	RN
Gallently, T.W.	Gnr.		RN	Orman, T.	A.B.	J24366 (Po)	RN
Gibson, T.T.R.	A.B.	J29990 (Dev)	RN	Oxenbury, S.	A.M.1	F24633	RNAS
Goldsworthy, W.	O.Std.	L4547 (Dev)	RN	Palmer, J.	Sto.1	K38313 (Dev)	RN
Goodwin, R.G.	A.M.2	F52189	RNAS	Pocock, F.	A.B.	J47759 (Cha)	RN
Grey, D.J.	A.B.	SS7028	RN	Popple, G.	A.B.	J19453 (Dev)	RN
Hall, E.	A.B.	SS3771 (Po)	RN	Powell, A.	Gnr.		RN
Hands, J.W.	A.B.	J17760 (Cha)	RN	Price, A.H.	A.M.1	F19846	RN
Harding, L.C.	O.Sea.	J73920 (Cha)	RN	Radley, E.C.	A.B.	J55797 (Cha)	RN
Harner, W.	P.O.	228795 (Dev)	RN	Redmond, T.	Sto.1	K33681 (Cha)	RN
Harris, T.P.	A.B.	J19845 (Cha)	RN	Ripley, T.H.	A.B.	J30094 (Po)	RN
Hayman, J.L.	Sto.1	K35627 (Dev)	RN	Roberts, T.	Sto.1	K27931 (Dev)	RN
Hickey, A.E.	A.B.	J26829 (Cha)	RN	Robinson, A.	S.B.A.	M3682 (Cha)	RN
Hide, F.H.	A.B.	J3075 (Cha)	RN	Robinson, E.	A.B.	SS1079 (Po)	RN
Higgins, P.J.	Sto.1	K16114 (Dev)	RN	Rose, John	A.B.	J31447 (Cha)	RN
Hilling, A.J.	A.B.	J17893 (Po)	RN	Rosoman, R.R.	Lt-Cdr.		RN
Hilton-Young, E.	Lt.		RNVR	Rowlands, R.	A.B,	233615 (Dev)	RN
Hindle, H.C.	O.Sig.	J41704 (Cha)	RN	Ryan, E.	O.Sea.	B/Z10394	RNVR
Hobden, G.	Sto. P.O.	281687 (Cha)	RN	Salter, F.W.	A.B.	J14727 (Po)	RN
Horton, W.	A.B.	J15666 (Po)	RN	Sanderson, G.H.	S.R.A.	M15237	RN
Howell. B	P.O.	J1661 (Cha)	RN	Sandford, R.D.	Lt.		RN
Howett, A.H.	A.B.	194255 (Cha)	RN	Selth, V.	L.Sto.	K18532 (Cha)	RN
Humphreys, A.J.	A.M.1	F13698	RNAS	Smith, A.E.	Sto.1	K38079 (Cha)	RN
Hutton, J.S.	A.M.2	F51617	RNAS	Smith, J.H.E.	A.B.	234183 (Po)	RN
Ireland, J.B.	A.B.	SS7025 (Po)	RN	Sneyd, R.S.	Cdr.		RN
Jackson, H	P.O.1	213767 (Cha)	RN	Stapleton, A.G.	A.B.	J39822 (Po)	RN

Stephenson, G.	Sig.	J41564 (Cha)	RN	Walker, H.T.C.	Lt.		RN
Stone, B.C.	A.B.	J17646 (Dev)	RN	Warrington, G.	A.M.1	F26702	RNAS
Sullivan, A.	Sto.1	K25552 (Cha)	RN	Watters, D.	A.B.	C/Z6739	RNVR
Summerhayes, F.C.	A.B.	J17594 (Dev)	RN	Wells, A.	Sig.	J41825 (Dev)	RN
Taylor, E.B.	A.B.	J22888 (Dev)	RN	Wells, A.W.	L.Ck.Mte.	M2748 (Cha)	RN
Taylor, W.E.	A.B.	J35414 (Po)	RN	Whincup, A.H.	A.B.	SS3489 (Cha)	RN
Tebbutt, W.A.	A.B.	J35028 (Po)	RN	White, E.L.	A.B.	J16608 (Dev)	RN
Terney, F.J.	A.M.1	F27308	RNAS	White, F.	Sto.1	SS115252 (Dev)	RN
Terry, A.A.	L.Sto.	K20132 (Cha)	RN	Wilson, W.J.	A.B.	J26879 (Cha)	RN
Terry, T.	L.Sto.	SS110321 (Cha)	RN	Winfield, C.T.	L.Sea.	223785 (Po)	RN
Tillett, J.	A.B.	227259 (Cha)	RN	Wood, F.	A.B.	J24591 (Po)	RN
Trippier, F.	A.M.1	F12814	RN	Woodroofe, F.J.	A.B.	J38918 (Dev)	RN
Turk, E.	Ch.M.M.	MB2011	RNVR	Worth, G.T.	A.B.	J61680 (Po)	RN
Turner, C.	A.B.	161836 (Dev)	RN	Youlton, E.G.	P.O.1	183625 (Dev)	RN
Vaux, P.E.	Lt.		RN				

ROYAL NAVAL CASUALTY NOTES

i.) Lea. Sea.Daniel Bowthorpe died of wounds 24.04.18.

ii.) Sto.1. John Cleal died of wounds 24.04.18.

iii.) A.B. Jesse Culmer died of wounds 24.04.18.

iv.) A.B. F. C. Fountain (Alias) died of Wounds 25.04.18. Frederick Charles Phillips served as Frederick Charles Fountain. He died aged 19, which suggests he enlisted under this alias because he may have been under age.

v.) L.Sea. Alexander Hick died of wounds 25.04.18.

vi.) A.B. Harold Jones died of wounds 24.04.18.

vii.) Sub-Lt. Maurice Lloyd died of wounds 24.04.18.

viii.) Sto..P.O. Frank Lucas died of wounds 24.04.18.

ix.) Dk.Hd Angus MacIntyre died of wounds 25.04.18.

x.) Sto.1. Sidney Nicholls died of wounds 24.04.18.

xi.) A.B. Alfred Taylor died of wounds 24.04.18.

xii.) A.B. William Taylor died of wounds 11.06.18.

xiii.) A.B. Harold Watson died of wounds 03.05.18.

xiv.) A.B. Reginald Weeks died of wounds 24.05.18.

xv.) A.B. George Willmore died of wounds 24.04.18.

ROYAL MARINES PERSONNEL KILLED DURING TRAINING
FOR RAID ON ZEEBRUGGE 1ST APRIL 1918

NAME	RANK	SERVICE NO.	SHIP/UNIT	AGE	CEMETERY/ GRAVE
Aldridge Albert	Gnr	RMA/14445	RMA	21	Deal Cemetery (2.1220)
Belfield Fred	Gnr	RMA/14455	RMA	U	Deal Cemetery (2.1222)
Cassey, Ernest	Gnr	RMA/13157	RMA	31	Leicester (Gilroes) Cemetery
Large Arthur	Gnr	RMA/13704	RMA	26	Deal Cemetery (2.1223)
Houchen Samuel	Gnr	RMA/14401	RMA	26	Deal Cemetery (2.1221)

ROYAL MARINES PERSONNEL KILLED DURING RAID ON ZEEBRUGGE 23RD APRIL 1918

NAME	RANK	SERVICE NO.	SHIP/UNIT	AGE	CEMETERY/ GRAVE
Adams, Roy	Pte	CH/21203	RMLI	18	Lydd (All Saints) Churchyard, Kent
Aldridge, Richard	Pte. i.)	PLY/1898(S)	RMLI	29	Birkenhead (Flaybrick Hill)
Atkinson, Arthur	Pte.	CH/9214	RMLI	U	Chatham Cemetery, Kent (XX.230)
Attwood, Ernest	Pte.	PLY/13578	RMLI	U	Dover, St. James's Cemetery (P.W.46A)
Barnes, Henry	Pte.	PO/19273	RMLI	U	Marksbury (St. Peter) Churchyard, Somerset.
Batt, E	Pte.	PO/9317	RMLI	38	Flushing (Vlissingen) North. Cem. Holland
Berry, Alfred	Pte. ii.)	PO/18840	RMLI	20	Uckfield Cemetery, Sussex.
Bostock, John	Pte.	CH/19897	RMLI	24	Deal Cemetery, Kent (AM.O.6)
Brewer, George	Cpl.	RMA.11430	RMA	31	Dover, St. James's Cemetery (P.W.22A)
Browne, Harold	Gnr.	RMA.14605	RMA	21	Dover, St. James's Cemetery (P.W.67A)
Burnell, Arthur	Pte. iii.)	PO/18773	RMLI	19	Scunthorpe Cemetery, Lincolnshire.
Butler, F	Pte.	CH/2092(S)	RMLI	U	Tooting (St. Nicholas Ch.) London
Butterworth, William	Pte.	PO/2140(S)	RMLI	38	Hereford Cemetery, Herefordshire
Clarke, Harry	Pte.	PO/18205	RMLI	17	Portsmouth (Kingston) Cem. Hampshire
Colligan, James	Pte.	PLY/14384	RMLI	28	Plymouth Naval Mem. (Panel 29, NKG).
Conkey, Henry	Pte. iv.)	PLY/16188	RMLI	19	Dover, St. James's Cemetery (P.W.45A)
Coombs, Ernest	Pte	PO/19845	RMLI	19	Dover, St. James's Cemetery (P.W.38A)
Cordner, Alexander	Maj.		RMLI	U	Whitchurch (St.Andrew) Ch. Devon
Cornforth, William	Pte.	CH/19029	RMLI	20	Coxwold (St. Michael) Ch. Yorkshire
Cowley, William	Gnr.	RMA.13151	RMA	22	Fulham Palace Road Cemetery, London
Croft, Thomas	Pte.	CH/17698	RMLI	25	Stone Cemetery, Staffordshire
Dale, Joseph	Pte.	CH/2101(S)	RMLI	24	Hartlepool Stranton Cemetery
Davies, Henry	Pte	CH/21211	RMLI	19	Dover, St. James's Cemetery (P.W.47A)
Demery, David	Pte.	PLY/18986	RMLI	19	Dover, St. James's Cemetery (P.W.8A)
Dollery, W	Lt.		RMLI	U	Gosport (Ann's Hill) Cemetery, Hampshire
Drury, Leonard	Pte.	CH/19162	RMLI	19	Chatham Cemetery (UU. 361)
Eagles, Charles	Maj.		RMLI	34	Coughton Church Cemetery, Warwickshire
Ede, William	Pte.	PLY/18154	RMLI	21	Dover, St. James's Cemetery (P.W.9A)
Edney, Albert	Pte.	CH/21257	RMLI	19	City of London Cemetery, Manor Park, Essex
Eldridge, Thomas	Pte.	CH/11534	RMLI	36	Dover, St. James's Cemetery (P.W.34A)
Elliot, Bertram (DSO)	Lt-Col.		RMLI	U	Chatham Cemetery (E.345)
Freeman, Fred	Pte.	PLY/16308	RMLI	U	Highcliffe (St. Mark) Ch. Hampshire
Garland, Isaac	Sgt.	PO/15218	RMLI	29	Portsmouth Naval Mem. (Panel 30, NKG)
Gatehouse, Reginald	Pte.	CH/19258	RMLI	19	Earley (St. Peter) Ch. Berkshire
Giles, Samuel	Pte.	PLY/16489	RMLI	19	Grangemouth (Grandsable) Cem. Stirling.
Goulden, W	Pte.	CH/21771	RMLI	19	Birmingham Whitton Cem. Warwickshire
Green, A.W.	Gnr. v.)	RMA.14077	RMA	22	Gillingham (Woodlands) Cemetery, Kent
Hand, Cecil	Gnr.	RMA.15026	RMA	18	Dover, St. James's Cemetery (P.W.24A)
Harbour, Wiliam	Pte.	CH/16516	RMLI	U	Gillingham (Woodlands) Cemetery, Kent
Harper, Leonard	Pte.	PO/2137(S)	RMLI	U	Camberwell Old Cemetery, London
Heffernan, Charles	L.Cpl.Bglr.	CH/137357	RMLI	38	Dover, St. James's Cemetery (P.W.30A)
Henderson, F	Pte.	PLY/2404(S)	RMLI	U	Wallsend Church Bank Cem Northumberland
Hewlett, G.H.	Gnr. vi.)	RMA.13981	RMA	28	Gillingham (Woodlands) Cemetery, Kent
Hildred, Bertie	Pte. vii.)	CH/19730	RMLI	17	Gillingham (Woodlands) Cemetery, Kent.
Holder, Harry	Pte.	CH/19547	RMLI	19	Gillingham (Woodlands) Cemetery, Kent.
Hudson, Walter	Gnr.	RMA.15450	RMA	18	Kensal Green (All Souls) Cem. London

Huggins, William	Pte.	PO/12926	RMLI	33	Gosport (Ann's Hill) Cemetery, Hampshire
Hurley, Benjamin	Pte.	CH/2417(S)	RMLI	19	Woodgrange Park Cemetery, East Ham, Essex
Hurst, Gerald	Gnr.	RMA.15033	RMA	19	Dover, St. James's Cemetery (P.W.26A)
Inskip, Sydney	Lt.		RMLI	22	City of London Cemetery, Manor Park, Essex
Jackson, Joseph	Lt.		RMLI	23	Manchester Southern Cemetery Lancashire
Jackson, Stanley	Pte.	PO/515(S)	RMLI	27	Dover, St. James's Cemetery (P.W.23A)
Jackson, Tom	Pte.	PLY/17316	RMLI	20	Immingham (St. Andrew) Ch. Lincs.
James, Stanley	Pte.	CH/17833	RMLI	U	Highgate Cemetery, London 157.4975
Jones, G.	Pte.	CH/20137	RMLI	20	City of London & Tower Hamlets Cem Lon.
Jones, John	Cpl.	CH/19114	RMLI	21	Dover, St. James's Cemetery (P.W.66A)
Jones, R	Pte.	CH/2278(S)	RMLI	U	Llanrhaiadr-yn-mochnant (St.Dogfan) Ch.
Lane, George	Pte. viii.)	PO/9337	RMLI	37	New Fishbourne (SS Mary & Peter) Ch.
Latimer, David	Pte.	CH/21084	RMLI	18	Newcastle-upon-Tyne (All Saints) Cem.
Linkin, Percy	Pte.	CH/17284	RMLI	28	Islington Cemetery, Middlesex
Loxley, Victor	Pte.	PO/1921(S)	RMLI	20	Oswaldtwistle (Immanuel) Ch. Lancs.
Mann, William	Gnr.	RMA.14126	RMA	20	Dover, St. James's Cemetery (P.W.17A)
Mason, Alexander	Pte.	CH/20357	RMLI	20	Embleton (Spitalford) Cem. Northumberland
Matthews, Albert	Pte.	PLY/16141	RMLI	24	Dover, St. James's Cemetery (P.W.14A)
May, William	Pte.	CH/18145	RMLI	22	East London Cemetery, Plaistow, Essex.
Mayled, Victor	Pte.	PLY/18934	RMLI	19	Dover, St. James's Cemetery (P.W.522)
Mercer, Harold	Pte.	CH/2055(S)	RMLI	20	Burnley Cemetery, Lancashire.
Merritt, Frank	L.Cpl	PLY/9984	RMLI	39	Dover, St. James's Cemetery (P.W.40A)
Middleton, George	Gnr.	RMA.13064	RMA	22	Bristol (Arnos Vale) Cemetery
Misselbrook, Alfred	Pte.	CH/21177	RMLI	U	Walthamstow (Queens Road Cemetery)
Moore, Thomas	Pte.	PLY/9334	RMLI	35	Plymouth Naval Mem. (Panel 29, NKG)
Neate, Reginald	Cpl.	CH/18066	RMLI	22	Castle Coombe (St. Andrew) Chyd, Wilts.
O'Neil, Hugh	Pte.	CH/18487	RMLI	26	Dover, St. James's Cemetery (P.W.SSA)
Omerod, Vincent	Gnr.	RMA/14785	RMA	20	Dover, St. James's Cemetery (P.W.15A)
O'Sullivan, D	Pte.	CH/21243	RMLI	20	Flushing (Vlissingen) Northern Cem. Hol.
Osborne, George	Cpl.	PLY/16683	RMLI	22	Zeebrugge Churchyard (Grave 171).
Packer, William	Gnr.	RMA.1479(S)	RMA	37	Dover, St. James's Cemetery (P.W.28A)
Parks, George	Pte.	CH/21276	RMLI	19	Folkestone Old Cemetery
Pearse, Robert	Gnr.	RMA.13569	RMA	22	Dover, St. James's Cemetery (P.W.25A)
Prangnell, Harold	Pte.	CH/19762	RMLI	U	Chatham Cemetery Kent, (HH.674)
Reeder, Charles	Pte.	CH/17982	RMLI	U	Gillingham (Woodlands) Cemetery, Kent.
Rigby, Charles	Lt.		RMA	23	Hertingfordbury (St. Mary Ch) Herts
Roberts, Harry	Pte.	PLY/1881(S)	RMLI	28	Llandudno (St. Tudno) Ch. Wales
Rolfe, Frank	Pte.	CH/2580(S)	RMLI	19	Dover, St. James's Cemetery (P.W.1A)
Rumsby, William	Gnr.	RMA.13753	RMA	21	Dover, St. James's Cemetery (P.W.10A)
Russell, Robert	Gnr.	RMA.14196	RMA	25	Dover, St. James's Cemetery (P.W.11A)
Scott, Walter	Pte.	CH/2480(S)	RMLI	19	Larkfield (Holy Trinity) Churchyard, Kent.
Shaw, R	Pte.	CH/21108	RMLI	U	Worcester Park (St. Philip) Ch. Surrey
Sillitoe, W	Lt.		RMLI	22	Deal Cemetery, Kent (A.M.0.5)
Simmons, T	Gnr. ix.)	RMA.14066	RMA	25	Stoke-on-Trent (Hartshill) Cemetery Staffs.
Sparkes, Bertram	Sgt.	CH/16534	RMLI	25	Dover, St. James's Cemetery (P.W.33A)
Spiers, William	Pte.	PLY/1890(S)	RMLI	26	Dover, St. James's Cemetery (P.W.27A)
Smith, George	Pte.	PLY/11530	RMLI	33	Nottingham (New Basford) Cemetery, Notts
Smith, Samuel	Cpl.	PO/14547	RMLI	29	Meonstoke (St. Andrew) Churchyard, Hants.
Sneyd, T	Pte.	CH/14455	RMLI	U	Cement House Cem. Langemark, Belgium.
Stanton, Robert	Lt. x.)		RMLI	21	Market Deeping Cemetery, Lincolnshire
Steer, Charles	Cpl.	CH/16666	RMLI	U	Hendon Cemetery, Middlesex.

Sunshine, Frederick	Pte.	CH/19027	RMLI	20	Abney Park Cemetery, London
Swan, Frederick	Pte.	CH/19349	RMLI	19	Dover, St. James's Cemetery (P.W.16A)
Thatcher, William	Pte.	CH/2093(S)	RMLI	30	Bradford (Scholemoor) Cemetery, Yorks.
Thomas, Haydn	Pte.	PLY/18127	RMLI	24	Dover, St. James's Cemetery (P.W.36A)
Thwaites, Albert	Pte.	CH/19653	RMLI	22	Dover, St. James's Cemetery (P.W.32A)
Tickner, Frederick	Pte.	PO/18066	RMLI	18	Dover, St. James's Cemetery (P.W.54A)
Tidman, James	Gnr.	RMA.13251	RMA	22	Dover, St. James's Cemetery (P.W.50A)
Towers, Gilbert	Gnr.	RMA.13244	RMA	22	Dover, St. James's Cemetery (P.W.56A)
Tuckey, Charles	Capt.		RMLI	23	Zeebrugge Churchyard (Grave 1)
Tysoe, Stanley	Pte.	PLY/18795	RMLI	19	Wootton (St. Mary) & Ext. Oxfordshire.
Vine, Sidney	Gnr.	RMA.10769	RMA	18	Dover, St. James's Cemetery (P.W.21A)
Walling, A.	Pte.	PLY/10222	RMLI	U	St. Mary Church, Torbay.
Ware, Herbert	Pte. xi.)	CH/19550	RMLI	U	Gillingham (Woodlands) Cemetery, Kent.
West, G.	Pte.	CH/13569	RMLI	32	City of London & Tower Hamlets Cem. Lon
White, Joseph	Gnr.	RMA.14601	RMA	20	Leeds (Lawns Wood) Cemetery, Leeds.
Whitley, Walter	Pte.	PO/2594(S)	RMLI	22	Mold Cemetery
Wickham, William	Pte. xii.)	PO/18806	RMLI	20	Nutley (St. James's the Less) Ch. Sussex.
Willavise, William	Pte.	PLY/17462	RMLI	20	Dover, St. James's Cemetery (P.W.20A)
Wickwar, Edward	Pte.	PO/18816	RMLI	22	Dover, St. James's Cemetery (P.W.3A)
Wood, George	Pte.	CH/19473	RMLI	20	Manchester (Gorton) Cemetery, Lancashire.

ROYAL MARINES PERSONNEL WOUNDED DURING RAID ON ZEEBRUGGE 23RD APRIL 1918

NAME	RANK	SERVICE NO.	SHIP/UNIT
Adam, J.W	Pte.	PLY/16271	RMLI
Airey, W.G.	Pte.	CH.21204	RMLI
Alexander, P	Pte.	PO/2106(S)	RMLI
Allbones, C	Pte.	CH/19467	RMLI
Astley, O	Pte.	CH/18022	RMLI
Atkinson, J.D.	Pte.	CH/21210	RMLI
Baines, W	Pte.	CH/19104	RMLI
Baker, D.F.G.	Pte.	PO/18680	RMLI
Barry, F.	Pte.	CH/14008	RMLI
Barter, R.R.	Pte.	PO/17313	RMLI
Baum, H.E.	Pte.	PLY/18714	RMLI
Baxter, P.	Pte.	CH/18016	RMLI
Beckford, J.A.	Pte.	PLY/17401	RMLI
Bell, S.	Pte.	PLY/17301(S)	RMLI
Belleone, A.	Pte.	CH/16870	RMLI
Beresford, C.	Cpl	CH/16581	RMLI
Blake, H.C.	Pte.	CH/19415	RMLI
Bloxsom, W.C.	2nd Lt.		RMLI
Bold, C.	Pte	PO/19883	RMLI
Booth, R W	Pte.	CH/2306(S)	RMLI
Bowie, S.	Pte.	CH/2416(S)	RMLI
Branson, J.H.	Pte.	CH/17636	RMLI
Broad, G.J.	Pte.	CH/2029(S)	RMLI
Brooker H.H.T.	Pte.	CH/21153	RMLI
Brown, G.A.	Pte.	PO/16158	RMLI
Brown, W.C.	Pte.	PLY/15712	RMLI
Bulmer, H.E.	Pte.	CH/21120	RMLI
Bushell, W	Pte.	PLY/16341	RMLI
Camfield, H.H.R.	Sgt.	PO/14166	RMLI
Chambers, T.H.	Sgt.	CH/15756	RMLI
Charters, E.	Pte.	PLY/2579(S)	RMLI
Childs, L.W.	Gnr.	RMA. 15417	RMA
Chittle, A.H.	Pte.	CH/15232	RMLI
Clacey, C.P.	Pte.	PLY/2491(S)	RMLI
Clark, A.G.	Pte.	PLY/16838	RMLI
Clark, J.	Pte.	PO/19888	RMLI
Clarke, W.P.	Pte.	CH/17347	RMLI
Clist, J.	Pte.	PLY/16764	RMLI
Collins, F.J.	Pte.	PLY/1970(S)	RMLI
Conybeare, C.B.	Capt.		RMLI
Cooke, T.F.V	Lt.		RMLI
Cope, G.	Pte.	CH/19497	RMLI
Coster, G.W.	Pte.	CH/21130	RMLI
Daly, B.D.	Pte.	PO/17312	RMLI
Daniel, J.B.	Pte.	PLY/16619	RMLI
Darhy, T.	Pte.	PLY/16701	RMLI
Davies, E.L.	Pte.	PLY/15366	RMLI
Deed, J.M.	Pte.	PLY/12337	RMLI

Name	Rank	Number	Unit
Del.Strother	Capt.		RMLI
Dewhurst, D.W.	Cpl.	PLY/16354	RMLI
Donnelly, J.	Pte.	CH/19039	RMLI
Eden, J.S.	Pte.	CH/18374	RMLI
Edgar, G.W.	Pte.	CH/1288(S)	RMLI
Edge, J.	Pte.	PLY/18308	RMLI
Erskine, A.C.	Pte.	PLY/1870(S)	RMLI
Finch, N.	Sgt.	RMA.12151	RMLI
Finney, J.	Pte.	PLY/2492(S)	RMLI
Fitzpatrick, F.	Pte.	CH/16634	RMLI
Fort, S.H.	Pte.	CH/18387	RMLI
Franks, B.H.	Pte.	CH/19906	RMLI
Frew, W.	Pte.	RMA.14146	RMLI
Fryer, J.H.	Pte.	PLY/15585	RMLI
Gale, C.M.	Pte.	PO/19915	RMLI
Gallin, W.G.	Pte.	PLY/15290	RMLI
Gamblin, F.	Cpl.	CH/17100	RMLI
Gibson, W.S.	Pte.	PLY/1907(S)	RMLI
Gilbert, R.S.	Pte.	PO/18254	RMLI
Gillingham, W.S.	Pte.	PO/16776	RMLI
Gleed, G.W.	Pte.	PLY/17734	RMLI
Goddard, C.W.B.	Pte.	CH/18246	RMLI
Goodchild, F.W.	Cpl.	CH/14864	RMLI
Gordon, A.R.	Pte.	CH/20545	RMLI
Graham, G.	Pte.	PLY/15806	RMLI
Grant, H.H.	Pte.	PO/7873	RMLI
Gumm, A.P.	Cpl.	PLY/15119	RMLI
Hailstone, W.G.	Gnr.	RMA.14857	RMA
Hall, G.W.	Pte.	PLY/7413	RMLI
Haly, John	Pte.	CH/18243	RMLI
Hardman, J.	Pte.	PLY/2493(S)	RMLI
Harris, P.	Pte.	CH/18113	RMLI
Hart, P.J.	Pte.	CH/17921	RMLI
Hartnell, G.J.	Pte.	PLY/1972(S)	RMLI
Harvey, A.	Pte. xiii.)	PLY/15306	RMLI
Hedges, R.A.	Sgt.	CH/14651	RMLI
Hewitt, G.J.H.	Cpl.	PO/15858	RMLI
Hill, E.	Pte.	PLY/2510(S)	RMLI
Hinchcliffe, J.H.	Pte.	RMA.13936	RMA
Hitchcock, H.B.	Pte.	CH/21190	RMLI
Holding, Leonard	Pte.	CH/2565(S)	RMLI
Hole, F.	Pte.	PLY/15729	RMLI
Holmes, M.	Pte.	PLY/15973	RMLI
Hore, F.J.	Lt		RMLI
Houston, W.	Pte.	PLY/2588(S)	RMLI
Ireland, S.J.	Pte.	PLY/1980(S)	RMLI
Janes, A.F.	Pte.	PLY/15988	RMLI
Janes, S.	Pte.	CH/17833	RMLI
Jeffery, W.J.	Pte.	PO/19933	RMLI
Johns, C.H.	Pte.	CH/13706	RMLI
Jones, H	Pte.	PLY/16900	RMLI
Keaveny. M.	Pte. xiv.)	PLY/1977(S)	RMLI
Kelly, F.A.	Pte.	PO/17971	RMLI
Kelso, C.	Pte.	PO/15834	RMLI
Kember, J.E.	Pte.	CH/15357	RMLI
Kerr, R.	Pte.	PLY/17297	RMLI
Knowles, T.	Pte.	PLY/16195	RMLI
Lawrence, A.	Pte.	PO/19900	RMLI
Lee, A.V.	Pte.	PLY/17591	RMLI
Letheren, F.W.T.	Pte.	PLY/17065	RMLI
Levatt, H.B.	2nd.Lt.		RMLI
Lewis, R.R.	Pte.	PLY/1916(S)	RMLI
Lloyd, J.F.	Pte.	CH/2405(S)	RMLI
Lock, A.E.	Pte.	CH/2418(S)	RMLI
Locker, G.H.	Cpl.	PLY/11496	RMLI
Lovatt, H.B.	2nd.Lt.		RMLI
Lucas, W.	Gnr.	RMA.13867	RMLI
Lynch, C.F.	L.Cpl.	PLY/18248	RMLI
McDonald,	Pte.	PLY/13352	RMLI
McKenzie, R.J.	Pte.	CH/2278(S)	RMLI
MacAskill, H.	Pte.	CH/2276(S)	RMLI
MacPherson.A.	Pte.	PLY/2509(S)	RMLI
Maddocks. L.	Pte.	PLY/2501(S)	RMLI
Manners, W.G.	Pte.	CH/2090(S)	RMLI
Manning, H.	Pte.	PO/17926	RMLI
Marfleet, A.	Pte.	CH/2410(S)	RMLI
Marriott, C.	Pte.	PO/159(S)	RMLI
Martyn, C.H.	Pte.	CH/1903(S)	RMLI
May, A.G.	Cpl.	CH/13289	RMLI
Milton, A.S.	Pte.	CH/17093	RMLI
Milton, F.	Pte.	PLY/15499	RMLI
Mitchinson, G.H,	Cpl.	CH/17117	RMLI
Mooney, R.	Pte.	PLY/17992	RMLI
Moran, G.	Pte.	PLY/19114	RMLI
Morrow, A.W.	Bglr.	PO/16577	RMLI
Morse, J.W.	Pte.	CH/2073(S)	RMLI
Moss, J.	Pte.	CH/2256(S)	RMLI
Mundy, F.W.	Pte.	PLY/15482	RMLI
Murfin, W.	Pte.	CH/19883	RMLI
Narracott, F.K.	Pte.	PLY/2508(S)	RMLI
Noyce, L.	Pte.	PO/18628	RMLI
Noyes, D.J.	Gnr.	RMA.14241	RMA
Oakden, A.	Pte.	PLY/18128	RMLI
Painter, R.	Pte.	PLY/11543	RMLI
Palmer, J.W.	Gnr.	RMA.14701	RMA
Parker, L.C.	Cpl.	PLY/16948	RMLI
Patston, C.F.	Pte.	PO/17861	RMLI
Pepper, A.T.	Pte.	PO/19719	RMLI
Phillips, A.J.	Pte.	PLY/17329	RMLI
Pitcher, A.	Pte.	CH/14311	RMLI
Pook, J.	Pte.	PLY/9256	RMLI
Poole, Henry	Pte.	PO/2605(S)	RMLI

Potter, J.L.	Cpl.	PLY/15422	RMLI	Taylor, A.	Sgt.	PO/14899	RMLI
Press, J.D.L.	Pte.	PO/15394	RMLI	Taylor, James	Pte.	CH/2562(S)	RMLI
Prince, A.H.	Pte.	CH/17760	RMLI	Thatcher, C.J.	Sgt.Maj.		RMLI
Quarrington, R.E.	Pte.	CH/2392(S)	RMLI	Thompson, T.E.	Pte.	PLY/17768	RMLI
Radford, F.	1.Sgt.	PLY/14991	RMLI	Thomson, W.J.	Sgt.	CH/15438	RMLI
Rawlinson, W.	Cpl.	PLY/18040	RMLI	Toach, A.W.	Pte.	PLY/2494(S)	RMLI
Regan, Frank	Cpl.	PO/16571	RMLI	Turner, J.	Pte.	CH/2086(S)	RMLI
Rhind, E.H.	Pte.	PLY/2153(S)	RMLI	Underwood, G.R.	Pte.	CH/18153	RMLI
Ritter, R.P.	Pte.	PLY/1882(S)	RMLI	Wadd, J.H.	Pte.	PLY/14090	RMLI
Rodgers, J.	Pte.	CH/21256	RMLI	Wakefield, W.J.	Pte.	PO/18387	RMLI
Rose, B.F.	Pte.	CH/19033	RMLI	Ward, T.	Pte.	CH/18454	RMLI
Sandy, H.S.	Pte.	PO/2031(S)	RMLI	Watkins, B.	Pte.	CH/21157	RMLI
Scarrett, W.	Pte.	PO/2481(S)	RMLI	Welsby, C.	Cpl.	CH/17510	RMLI
Scott, T.I.	Pte.	CH/13625	RMLI	Wheatley, C.B.	Pte.	PLY/2525(S)	RMLI
Scotton, H.W.R.	Gnr.	RMA.13835	RMA	Wheeler, C.S.	Pte.	PO/1967(S)	RMLI
Seal, N.W.	Pte.	PLY/2577(S)	RMLI	White, F.T.	Pte.	PLY/1913(S)	RMLI
Skelton, W.M.	Pte.	PLY/10001	RMLI	White, W.H.	Pte.	PLY/16494	RMLI
Smith, A.S.	Pte.	CH/2049(S)	RMLI	Whitelegge, J.	Pte.	PLY/15998	RMLI
Smith, R.C.	Pte.	PO/17142	RMLI	Whittle, J.	Pte.	CH/21140	RMLI
Smith, W.	Pte.	PLY/10404	RMLI	Williams, A.W.T.	Cpl.	RMA.12915	RMA
Snelling, A.R.	Sgt.	CH/15731	RMLI	Williams, E.H.	Pte.	PLY/15447	RMLI
Somners, H.J.	Gnr.	RMA.14697	RMA	Williamson, J.C.	C.Sgt.	PLY/8123	RMLI
Stanfield, M.	Pte.	CH/18648	RMLI	Wiltshire, A.H.	Pte.	PO/18359	RMLI
Stark, F.	Pte.	PO/17832	RMLI	Wood, W.	Pte.	PLY/16909	RMLI
Stewart, A.	Pte.	PLY/16586	RMLI	Woodhouse, W.G.	Pte.	PLY/2495(S)	RMLI
Stewart, A.E.	Pte.	CH/17150	RMLI	Wright, B.	C.Sgt.	PO/10895	RMLI
Street, F.J.	Pte.	PO/1853(S)	RMLI	Wright, T.V.	Pte.	PLY/18257	RMLI
Sutton, G.	Gnr.	RMA.13882	RMA				

NOTES ON RMLI & RMA CASUALTIES

i.) Pte. Richard Aldridge RMLI died of wounds 04.05.18.

ii.) Pte. Alfred Berry RMLI died of wounds 25.04.18.

iii.) Pte. Arthur Burnell RMLI DOW 24.04.18

iv.) Pte. Henry Conkey RMLI served in RMLI as Henry Campbell for five years. The reason for serving under an alias is because when he enlisted at 14 he was under age.

v.) Gnr. A. W. Green RMA died of wounds 17.05.18

vi.) Gnr G. H. Hewlett RMA died of wounds 18.05.18.

vii.) Pte. Bertie Hildred RMLI died of wounds 20.05.18.

viii.) Pte. George Lane RMLI died of wounds 24.04.18.

ix.) Gnr. T. Simmons RMA died of wounds 20.05.18.

x.) Lt. Robert Stanton died of wounds 28.04.18.

xi.) Pte. Herbert Ware died of wounds 25.04.18.

xii.) Pte. William Wickham died of wounds 24.04.18.

xiii.) Pte. Albert Harvey RMLI died 28.06.18.

xiv.) Pte. M. Keaveny RMLI died 04.10.18. Buried Murmansk New British Cemetery.

GERMAN PERSONNEL KILLED

It is difficult to ascertain the number of German casualties during the Zeebrugge Raid, but according to German records and accounts of the raid the number reported is incredibly small. The slight casualties sustained by the Germans can be supported by the fact that there is only a small number of German naval personnel who were killed on 23rd April 1918 who are buried in Zeebrugge Churchyard. The names are:

George Rau Artmat	23.4.18
Joseph Miltze OB MTRATI	23.4.18
Eric Hagemann See Offz.anw	23.4.18
Otto Kuhn TMTR	23.4.18
Berthold Schulz T.M.T.R.	23.4.18
Otto Bauer T.P.MATR	23.4.18
Hermann Kunne T.M.T.R.	23.4.18

However, other German casualties may have been repatriated home to Germany for burial, or buried in other German cemeteries.

APPENDIX 3

HONOURS & AWARDS

VICTORIA CROSS

Captain Alfred Carpenter, RN	HMS Vindictive
Captain Edward Bamford, DSO RMLI.	No.7 Platoon, B Company, 4th Battalion RMLI
Lieutenant Commander George Bradford RN	HMS Iris
Lieutenant Percy Dean RNVR	HMML 282
Sergeant Norman Finch RMLI. RMA 12151	Royal Marines Artillery
Lieutenant Commander Arthur Harrison RN	Royal Naval Landing Party
Able Seaman Albert McKenzie RN J31736	B Company, Royal Naval Landing Party
Lieutenant Richard Sandford, RN	HM Submarine C3

DISTINGUISHED SERVICE ORDER

Lieutenant John Annesley RN	Coastal Motor Boat Commander
Lieutenant Edward Billyard-Leake RN	HMS Iphigenia
Eng. Lieutenant Commander Ronald Boddie RN	HMS Thetis
Lieutenant Stuart Bonham-Carter RN	HMS Intrepid
Lieutenant Harold Campbell RN	HMS Daffodil
Captain Arthur Chater	Adjutant, 4th Battalion RMLI
Lieutenant Theodore Cooke	No.5 Platoon, B Company, 4th Battalion RMLI
Captain Reginald Dallas Brooks	Royal Marines Artillery
Lieutenant Cecil Dickinson RN	Royal Naval Landing Party
Lieutenant Commander Kenneth Helyar RN	HMS North Star
Lieutenant Oscar Henderson RN	HMS Iris
Lieutenant John Howell-Price DSC RNR	HM Submarine C3
Lieutenant Hugh Littleton RNVR	HMML 526
Commander Edward Osborne RN	RN Gunnery Officer (Staff VA Dover) HMS Vindictive
Chaplain Reverend Charles Peshall RN	HMS Vindictive
Surgeon Frank Pocock MC RN	HMS Iris
Lieutenant Arthur Welman DSC RN	Coastal Motor Boat Flotilla Commander

DISTINGUISHED SERVICE CROSS

Lieutenant George Belben RN	HMS Thetis
Sub-Lieutenant Leslie Blake RNR	CMB 7
Lieutenant George Bowen RNVR	HMML 110
Lieutenant Cuthbert Bowlby RN	CMB 26B
Surgeon William Clegg RN	HMS Vindictive

Lieutenant Alan Cory-Wright RN	HMS Intrepid
Artificer Engineer Wiliam Edgar RAN	HMS Iris
Gunner Thomas Galletly RN	HMS North Star
Lieutenant Leopold Hegarty RNR	HMS Daffodil
Acting Sergeant Major Ernest Kelly CH/10068	CSM No.1 Platoon A Company 4th Battalion RMLI
Lieutenant Francis Lambert RN	HMS Thetis
Lieutenant Charles Lamplough RMLI	No.9 Platoon, C Company, 4th Battalion RMLI
Lieutenant Leonard Lee RNVR	ML 110 personnel
Sub Lieutenant Maurice Lloyd DSC RN (Received bar)	HMS Iphigenia
Captain John Palmer DSC RMLI (Received bar)	2nd ic C Company, 4th Battalion RMLI
Sub Lieutenant Cedric Outhwaite RNVR	CMB 5
Lieutenant John Robinson RNVR	HMML 424
Lieutenant Harold Rogers RNR	HMS Daffodil
Artificer Engineer William Sutton RN	HMS Daffodil
Sergeant-Major Charles Thatcher R.M.L.I.	4th Battalion RMLI
Lieutenant George Underhill RMLI	No.12 Platoon, C Company, 4th Battalion Mole RMLI
Mate Sidney West RN	HMS Iphigenia
Lieutenant Keith Wright RNVR	HMML 282
Lieutenant Philip Vaux RN	HMS Iphigenia

CONSPICUOUS GALLANTRY MEDAL

Chief Motor Mechanic James Attwood RNVR MB 1915	ML 283
Stoker 1st Class Henry Bendall RN K.5343 (Po)	HM Submarine C3
Signaller Thomas Bryant RN 215297 (Po)	HMS Iris
Leading Seaman William Cleaver RN 221196 (Po)	M Submarine C3
Leading Seaman Albert Davis RN 189243 (Ch)	HMS Iphigenia
Chief Motor Mechanic Sydney Fox RNVR MB 1872	ML 282
Chief Engine Room Artificer Frank Gale RN 272503 (Ch)	HMS Thetis
Private William Hopewell RMLI PLY/15995	No.9 Platoon, C Company, 4th Battalion RMLI
Petty Officer Walter Harner RN 228795 (Dev)	HM Submarine C3
Sergeant Frank Knill RMA 12738	Trench Mortar Section RMA
Able Seaman Ferdinand Lake RN J22273 (Po)	HMS Iris
Private John Press RMLI PO/15394	No.5 Platoon, B Company, 4th Battalion RMLI
Engine Room Artificer 3rd Class Alan Roxburgh RN 272442 (Ch)	HM Submarine C3
Petty Officer David Smith RN 225904 (Po)	HMS Iris
Leading Deckhand William Weeks RNR 13682 DA	ML 282
Petty Officer Edwin Youlton RN 183625 (Po)	HMS Vindictive

DISTINGUISHED SERVICE MEDAL

Private John Adam RMLI PLY/16271	No.9 Platoon, C Company, 4th Battalion RMLI
Chief Motor Mechanic Roy Alexander RNVR 1839	Picket Boats, Motor Launches and Motor Boats
Petty Officer George Antell RN 232634 (Dev)	Royal Naval Landing Party (A Company)
Chief Air Mechanic Clifford Armitage RNAS F6981	HMS Vindictive
Engine Room Artificer Harry Baker RN 271447 (Dev)	HMS Daffodil
Able Seaman Herbert Bambridge RN J3947 (Ch)	HMS Intrepid
Leading Seaman William Bassett RN 227412 (Dev)	HMS Iris
Plumber Charles Batho R.N. M6328 (Ch)	HMS Iphigenia

Able Seaman William Bishop RN J40117 (Dev)	Royal Naval Landing Party (C Company)
Petty Officer Charles Biss DSM RN 183877 (Received bar)	Royal Naval Landing Party (C Company)
Deckhand Frank Bowles RNR 3938 SD	Picket Boats, Motor Launches and Motor Boats
Deckhand Albert Brooks RNR 16116 DA	Picket Boats, Motor Launches and Motor Boats
Sergeant Crispin Budd RMLI PO/15765	Machine Gun Section, 4th Battalion RMLI
Engine Room Artificer 3rd Class Arthur Burton RN M7269 (Ch)	HMS Iphigenia
Able Seaman Walter Butler RN J16311 (Po)	Royal Naval Landing Party (C Company)
Sergeant Reginald Burt RMLI PO/15162	No.5 Platoon, B Company, 4th Battalion RMLI
Leading Seaman George Bush RAN 7018	Royal Naval Landing Party (A Company)
Stoker Victor Bush RN K23345 (Dev)	HMS Iphigenia
Chief Petty Officer George Cann ON 174002 (Cha)	Not known.
Able Seaman Andrew Carnochan RN J32306 (Ch)	Royal Naval Landing Party (D Company)
Chief Engine Room Artificer George Carter RN 270392 (Ch)	HMS North Star
Engine Room Artificer 4th Class Norman Carroll RN M17679 (Ch)	HMS Vindictive
Able Seaman Robert Catchpole RN 222758 (Ch)	HMS Phoebe
Engine Room Artificer 3rd Class Herbert Cavanagh RN M1111 (Po)	HMS Vindictive
Leading Seaman William Childs RN J20481 (Po)	Royal Naval Landing Party (B Company)
Private Albert Clark RMLI PLY/16838	No.12 Platoon, C Company, 4th Battalion RMLI
Able Seaman William Clark RNVR Clyde 3/1495	Royal Naval Landing Party (A Company)
Signaller Harold Clinch RN J34097 (Ch)	HMS Thetis
Petty Officer Robert Cockburn RN J4132 (Ch)	HMS North Star
Deckhand Charles Cowling RNR 13973 DA	Picket Boats, Motor Launches and Motor Boats
Petty Officer James Cownie RN 239385 (Dev)	HMS Daffodil
Stoker 1st Class William Crawford RN K34438	HMS Vindictive
Petty Officer Thomas Crust RN J2018 (Ch)	Picket Boats, Motor Launches and Motor Boats
Leading Deckhand Percy Dalman RNR 5001 SD	Picket Boats, Motor Launches and Motor Boats
Mater at Arms Charles Dunkason RN 191301 (Po)	HMS Vindictive
Stoker Frederick Easter RN 224844 (Ch)	HMS Daffodil
Yeoman Signals Alfred Elliot RN 229352 (Ch)	HMS Warwick
Armourer Arthur Evans RN M7148 (Ch)	HMS Vindictive
Able Seaman Harold Eves RN J15626 (Dev)	Royal Naval Landing Party (A Company)
Chief Engine Room Artificer Thomas Farrell RN 270955 (Ch)	HMS Intrepid
Engine Room Artificer 2nd Class John Ferguson RN M12154 (Ch)	HMS Intrepid
Chief Petty Officer Frederick Forster R.N. 182600 (Ch)	HMS Phoebe
Deckhand William Francis RNR 13899 DA	Picket Boats, Motor Launches and Motor Boats
Leading Stoker Frederick Freestone RN K7324 (Ch)	HMS Thetis
Leading Signaller Albert Gamby RN J11326 (Ch)	HMS Vindictive
Able Seaman Arthur Geddes RN J30822 (Ch)	HMS Vindictive
Armourer Herbert Gibson RN M3735 (Ch)	HMS Iphigenia
Private William Gilkes RMLI CH/15525	No. 3 Platoon, A Company, 4th Battalion RMLI
Deckhand William Golding RNR 4488 SD	Picket Boats, Motor Launches and Motor Boats
Leading Deckhand Arthur Grain RNR 3212 SD	Picket Boats, Motor Launches and Motor Boats
Bugler Leonard Guttridge RMLI PO/16989	No.5 Platoon, B Company, 4th Battalion RMLI
Chief Petty Officer Robert Hall RN 161596 (Ch)	HMS North Star
Leading Telegraphist William Halsey RN J24951 (Ch)	Picket Boats, Motor Launches and Motor Boats
Engine Room Artificer 5th Class Herbert Harris RN M6218 (Po)	HMS Vindictive
Stoker Thomas Haw RN 306429 (Po)	HMS Vindictive
Leading Seaman Veines Hawkins RN J15592 (Po)	Royal Naval Landing Party (C Company)
Stoker 1st Class James Hayman RN K35627	HMS Vindictive
Gunner Edward Hearn RMA 12169	RMA Detachment
Leading Deckhand James Heaver RNR 3029 SD	Picket Boats, Motor Launches and Motor Boats

Sergeant George Hewitt RMLI PO/15858	No.8 Platoon, B Company, 4th Battalion RMLI
Able Seaman Frederick Hide RN J3075 (Ch)	HMS Intrepid
Chief Motor Mechanic Stanley Hill RNVR MB 1473	Picket Boats, Motor Launches and Motor Boats
Chief Motor Mechanic Frederick Holmes RNVR MB 1668	Picket Boats, Motor Launches and Motor Boats
Petty Officer Percy Inge RN J1840 (Ch)	HMS Intrepid
Petty Officer Herbert Jackson RN 213767 (Ch)	HMS Vindictive
Chief Petty Officer Henry Jeffries RN 178838 (Ch)	HMS Iphigenia
Chief Engine Room Artificer 2nd Class Ernest Johnson RN 271752 (Ch)	HMS Iphigenia
Deckhand Frank Johnson RNR 15397 DA	Picket Boats, Motor Launches and Motor Boats
Stoker 1st Class Walter Joy RN K12668 (Ch)	HMS Iphigenia
Petty Officer Frederick Joyce RN J522 (Po)	Royal Naval Landing Party (B Company)
Able Seaman Francis Kelland RN J30116 (Dev)	Royal Naval Landing Party (D Company)
Able Seaman Leonard King RN J.41060 (Ch)	HMS Iphigenia
Corporal William Kingshott RMLI PLY/14785	No.12 Platoon, C Company, 4th Battalion RMLI
Private Leonard Lane RMLI PO/16430	No.8 Platoon, B Company, 4th Battalion RMLI
Able Seaman Frederick Larby RN J27317 (Po)	Royal Naval Landing Party (A Company)
Deckhand Charles Lawrence RNR 13039 DA	Picket Boats, Motor Launches and Motor Boats
Private Victor Lee RMLI PLY/17591	No.12 Platoon, C Company, 4th Battalion RMLI
Able Seaman William Lodwick RN J17820 (Dev)	Royal Naval Landing Party (A Company)
Stoker Petty Officer Henry Mabb RN K1043 (Ch)	HMS Iris
Able Seaman Richard Makey RN 219228 (Po)	HMS Vindictive
Private Charles Martyn RMLI PLY/1903(S)	HMS Iris, Machine Gun Section, 4th Bttn RMLI
Leading Deckhand Donald McAllister RNR 1890 SD	Picket Boats, Motor Launches and Motor Boats
Gunner Norman McPhee RMA 14124	RMA Detachment
Petty Officer Alfred Messer RN 228561 (Po)	HMS Thetis
Able Seaman Horace Nash RN J19150 (Po)	Royal Naval Landing Party (A Company)
Engine Room Artificer 3rd Class Stanley Odam RN M3166 (Dev)	HMS Iris
SBS Arthur Page RN M960 (Ch)	HMS Vindictive
Signaller Clement Page RNVR Lon/Z 3892	Picket Boats, Motor Launches and Motor Boats
Stoker John Palmer RN K38313 (Dev)	HMS Intrepid
Chief Motor Mechanic Howard Pank RNVR 836	Picket Boats, Motor Launches and Motor Boats
Petty Officer George Pemberton RNAS F13706	HMS Daffodil
Motor Mechanic Robert Pratten RNVR MB 2085	Picket Boats, Motor Launches and Motor Boats
Private Herbert Proctor RMLI PO/15752	No. 8 Platoon , B Company, 4th Battalion RMLI
Chief Motor Mechanic Charles Pulsford RNVR MB 1858	Picket Boats, Motor Launches and Motor Boats
Lance Sergeant Frank Radford RMLI PLY/14991	No.9 Platoon, C Company, 4th Battalion RMLI
Able Seaman Edgar Radley RN J55797 (Ch)	HMS Thetis
Stoker Petty Officer Henry Rainbow RN 296938 (Ch)	HMS Phoebe
Leading Seaman John Reynolds RN J1639 (Ch)	Royal Naval Landing Party (A Company)
Able Seaman Thomas Ripley RN J30094 (Po)	Royal Naval Landing Party (B Company)
Leading Seaman Dalmorton Rudd RAN 3389	Royal Naval Landing Party (A Company)
Chief Stoker Alfred Sago RN 281683 (Ch)	HMS Vindictive
Leading Seaman George Shiner RN 234467 (Dev)	Royal Naval Landing Party (D Company)
Air Mechanic 1st Grade John Shrewsbury RNAS F20056	Picket Boats, Motor Launches and Motor Boats
Deckhand Cyril Slough RNR 16793 DA	Picket Boats, Motor Launches and Motor Boats
Stoker Petty Officer Albert Smith RN 303896 (Ch)	HMS Intrepid
Engine Room Artificer Herbert Smith RN 271777 (Ch)	HMS Intrepid
Stoker Joseph Smith RN K24538 (Dev)	HMS Vindictive
Chief Motor Mechanic Leslie Spillman RNVR MB 2306	Picket Boats, Motor Launches and Motor Boats
Able Seaman George Staples RAN 2858	Royal Naval Landing Party (A Company)
Leading Stoker Edwin Starks RN K6588 (Po)	Picket Boats, Motor Launches and Motor Boats

Signaller John Stewart RN J3450 (Ch) — Picket Boats, Motor Launches and Motor Boats

Able Seaman Benjamin Stone RN J17646 (Dev) — Royal Naval Landing Party (B Company)

Able Seaman Frederick Summerhayes RN J17594 (Dev) — Royal Naval Landing Party (B Company)

Stoker George Summers RN SS111550 (Ch) — HMS Thetis

Chief Petty Officer Andrew Tagg DSM RN (Received bar) 167336 (Ch) — HMS Intrepid

Petty Officer Ernest Tanner RN J.16136 (Ch) — HMS Thetis

Sergeant William Taylor RMLI PLY/11411 — No. 9 Platoon, C Company, 4th Battalion RMLI

Engine Room Artificer 4th Class Alan Thomas RN M16493 (Dev) — HMS Vindictive

Leading Seaman Edward Thompson RN J18760 (Ch) — Royal Naval Landing Party (C Company)

Sergeant William Thomson RMLI CH/15438 — Machine Gun Section, 4th Battalion R.M.L.I.

Chief Motor Mechanic Harold Thornton RNVR MB 596 — Picket Boats, Motor Launches and Motor Boats

Able Seaman Thomas Tusler RN J24729 (Po) — Royal Naval Landing Party (D Company)

Private Walter Wakefield RMLI PO/18387 — No.5 Platoon, B Company, 4th Battalion RMLI

Deckhand William Warnes RNR 4554 SD — Picket Boats, Motor Launches and Motor Boats

Petty Officer John Webb RN 210040 (Po) — Royal Naval Landing Party (C Company)

Corporal Bert Wells RMLI PLY/12841 — No.7 Platoon, B Company, 4th Battalion RMLI

Petty Officer Henry Wenman RN 226886 (Po) — Royal Naval Landing Party (D Company)

Able Seaman Albert West RN J32673 (Ch) — Royal Naval Landing Party (B Company)

Able Seaman Frank White RN J12608 (Po) — Royal Naval Landing Party (B Company)

Chief Motor Mechanic Edward Whitmarsh RNVR MB 1891 — Picket Boats, Motor Launches and Motor Boats

Leading Deckhand William Wigg DSM RNR (Received bar) 2722 SD — HMML 532

Chief Motor Mechanic Arthur Wilkins RNVR MB 1808 — Picket Boats, Motor Launches and Motor Boats

Chief Motor Mechanic Edward Windley RNVR MB 1457 — Picket Boats, Motor Launches and Motor Boats

Leading Seaman Charles Winfield RN 223785 (Po) — HMS Thetis

Petty Officer Thomas Wood RN 171903 (Ch) — HMS Vindictive

Chief Motor Mechanic Howard Wolfe RNVR 1204 — Picket Boats, Motor Launches and Motor Boats

Able Seaman Frederick Woodroofe RN J38918 (Dev) — HMS Iphigenia

Sergeant Harry Wright RMLI PLY/14423 — No.10 Platoon, C Company, 4th Battalion RMLI

Stoker Petty Officer James Wynn RN K1660 (Po) — HMS Thetis

ABBREVIATIONS

HMML	His Majesty's Motor Launch
RMA	Royal Marines Artillery
RMLI	Royal Marines Light Infantry
RN	Royal Navy
RNAS	Royal Naval Air Station
RNR	Royal Naval Reserve
RNVR	Royal Naval Volunteer Reserve

(For the sake of clarity, the itaiic conventions are not followed in the appendices.)

APPENDIX 4

LIST OF FLANDERS-BASED GERMAN SUBMARINES LOST DURING WW1

DATE	U-BOAT	COMMANDER	CAUSE OF LOSS	LOCATION
30th June 1915	UC 2	O/L K. Mey	Destroyed by detonation of own mine.	Off Yarmouth
15th August 1915	UB 4	O/L K Groß	Sunk by gunfire from the Q-ship HMS Inverlyon.	Off Yarmouth
October 1915	UC 9	O/L P. Schürmann	Destroyed by detonation of own mine.	East of Longsands L.V.
6th November 1915	UC 8	O/L W.G. Schmidt	Run aground off Terschelling. Interned by Holland.	Terschelling, Holland
5th April 1916	UB 26	O/L W. Smiths	Entangled in the nets of the British drifter Endurance at Le Havre. The French torpedo boat Trombe dropped three bombs near to UB 26, which forced Smith and his 21 crew to surface and surrender to the Allies. UB 26 later served the French navy as the Roland Morillot.	Le Havre
23rd April 1916	UC 3	O/L G. Kreysern	Entangled in mine nets of smack Cheero.	Norfolk coast
24th April 1916	UB 13	O/L A. Metz	Bombed by drifter.	Off Walcheren
27th April 1916	UC 5	O/L H Mohrbutter	Run aground off Harwich.	Off Harwich
6th July 1916	UC 7	O/L G. Haag	Depth charged by motor boat HMS Salmon.	Off Lowerstoft.
21st August 1916	UC 10	K/L W. Albrecht	Torpedoed by HM Submarine E54	Off Schouwen Bank
30th November 1916	UB 19	O/L E. Noodt	Gunfire from Q boat HMS Penshurst.	English Channel
4th December 1916	UC 19	O/L A Nitzsche	Sunk by depth charges from HMS Lewellyn.	Dover Straits
6th December 1916	UB 29	O/L E. Platsch	Sunk by depth charges from HMS Ariel.	South of Ireland
14th January 1917	UB 37	O/L P. Günther	Gunfire from Q boat HMS Penshurst.	English Channel
8th February 1917	UC 39	O/L O. Ehrentraut	Gunfire from HMS Thrasher.	Off Flamborough Head
8th February 1917	UC 46	O/L F. Moecke	Rammed by destroyer HMS Liberty.	Dover Straits
19th February 1917	UC 18	O/L W. Kiel	Gunfire from Q ship HMS Lady Olive.	English Channel
23rd February 1917	UC 32	O/L H. Breyer	Sunk by own mines	Off Sunderland
13th March 1917	UB 6	O/L Steckelberg	Ran aground at Hellevoetsluis. Interned by the Dutch.	Hellevoetsluis
5th April 1917	UC 68	O/L H. Degetau	Sank by a torpedo from HM Submarine C7.	Schouwen Bank
19th April 1917	UC 30	O/L H. Stenzler	Mined.	North Sea
9th May 1917	UC 26	O/L Graf von Schmettow	Rammed and depth charged by destroyer HMS Milne.	Straits of Dover
17th May 1917	UB 39	O/L H Küstner	Gunfire from Q boat HMS Glen.	Off Isle of Wight
20th May 1917	UC 36	K/L G Buch	Bombed by seaplane 8663.	Off W. Hinder L.V.
7th June 1917	UC 29	K/L E. Rosenow	Gunfire from Q Ship HMS Pargust	Southern Irish coast
12th June 1917	UC 66	O/L S. Pustkuchen	Depth charged by trawler HMT Sea King.	Off Lizard
24th June 1917	UB 36	O/L von Keyserlinck	Rammed by French steamer Moliere.	Off Ushant
24th July 1917	UC 1	O/L Mildenstein	Bombed by seaplanes.	Thames estuary
26th July 1917	UC 61	K/L G. Gerth	Stranded and scuttled.	Cape Gris Nez, Dover Straits
29th July 1917	UB 20	O/L H Glimpf	Bombed by seaplanes.	Off Zeebrugge
29th July 1917	UB 27	O/L von Stein	Rammed and depth charged by HMS Halcyon.	Off Harwich

30th July 1917	UB 23	O/L H. Niemer	Interned at Corunna, Spain after being depth charged by the patrol boat HMS PC-60.	Corunna, Spain
4th August 1917	UC 44	K/L Tebbenjohanns	Sunk by German mines	Waterford
18th August 1917	UB 32	O/L B. von Ditfurth	Bombed by seaplanes.	Off Cape Barfleur
10th September 1917	UC 42	O/L H. Müller	Sunk by own mines	Off cork
22nd September 1917	UC 72	O/L E. Voigt	Bombed by seaplanes.	Near Sunk L.V.
27th September 1917	UC 21	O/L von Zerboni di Sposetti	Sunk by mine nets.	North Foreland
28th September 1917	UC 6	O/L G. Reichenbach	Bombed by seaplanes.	Near Sunk L.V.
3rd October 1917	UC 14	O/L der Re. Feddersen	Mined off Zeebrugge.	Off Zeebrugge
19th October 1917	UC 62	O/L M. Schmitz	Torpedoed by HM Submarine E45.	East of Lowerstoft
23rd October 1917	UC 16	O/L G. Reimarus	Depth charged by HMS Melampus.	English Channel
1st November 1917	UC 63	O/L von Heydebreck	Torpedoed by HM Submarine E 52.	English Channel
3rd November 1917	UC 65	K/L K. Lafrenz	Torpedoed by HM Submarine C15.	English Channel
13th November 1917	UC 51	O/L G. Galster	Possible sinking by gunfire from HMS Firedrake.	Off Lowerstoft.
17th November 1917	UB 18	O/L G. Niemeyer	Mined.	Start Point
18th November 1917	UC 47	O/L Wigankow	Rammed and depth charged by P 57.	Off Flamborough Head
2nd December 1917	UB 81	O/L L. Salzwedel	Mined.	Isle of Wight
6th December 1917	UC 69	O/L H. Thielmann	Accidental collision with U 96.	Cape Barfleur
19th December 1917	UB 56	O/L H. Valentiner	Mined in Dover Barrage.	Straits of Dover.
26th January 1918	UB 35	O/L K Stöter	Depth charged by HMS Leven.	Straits of Dover
4th February 1918	UC 50	K/L R Seuffer	Depth charged by HMS Zubian.	English Channel
8th February 1918	UB 38	O/L G Bachmann	Mined.	Dover Barrage
25th February 1918	UB 17	O/L A Branscheid	Depth charged by HMS Onslow.	English Channel
10th March 1918	UB 58	O/L W Löwe	Mined.	Dover Barrage
11th March 1918	UB 54	O/L E. Hecht	Depth charged by HMS Sturgeon.	Off Lincolnshire Coast
24th March 1918	UC 48	O/L H Lorenz	Damaged by depth charges from RMS Loyal on 20th March. Interned at Corunna, Spain.	Spain
11th April 1918	UB 33	O/L F Gregor	Mined.	Dover Barrage
22nd April 1918	UB 55	O/L R Wenninger	Mined.	Dover Barrage
2nd May 1918	UB 31	O/L der Res. W Braun	Depth charged by drifters.	Straits of Dover
2nd May 1918	UC 78	K/L H Kukat	Depth charged by drifters.	Dover Straits.
9th May 1918	UB 78	O/L A Stoßberg	Rammed by transport SS Queen Alexandra.	Cherbourg.
10th May 1918	UB 16	O/L von der Lühe	Torpedoed by HM Submarine E 34.	Off Essex coast
24th May 1918	UC 56	K/L W. Kiesewetter	Damaged by USS Christabel and interned at Santander, Spain.	Santander, Spain
26th May 1918	UB 74	O/L E Steindorff	Depth charged by HM Yacht Lorna.	Portland
31st May 1918	UC 75	O/L W Schmitz	Rammed and gunfire from HMS Fairy.	Yorkshire coast
20th June 1918	UC 64	O/L F Schwartz	Mined.	Dover barrage
26th June 1918	UC 11	O/L K Utke	Mined.	Harwich
10th July 1918	UC 77	O/L H Ries	Depth charged by trawlers.	Straits of Dover
19th July 1918	UB 110	K/L W Fürbringer	Damaged by depth charges then rammed by HMS Garry.	Off Durham Coast
27th July 1918	UB 107	K/L von Pittwitz und Gaffron	Depth charged by trawlers.	Off Scarborough
27th July 1918	UB 108	K/L W Amberger	Missing. Presumed mined.	English Channel
8th August 1918	UC 49	O/L H Kükenthal	Depth charged by HMS Oppossum.	Start Point
13th August 1918	UB 30	O/L R Stier	Rammed and depth charged by trawler.	Whitby
14th August 1918	UB 57	O/L J Losz	Mined.	Zeebrugge

28th August 1918	UC 70	O/L K Dobberstein	Depth charged by HMS Ouse.	Whitby
28th August 1918	UB 12	O/L E Schöller	Mined.	Heligoland
29th August 1918	UB 109	K/L Ramien	Mined.	Dover Barrage
16th September 1918	UB 103	K/L P Hundius	Depth charged.	Straits of Dover
19th September 1918	UB 104	O/L T Bieber	Mined.	Northern barrage
29th September 1918	UB 115	O/L R Thomsen	Depth charged by HMS Star and Ouse.	North east coast
14th September 1918	UB 113	O/L U Pilzeder	Missing.	English Channel
1st October 1918	UB 10	W Stüben	Scuttled.	Flanders
2nd October 1918	UB 40	O/L H Emsmann	Scuttled.	Flanders
2nd October 1918	UB 59	K/L E Waßner	Scuttled.	Flanders
5th October 1918	UC 4	O/L E Schmidt	Scuttled.	Flanders

Sources: Public Record Office: German Submarine Losses Report ADM 116/1601A. *German Submarine War 1914–1918* by R.H. Gibson and Maurice Prendergast

BIBLIOGRAPHY

PUBLISHED SOURCES

The following sources have greatly assisted me in the research and writing of this book.

Arthur, Max, *Lost Voices of the Royal Navy*, Hodder & Stoughton, 2005.
Aspinall-Oglander, Cecil: *Roger Keyes*, Hogarth Press, 1951.
Aston, Sir George, *The Secret Service*, Faber & Faber Limited, 1933.
Brooks, Geoffrey, *Fips: Legendary U-Boat Commander, 1915-1918*, Pen & Sword, 1999.
Campbell VC, DSO, Rear Admiral Gordon, *My Mystery Ships*, Periscope Publishing Ltd, 2002.
Carlyon, L.A.,*Gallipoli*, Bantam books, 2003.
Carpenter, A.F.B. Captain VC RN, *The Blocking of Zeebrugge*, Herbert Jenkins Limited, 1925.
Carr, William Guy. *Out of the Mists*, Hutchinson & Co. 1940.
Churchill, Winston, *The World Crisis 1911–1918*, Odhams Press, Limited 1938.
Dean, Gregory, *On the War Path in Bruges*, Dienst Museum, Bruges.
Gibson, R.H. & Prendergast, Maurice, *The German Submarine War 1914–18*, Naval & Military Press, 2003.
Hammerton, Sir J., *The Great War, I Was There*, The Amalgamated Press Ltd, London, 1938.
Heathcote, T.A., *The British Admirals of the Fleet 1734–1995*, Leo Cooper, 2002.
Hilton-Young MP, Edward, *By Sea and Land, Some Naval Doings*, T.C. & E.C. Jack Ltd, 1920.
Hislam, Percival, *How We Twisted the Dragon's Tail*, Hutchinson & Co, 1918.
Jerrold, Douglas, *The Royal Naval Division*, Naval & Military Press, 1923
Keble, Howard, *The Zeebrugge Affair*, George H. Doran Company, 1918.
Keyes, Sir Roger, Admiral of the Fleet RN, *The Naval Memoirs 1916–1918*, Thornton Butterworth Ltd, 1935.
Lake, Deborah, *The Zeebrugge and Ostend Raids 1918*, Leo Cooper, 2002.
Lloyd George, David, *War Memoirs of David Lloyd George*, Odhams Press, 1938.
Peshall, C. Rev and Stewart, Commander A., *The Immortal Gamble*, A&C Black Ltd, 1918.
Pitt, Barrie, *Zeebrugge*, Cassell, 1958.
Schultz, Captain Karl, 'The British Assault on the German Bases Ostend and Zeebrugge', Naval Archives, 1929.
Stinglhamber, DSO, Colonel G.M., *The Story of Zeebrugge with an account of The Blocking of Zeebrugge*, privately published, 1928.
Thomas, Lowell, *Raiders of the Deep*, Periscope Publishing Limited, 1928.
Warner, Philip, *The Zeebrugge Raid*, William Kimber, 1978.

UNPUBLISHED SOURCES

Petty Officer Harry Adams papers (Courtesy John Soanes).
Engineer Lieutenant Ronald Boddie papers (Courtesy Boddie family).
Lieutenant Commander George Bradford papers (Courtesy Jonathan L. Bradford Cremer).

Private Arthur Burnell papers (Courtesy Burnell family).

Lieutenant Harold Campbell papers (Courtesy Michael Anson).

Private Jim Clist interview (Courtesy David Clist).

Lieutenant Alan Cory-Wright papers (Coutesy Godfrey Cory-Wright).

Leading Seaman Edward Gilkerson papers (Courtesy Rodney Gilkerson).

Private Alexander Gordon papers (Courtesy Kevin Gordon).

Lieutenant Hope Inskip papers (Courtesy Dave Eastman).

Midshipman David Morris (Author's collection).

Corporal George Moyse (Courtesy Ron Moyse & Peter White).

Ordinary Seaman William O'Hara papers (Author's collection).

Private Harold Prangnell papers (Courtesy Sheila Kitchener).

Lieutenant George Spencer papers (Courtesy the late Hannah Spencer, Iris Mary Spencer Latour and Catherine Latour).

Private Lewis Stoddart papers (Courtsy Bryan Stoddart).

Able Seaman Frederick Summerhayes papers (Courtesy Dennis Summerhayes).

Private Beau Tracey interview (Courtesy Richard Davison).

Lieutenant Commander James Young papers (Author's collection).

NATIONAL ARCHIVES

ADM 1/8423/152 (HMS Mohawk explosion casualty report 1915)

CAB 45/268 (Admiral Sir Roger Keyes' original letters and comments on the Eastern Mediterranean (Dardanelles and Gallipoli), the Ostend and Zeebrugge raid, and the Dover Straits, 1915–1930).

CAB 45/272 (Zeebrugge correspondence reports, 1918-19).

ADM 196/63 (Major G S Hobson' service record).

ADM 137 / 3894 (Reports on Zeebrugge and Ostend operations April May 1918).

ADM 116/1656 (Operations against Zeebrugge casualties 25th April 1918).

AIR 1/56/15/9/50 (Daily summaries – Dover Patrol serials 34-112).

AIR 1/2393/249/2 (Lecture paper on the blockading operations at Zeebrugge and Ostend).

ADM 137 / 3876 (Interrogation of survivors of German submarines).

ADM 137/3874 (Interrogation of survivors of German submarines re: UB 109).

ADM 116/1601A (German submarine operations in home waters 1917-18).

WO 339/58056 (re: Lt. A Eastlake)

ADM 337/127 P298 (Commander Patrick Harrington Edwards Service Record)

ADM 273 Vol.4/35 Wing Commander Frank Brock's service record

ADM 196/ P247-8 Sergeant Charles Thatcher's service record

ADM 339/3 Surgeon Frank Pocock's Service Record

ADM 1/8455/92 (Loss of submarine E22).

ADM 1/8525/142. Naval Raids on Zeebrugge & Ostende April & May 1918.

ADM 173/1498. Submarine E34 Report.

ADM 196/98 P103: Lieutenant Willie Sillitoe's service record.

NEWSPAPERS

Accrington Observer & *Accrington Times*, 4th May 1918.

The *Ashton Reporter*, Saturday 4th May 1918.

Blackburn Times 27th April 1918.

The *Blackpool Times*, 27th April 1918.

Bristol Times & *Bristol Mirror*, 1st May 1918.

The *Burnley News*, 1st May 1918.
Chatham News, Rochester News & Gillingham News, Saturday 27th April 1918.
Cornhill, December 1918.
Daily Mail, 24th April 1918.
The *Daily Chronicle*, 27th April 1918.
Daily Sketch 30th April, 1st May 1918.
Daily Telegraph, 22nd April 1968.
Dartford Chronicle & District Times, 10th May 1918.
Downham Market Gazette, 4th May 1918.
Folkestone, Hythe, Sandgate & Cheriton Herald, 4th May 1918.
Halifax Courier, 4th May 1918.
Hampshire Telegraph & Post, 26th April 1918.
Jersey Weekly Post, 10th January 1959.
The *Liverpool Chronicle*, 29th April 1918.
The *Newcastle Daily Chronicle*, 29th April, 2nd May 1918.
The *Newcastle Journal* September 29th 1975.
Northern Daily Mail, 27th April 1918 (*Hartlepool Mail*).
North Wales Chronicle, 2nd May 1941.
Nottingham Journal & Express, 30th April 1918.
The *Southend Standard*, 2nd May 1918.
South Wales Daily News, 27th, 29th, 30th April 1918.
The *Sunday Graphic and Sunday News* 1935.
Thanet Times 3rd May 1918.
Thomson's Weekly News 4th May 1918.
The *Times*, 7th September 1972, April 1918.

IMPERIAL WAR MUSEUM DOCUMENTS DEPARTMENT

IWM Ref. 96/47/1 Engineer Lieutenant Ronald.C. Boddie RN.
IWM Ref: 02/30/1, Lance Corporal George Calverley RMLI.
IWM Ref: P447, Lieutenant Vaux RN.
IWM Ref: 74/101/1, Captain A.R. Chater, RMLI.
IWM Ref. 91/11/1 Acting 1st Class Mechanic W.H. Gough RNAS.

IMPERIAL WAR MUSEUM SOUND DEPARTMENT

Private Jordan Daniel 8552
W E D Wardrop DFM 29
Emily Rumbold 576
Hans Howaldt 4139

ROYAL MARINES MUSEUM

Sergeant Wright, Royal Marine Museum Archives ARCH 10/2/W
Sergeant Wright Royal Marines Museum Archives ARCH 11/12/5(5)
Sergeant Wright Royal Marines Museum Archives ARCH 11/13/1(2)
Private Philip Hodgson RM ARCH 7/17/2
Lieutenant C. Lamplough No. 9 Platoon Royal Marines Museum (ARCH 11/13/79)

4th Battalion Royal Marines Light Infantry War Diary
Letter from Lieutenant Colonel Elliot to Adjutant General, Brigadier-General H.S. Neville White, 23rd March 1918.
Brigadier General Neville White report dated 23rd March 1918.
Stokes Mortar Accident Report

AUSTRALIAN WAR MEMORIAL

Stoker N. McCrory, Royal Australian Navy, H.M.A.S. *Australia* AWM Ref: 1 DRL 0429

ROYAL NAVAL MUSEUM

Royal Naval Museum RNM, Ad. Lib. MSS 217. Papers of Captain Herbert Grant.

DOVER MUSEUM

Leading Seaman H.C. Beaumont

BUNDESARCHIV

Bundesarchiv BA-MA, RM 120 / 275
Bundesarchiv 270 / 125 P190

IN FLANDER'S FIELDS MUSEUM, YPRES, BELGIUM

Anonymous nun's account – Zeebrugge Raid.

LIDDELL COLLECTION, UNIVERSITY OF LEEDS ARCHIVES

RNMN (REC) 037 HENRY GROOTHIUS
RNMN (REC) 008 Name: BASCOMBE, H F

THE LONDON GAZETTE

The London Gazette on 1 January 1916, 6th September 1916, 23rd July 1918, 28th August 1918, 11th January 1919, 3rd February, 18th February 1919, 17th March 1919, 20th November 1918

MAGAZINES

Globe & Laurel 1918.
Private James Feeney, Royal Marines Museum *Globe & Laurel* April 1919
Lieutenant F.J.Hore, Royal Marines Museum *Globe & Laurel* 1918

Cross & Cockade
Air Mechanic Sidney Hesse Account (Peter Chapman via Sidney Hesse).

PHOTOGRAPHIC SOURCES AND ACKNOWLEDGEMENTS

FRONT COVER: Above, POWs, IWM, see p153; Below, *Vindictive* and *Daffodil* at the Mole. The painting hangs in Zeebrugge Town Hall.

CHAPTER 1 – THE FLANDERS FLOTILLA

Page

16 U 24 sinking HMS *Formidable* off the Dorset coast on 1st January 1915. (Postcard, Author's collection).

17 HMS *Formidable*. (Postcard J Welch & Sons, Photographic Publishers, Portsmouth, Author's collection).

18 Admiral Ludwig von Schröder. (Postcard, Author's collection).

21 German submarine approaching the Mole at Zeebrugge. (Author's collection).

21 UC-66 leaving the canal at Zeebrugge during June 1917. (Courtesy In Flanders Fields Museum).

22 Entrance to the Zeebrugge sluices. (Postcard, Authors collection).

22 Entrance to the Bruges canal at Zeebrugge. (Postcard, Author's collection).

23 Entrance to the Bruges canal at Zeebrugge, 2006. (Author's collection).

23 German submarines at Bruges. (Author's collection).

23 German submarine pens at Bruges. (Author's collection).

24 Torpedo Boats from the Flanders Flotilla berthed at Bruges. (Author's Collection).

25 Aerial view of the German Naval Base, Bruges, home of the Flanders Flotilla. (Author's collection).

26 The Bruges canal from Zeebrugge lock gates, November 2006. (Author's collection).

26 German submarine in the Bruges canal. (Author's collection).

26 Bruges canal in 2003 (Author's Collection).

26 German submarine waiting to pass through the lock gates at Zeebrugge prior to patrol for Allied shipping. (Author's collection).

27 The lock gates at Zeebrugge pictured in November 2006. (Author's collection).

27 Three photos of German submarines moored alongside the Mole at Zeebrugge. (Author's collection).

28 German destroyers and submarine berthed alongside the inner Mole at Zeebrugge. (Author's collection).

28 German submarine departs the Mole after patrol in the English Channel, heading for the entrance to the Bruges canal in top left corner of photo. (Author's collection).

28 German Torpedo Boats at Zeebrugge, 1917. (Author's collection).

29 Three photos of German submarines berthing alongside the Mole at Zeebrugge. (Author's collection).

31 Captured Submarine UC-5 (Crown Copyright).

32 British sailors onboard captured Flanders Submarine UC-5. (Postcard, Author's collection).

34 Kapitänleutnant Otto Steinbrinck (Photo from U-boote Am Feind 1937).

35 Captured German Submarine UC-5 pictured in the River Thames. UC-5 was displayed to the public at Temple. (Author's collection).

180 Zeebrugge Churchyard. (Author's collection).

180 Funeral of seven German personnel killed during the Zeebrugge Raid at Zeebrugge Churchyard. (Author's collection).

181 Memorial to the Missing, Zeebrugge Churchyard (Author's collection).

CHAPTER 14 – ASSESSMENT

185 View of blockships from a passing German submarine at Zeebrugge at high water. (Courtesy Johan Ryheul).

188 The Flanders Flotilla UB 88 in the Panama Canal region photographed in 1919. (Author's collection).

191 Vice Admiral Sir Roger Keyes and Sir Douglas Haig received by the Recorder of Dover. (Author's collection).

CHAPTER 15 – THEY WERE ON THE *VINDICTIVE*

193 Captain Carpenter VC (officer with arm in sling) with sailors and Royal Marines who took part in the raid on Zeebrugge at Dover. (Photo IWM Q 61351).

194 Stoker John Connick ('The *Ashton Reporter*, Saturday 4th May 1918. Courtesy *Ashton Reporter*).

194 Able Seaman Frederick Bowlt, (The *Dover Express And East Kent News*, Friday 10th May 1918. Courtesy *Herald Express*, Kent Regional Newspapers).

195 Lieutenant Eastlake (The *Daily Graphic*, Wednesday 1st May, Page 3).

195 Clifford Armitage, pictured as a Leading Mechanic in 1916. (Photo courtesy Philip Gough).

196 Rear of the Flame-thrower hut where Lieutenant Eastlake, Chief Petty Officer Clifford Armitage and Air Mechanic John Lomax were positioned during the Zeebrugge Raid. (Author's collection).

196 1st Class Air Mechanic John Lomax, RNAS. (*Blackburn Times*, 27th April 1918)

196 Plumber Alexander Horne (Courtesy Linda Kelly).

197 Petty Officer Herbert Britton (The *Southend Standard*, 2nd May 1918. Courtesy of the *Southend Standard* (Echo Newspapers)).

198 Leading Seaman Fred Kimber (Courtesy Sally Purchase).

198 Leading Seaman William Marling (Courtesy Steve Marling).

198 1st Class Stoker Frederick Pooley Photo, *Dartford Chronicle & District Times*, 10th May 1918. (By kind permission Kentish Times Newspapers).

198 Leading Seaman Daniel Bowthorpe, (Downham Market Gazette, 4th May 1918. By kind permission of the *Eastern Daily Press*).

199 Stoker William Hancock, pictured shortly before the Zeebrugge raid while he was serving aboard HMS *Repulse* in 1917. (Photo courtesy Diane Ellison).

200 Chaplain Charles Peshall DSO CBE. (Photo courtesy Edward Peshall).

201 Steward's Assistant Percy Kenworthy (The *Ashton Reporter*, Saturday 4th May 1918. Courtesy *Ashton Reporter*).

202 Master at Arms Charles Dunkason DSM, (Photo Courtesy Michael Dunkason).

202 Charles Dunkason receiving the DSM at Portsmouth after the Zeebrugge Raid. (Photo Courtesy Michael Dunkason).

203 Harry and Walter Bennewith (Photo courtesy Neville and Ian Bennewith).

204 Leading Seaman Edward Gilkerson. (Photo courtesy Rodney Gilkerson).

205 Grave of Leading Seaman Edward Gilkerson at St. James's's Cemetery, Dover. (Author's collection).

205 Leading Seaman Edward Gilkerson (third from left) Stoker Ernest Thornton (first left) and Able Seaman William Frost (second from left) aboard HMS *King George V*. William Frost was wounded

aboard HMS *Iris* and lost his right leg during the Zeebrugge raid. Stoker Ernest Thornton formed part of the blockship crew aboard HMS *Iphigenia*. (Photo courtesy of Linda Butcher).

206 Lieutenant Charles Rigby (Author's collection).

206 *Vindictive* after her return from Zeebrugge. (Author's collection).

207 Sergeant Norman Finch VC (Royal Marines Museum).

207 Sergeant Finch VC (left) and CSM Barker (right) place a wreath in the shape of *Vindictive* in violets at the base of the Zeebrugge Memorial unveiled by King Albert. (Author's collection).

208 Gunner Vincent Ormerod (Photo courtesy Jim Clay).

CHAPTER 16 – THEY STORMED THE MOLE

209 Commander Patrick Harrington Edwards, (*Daily Graphic*, April 26th 1918, p7).

211 Lt Harrison VC before promotion to Lieutenant Commander. (Courtesy John Soanes).

211 Able Seaman Frederick Summerhayes (Photo courtesy of Dennis Summerhayes).

212 Royal Naval Landing Party 1918 (Author's collection).

212 Able Seaman Hubert Helliar (Courtesy Neil and Heather Helliar).

213 Able Seaman Edward Tolra, (*Daily Sketch*, 1st May 1918).

213 Able Seaman Charles Pooley (*South Wales Daily News*, 27th April 1918).

214 Memorial card dedicated to A.B. D. Drummond after the Zeebrugge raid. (Author's collection).

215 Leading Seaman George Antell pictured in 1913. (Photo courtesy Mr. George Antell).

215 Petty Officer George Antell sitting between his two sisters while convalescing from wounds sustained at Zeebrugge. Note that he has lost a finger from his right hand. (Photo courtesy Mr. George Antell).

216 Able Seaman Harry Gillard wearing HMAS *Australia* cap ribbon. (Courtesy Gillard family).

217 Able Seaman Walter Taylor pictured in 1926 on his wedding day. (Photo courtesy Richard Taylor).

218 Able Seaman Fred Berry (Photo courtesy of Danny Webber).

219 Telegram sent to Fred's mother, Mrs. Harriett Berry informing that her son was wounded on 23rd April 1918 aboard HMS *Vindictive*. (Courtesy Danny Webber).

219 Able Seaman Fred Larby wearing Royal Naval uniform. (Photo courtesy daughter, Marlene Gostelow).

220 Able Seaman Fred Larby pictured with boxing trophies that he won in Royal Naval Boxing tournaments. (Photo courtesy daughter, Marlene Gostelow).

220 Leading Seaman Ellams, (Courtesy of the *Warrington Guardian*, 4th May 1918).

221 Able Seaman William Botley. (Courtesy Ian Botley).

221 Seaman Francis Kelland. Photo taken when he served with the Fore Transmitting Station Crew aboard HMS *Conqueror* in 1914. (Courtesy Ivor Kelland).

222 Francis Kelland pictured left with walking stick recovering after the Zeebrugge raid at a convalescent home at Harting. The other two unidentified men may have been wounded at Zeebrugge. The sailor on the right has lost his right arm from the elbow. (Photo courtesy Ivor Kelland).

222 Photo of Francis Kelland taken before the Zeebrugge raid with fellow Zeebrugge raiders (from left to right) Able Seamen Beare, Ahern and Matthews. (Photo courtesy Ivor Kelland).

222 Wing Commander Frank Brock OBE (Author's collection).

223 HMS *Daffodil IV* demonstration of patent fog producing apparatus. (R&H Robbins Ltd. Liverpool).

224 German personnel stand next to searchlight and one of the metal tubes on the Mole at Zeebrugge which so intrigued Brock. (Author's collection).

225 Two British Zeebrugge Raiders lie dead on the Mole, pictured after the raid. The body nearest to the camera could be Lieutenant Commander Brock. (Photo courtesy Alain van Geeteruyen).

226 Leading Mechanic John Frederick Wilkinson. (Photo courtesy Geraldine Thompson, Manchester Royal Infirmary).

227 Air Mechanic Francis Donovan, pictured in his role as Chairman of the Zeebrugge Association. (Courtesy, Dominic Walsh).

228 William Gough, pictured after World War One. (Photo courtesy Philip Gough).

229 Mayor of Southwark escorting Able Seaman Albert McKenzie to his home off the Old Kent Road on his return from Buckingham Palace, where he received the VC for the part he played in the Zeebrugge exploit from King George V (Dover Museum d15504).

230 Sergeant Major Charles Thatcher DSC (Dover Museum d15509).

230 Fight on the Mole, 23rd April 1918, by D. Macpherson. (Author's collection).

231 Captain Arthur Chater DSO (Royal Marines Museum Ref: 2/10/15(2)).

232 Captain Edward Bamford VC DSO (Photo from *How We Twisted the Dragon's Tail*, Percival Hislam, 1918).

233 The Friedrichsort Leitstand on the Mole after the raid. (Courtesy Johan Ryheul).

233 Zeebrugge Mole, morning 23rd April 1918 (hours after the raid). (Courtesy Johan Ryheul).

234 Lieutenant Theodore Cooke DSO (Photo courtesy Mrs. Doreen Burrow).

235 Lieutenant Theodore Cooke and No.5 Platoon RMLI that took part in the Zeebrugge raid. (Photo courtesy Royal Marines Museum Archive 2/10/15(1)).

235 Private Arthur Burnell, looking very proud wearing his RMLI uniform, soon after he enlisted. (Photo courtesy Stewart Burnell).

236 Private Arthur Burnell. (Photo courtesy Lynne and Frieda Burnell).

236 Private Arthur Burnell's grave in Scunthorpe Cemetery. (Photo courtesy Lynne and Frieda Burnell).

236 Private Arthur Burnell, pictured left. (Photo courtesy Lynne and Frieda Burnell).

237 Private William Warren. (Courtesy Mary and Mark Twells).

237 William Gallin pictured while serving as a Royal Marines Policeman at Plymouth Dockyard. (Courtesy Brian Brown).

237 Private Frank Kendall Narracott, (Photo from The *Southend Standard*, 2nd May 1918, p6).

238 No.9 Platoon, C Company, 4th Battalion Royal Marine Light Infantry photographed at Deal prior to the Zeebrugge Raid. (Photo, Royal Marines Museum ref: 13/11/56(26)).

238 Private William Hopewell. (Photo courtesy Betty Thornton & Tony Hopewell).

239 Private Samuel Hopson. (Photo courtesy Karen Morris).

239 Private Archie Toach, (Photo courtesy Gordon Toach).

239 Bugler Frederick Greenway (Photo Courtesy Tom Greenway).

240 German guns on the Mole at Zeebrugge, This is a view of the guns and crew quarters of the Hafenkopf Battery on Zeebrugge Mole. Ten men from this battery were sent by Schütte to confront the British raiders. (Postcard, Author's collection).

240 Private Tommy Keegan (Courtesy Mr. Des Donovan).

240 Private Thomas Jackson (Photo courtesy Jim Clay).

241 Sergeant Harry Wright, photo taken as a POW. (Royal Marines Museum Archive 7/17/2/(87)).

241 No. 10 Platoon, C Company Royal Marines Light Infantry (Royal Marines Museum Archive 2/10/15(3)).

242 Private William Bushell, (Photo The *Walsall Observer & South Staffordshire Chronicle*, Saturday 4th May 1918. Courtesy Trinity Mirror Midlands Weekly Newspapers).

242 Private Ernest Rhind (Photo courtesy Nigel Rhind).

242 Corporal George Moyse (Photo, Courtesy Ron Moyse).

243 Percy Gumm (Courtesy Brian Gumm).

244 Private John Edge (Blackburn Weekly Telegraph, 4th May 1918).

244 Private William Cuthbert (Photo courtesy Dorothy Cardoo and Michael McLaren).

245 No.12 Platoon pictured before the Zeebrugge Raid at Deal. (Royal Marines Museum Archive 2/10/15(6)).

245 Captain Charles Conybeare (Royal Marines Museum Ref: 2/10/15(2)).

246 Private John Kember (The *Thanet Times*, 3rd May 1918. Courtesy *Thanet Times*).

246 Private Lewis Stoddart pictured at Deal, Kent. (Courtesy of Bryan Stoddart)

247 Private Maurice French (Photo courtesy Graham Marsden).

247 Private John Weaver (Photo courtesy Andrew Bruton).

271 Petty Officer James Cownie DSM. (*South Wales Daily News*, 29th April 1918).

272 HMS *Daffodil*, flying the White Ensign. (Author's collection.)

272 *Daffodil* after the Zeebrugge Raid (Photo by J H Mumford, New Brighton, Author's collection).

CHAPTER 19 – THEY WERE ON THE *IRIS*

273 Commander Oscar Henderson CVO CBE DSO RN photographed in 1935. (Courtesy Captain O. W. J. Henderson).

274 HMS *Iris* pictured at Dover after the Zeebrugge Raid. (Courtesy Captain O. W. J. Henderson).

274 Major Charles Eagles (*The Distinguished Service Order 1916 – 1923*, Naval & Military Press)

274 Ordinary Seaman Henry Hollis, (*Southampton and District Pictorial*, 16th May 1918, p7).

274 Able Seaman John Ahern, (Courtesy Ivor Kelland)

275 Surgeon Frank Pocock DSO MC ((Royal Marines Museum. Ref: 2/10/15(2)).

275 Grave of Surgeon Frank Pocock, Lourval Military Cemetery, France. (Author's collection).

275 Lieutenant Commander George Bradford VC (Photo courtesy of Jonathan L Bradford Cremer).

276 Grave of Lieutenant Commander George Bradford VC, Blankenberge Town Cemetery, Belgium (Grave A.5). (Author's collection).

277 Air Mechanic 1st Class George Warrington, courtesy Andrew Warrington.

277 Able Seaman William Frost (Courtesy Linda Butcher).

277 Lieutenant George Spencer DSC RNR (Courtesy Iris Mary Spencer Latour and the late Hannah Spencer)

278 Mersey ferry *Iris* after Zeebrugge (Real Photographs Co Ltd, Victoria House, Hoghton Street, Southport, Author's collection).

278 'HMS Iris, Bridge and fore-deck wrecked, Bridge End'. Position where Commander Valentine Gibbs and Lieutenant Spencer received their mortal wounds. (R&H Robbins Ltd, Liverpool. Author's collection)

279 Lieutenant William Henry Vaughan Edgar DSC, RAN, with a party of civilians on HMAS *Australia*. (Australian War Memorial Reference: P02214.001).

279 Petty Officer Henry Mabb DSM. (Courtesy Patricia Webber & Gordon Mabb).

279 Private Ernest 'Beau' Tracey. (Courtesy Richard Davison).

280 No.1 Platoon, A Company, 4th Royal Marine Light Infantry Battalion RM Museum Archive 2/10/15(9).

280 Private Harold Mercer, (Photo from the *Burnley News*, 1st May 1918 Page 4). (Courtesy Margaret Parsons, *Burnley Express & News*).

280 Private George Laming (Photo from *The Dover Express And East Kent News*, Friday 17th May 1918. Courtesy Simon Finlay Kent Regional Newspapers).

281 Private George Parks (Photo *Folkestone, Hythe, Sandgate & Cheriton Herald*, 4th May 1918. (Courtesy Simon Finlay, Kent Regional Newspapers).

281 Private Percy Linkin, (Courtesy John Linkin).

281 Lieutenant Hope Inskip. Royal Marines Museum Archive 2/10/15(9).

282 Private Charles Allbones. (Photo courtesy Diane and Brian Allbones).

283 Alexander Gordon pictured during and after the War. (Photo courtesy Kevin Gordon).

283 Lance Corporal George Calverley. (Photo courtesy Nigel Calverley).

285 Survivors of the Zeebrugge Raid at Chatham barracks. This photo was amongst Lance Corporal George Calverley's possessions. (Photo courtesy Nigel Calverley).

286 Private Fred Hoath (Courtesy Mr. Neville Hoath).

287 Private Fred Hoath (seated) with fellow Zeebrugge raider Private Stanley Hobbins. Taken on Fred's wedding day when Private Hobbins acted as his best man. (Photo courtesy Mr. Neville Hoath).

288 Private Parowmas Harris is pictured standing. (Courtesy Jacqueline Oldman).

CHAPTER 20 – THEY WERE ON THE SUPPORT VESSELS

CHAPTER 21 – THE MONUMENTS

INDEX